THE LIFE OF
John Hamilton Reynolds

PUBLISHED FOR THE UNIVERSITY OF VERMONT BY
UNIVERSITY PRESS OF NEW ENGLAND
Hanover and London, 1984

THE LIFE OF

John Hamilton Reynolds

Leonidas M. Jones

UNIVERSITY PRESS OF NEW ENGLAND

The publication of this book has been made possible
by grants from the Andrew W. Mellon Foundation
and the Hyder E. Rollins Fund of Harvard University.

LIBRARY OF CONGRESS CATALOGING IN PUBLICATION DATA

Jones, Leonidas M.
    The life of John Hamilton Reynolds.

    Includes bibliographical references and index.
    1. Reynolds, John Hamilton, 1794–1852.   2. Poets,
English—19th century—Biography.   3. Keats, John, 1795–
1821—Friends and associates.   I. Title.
PR5221.R5Z74   1984   821'.7 [B]   83-40558
ISBN 0-87451-293-X

To
Willard B. Pope

Contents

Preface

JOHN HAMILTON REYNOLDS was one of those rare, magical personalities who attracted men of genius and, in turn, stimulated the development of their talents. John Keats called him brother and valued him as a collaborator in exploring poetic principles and planning poems. He was William Hazlitt's most ardent disciple and for a time his close friend. He hypnotized John Clare and charmed Thomas Hood into a bond of intimate friendship that endured for many years. Although Reynolds's own early meteoric career faded to near tragedy in his last years as he failed to fulfill the glowing promise of his youth, the life of such a man, offering much that is enlightening as well as much that is moving, deserves close and thorough scrutiny.

During the many years that I have enjoyed researching the life of Reynolds, I have been fortunate in the generous help I received from others. The dedication testifies only in part to the unselfish assistance that my colleague Willard B. Pope has given me for over thirty years. Having himself researched John Hamilton Reynolds masterfully, as well as Benjamin Robert Haydon, for his Harvard doctoral dissertation, he focussed his own productive scholarship on Haydon and guided me in further investigation of Reynolds. My debt is large to Walter Jackson Bate, whose encouragement has been a never failing support.

This biography is built on the solid foundation laid by scholars over the last half century. Reynolds was only a name in Keats's letters when George L. Marsh began the process of restoring him to his modest, but deserved place in literature. Hyder E. Rollins provided in *The Keats Circle* the central storehouse of documents for study of all Keats's friends, including Reynolds. Robert Gittings's great biography of Keats furnished vital insights into Reynolds, his family, and friends, and his article specifically devoted to Reynolds in *Ariel* (1970, I, 7-17) revealed the facts of his family in the eighteenth century. Peter F. Morgan has for thirty years kept me informed by correspondence of his discoveries about Reynolds acquired in the process of his research into Thomas Hood. In the last few years three scholars have expanded the published record of Reynolds' letters markedly: Joanna Richardson in *Letters from Lambeth* (1981) and John Clubbe and Anne Kaier in articles in the *Keats-Shelley Journal* (1981, XXX, 152-181, 182-190). Frank P. Riga's and Charles A. Prance's *Index to the London Magazine* (1978) was invaluable for the assessment of Reynolds's contribution to the greatest of all British literary periodicals.

I am grateful to the numerous librarians and libraries that have afforded me essential services, in many cases extending over long periods of years: Mrs. Christina Gee, Assistant Curator, and the Keats House, Hampstead; the Houghton Library at Harvard; the Beinecke Library at Yale; the Bailey-Howe Library at the University of Vermont; the British Library; the National Library of Scotland; C. Hurst of Special Collections and the Bodleian Library; Seymour Adelman and the Bryn Mawr Library; and Bennet Hatch of Special Collections and the University of Massachusetts Library.

Archives and public records have provided much new evidence, and I thank all those who have helped me to explore them: Mrs. Marian Halford, Archivist, and Mrs. Janette Shepherd, Assistant Archivist, Shropshire County Records Office, Shrewsbury; James B. Lawson, Librarian of Shrewsbury School; Vaughan Heis, Assistant Archivist, the Minet Library, London; and J. W. Bastin, genealogist.

Among the other individuals who have assisted me, I am especially grateful to Mrs. G. Dora Hessell of Papakura, New Zealand, a descendant of the Reynolds family who was remarkably generous with time and effort in sending me information from the family papers and the photograph of the portrait of Charlotte Reynolds by William Hilton. My thanks go to my colleague, A. Inskip Dickerson, for checking the catalogues of libraries in Scotland for me while he was on sabbatical. And it is a pleasure to express my appreciation to Joseph C. Grigeley of Oxford for the Reynolds note to Horace Twiss and for helpful correspondence about John Martin's copy of *The Inquirer*. After the completion of the manuscript of this book, Mr. Grigeley's thorough account of the volume appeared in the *Keats-Shelley Memorial Bulletin* (1982, XXXIII, 49-61).

I thank the American Council of Learned Societies for a grant for travel to England and the University of Vermont for an Institutional Research Grant for the typing. Judith Cota and Evelyn Kyle earned my gratitude by typing the manuscript.

L. M. J.

THE LIFE OF

John Hamilton Reynolds

CHAPTER 1

Childhood

JOHN HAMILTON REYNOLDS's paternal ancestors were of humble origin. His great-grandfather, Thomas Reynolds, was a tanner in Tottenham. His grandfather, Noble Reynolds, was bound as a barber's apprentice in 1733, the public charity of the parish of Tottenham paying his fee of five pounds. After an apprenticeship of seven years, he was admitted to the Barbers' Company in 1740; he did not prosper because his election to the Livery of the Barbers' Company was delayed for twenty-four years.[1] Some three years earlier he had married a second wife, Susannah Beardsell, at St. Olave's Church in Hart Street on 2 June 1761; and from that marriage his only son, George C., was born on 7 January 1765[2] and baptized at St. Olave's Church on 20 January.[3] Noble Reynolds must have died in straitened circumstances, for in February 1781, after his death, the Court of the Barbers' Company allocated the Michael Tans charitable legacy to Susannah Reynolds as "a poor Liveryman's widow."[4]

George Reynolds attended Christ's Hospital as a charity student from March 1774 to October 1779, leaving at the age of fourteen. The family of Noble and Susannah Reynolds lived at St. Michael's, Cornhill,[5] but by February 1788 George resided at Kingsland, near Hackney and Tottenham, the region of his family's origin.[6] It seems probable, as Robert Gittings conjectured, that he began early his life-long career as a schoolmaster, teaching in one or more of the many new schools established in the Hackney region in the latter half of the eighteenth century.[7]

On his twenty-fifth birthday George Reynolds married the twenty-nine-year-old Charlotte Cox in St. Mary le Bone Church, the register being signed by two of her relatives, Jane Cox and John Hamilton.[8] Perhaps this Jane Cox was Charlotte's mother, who was still alive in 1808 and vigorous enough to travel from London to Bristol for a three-month visit.[9] Charlotte's family connections were more distinguished than her husband's; though the precise relationships are not clear, she was in some manner related to the famous William

Beckford and the sporting writer Peter Beckford, descendants of the Hamilton family. Charlotte's mother had been proud of these relatives, however remote the kinship, naming her only son William Beckford Cox. Charlotte continued the pattern by naming her son John Hamilton and her third daughter Eliza Beckford.[10]

George Reynolds lived at Wandsworth in Surrey at the time of his marriage, while Charlotte Cox before her marriage resided in St. Mary le Bone parish, presumably with her mother.[11] Evidently the couple lived in St. Mary le Bone parish while George taught at unidentified London schools, at least until their first child, Jane, born on 6 November 1791, was baptized at St. Mary le Bone on 28 November.[12] Some time thereafter they moved to Shrewsbury, where George taught at an unnamed school. Their second child and only son, John Hamilton Reynolds, was born in Shrewsbury on 9 September 1794 and baptized in St. Mary's Church on 29 September. The three daughters who followed were also baptized in St. Mary's: Marianne, born 23 February 1797; Eliza, birth date unknown, baptized 20 November 1799; and Charlotte, born 12 May 1802.[13]

George Reynolds began teaching at Shrewsbury School in September 1797,[14] shortly before Samuel Butler, grandfather of the novelist and later an Anglican bishop, began his long service as headmaster there. The only evidence of any relationship between Butler and the Reynoldses is too slight to be very meaningful: in a letter years later John Hamilton Reynolds called him "pompous."[15]

One of George Reynolds's pupils, John Freeman Milward Dovaston, became a close friend of the family, and this friendship continued for many years. Dovaston was the only child of a wealthy landowner of the same name, whose estate, called the Nursery, was located at West Felton between Shrewsbury and Oswestry. When admitted to the school in October 1798, Dovaston met John Hamilton Reynolds. Although ten years older than his teacher's son, Dovaston was drawn to the boy, and spent many happy hours with him in and around Shrewsbury.[16] By the time Dovaston left for Christ Church, Oxford, before 1804,[17] the two had become fast friends.

Willard B. Pope was surely correct in supposing that Reynolds attended some other school in Shrewsbury before he entered Shrewsbury School on 24 January 1803 along with fifteen other boys, for it is highly unlikely that his schoolmaster father and his very literate mother would delay beginning his education until he was nine.[18] At

Miniature of John Hamilton Reynolds by Joseph Severn c. 1817
in the Keats House, Hampstead.

any rate, from his ninth through his eleventh year, Reynolds attended Shrewsbury School. Two poems by Reynolds in the *London Magazine* cast some light on what life was like there for young students: "A Parthian Peep at Life, an Epistle to R[ichard] A[llen]," recalling joyously shared schoolboy activities, and "Stanzas to the Memory of Richard Allen," lamenting the schoolmate buried in a "country church-yard" where they had played as boys.[19] Reynolds drew on his own experiences at school, though nostalgia may have colored some details. The activities were by no means surprising— indeed they were what one expects of schoolboys. In "A Parthian Peep," he recalled playing on the walls, shooting marbles on the playground under the trees, reading romances in the shade, playing on the bank of the Severn, looking for birds' nests, stealing crab apples, and attending a school party with country dancing. In "Stanzas to the Memory of Richard Allen," he added recollections of "wild Thursday afternoon" (evidently a half holiday), hunting, fishing, swimming, playing ball and prisoner's base, rolling hoops, climbing trees, and stealing apricots for a "pillow treat."

A third Reynolds poem in the *London,* "Old Ballads," also referred to Shrewsbury School and revealed how early folk ballads began to influence him. After reading the ballads "under the playground tree," he told the stories of *Chevy Chase* and Richard Plantagenet at night to the other students; the stories seemed all the more interesting to boys who should have been in bed asleep.[20]

Reynolds's fullest account of life at Shrewsbury School appeared in *The Fancy* (1820), but one must be more wary than John Masefield, who accepted the experiences described there as Reynolds's own.[21] Although the character of Peter Corcoran echoed Reynolds's life in many ways—both were born in September 1794, both attended Shrewsbury School, both had an avid interest in sports, and both were aspiring poets—the book was mock autobiography. Its theme, treated both comically and sentimentally, was the moral decay of Peter Corcoran, ending in Corcoran's rejection by his beloved because of his increasing addiction to sports, especially the unsavory boxing. Anticipation of that theme doubtless led Reynolds to exaggerate some of his own misconduct and to add offenses of which he was innocent: young Peter tore grammars, broke bounds, pilfered orchards, fought, and swore. As the traditional servant to an older boy, he cleaned shoes, set the tea utensils, and prepared special treats for the older boy's supper. Corcoran slipped out of his bedroom window at night to steal fruit for his boy-master's tart, and he carried the older boy's fighting cocks in a bag to a nearby field. Like Huck Finn and Tom Sawyer, he liked nighttime adventures, stealing out by moonlight to fish for trout and swim in the Severn. Because he did not study industriously, the headmaster punished him frequently with the rod, but his tutor—and this was Reynolds's own tutor, the Reverend John Sheil—was kind and assiduous in counseling him and caring for him.[22] Although we cannot know that all these experiences were Reynolds's own, they provide a sense of what life was like at Shrewsbury School.

Three other features of Peter Corcoran are significant because the same traits in the later Reynolds argue that they were based on personal schoolboy experience: the writing of verse, the desire for fame, and the sharp wit. Peter began writing verse at school; he lampooned his boyish enemies and penned melancholy and heroic songs. The applause these efforts won from his schoolfellows stirred early his craving for fame. He fought with schoolmates for glory, as well as for love of battle. His wit won notice: no one could surpass him in smart remarks to the maid or the master's daughter.

George Reynolds left Shrewsbury School at midsummer 1805, receiving his last salary payment for only three-quarters of the year at that time; the family arrived in London before 21 October 1805 because Reynolds remembered vividly seeing Lord Nelson in the Strand before the Battle of Trafalgar.[23] One of George Reynolds's reasons for returning to London can be inferred from his son's letter of 1820 to John Taylor: "My father among his various places of *emolument* hold[s] the place of Writing Master to the Asylum & he *has* held it for the last 15 years.—Some of the Managers of this concern are now proposing to lop his trifling salary of £50 per annum down to £30—on the economy *lay*."[24] Though the £50 salary seemed trifling to John Reynolds in 1820, it was undoubtedly attractive to George in 1805, when he had received only £11 annually from Shrewsbury School.

While George Reynolds's employment by the Lambeth Female Asylum was one reason for moving to London, an even greater attraction for Reynolds was a job at the Lambeth Boys Parochial School, which supplied him with a large house for his family, attached to the old school building, and an annual schoolmaster's salary of £120. The additional £50 a year he received as writing master of the Female Asylum enabled him to support the family comfortably.[25]

Founded by Major Richard Lawrence in 1661, the Lambeth Boys Parochial School expanded in 1754 by combining with another school that had been established in 1731. From fifty-four boys in 1754, the school grew until the number reached four hundred in 1809.[26] At the time of the 1754 union, the schoolhouse with attached quarters for the schoolmaster's family had been completely rebuilt. Located on the road leading to Kennington in the Lambeth-green, this was the building into which the Reynoldses moved their family.

With the Boys Parochial School as his primary responsibility, George Reynolds spent a smaller portion of his time as writing master at the Lambeth Female Asylum. Founded by Sir John Fielding in 1758 to provide education and domestic training for destitute orphans, the asylum occupied a large building in Lambeth Marsh. About two hundred girls, from the ages of nine to fifteen, were taught reading, writing, sewing, and cooking to prepare them to become either housewives or domestic servants. William Blake lived near this asylum before 1800 and sympathized with the orphans "labouring at the Whirling Wheel" of their assigned academic and practical work.[27]

George Reynolds was an expert in Dr. Andrew Bell's Madras system of instruction, which employed selected students to teach other students. Since the professional staff could be kept to a bare minimum, the system was very economical and spread rapidly in the first two decades of the nineteenth century. Both Wordsworth and Southey were enthusiastic champions; Wordsworth did some volunteer teaching according to its principles in a school in the Lake District, and Southey wrote a laudatory biography of Dr. Bell, an Anglican clergyman who allied his system firmly with the established church. A competitor named Lancaster, who had originally borrowed the feature of student instruction from Bell, drew much of his support from dissenters. In time, controversy between the two rivals became so heated that young John grew sick of the polemics in the newspapers and magazines. Eventually some parents balked at the practice of cutting corners with their children's education in order to save money,[28] but by 1805 the Bell system had met little resistance, and George Reynolds introduced it smoothly into the Lambeth Boys

Parochial School, receiving the glowing approbation of Dr. Bell himself. George was proud to report to his old pupil Dovaston, "Dr. Bell visits us frequently."[29]

George Reynolds also worked for the school from which he received his own education, Christ's Hospital. His son noted that he had "various places of *emolument.*" When he was later elected head writing master at Christ's Hospital in May 1817, one of the requirements was that a candidate had previously served seven years as an usher in the school.[30] Some of that time could have been served after he left the Lambeth Boys Parochial School about 1816, but not all of it. He may have been employed at Christ's Hospital as an usher before he left London for Shrewsbury, or he may have done some work from 1805 through 1815 in addition to his duties at the Boys Parochial School and the Female Asylum. He was an extremely industrious man. His wife's and his son's letters to Dovaston abounded with remarks about how busy he was with his teaching duties, how exhausted he was, and how fearful they were that he might damage his health by overwork.

Christ's Hospital adopted Bell's system of instruction,[31] and the board of governors chose George Reynolds to introduce the plan into its Hertford branch in August 1809, a mission that pleased young John, since he was allowed to accompany his father for the visit. George received a stipend of £20 and a letter of thanks from the governors. His efforts were "crown'd with success, as the Masters enterd with spirit into the plan as well as the Boys."[32]

George and Charlotte Reynolds chose for their promising son an excellent school, St. Paul's, whose most famous pupil had been John Milton. When John Reynolds entered the school on 4 March 1806 at the age of eleven,[33] he must have passed over some of the lowest of the eight forms because of his earlier three years at Shrewsbury School. By the time St. Paul's students reached the highest form, they were "generally good grammarians and orators, and well instructed in Latin, Greek, and Hebrew."[34] Reynolds's letters, published prose, and translations of Latin poetry confirm the claim that St. Paul's produced able Latinists. He may have received some rudimentary training in Greek, though his letters to Dovaston show that he acquired most of his knowledge of that language from independent study after he left St. Paul's. If he learned any Hebrew, the only reflection of it was the one Hebrew word he included in *The Fancy.*

His master at St. Paul's was Richard Edwards, a graduate of the school and of Cambridge, who served as surmaster from 1806 through 1823.[35] Recognizing the potential of his young student, Edwards supplemented the curriculum of St. Paul's by providing him with a ticket to the Surrey Institution. There he could listen to lectures in the sciences, such as the one on electricity which he found "both useful and amusing," and he could use "a very good library."[36]

The ill health that dogged Reynolds most of his life began while he was at St. Paul's; in the summer of 1808 he contracted a mysterious malady, which neither his mother nor apparently the doctor could identify. An "attack in his Bowels," "a vile cough," and severe loss of weight combined with sudden adolescent growth made him seem skin and bones. Much as they disliked his loss of a quarter from school, his parents, fearing for his life, followed medical advice and sent him out of town for seven weeks.[37]

Among his schoolfellows at St. Paul's was Richard Harris Barham, in later life author of *The Ingoldsby Legends* and a friend of Reynolds.[38] But Barham probably did not know Reynolds well at school, since he was six years Reynolds's senior and entered Oxford in 1807, the year after Reynolds's arrival at St. Paul's. By some curious chance, Richard Allen, son of a Harley, Shropshire farmer, who had been a close friend of Reynolds at Shrewsbury School, enrolled at St. Paul's seven months after Reynolds, at the age of eleven.[39]

The engaging personality that later charmed John Keats, John Clare, Thomas Hood, and many another won John Hamilton Reynolds close friends at St. Paul's as well, though their identities are now lost, since Reynolds referred to them without names in his letters to Dovaston. In the spring of 1809 Reynolds spent a week's vacation, and in the fall an entire month, at the home of a friend in Stanmore in Middlesex.[40] During the latter visit he participated as actively as he could in field sports, though he was hampered by "a deal of advice," doubtless from his mother, "not to touch a gun not even if it is not loaded because it might go off." With another schoolmate he raised pigeons and rabbits for sale, proudly announcing, "I am turn'd merchant."[41]

He seems to have succeeded reasonably well with his studies at St. Paul's. Before the one examination mentioned in the letters, he was apprehensive, wishing in vain for a London visit and assistance in preparation from his mentor Dovaston—but nervousness would be normal for even a good student. In December 1808 Reynolds reported winning a prize for an essay submitted to a school other than St. Paul's, though he was surprised to find that the school magazine gave him the reward without printing the essay. In February 1809 he won a second prize for an essay submitted to a school magazine.[42]

Delighting in the eighteenth-century essayists, especially those who published in the *Spectator,* Reynolds, while still at St. Paul's, began writing essays both for his own pleasure and for the enjoyment of his family and friends. He also managed and wrote for manuscript newspapers and magazines, but he could not foresee that his writing would ever be more than a pleasant avocation. When he was fourteen he realized he would soon have to abandon this hobby for some stable and remunerative work.[43]

Students during this period who lacked the resources to attend a university usually left school at the age of fourteen or fifteen to enter upon some suitable vocation. Reynolds's father had left Christ's Hospital when he was fourteen; and so Reynolds left St. Paul's on 10 September 1809, one day after his fifteenth birthday. It was an emotional experience; as he reported to Dovaston, "Yesterday we all left off at St. Pauls School for the Holidays I quitted for good and I must say I felt some thing rise in my throat when I shut the school door I was pleased to hear (the) one master say he was sorry I was going and another that I had always behaved greatly to his satisfaction."[44]

After the Reynoldses had lived less than three years in the house attached to the Lambeth Boys Parochial School, the board of governors, following protracted committee meetings, decided that it was impractical to repair the old building, which had last been renovated in 1754. Instead, by March 1808 they planned to raze the old building and to erect an entirely new schoolhouse, including quarters for the master's family, on the same site. While the new building was being constructed, the Reynolds family and the school moved temporarily to a large building, formerly Williams's Auction Rooms, across the street from the Lambeth Female Asylum. In anticipation of the comfortable new school, George Reynolds sent his friend Dovaston a detailed sketch of it with one room marked "Elbow room for Dov"; by 23 September 1808 the building was completed, and the Reynoldses had moved in.[45]

The character of George Reynolds has always been in shadow;

those who have sought to interpret it have had to rely in large part on negative evidence. Keats never once mentioned George in his letters despite all the time spent in various Reynolds houses. This omission implies that George was seldom home, perhaps because he was so occupied with his work, and that when he was occasionally home, he was quiet and unassertive. His grandsons' report that he had "a rooted objection to having his personal appearance delineated in any way" confirmed his reticence.[46] His granddaughter's anecdote has revealed his sense of humor. When some boys were caught stealing Hood's apples, Reynolds pretended to be a magistrate and carried the practical joke to such an extreme that the boys thought they were really being convicted.[47]

The Reynolds family letters to Dovaston do not change radically the view of George Reynolds derived from other evidence, but they show more strength behind his mild manners than has been realized. Dedicated to the Bell system of education, he was zealous in implementing it and proud of his success. He quoted with satisfaction Bell's handwritten praise in a presentation copy of Bell's book: "To Mr Geo. Reynolds,—Master of Lambeth School, in grateful acknowledgement of his Faithful, Able and Willing Services in the Cause of Education and religious Instruction on the Madras-System from the Author." And he was justifiably pleased by the printed tribute in the same book: "Of which there is a memorable example in the Boys Charity School at Lambeth, where Mr Reynolds the Schoolmaster, found and made no difficulty but carried every instruction into immediate effect with equal ease and success."[48] He was gratified that Christ's Hospital recognized him as an expert and sent him to its Hertford branch to install its system during the first two weeks of August 1809.[49]

He was not only a teacher and educational administrator, but also an author of textbooks. Though his books were utilitarian, they received some recognition at the time. The first of his six books, *The Simple Rules of Arithmetic, in Questions and Answers . . . On Dr. Bell's Plan,* so impressed Mrs. Sarah Trimmer, friend of Dr. Johnson and recognized authority on education, that she wrote him she planned to do everything she could to advance his work even though it meant sacrificing her own publications based on different principles. He invented a set of "frames" (evidently printed placards) for the student teachers to use in indoctrinating the pupils; he was so confident of the system's value that he submitted a model of it to the Society of Arts and Sciences. When Dovaston visited him in Lambeth, he proudly displayed to his friend his educational system in operation.[50]

George Reynolds was both patient and tenacious. His son described a scene which he endured for many years: "My father . . . has now in the School about 400 boys . . . who when you set your head into it instantly makes your pate dizzy. I wonder how my father bears it."[51] When a party attempted in 1815 to displace Reynolds, he and his son fought hard to retain his position and eventually they triumphed.[52]

Despite the crushing burden of heavy work, Reynolds found time to be attentive to his children; it was he who took them to the theater, the opera, and Astley's Amphitheatre while Charlotte remained at home. He solaced his fatigue in the evenings listening to Jane play the piano, and he enjoyed watching the children prepare for amateur theatricals staged at his house or that of the children's cousins (probably the Butlers). When his son sought reviews of a friend's book, the father's friendship with publisher John Hatchard provided an opportunity for favorable notice in a magazine. When John completed his first book, it was George who went to John Murray and started the process leading to Byron's favorable judgment and to publication, although the son impulsively, and probably unwisely, sought other publishers.[53]

More soft-spoken than his wife, more a listener than a talker, he recognized his wife's good sense and forcefulness and allowed her to contribute to the well-being of his family. He participated actively in guiding his children: promising to buy extra books recommended for John, supplying the materials necessary for Jane's development in music, removing his son from St. Paul's when he reached fifteen, encouraging him to select a vocation, agreeing to provide all the special vocational instruction that he could, and conferring with his son about different clerical positions until they fixed upon the most suitable one. He and his wife almost always agreed in guiding their son, but in the one recorded case where they disagreed, it was his view that prevailed. When John borrowed £5 from Dovaston and had to delay repayment because of imprudent book buying, Charlotte wanted to repay the debt immediately with family money. George insisted that John must learn the consequences of his own actions and suffer some discomfort so that in the future he would be more prudent. Sensing she had been looking for the easy way out, Charlotte wisely abided by his decision.[54]

There is no evidence that she ever threw in George's face her more distinguished family connections, nor did she ridicule his humble origin. Aside from three references to her "valued mother,"[55] she never mentioned her family background in her letters. Instead, her letters were full of pride in George's achievements and his championing of the Bell system over the competing Lancaster plan. She did once annoy a guest, Ralph Rylance, by talking repeatedly about the family's "connexions," but they undoubtedly included George's connections with Dr. Bell, the governors of Christ's Hospital, the Archbishop of Canterbury (to whom George dedicated his second textbook—his steward was a close family friend), Lord Radstock, who came to observe the Bell system in operation,[56] and prosperous booksellers like John Murray and John Hatchard, as well as her family. George's connections were more meaningful to her than her "family position."

A strong and forceful woman, Charlotte accepted full responsibility for the management of the household. After they moved from the temporary housing into the new living quarters of the Lambeth Boys Parochial School, it was she who worried about getting the paperhangers to put the finishing touches on the interior. She directed the domestic servants and grumbled about their inefficiency. Often ill herself, she nursed her children through frequent serious illnesses. She exerted firm control over her children. When John was fifteen, she read his letters and would not let him send those which she judged to be careless or frivolous.[57] When Jane tried to tell her mother that a piece of sheet music she planned to send to Dovaston was not worth sending, Charlotte took a position that sounded characteristic: I have spoken, and that is that.[58]

But tolerance and love shone through this firm direction. Her account of how she struggled to write a letter in the midst of distractions by her children is a memorable example:

I dare say when you see my bratlings again you will perceive them much grown. —to me they seem infinitely taller, but in my eyes they are ever improving I am too partial, & too blind to their little defects—I will just tell you in what manner I am writing. —Jane is reading the book I laid down [*Don Quixote*] when I began this letter—the consequence is, that

Portrait of Charlotte Reynolds, the elder, by William Hilton, owned by Mrs. G. Dora Hessell of Papakura, New Zealand.

she every now & then breaks forth into such noisy laughter that I am in doubt whether she may not be a little beside herself. Eliza & Charlotte are in full speed after the Cat with a ball. & Marianne tormented with a vile cold which is attended with a perpetual sneezing. I leave you to judge with such a confusion of sounds what state this flimsy brain must be in for writing—[59]

Despite the distractions of her children and the demands of managing the household, she wrote a great many letters, though only a small fraction of them has been preserved. Since George had little time and disliked writing letters, he turned over most of the correspondence to her; she and her son wrote nearly all the letters to Dovaston.[60] She corresponded for over twenty-five years with her best friend, Jane Mackay, in Bath.[61] She wrote repeatedly that the recipient of her letters must not expect profundity, what she wrote was nonsense—but that was only modesty. Her letters were thoughtful, lively, sometimes humorous, and always interesting.

She valued candor, insisting that others speak their minds even if their views were unfavorable. She recognized the danger of her own bias in assessing her children and sought to guard against it. She was forthright. She once asked for a present of game, since she wanted it, even after other members of the family had advised her that it was not polite. She was loquacious. She chattered too much, but she also had the good sense to realize the tendency and keep it within bounds. Above all, she was loving. When a family friend failed to mention her husband in two consecutive letters, she reminded him, "I am not a widow," and ordered him to mention George next time. She was well aware that most of her life consisted of her family when she wrote, "our Children are well, I think you like them which is the cause I note them, indeed I believe there is another reason and a very powerful one—that I love them so myself. I should not feel happy if I did not notice them to you. I scarce ever write a letter but they are brought in, in some way, however awkwardly but you know 'Dame Reynolds' is an old fashioned creature firm in Love to her family."[62]

The family friend to whom this passage was addressed, John Freeman Milward Dovaston, had resumed his schoolboy friendship with the Reynolds family. After leaving Shrewsbury School, Dovaston had enrolled at Christ Church, Oxford where he took the B.A. in 1804 and the M.A. in 1807. In June 1807 he was called to the bar at the

Middle Temple. While in London, he practiced law and also served as theatrical critic for a morning newspaper. He now visited the master's house in the Lambeth Boys Parochial School very often, amusing the quiet George with his witty conversation as he smoked his pipe and drank George's ale, entertaining Charlotte by playing the piano, and endearing himself to all the children with his round face, snub nose, and playful manner. In later years some less attractive features of his character emerged, but they were not evident at this time. Dovaston wrote English and Latin verses, played the piano and organ, and composed music for songs. His love of music led to friendship with the London bookseller George Walker, who specialized in sheet music.

Dovaston left London early in 1808 to return to Shropshire to care for his fatally ill father. He wrote George and Charlotte, describing his trip and the condition of his father; she replied on 9 March 1808, advising what food and wine to give the patient to bring him through his illness. Her advice was to no avail; John F. M. Dovaston died in early April, and his son inherited the estate at West Felton, where he lived for the rest of his life, pleading his law cases at Shire Hall in Shrewsbury and superintending the bees and apple trees that were the chief producers at the Nursery. He was a wealthy man who lived a relaxed rural life surrounded by a host of friends such as his neighbor Thomas Yates and an Oswestry doctor, John Evans, who had also been a friend of the Reynolds family when they lived in Shrewsbury.

Dovaston was a very eligible bachelor, and the attitude of his neighbors and friends illustrated perfectly Jane Austen's ironic epigram, "It is a truth universally acknowledged, that a single man in possession of a good fortune must be in want of a wife." His housekeeper named Molly, however, kept Dovaston so comfortable that Charlotte once said he did not need a wife so long as he had Molly. Gossipers were so persistent that at one time rumor had him married. Charlotte could write him jokingly, "& now for a bit of news for you—you are Married."[63] But he disappointed all the matchmakers by never marrying. With no need to add to his income with his pen, he published gratis in the Oswestry *Herald,* the Shrewsbury *Chronicle,* and the *Gentleman's Magazine.*

A year before he left St. Paul's, John Reynolds had pondered the vocation he would choose, writing Dovaston that he knew his manu-

script newspapers and magazines were mere pastimes and that he
would soon have to settle on some more mundane pursuit. After his
return from the trip to Hertford with his father in August 1809, he
thought he had made his determination—he would become a surveyor. His parents regarded it as a respectable occupation, and it
seemed within his grasp since his father could instruct him in pre-
vocational studies, he could take additional lessons in drawing, and,
though the fee for an apprenticeship might be difficult, it could be
managed.[64] He doubtless discussed the matter with his friend Frank
Squibb, who later did prepare to become a surveyor. Reynolds's
mother asked Dovaston for counsel in the matter, though she ruled
out any attempt to dissuade him from surveying, since she believed
he had seriously made up his mind. But nothing came of this carefully considered plan.

After leaving St. Paul's in 1809, John spent part of September with
a former schoolmate in Stanmore and then returned to Lambeth to
amuse himself. The Reynolds children had three close friends, William, Frank, and George Squibb, whose father G. Squibb, an auctioneer,[65] had a house in Ealing within walking distance of the Lambeth Boys Parochial School. Frank Squibb was three years older than
John;[66] William Squibb was close to Frank's age; and George was the
youngest. The Reynolds and Squibb children were in and out of
each other's houses constantly, singing, playing, and arguing good-
naturedly.

A favorite pastime was to stage amateur theatricals at their homes,
most often around Christmastime. This year the preparation began
early. The evening of 10 October 1809 found the living room filled,
with George writing to Dovaston, Charlotte and a female guest doing needlework, and "the Children painting Scenery for a new Theatre John the principal Artist—. ⟨Wh⟩ round a comfortable fire."[67]
Dovaston, who had evidently acted in their private theatricals when
he lived in London, planned to visit them around Christmas and
promised to play a part in their performance. John joked, "You may
depend upon good wages I (*the Manager*) k[n]owing you to be a
good performer."[68] John, Dovaston, William and Frank Squibb, and
probably some of the other young people acted Samuel Foote's *The
Mayor of Garratt* (1763) at the Squibbs' house in Ealing. Good-
natured Dovaston accepted a female part and played Mrs. Bruin so

hilariously that both families remembered the performance for a long time. Eight months later the Squibbs asked to be remembered to "Mrs. Bruin."[69]

So close to the Reynolds family as to be almost an adopted relative, Dovaston served as a mentor to John and Jane for years. Replying promptly to John's letters, usually within a few weeks and often within a couple of days, he guided him in his reading of Latin classics (John must read Ovid in the original and not in translation, and Sallust was too difficult for one his age), encouraged him to study Greek, and criticized John's writing when he grew careless in some letters. He followed closely Jane's development on the piano and organ, providing expert advice on the quality of the composers whose work she considered playing, writing new words for "Pinkney House" when the old words seemed unsatisfactory, and sending her copies of his own music as he wrote it.

After Dovaston returned to Shropshire early in 1810, John busied himself for a time with various pleasures. He sent Dovaston a hamper of busts of the poets, no doubt at Dovaston's request. He shopped for books, buying a copy of the *Bath Guide* and an edition of *Dinarbas,* and glorying especially in Tonson's edition of the *Spectator* and the *Guardian,* which he bought at Squibb's auction room. John and some friends, doubtless including the Squibbs, began issuing a manuscript collection of essays entitled the "Inspector," which they continued for at least six months. John requested essays from Dovaston for the work, and Dovaston sent one.[70] He opened yet another theater, apparently at the Reynolds house, for which he composed and delivered a prefatory address.[71]

These diversions, innocent and educational though they were, must have made his parents uneasy, for he was fifteen, had been out of school for six months, and still had found no work to pay for his support. Finally in March 1810 he took a job that he immediately disliked. As a clerk in the office of the *Day* newspaper, he was confined to a stuffy and noisy room, doing the most pedestrian kind of clerical work, and denied any part in writing for the paper, which he longed to do. He grew so desperate that on 10 May 1810 he had the temerity to ask Dovaston to use his influence with B. Wood, editor of the Shrewsbury *Chronicle,* to secure him a place as the paper's London correspondent—this from a fifteen-year-old boy. Dovaston was doubtless startled by this request; he certainly disapproved and expressed his displeasure to Charlotte, who agreed that John had done wrong and deserved rebuke.[72]

The wildness of his attempt to escape may have served a purpose in alerting his parents to how miserable the drudgery was making him. John and his father immediately began searching around for another position. John resigned from the *Day,* considered for a time a clerkship to a conveyancer, but accepted instead in early July 1810 a place as clerk in the Amicable Society for a Perpetual Assurance, located in Sergeant's Inn, Fleet Street.[73] There the work was far less cramping and deadening to his spirit. His employer, Mr. Pensam, was "a good man easily satisfied yet punctual to Business."[74] Certainly the firm promised stability: the Amicable Society, founded in 1705, was the world's oldest life insurance company.[75] Reynolds was the third of three clerks. In addition to the usual office paper work, he witnessed the declarations of customers who contracted for insurance policies.[76] Office discipline must have been relaxed since after the summer of 1810 he wrote nearly all his letters to Dovaston from the office, and he had Dovaston address all letters to him there so that he would receive them sooner. His salary was £100 a year paid quarterly[77]—rather handsome for a fifteen-year-old when compared with the £170 total of his father's two major salaries, though the sale of textbooks and teaching frames supplemented his father's income. Reynolds had found the steady employment he needed, and it was to last for six years until April 1816.

It is uncertain whether Reynolds wrote in 1809 the essays, letters, and poems signed J. H. R. and almost always dated from Sudbury, Suffolk, published in Rudolph Ackermann's *Repository of Arts, Literature, Fashions* and in his *Poetical Magazine,* which printed the overflow from the *Repository.*[78] Young Reynolds may have mailed these pieces from Sudbury. He, his mother, Jane, and the other girls sometimes left Lambeth to go to "the Country" for reasons of health or pleasure. The Reynolds family may have had a relative or close friend who owned a place near Sudbury which they were free to visit whenever they pleased. The quality of the material in the *Repository* and *Poetical Magazine* does not argue against authorship by a fourteen- and fifteen-year-old boy. For example, the ponderous moralizing in "On the Inconveniences of Beauty" sounds juvenile enough to be unintentionally comic: females who are not beautiful are fortunate because beauty is likely to make them conceited and to deflect them from virtue.[79] Reynolds was certainly precocious enough to have written all these pieces; he may have selected them to be printed from the manuscript magazines and newspapers that he circulated from 1808 through 1810. His letters to Dovaston reveal that he did write the poems printed in the *Repository* in 1812 and 1813, but none of the later poems has a Sudbury location. It is quite possible that some other Sudbury resident with the same initials wrote the material published in 1809. Unless a definite link can be established between the Reynolds family and Sudbury, the authorship must remain doubtful.

A frequent visitor to the hospitable Reynolds home in 1810 was the Reverend John Sheil, John's old tutor at Shrewsbury School, who had married and moved to London. When the Reynoldses told him Dovaston was annoyed that Sheil had allowed their correspondence to lapse, he wrote Dovaston a charming letter including a glowing tribute to the Reynolds family: "Yet I like the town; but I think it would be different without the Reynolds'. I shall say nothing of them, for you know them well; besides I have no time to cull words and hunt expressions, & unless I did so, I could not shew you what I feel & see. Believe me it is at Lambeth only, that I feel happy; and when prompted to curse Shrewsbury School & all its concerns, but particularly my connection with it, I think of this friendship, my murmurs are all hushed, and I fancy myself overpaid for all my uneasiness."[80]

Reynolds sometimes chafed at being a "most compleat Cockney Clerk,"[81] but the company of the kindly Sheil for a time and later other companions and activities kept him happy for the next two years. He continued his interest in the theater, which was at first boyishly undiscriminating. When his father took him to see *The Blood Red Knight* at Astley's Royal Amphitheatre, he was "much pleased" with "the last Scene a Battle upon real Horses in Armour," all bathed in "Blue light." Not until later did his mother's and the newspapers' objections make him realize that such spectacles with horses and elephants on stage might debase the drama. He enjoyed popular comedies like *All in the Wrong,* as well as *Hamlet* and *Julius Caesar.* His pleasure in private theatricals continuing, he acted in one of Colman's plays performed at the Squibb house in the fall of 1810. Shortly thereafter he produced Tobin's *Honey Moon* at the Reynolds house, acting the Duke Aranza himself. On New

Year's Eve 1810, Tobin's *Honey Moon* was repeated, followed by *Sylvester Daggerwood* with Reynolds as the hero and a farce, *Who's the Duke,* with himself as Old Doiley. For the last performance, Reynolds requested and Dovaston sent within a few days a hastily written prologue. It was doggerel, but it struck just the right note and pleased family and friends greatly. The next fall when Reynolds produced Sheridan's *The Rivals,* he remembered the pleasure Dovaston's prologue had given and requested a second, but by that time Dovaston was temporarily miffed with the Reynoldses and did not oblige.[82]

During this time Reynolds proceeded with his independent study and reading. He worked at Greek, using a grammar written in English rather than Latin, and when Dovaston objected to this departure from the practice he had known at Shrewsbury School and Oxford, Reynolds remained unpersuaded and defended his use of the grammar written in English. He liked the sound of Greek and planned to persevere until he reached his ultimate goal, to read Homer in the original. In his reading of contemporaries, he followed the fashion by reveling in Walter Scott and Thomas Campbell's *Gertrude of Wyoming.* He considered, but postponed, buying a new edition of Shakespeare derived from George Steevens's text.[83]

Not all his spare time went to the theater, professional and private, and to study and reading. He spent some evenings singing with friends as Jane accompanied on the piano. He returned to the fishing he had enjoyed in Shrewsbury and spent daylight hours on Sundays and holidays pursuing the sport. He played cricket, at one time snapping the leader in his foot.[84] He attended the anniversary dinner of the Amicable Society, both hampered and supported by his mother's ambiguous attitude toward it. She feared the drinking at the dinner might lead him astray, and yet she recognized so clearly his obligation to attend that she wrote the anniversary address delivered there.[85]

Although Dovaston early in his life was a genial, generous, and loving man, he already had streaks of touchiness and suspicion, which surfaced only in small ways. He was a bachelor who could behave curiously like the spouse who continually seeks reassurance by saying, "You don't love me anymore." At times it seemed to him as if his warm friendship with the Reynoldses was one-sided because they did not return his affection sufficiently. He almost always answered their letters within a few days or weeks (his letters are not preserved, but he endorsed the Reynolds letters which he saved so carefully with the dates of his replies); they delayed their replies for many weeks and even months. He had visited them three times for extended periods, staying in their house while he was in London (September 1808, January 1809, and November and December 1809);[86] not one of them had accepted any of his repeated invitations to visit him in his commodious house in Shropshire. George had carried out one commission for him by going to the Middle Temple to inquire of Randall Norris, whom George knew as a governor of Christ's Hospital, what Dovaston needed to do about his membership in the law society there,[87] but that was their only reciprocation for the presents of poultry and game with which he showered them. He began to complain of "the daily diminution of [my] powers to please at Lambeth."[88] Charlotte tried to reassure him.

why should you pester your brains with Ideas such as these, unless when you examine your Bosom you call to recollection any conduct for which you can blame yourself. if you can, or do, I believe I may say you think more of it than any one here does. for we remain the same happy united family we were before you press'd our threshold, & I trust shall ever remain so, & you seem to wish us to beleive you the same friend, then, what occasion for all these doubts & fears—[89]

Dovaston thought John should have visited him at West Felton instead of wasting his time at the *Day* newspaper on work that he hated. Charlotte replied sensibly that such a visit would have been impossible at the crucial time after John left school; though the first job had been a bad one, it was better than doing nothing, and the process of exploring employment had led to his present satisfactory place at the Amicable. But Dovaston was not completely satisfied.

A year later he wrote the Reynoldses that he planned to visit them in Lambeth in the fall of 1811. John was delighted and encouraged him, but Charlotte had to inform him in her usual forthright way that she could no longer supply him with a bedroom because Jane had become a music teacher and had been allowed to turn the spare bedroom into a studio where she could teach her pupils. She hastened to add that she hoped he would make the trip, find a room elsewhere, and take all his meals and spend as many of his waking hours as possible with them.[90] But Dovaston was hurt by this departure from the established pattern of his visits. He did not go to London, and it seems likely that a chance remark by John in a letter written the same day as his mother's increased his irritation. John wrote that his mother's best friend, Jane Mackay, was coming from Bath for a visit and that he hoped the two would be there at the same time so they could meet. It is not certain Jane Mackay stayed in the Reynolds house, but Dovaston must have wondered whether she did and must have suspected that another friend was being preferred over him. Not only did he refuse to go to London, but he did not reply to their letters for many months, and then not until both John and Charlotte had written him again. And when he received Charlotte's second letter, he waited almost two months to reply. He also did not send the copy of the engraved Breidden Society Glees and Chorus which he had promised before he had been told he would not have a room.[91]

CHAPTER 2

London and Shropshire—
Summer 1812–Summer 1813

Dovaston's annoyance over the room incident lingered. Though Charlotte later invited him several times to visit their house in Lambeth, he never stayed with them in London again. Nevertheless, he still valued his friendship with the Reynolds family. He had invited John many times to visit him at West Felton, but John had always had to decline because of the expense and because of his employment at the Amicable. He had longed to visit Dovaston ever since Dovaston inherited the estate from his father. Soon after he began working at the Amicable, he started saving £5 from each quarterly £25 payment of his salary to cover the expenses of a trip. In the summer of 1812 when he had saved enough to make the trip possible, he wrote Dovaston that he planned to visit, and Dovaston replied promptly "to invite him here."[1] John applied to his employer, Mr. Pensam, for immediate leave instead of the appointed vacation time in September; Pensam refused the request because of business pressures at the time, but he advanced the date of John's vacation to 10 August. John wrote Dovaston that he would come in the middle of August unless Dovaston planned to be away from home at the time, and, when Dovaston did not reply promptly, John wrote again after nine days, eager for Dovaston's answer.[2] Dovaston repeated his warm invitation for mid-August, and the long-cherished dream became a reality.

Taking with him music for Dovaston, a letter from his mother, and news of a victory by Wellington in Spain, he left by the mail on Sunday evening, 16 August, for Shrewsbury, riding on the outside of the coach. His mother's fear that his customary fit of drowsiness about eleven o'clock might cause him to fall off the coach[3] proving groundless, he arrived safely on Monday at Shrewsbury, where Dovaston met him with a horse and gig and they drove on to West Felton. After a brief visit with another old family friend named Gribble,

Dovaston took him on an excursion across the border into Wales to see Lynellys, the Ogo, and the Rocks of Blodwell.[4] John's memory of the Blodwell Rocks prompted him two years later to write "A Recollection," a fifty-seven-line blank-verse poem printed along with *The Eden of Imagination*.[5] Even more important, during the trip he saw "the flounced frock and white stocking" of *"Peg o'the Pant"* (nickname for a local Welsh beauty?) that led him later to write one of his finest poems, "Margaret," published in *The Naiad*.[6]

At the Nursery, Reynolds met for the first time another London friend of Dovaston's. Born on 30 March 1782[7] in Bolton, Lancashire, Ralph Rylance gained some local distinction as a young scholar in the church school he attended there. Apprenticed to a weaver long enough to master the trade, he continued his literary interests and brought his talents to the attention of the Liverpool scholar William Roscoe, who became his patron and in later life his close friend. Roscoe arranged further education for Rylance with the classicist John Lemprière at his school in Abingdon, where Rylance distinguished himself as a linguist, mastering Greek and Latin and beginning the study of contemporary languages which he later broadened to a knowledge of eighteen. In 1805, at the age of twenty-three, he wrote a play that pleased Roscoe so much he rewarded Rylance with twelve guineas and secured him a place as employee of the London printer and versifier, John McCreery. After learning the bookseller's trade during a year with McCreery, Rylance set himself up as a literary man-of-all-work, a hack who was amazingly versatile in turning to financial account any facet of the book trade, no matter how lowly.[8] He served as ghostwriter, first through Cadell and Davies and later through Longmans, for any wealthy man who wanted the honor of authorship without doing the work. He wrote official agricultural reports, medical treatises, and other scientific studies. He translated from French, German, Italian, Spanish, and Portuguese. He advised publishers on the soundness of manuscripts offered for publication. He wrote political pamphlets and jokes and fillers for magazines. He supplied obituaries, statistics, and indexes for journals. He tutored in French and gave lessons in English to Argentine diplomats. A man of remarkable talents, he was willing to perform any task to support himself and his mother, with whom he lived at this time at 34 Newman Street.

In the autumn of 1810 Rylance had first met Dovaston while traveling through the county securing materials for the Shropshire section of *The Beauties of England and Wales,* a work he was ghost-writing in part for the Reverend Joseph M. Nightingale, a Unitarian minister in London. In 1812, closer in age to Dovaston than the eighteen-year-old Reynolds, he had not known Dovaston as long as Reynolds had, but his shrewdness, wit, and deference to the country squire had earned him friendship that led to many extended visits to West Felton.

Though Rylance did not usually make a good first impression, he did on this occasion, and he and Reynolds quickly became good friends. The three relaxed and enjoyed themselves in Dovaston's comfortable house and spacious grounds, when they were not visiting Dovaston's neighbors, Mr. Davenport and Mrs. Turner.[9] For the first time Reynolds read Dovaston's completed poem, *Fitzgwarine,* of which he had seen only passages copied into letters. They discussed Rylance's plans for a poem about the time of Henry IV and Hotspur to be called "St. Magdalene's Eve," and Reynolds read aloud from his own manuscript poems. In high spirits they improvised a continuation of the *Spectator* with Dovaston as Sir Roger de Coverley, Rylance as the Spectator, and Reynolds as Will Wimble. Reynolds's delight was complete, "I never spent a happier fortnight in my life."[10]

Reynolds's return from this idyllic vacation was an anticlimax. On 31 August he left Rylance with Dovaston, commissioned to deliver in London letters to Rylance's friend and collaborator Reverend Joseph Nightingale, to Rylance's mother, and to Mrs. Turner's son. Riding on the outside of the coach during the daylight hours, but managing to get inside at night, he was repelled by the vulgarity and stupidity of his fellow passengers. The "knaves and fools" who mouthed clichés about weather and crops were bad enough, but worse was an Irishman who was taking his gibbering, insane wife to London with absurd hope that the London air would cure her. But the sight of home revived him; he bolted into the Reynolds house on 1 September at six o'clock in the evening and poured out the wonders of his visit to the assembled family until eleven.[11]

Rylance and Reynolds continued their friendship in London. On his return from Shropshire, Rylance stopped by the Amicable office in Fleet Street to deliver Dovaston's letters and to tell John of the adventures he and Dovaston had had after Reynolds left and of the "rhyming dialogues" that they had written. Accepting the invitation Charlotte had extended to him by mail while he was still with Dovaston, Rylance dined on 5 September at the Reynolds home, where he was most impressed by the beauty of fifteen-year-old Marianne. His testimony revealed that she already displayed the beauty that Charles Dilke was to praise in later years: "We had excellent viands, wine & music. Mary Anne is a goddess in stature and form,— the prettiest dove-like eyes and sweetest mouth I ever gazed upon."[12]

Reynolds was "anxious that Rylance should be suited." When Rylance dined again with the family on Monday, 14 September, Reynolds arranged the guest list to make the occasion satisfying for him. To balance one dull guest, "a Gentleman that has travelled a great deal but very honestly brought little away from the various places he has seen," he also invited his uncle, probably Charles Butler, "(a very clever Man) and one who has a tolerable share of Taste for the ancient & modern classics."[13] Rylance was gratified by the attention and Charlotte was pleased to add him to the list of family friends.

During his frequent visits with the family, Rylance became smitten with Jane. Though he was struck by the beauty of fifteen-year-old Marianne, she was too young for his thirty years, and he turned more seriously to twenty-one-year-old Jane. He wrote Dovaston, "Dare I tell you a secret that I have half a mind to fall in love with that Jane Reynolds—I supped there on Friday night and then the idea partly struck me for the second time. I can't tell how it will be. . . . The maid hath much that man desireth in a wife." His amorous interest continued for at least six months; to a report to Dovaston that he was giving her French lessons, he appended the joking query, "Abelard?"[14] But either from Rylance's faint heart or Jane's lack of response, nothing further developed between them.

Reynolds remained close to Rylance for a year-and-a-half, following all Rylance's political activities in support of the candidacy of Percival Lewis, who ran for the House of Commons for Radnor in Wales in the fall of 1812. Rylance conferred with Lewis in London, traveled to Wales on his behalf, once being overturned but uninjured in the Gloucester mail, and engaged Dovaston as legal counsel to join him in Wales to support Lewis's campaign.[15] Reynolds facilitated Rylance's correspondence with Dovaston by securing a frank for him, read the first part of "St. Magdalene's Eve" as soon as

Rylance had written it, dined with Rylance and his mother in their house in 34 Newman Street, and assisted Rylance with his index to the *Edinburgh Review*.[16] He was drawn to Rylance because he and Dovaston were the only two of his correspondents who shared his love of poetry.[17]

Reynolds was young and undiscriminating enough to overvalue *Fitzgwarine,* Dovaston's attempt to capitalize on the Walter Scott vogue by shifting the scene of a medieval metrical romance from the Scottish to the Welsh border. He promised Dovaston that he would make every effort to ensure public attention,[18] and he kept his promise. As soon as the work was published, Reynolds persuaded three of his friends to buy copies, and he reviewed it favorably in the *Gentleman's Magazine,* at first concealing his authorship of the review from Dovaston. When Dovaston learned from Rylance that Reynolds wrote the review, Dovaston blamed him for an error; Reynolds explained the mistake as the result of not having the volume with him when the editor John Nichols pressed him to finish the review.[19]

Reynolds praised *Fitzgwarine* highly in a review in Asperne's *European Magazine,* calling the work his "most spirited prose performance" to date.[20] He tried to review the work in Ackermann's *Repository of Arts, Literature, Fashions,* reporting to Dovaston that he was confident the review would be accepted because Ackermann was very attentive to him and always printed what he sent, but Reynolds had forgotten that the *Repository* printed only news of works in progress and excluded reviews.[21] He considered using his father's influence with the bookseller John Hatchard to arrange a review in the *British Critic,* but delayed because he lacked an extra copy of *Fitzgwarine* to send, and finally decided that the magazine was not influential enough to warrant the trouble. The *Monthly Review* annoyed him by damning *Fitzgwarine,* but he assured Dovaston that no one would be swayed by the journal notorious for ruining Henry Kirke White's life by attacking his youthful poetry. Robert Southey's defense of Kirke White and attack on the *Monthly* is still rather well-known to literary scholars.[22]

Knowing the journalistic ropes, Reynolds realized that what would count most would be a review in either the Whig *Edinburgh* or the Tory *Quarterly,* the most powerful journals in the land. He despaired of the *Edinburgh* because *Fitzgwarine* was in the new, somewhat irregular "Romantic" mode, and he understood Francis Jeffrey's conservative poetic position. He hoped for favorable treatment in the *Quarterly,* waiting eagerly for one issue, only to find that it ignored Dovaston.[23] He then sent a copy privately to Octavius Gilchrist, a mainstay of the *Quarterly* and an old friend of Dovaston's, but to their surprise the maneuver failed to secure any notice of *Fitzgwarine.*[24] Reynolds welcomed the praise of the antiquarians William Roscoe and John Britton, though he must have known that their tributes, pleasing as they were to Dovaston, would have little influence on sales.[25] He even took the small practical step of reminding the bookseller George Walker that he ought to promote the sale of his friend Dovaston's book.[26] That *Fitzgwarine* achieved only limited success was certainly not Reynolds's fault; he had done everything that a nineteen-year-old could reasonably be expected to do.

While he was promoting *Fitzgwarine,* Reynolds also provided other services for Dovaston. He promised to transact any business in London that Dovaston wished and sent him George Crabbe's *Tales in Verse* (1812), which Reynolds recommended highly and later defended stoutly against the disparaging comments of Dovaston and Rylance.[27] He gave Dovaston his own duplicate copy of Francis Hodgson's *Lady Jane Grey* and bought a copy of Beresford's *Miseries of Life* for him.[28] He searched for a copy of Burton's *Anatomy of Melancholy,* reported the price of Hayley's *Life of Cooper,* doubted that so old a book as *The System of Nature* could be found, and offered to send James and Horace Smith's *Rejected Addresses* and Byron's *Giaour.*[29] He copied and sent William Spencer's translation of *Leonora* and his own manuscript essays "Reflections of Posthumous Fame among the Ancients" and "On Flowers."[30] Although Dovaston paid for all the books but one, he had reason to be grateful to Reynolds for the time and energy expended in his service.

Reynolds was as close to Dovaston as a nineteen-year-old could be to a man, twelve years older, who maintained the stance of mature adviser. He could joke about Dovaston's single state and tease him about a friend of the Reynolds family—as long as Dovaston's "favorite" Miss Box was not married, there was still some hope.[31] But he did not reveal to Dovaston until nearly two years later a sharp blow to his own heart which occurred at this time. It was too personal and too painful. His first sweetheart died in the bloom of her youth, probably before 24 May 1813, when a poem included in a letter seemed to hint at her death. The poem is among the best of Reynolds's early efforts, faintly reminiscent of Shelley's finer brief lyrics:

1

Can a rosy lip or a sparkling eye,
    rivet the lover's heart;
Will not at last their memories die,
    And their fading Charms depart:
For oh! when a mind is wanting there,
    Will Beauty requite? ah never!
The remembrance of lips tho' sweet & fair,
    Time will sever.

2

Ah many a flower of color bright,
    Delights the eye while thriving;
But it only pleases the passing sight,
    And only attracts while living:
⟨But⟩ The Rose still remains admir'd when dead
And its fragrance serves to discover
That virtue lives when Beauty is fled
And Life is over.[32]

Reynolds told Dovaston that he wrote the poem "for a slow movement of Haydn," and it is called "Lines Written to one of Haydn's Airs" in the copies in the Leigh Browne-Lockyer Collection. No one would suspect that a real death lay behind the poignant second stanza—indeed it may be coincidence, and the passage nothing more than general moralizing.

But it is certain that his sweetheart died before 15 August 1813, the date given to the following poem published in the *Repository:*

To *.*.******.

The air is still, the day is gone,
    I turn aside to weep;
And meet it is that I alone,
    With tears, thy watch should keep.
    Oh! sacred is thy mystic sleep,
And ne'er should sigh or groan
    Molest thy urn, where death-flow'rs creep,
In green gloom, round the stone.

I will not sigh, that fools may hear,
    I will not weep aloud;

I will not shed the dewy tear
 Before the heartless crowd;—
But I will sorrow o'er thy shrowd,
Alone in death be near,
 Bend o'er thee like a winter cloud,
And mourn upon thy bier.

J. H. R.
West Felton, Aug. 15, 1813.[33]

There seems no way to identify the dead girl with certainty, but later poems produce a surprising number of revelations. "Stanzas to ** ****** (" 'Tis past; the dream of life is oer"), published in the *Inquirer* (May 1814, p. 104), confirms the indication of the two initials that she was known by two Christian names rather than one, something like Anna Maria or Mary Ellen. The six stars for the surname in both poems indicate that it had six letters. We can conclude that she was a Londoner because "Stanzas to ** ******" states that he viewed her body after death and visited her grave often alone at night. She was loved both by Reynolds and by his future wife, Eliza Powell Drewe, whom she resembled. In a letter to Dovaston of 10 October 1814, he included a poem lamenting the death of the girl and addressed almost certainly to Eliza Powell Drewe, "written to a Young Lady (at her desire) upon the death of a youthful friend of ⟨words cancelled heavily and illegibly⟩ hers and mine."[34] In a poem addressed to Eliza Drewe in the *Champion* of 22 December 1816, he recounted how he gazed upon Eliza's face until her similarity to the other girl conjured up an image of the dead:

I wander'd back to brighter hours,
 And mused on one resembling thee;—
To moments fled like summer showers,
 When eyes were tearless,—hopes were free.

I gazed on thee, and thought on one,
 Who was so like thee in her mirth,—
That life, it might be deem'd, had won
 Her spirit to return to earth.

I gaz'd on her, in watching thee,—
 I heard her voice once more in thine,—
Her beauty beam'd again on me,
 When thy dark eyes encounter'd mine.

There was no feature of thy face,
But Memory knew its beauty well;—
There was no wild or simple grace
Of form, but charm'd me as a spell.

I felt thy presence—feel it now,
My ruffled passions deeply thrill;—
It was not in thy thoughts, that thou
Had touch'd a chord that long was still.[35]

Finally, in "To Ella," published in the *Champion* of 30 June 1816, he told how once, forgetting that Eliza also loved the dead girl, he mentioned her and caused Eliza to weep. He resolved in the future to grieve silently to spare her such pain. The later poems leave no doubt that Eliza Drewe also loved his first sweetheart. One suspects from the marked resemblance between the dead girl and Eliza that they were relatives, and from the six letters of the surname that she was a daughter of the Squibb or Butler family, who died early in 1813. Eliza seems to have been a relative of a London family close to the Reynoldses, but no records have been discovered to establish the connection.

Benjamin Bailey, whom Reynolds knew by 1813 if not before, had also known the dead girl. In 1815 or 1816 Haydon's depiction of Jairus's daughter in *Christ's Entry into Jerusalem* struck Bailey as such a likeness of Reynolds's first love who "died in her bloom" that he wrote a poem to marvel at it.[36] Bailey had seen the living girl, but her image was fixed firmly in his mind by her picture in Reynolds's room. Reynolds described the picture in stanza 5 of "Reproach Me Not" and perhaps referred to it in "Sonnet on the Picture of a Lady" in *The Garden of Florence*.[37]

While Reynolds's grief over the death of his first sweetheart was deep and long-lasting, he did not withdraw from active life because of it. Much of his time and attention from 1812 through early 1815 was given to the Zetosophian Society, a literary, cultural, and social club composed of fourteen young men, most of them "of very considerable genius."[38] The society was well established when Reynolds was elected to membership on 16 September 1812.[39] His friend Frank Squibb may have nominated him for election. In October 1816 John Martin listed the members at the time of the bitter feud that ended the society early in 1815 in this order: "W. Squibb, F Squibb,

Rice, B. Bailey, J. Burchell, J Reynolds, E[?] Hardesty, J. Cottle, Stanley, Archer, W. Seymour, and J. Martin."[40] W. and F. Squibb were Reynolds's close friends William and Frank Squibb; Rice, James Rice; B. Bailey, Benjamin Bailey; J. Burchell, perhaps William John Burchell, who wrote for the *Pamphleteer* after 1813 and who published books on Africa in 1819 and 1822;[41] J. Reynolds, the subject of this biography; Stanley, George Stanley, who wrote a sonnet on Haydon's portrait of Wordsworth for *Annals of the Fine Arts*[42] and was an auctioneer of paintings; Archer, Archibald Archer, portrait painter later known to Keats; W. Seymour, the Seymour who was later William Squibb's law partner,[43] and J. Martin, John Martin, copublisher of Reynolds's first two books, friend of Keats, and bibliographer. I have found no trace of E.[?] Hardesty or J. Cottle.

Three unknown members dropped out between 1813 and the dissolution of the society in early 1815, for Reynolds recorded on 3 March 1813 that there were fourteen members; Benjamin Bailey joined after that date in the summer of 1813, and Martin's list included only twelve members. Otherwise the membership remained stable.

The Zetosophian Society, the Greek name meaning "I seek wisdom," met every Wednesday evening. Each member was required to write and read an essay once a month.[44] On 14 April 1813, Reynolds delivered "Reflections on Posthumous Fame, and its effect upon the minds of the Ancients," an essay which he had taken pains in writing and was anxious to have well received.[45] On 18 August 1813, Benjamin Bailey delivered his "Introductory Address to the Zetosophian Society"; he was equally anxious and strove diligently to produce a sketch of the progress of learning from the ancients to the eighteenth century in seventeen competent Spenserian stanzas.[46] He had been elected within a month before this date, since the rule was that each member deliver an address once a month. Reynolds did not hear his address because he was visiting Dovaston in Shropshire at the time, but he had met Bailey in the spring of 1813 or earlier. Before 30 September 1813, Reynolds read another essay, this one "On Flowers."[47] These essays were the only ones recorded; of course there were many more. The title of another essay has been preserved—James Rice's "Essay on Swearing," which was so well received that it was privately printed, though not published.[48] Rice's humor would

Miniature of Benjamin Bailey by an unknown artist c. 1817
in the Keats House, Hampstead.

doubtless be much more satisfying to read than Bailey's grave verse treatise.

Proud of his membership in the Zetosophian Society, Reynolds went out of his way to mention it in his letters to Dovaston, referring to "One of our Zetosophians" and a "Brother Zetosophian" instead of using names.[49] He called the society "excellent" and reported with pleasure, "it is astonishing what information may be reaped from united endeavours."[50] Like Benjamin Franklin's Junto, it served a valuable educational function for a group of young men unable to attend college by combining study with sociability. Before he was elected, Reynolds was careful to brush up on his Latin and Greek, and the preparation of essays pressed him to read widely and purposefully in both the classical languages and English.[51]

Another society, social rather than educational, was almost as important to Dovaston as the Zetosophian was to Reynolds—the Breidden Society in Shropshire. Dovaston's father, John F. M. Dovaston, had founded it for the purpose of celebrating an annual festival on Breidden Hill with eating, drinking, smoking, poetry reading, toasting, singing, dancing, and much kissing sparked by a traditional "Kissing Stone." Until his death in 1808, the elder Dovaston conducted the summer festival every year without any formal organization. In 1809 Thomas Yates, who succeeded the elder Dovaston as president, arranged for written rules, which the younger Dovaston recorded. Every year thereafter the president named his successor for the following year before leaving the hill, and "the president's will being by him signified" was "in all cases [to] be held decisive law." But the president had to pay for these prerogatives since he alone was "at the whole Expence, and Trouble of providing a plain cold dinner; Rum, Brandy, and Beer." No laurel being available in the area, a poet laureate could not be created; instead, the abundant fern on the hill led to the substitution of poet ferneat, a post which vied in importance with that of queen of the hill, which the president filled by solemn pronouncement each year after selecting from the fair revelers. Dovaston was president, poet ferneat, and recorder in 1810; vice-president and poet ferneat in 1811; and poet ferneat in 1812.[52] Charlotte Reynolds's familiarity with the details of these festivals indicated that she and George had been among the sixty guests who participated annually before the Reynoldses left Shropshire in 1805.

After the visit with Dovaston in August 1812, Reynolds naturally wished to return, but his work at the Amicable, the expense, and a serious illness in February 1813 presented barriers. Dovaston invited him to spend part of the Christmas season of 1812 with him, but Reynolds had to decline.[53] In March 1813 his hospitable friend invited him well in advance to spend a week or two in the summer, but at that time he doubted that he could go.[54] Then Rylance's visit to Dovaston in April around Shakespeare's birthday reminded Reynolds of the rural pleasures and literary conversation he was missing and sparked his interest in returning. With the profits from his writing for the *Ladies Museum,* though he pointedly refrained from naming the magazine and admitting to Dovaston that he would publish in such a place, he planned to spend his August vacation from the Amicable in Shropshire.[55]

Rylance was supposed to furnish Dovaston with a poem for the annual festival of the Breidden Society, but by this time he was in Scotland, arranging for his index to the *Edinburgh Review,* and slow to communicate with Dovaston and Reynolds. To fill the gap, Reynolds sent Dovaston a poem for the Breidden Festival, "The Reflections of Mirth."[56] Dovaston was pleased with the poem, had Reynolds appointed Poet Ferneat for the year, and, after making a few small improvements, read it at the Breidden Festival on 12 July 1813, much to Reynolds's delight.[57] At the end of June 1813, Reynolds sought and received reassurance from Dovaston that he would be at home during August.[58]

Reynolds left on 7 August from Holborn on the Antient Briton for Shropshire, where he stayed until about 21 August.[59] This time Reynolds and Dovaston did not have the company of Rylance, who was still in Scotland. To console themselves, they wrote him a long joint letter, and Dovaston addressed a sonnet to him.[60] During this visit Reynolds met for the first time and admired Thomas Yates, who was also a friend of Rylance's. He again visited the old family friend, Mr. Gribble; if he followed his mother's advice, he made that visit at the time Dovaston was pleading his cases at the assizes in Shire Hall so as not to lose any more of Dovaston's company than necessary.

Dovaston took him on another excursion into Wales, where Reynolds wrote "Sonnet Written while viewing the Waterfall of Pistyl Rhaidyr, in North Wales," which he sent promptly to the *Reposi-*

tory.[61] He brought with him to the Nursery a set of satirical verses so pleasing to his host that Dovaston persuaded him to leave them behind to be copied. (Later Reynolds repented of the satire, convinced Dovaston to return it, and vowed never to write so ill-naturedly again.) He brought the letters Rylance had written him during the last year when Rylance was in Ludlow and Wales, and Dovaston found them so interesting that he kept them when Reynolds left. Their consultations about their own poetic plans were not very productive: Reynolds outlined his plan for a poem on "the Ninth Statue,"[62] which he never wrote, and Dovaston discussed a poem on Owen Glendower, which never materialized. On the day he left West Felton, Reynolds, arriving too late to take the coach for London, had to spend the night in Shrewsbury. There he called on the bookseller John Walton, from whom the proud Poet Ferneat secured a copy of the Shrewsbury *Chronicle* with the account of the last Breidden Society festival, at which his poem had been read.[63]

Back in London Reynolds resumed his clerical work at the Amicable during the day and returned to his rigorous program of study and reading in the evening. He had described his schedule for self-instruction to Dovaston: "I am now attending very closely to my Greek and Latin classics. I make it a point never to go to Bed 'till twelve, so that from 9 'till that time, I employ myself as above mentioned; or in carefully attending to our best English writers." During an occasional pause, he found writing his own verses, sometimes imitating Greek poets like Anacreon, and sometimes composing originally, "a pleasant relaxation to the more close study."[64] Rylance observed, however, that he was so popular at family gatherings and so much in demand by his friends that he was often deflected from this program of self-education.[65]

As an aid to study, he now bought from Dovaston's friend, the bookseller George Walker, Robert Bland's *Translations chiefly from the Greek Anthology*. Not finding in it a Greek poem that he and Dovaston had evidently read together and discussed at West Felton, he made two translations of it himself, one a literal rendering of the Greek and the other a loose version "in which an endeavour is made to give something of the point, ⟨&⟩ spirit & whim of the original."[66] He sent the translations to Dovaston for judgment and requested Dovaston's translation for him to compare with his own work.

Among contemporary publications, Reynolds's chief interest was in verse. He admired and shared with Dovaston Southey's *Curse of Kehama,* recommended to him by his mother's best friend Jane Mackay.[67] He read and imitated a section of Joanna Baillie's *Plays of the Passions,* and Francis Hodgson's *Lady Jane Grey* stirred his sympathy for that tragic character, which later led to one of his best *London Magazine* essays, "Bradgate Park, the Residence of Lady Jane Grey."[68] A special favorite with both Reynolds and Dovaston was Henry Kirke White; Reynolds "read him continually," and, when Dovaston praised "Clifton Grove," Reynolds concurred heartily.[69] Kirke White, for Reynolds, was similar to what Thomas Chatterton would later become for Keats. But of all living poets, the greatest influence on Reynolds at that time was Byron. Reynolds bought the third edition of *Childe Harold,* Cantos I and II, which he judged the best contemporary poem he had read.[70] He had long admired *English Bards and Scotch Reviewers* before his pocketbook allowed him to inquire about buying Dovaston's copy of the third edition—the first one with Byron's name on the title page.[71] He considered *The Giaour* the most striking of all the metrical romances; it was the poem he chose to imitate when he wrote his first book-length poem. He found in *The Bride of Abydos* the same fire as in the earlier metrical romances, but the plot seemed unduly cloudy.[72]

The short poems that Reynolds wrote in 1812 and 1813 provided him with the practice he needed to develop as a poet, and most of them gave him the encouragement of seeing his work in print. For the most part they deserved the criticism that Dovaston almost invariably gave them—both Reynolds and his mother welcomed the honesty of his strictures, but Charlotte once remarked plaintively that it might be well if Dovaston could find something favorable to say occasionally amidst all the condemnation. Reynolds was very modest about "Ode to Friendship," addressed to Dovaston and published in the *Gentleman's Magazine,*[73] and he had reason to be. He piled personification upon personification in the manner of William Collins without achieving anything like the superb control of tone that made Collins's odes successful. "The Lover's Dream," a free translation of Dovaston's "Somnium Amantis," is a little better; it is lively and pleasant to read, and its theatricality and lushness can be blamed on the original as much as on the translator. After sending Dovaston a copy and asking for criticism, Reynolds grew too impatient to wait for a reply and published it in the *Repository.*[74] He was embarrassed and forced to apologize when Dovaston damned it.[75] The adolescent praise of wine in "Anacreontic" deserved Dovaston's rejection, and Reynolds was correct in judging "The Warriour's Departure" as "Ideas confused—Rhymes miserable, Metre see-sawish, & tame execution."[76] "A Serenade," published in the *Repository,* is pictorial and musical, and the sonnet on Pistil Rhaidyr, written during his second visit to Dovaston and published in the *Repository,* is an energetic account of the waterfall, a wild goat, and an eagle, but neither poem is much better than hundreds of others submitted by aspiring poets to magazines.[77]

Three poems showed more promise. The "Stanzas," included above as the first poem that may have hinted at the death of Reynolds's sweetheart and published in the *Repository,* combined lovely imagery and flowing melody with careful control of tone to produce a memorable brief lyric. "The Reflections of Mirth, On the Eve of the Breidden Festival, for the Year 1813," though an occasional poem, rewards rereading with its color, its witty puns, and its ingenious rhyme reinforced by comic rhythm ("Time shall throw aside his scythe then; / Time shall bless the feast of Breidden."). Although "Sappho's Address to the Evening Star," written at this time, but not published until later in the *Inquirer,*[78] must finally be pronounced unsuccessful because of Reynolds's obvious attempt to derive pathos from Sappho's suicidal leap, the poem showed promise with its technical mastery of Reynolds's favorite Spenserian stanza and its careful "stationing," as Keats would have put it, of Sappho atop the crag. Although Reynolds perhaps had reason to worry that, as the admired Kirke White had said, he had "only the longing, without the *Afflatus,*"[79] he was only nineteen, and there were signs that he ought not to abandon his efforts to write fine poetry.

CHAPTER 3

A Quarrel with Dovaston, *Safie*, and *The Eden of Imagination*— Fall 1813–1814

O N HIS RETURN to London from his Shropshire vacation in late August 1813, Reynolds brought commissions to buy books and music for Dovaston. He packed up a Boccaccio, a waltz, and a bolero and tried to send them along with Longmans' shipment of books to Shrewsbury, but, when he found that the publisher had closed the current packing to any new items, he postponed sending them. By the end of September he had bought other books, including a set of Hunt's *Reflector,* but he learned from Longmans that the packages were so bulky he could send only part of them in the first shipment.[1] Dovaston had been generous in sending presents to the Reynoldses and hospitable in entertaining John during two summer vacations. Living at such a distance from London and needing a reliable friend to buy and to send him literary and musical materials, he expected that John would serve as his agent and attend to his desires promptly. Always meticulous in meeting his own responsibilities, both large and small, Dovaston had little sympathy for thoughtlessness or procrastination in others. With a considerable fortune and almost unlimited time for his own leisurely pursuits, he did not understand how hectic Reynolds's schedule was with his full-time clerical work ten hours a day, six days a week, his evening studies, his participation in the Zetosophian Society, his social obligations to friends, and now, added to all these regular activities, his composition of his first book-length poem, *Safie.* Reynolds neglected to send the remainder of the books, and Dovaston grew increasingly exasperated.

Underneath his beaming exterior, Dovaston harbored a curious jealousy of his two London friends. As the relationship between Rylance and Reynolds developed after they met in the summer of

1812, they exchanged letters when Rylance was out of town. Reynolds saved his friend's letters and took them to Shropshire for Dovaston to read when he visited in August 1813. Dovaston was so impressed with the letters that he persuaded Reynolds to leave them when he returned to London; Dovaston later wrote Reynolds requesting that he be allowed to keep the letters permanently. He accused Rylance of writing more interesting and valuable letters to Reynolds than to him, a charge Rylance denied rather brusquely. Surprised that Dovaston would suggest keeping letters not addressed to him, Reynolds refused his request with an emphasis that ruffled Dovaston's feelings. "As to the letters you talk of keeping I can only say that they are *prized particularly by me* and I cannot on any account allow you to keep them. If I had not thought much of them, they would not have been carried about with me. Pray return them:— I will (if you cannot get ⟨H⟩ a Frank) willingly pay the postage— The loss of them *I assure you* would very *much hurt me.*"[2]

Instead of complaining directly to Reynolds for the delay in sending the books, Dovaston wrote Rylance that he felt "ill naturedly indignant" at Reynolds's "pointed neglect," that he was astonished Reynolds should not take pleasure in doing anything at all for him, and that in the future he would not trouble Reynolds to do what he could easily hire someone else to do.[3] Reynolds had borrowed £5 from Dovaston and imprudently delayed repayment. Rylance showed Dovaston's sharp letter to both Reynolds and his mother. Charlotte was disturbed and wrote Dovaston to urge tolerance and mutual explanation.[4] Reynolds was offended and wrote warmly to protest, but his letter enraged Dovaston. Dovaston returned it to Reynolds with the most objectionable passages marked and with a counterblast appended. He wrote more fully to Charlotte, charging that her son had been "insolent" and arguing that he had returned the letter because it would be a "disgrace" to keep it with Reynolds's earlier, carefully preserved correspondence. Dovaston remarked sarcastically that after not answering his last letter to her for nearly four months, she had broken her silence only because she had an ulterior motive—to protect her interest and her son's interest with someone she had described as a man of property.

Charlotte had long loved Dovaston as a member of her family, but she had too much pride and spirit to brook so insulting a letter. Still she tried to joke him out of his anger, " 'Pray can you tell me if one

Mr Dovaston do live here' & if you to whom I am addressing myself be he.—I have receivd a letter ⟨bearing⟩ dated Nov 22^d bearing your signature, that I cannot conceive came from your hand." But she also met his attack head on and denounced it. She began to suspect that undercurrents in the three-way friendship among Dovaston, Reynolds, and Rylance were part of the problem. Quoting from Dovaston's letter, "as I lately told his better friend ⟨&⟩ to whom he owes all he now enjoys, he will find he has wrong'd one," she demanded frankness: "who is this better friend, & in what is he indebted to him—I question you as a friend & I look for your serious & honest answer. I know not of such friend as you speak."[5] She had not yet seen John's letter returned by Dovaston when she wrote, but she could not believe her son guilty of Dovaston's charge of insolence, and she would not want her son to submit to anyone's insults, including Dovaston's. She admitted she might have once or twice spoken of Dovaston in conversation as "a man of property," but she insisted vehemently that she had always valued him for his character, his intelligence, and his affection, not for his money. She tried to leave the way open for Dovaston to reply, and John wrote to express his amazement at Dovaston's explosion and to hope that they could both forgive and forget,[6] but Dovaston was so angry that he broke off all communication with the Reynoldses for five months.

After Dovaston had chastised him, Reynolds was human enough to look for a little revenge—he asked Rylance to report to Dovaston Lord Byron's praise of *Safie.* Rylance reported Reynolds's remarks but with an openness, indeed even a spitefulness, that Reynolds did not expect. "He said his favourable outset with Lord Byron would chagrin & torment you & wished me to write you word ⟨so⟩ of his favourable outset—waited till the upset & upshot ere I said a word." Reynolds had not intended that Rylance word the report in such a fashion as to embitter Dovaston; later in the same letter Rylance added, "John Reynolds says if you will write to him all will be reconciled."[7]

Rylance's strange candor was probably the result of his steady decline into complete insanity. He had been extremely depressed during the summer and early fall of 1813, living alone in Edinburgh where he knew almost no one except Archibald Constable, with whom he was arranging for the indexing of the *Edinburgh Review,* failing for many months to keep his promise to write to Reynolds, and finally writing a sour letter for which he apologized in a subsequent letter written jointly to Reynolds and Dovaston at West Felton. On Rylance's return to London, Reynolds noticed that there was something different about him, though there was nothing yet sufficiently irrational to sound an alarm.[8] In February 1814 Rylance set out on a lengthy visit to Shropshire. He had evidently shown some signs of mental imbalance before he left London, because the Roscoes in Liverpool thought that his mother should have kept him at home under "restrictions" until the mental derangement passed.[9]

He stopped first at Shrewsbury, where he planned to stay for a number of days with a friend, David Parkes, before proceeding to Dovaston's estate at West Felton. He behaved fairly well at Parkes's house, though he looked odd, until suddenly in the middle of the street he borrowed all the money Parkes had in his pocket and jumped into the coach to hurry to Dovaston's.[10] At Dovaston's place, the Nursery, he became completely insane despite all Dovaston's efforts to placate him and minister to him.[11] After a time he left, intending to travel north to Liverpool for a visit with his old friends the Roscoes. Dovaston wrote immediately to warn them of Rylance's condition. With much trepidation, the Roscoes prepared to care for the deranged friend,[12] but they were fortunately spared the burden. At Wigan on the way to Liverpool, Rylance received word that Archibald Constable was traveling to London and wished to see him on business; he abandoned his proposed visit with the Roscoes and returned at once to London.[13] Back in the city, his insanity continued; as William Roscoe reported to Dovaston on 3 May 1814, "You will be sorry to hear that R. Rylance has been again confined & shocked to be informed that he has lodged an information ag^t. M^cC[reery]—the printer, his old ⟨master⟩ employer & friend, for seditious words, under which M^cC— has been obliged to consult council. Infirmities are to be pitied; but this savours so strongly of a malicious & vindictive disposition that I ⟨have th⟩ should have thought myself inexcusable after the generosity & friendship you have shewn him, if I had not mentioned it for your future guidance."[14]

During the opening months of 1814, further problems developed between the Reynoldses and the intermittently irrational Rylance. Rylance dunned Reynolds for the fifteen shillings Dovaston had sent him to buy books. After having given Reynolds a copy of his index to the

Edinburgh Review in appreciation for Reynolds's assistance in preparing it, Rylance tried to collect another fifteen shillings for the copy. Perhaps acting on instruction from Dovaston, he sought to forgive Reynolds his £5 debt to Dovaston; the Reynoldses regarded that indirect offer of forgiveness of the debt as an impertinence by Rylance. The Reynoldses, who seem not to have realized Rylance's insanity at the time and to have charged his eccentric behavior to moral irresponsibility, finally refused to allow him into their house and returned all his letters and notes without comment.

About the beginning of April 1814, Rylance sent a request for Jane, whom he had tutored, to give him a recommendation as a teacher of French; included with the request was a letter from Dovaston to Rylance directing him to invite Reynolds to join Dovaston in Shropshire to celebrate Shakespeare's birthday. Charlotte returned the request and Dovaston's letter without a word of reply to Rylance. But since the invitation showed that Dovaston still retained some friendship for John, she and George decided she ought to explain to Dovaston why her son would not respond to the indirect invitation. She therefore wrote in measured, though not unfriendly, terms that she would not apologize, because she had nothing to apologize for, but that she believed Dovaston deserved an explanation. She blamed the break largely on Rylance, though she admitted that her son had been imprudent in not repaying the £5 loan promptly.[15]

Moved by Charlotte's letter, Dovaston immediately "wrote a hasty, and free Answer" of reconciliation to her.[16] He remained slightly annoyed with Reynolds, however, and did not communicate with him directly for another three months. Early in July, still unable to bring himself to mail a regular letter, he made the odd compromise of including a note to Reynolds in a letter to another London correspondent, directing that the note be sent by the metropolitan twopenny post. It was a brief but warm offer to resume their friendship on the old terms. Reynolds responded with warmth and affection to Dovaston's note,[17] and there were no signs of friction in the letters that followed during the next seven months. Rylance's name was conspicuously absent in all the letters thereafter, and Charlotte, having restored the friendship of the two with her letter of about 8 April 1814, never wrote Dovaston again.

Before the quarrel with Dovaston began, Reynolds had started work on his first book-length poem. For years he had written short poems, essays, and reviews for various magazines, but now at the age of nineteen he became more ambitious. In the early summer of 1813, he thought of using rhymed octosyllabics for some narrative poem. During his vacation in August, as he discussed the projected poem with Dovaston in Shropshire, he considered basing it on what he called several times "The Ninth Statue," apparently the ancient Persian tale of the "Ninth Statuette" from *Vikrama's Adventures,*[18] and using the Spenserian stanza throughout. On his return to London, the plan for a story based on the Ninth Statue grew in his mind; he wrote eleven introductory Spenserian stanzas (only ten were later printed); but he rejected the Spenserian stanza for the body of the poem and returned to his earlier idea of rhymed octosyllabics.[19] Then he dropped the idea of the Ninth Statue and devised his own simple plot for the poem of one thousand lines, completing it by the beginning of December. Rylance read it and told Reynolds he admired it, though his tone in reporting it to Dovaston indicated reservations which he did not reveal to the author.[20] At Reynolds's request, Rylance agreed to correct *Safie,* but before he could make the corrections, George Reynolds went to John Murray and secured his promise to consider it. Reynolds was so overjoyed that he sent the work to Murray without waiting for Rylance's refinements. The rest of Rylance's account is best presented in his own words:

He [Murray] sent it to Lord Byron who wrote a number of notes in a black kind of scrawl, approving & suggesting amendments in it and at the end of the Poem he wrote bravo bravissimo. Jack got it back with a note from Murray and says "will you print it if I correct it?" He said "I will."

Jack's mother asked me to come and sup there this night week (last Thursday week) to help him to correct it, but when I got there I found he had sent it uncorrected, of his own motion to Lord Byron, saying in a note he would call next day to learn whether Lord Byron would allow him to dedicate it to him. He called next night: Lord B. was gone to the play. "Any message?" "No"!! "No? I'll call to-morrow." "You must not call before twelve, for the servants are never up till eleven." He called; Lord Byron sent word down stairs that Lord Byron was gone into the country and had left Jack's Papers at Murrays. Jack went & quarreled with Murray and got his papers back; took them to another bookseller, the Lord knows who, for Jack does not tell me and I don't ask him; and now he says his "Safie, a Turkish tale" is to be out in ten days!!!![21]

The publishers of *Safie,* not known to Rylance, were James Caw-thorn and John Martin, the latter a young bookseller just twenty-two years old and Reynolds's fellow Zetosophian.

Like most of the reading public, Reynolds was swept away by *The Giaour,* published in June 1813. As he wrote R. M. Milnes late in life, *Safie* was "a downright imitation of Lord Byron," though there were some differences that undoubtedly contributed to its pop-ularity.[22] Reynolds objected to the complexity and obscurity of the plot in *The Bride of Abydos,* published in December 1813 after he had completed *Safie;* he might also have objected to the same quali-ties in *The Giaour,* with its unexplained shifts in speakers and its kaleidoscopic succession of scenes. He avoided those features in his own metrical romance by keeping his plot quite simple. Assad and his beloved Safie were blissful in their Persian paradise until the Turkish Guleph attacked with his band of marauders. Leaving his Turkish warriors to fight the defending Persians amid much clang-ing of weapons and flowing of blood, Guleph kidnapped Safie and raced away with her on horseback to his home region. After recover-ing from his wounds and grieving for a while, Assad set out with a band of warriors on a long journey to search for Safie. One evening in a Turkish town he heard a lute and a woman's voice singing, which he recognized as Safie's. "With horrid yell," Assad and his fol-lowers attacked the citadel, but the superior forces of the Turkish Guleph swiftly subdued and imprisoned them. In his dungeon the wounded and anguished Assad upbraided the faithless Safie, wrote a scroll addressed to her, and then committed suicide by stabbing him-self to the heart and pressing the wound to spray blood around the cell. In the twenty-page scroll, he celebrated Safie's beauty, recalled their earlier bliss, raged at her infidelity, insisted on his own un-swerving love, sent a forlorn message to his mother, and foresaw his own stark grave. Finally Safie mourned over the scroll until she died of a broken heart.

Except in his introduction, Reynolds used rapid octosyllabics in the same way as Byron: couplets, alternate rhymes, triplets, and occa-sional metrical variations. Reynolds's 90-line introduction in Spen-serian stanzas lamenting the enslaved state of the East and glorifying the beauty of its scenery and women paralleled Byron's 167-line in-troduction to *The Giaour* praising the beauty of Greece and con-trasting her ancient glory with her present enslavement. At times

Reynolds's introduction sounds similar to the subject matter of *The Giaour* presented through the sweeping Spenserian movement of the first two cantos of *Childe Harold.*

Some of Reynolds's borrowings from Byron were very close; he merely rearranged the same words or shifted to synonyms that were the thinnest kind of paraphrase. Byron's "Her hair in hyacinthine flow" (*The Giaour,* l. 496) became "A glossy flow of hyacinthine hair" (*Safie,* p. 5, stanza 5).[23] Byron's note to the line "Hyacinthine, in Arabic . . . as common a thought in the eastern poets as it was among the Greeks" became "The metaphor taken from the Hyacinth is very common with the Arabians, as it was with the Greeks." Byron's "The spur hath lanced" (The *Giaour,* l. 249) became "The spurs were lanced" (*Safie,* p. 17). Byron's note to "palampore" (*The Giaour,* l. 666), "The flowered shawls generally worn by persons of rank," became "A Palampore is a very elegant shawl, fancifully flowered, which is usually worn by persons of consequence" (*Safie,* note 8, p. 17). Byron's note, "The ataghan, a very long dagger worn with pistols in the belt" (*The Giaour,* note to l. 355) became "An Ataghan is a long dagger worn in the belt" (*Safie,* note 13, p. 32). Byron's dozen lines on the romance between the nightingale and the rose (*The Giaour,* ll. 21–33) were echoed by Reynolds's dozen lines on the same subject (*Safie,* pp. 27–28). Byron's 364-line final "confession" of the Giaour to the aged Friar had its counterpart in Reynolds's appended 342-line scroll in which Assad repeated his story and bewailed his lot.

Reynolds's differences from his master doubtless contributed to the short-lived popularity of *Safie.* The publisher James Cawthorn was "astonished" at its success, and letters of praise poured in from readers.[24] *Safie* was not the puzzling challenge to understand that *The Giaour* was; a reasonable attention was all that it required of the reader. And *Safie* was not immoral: if Byron had not been sympathetic to Reynolds, he might have called him, as he later did Bryan Waller Procter, "a sort of moral me." Unlike the Giaour, Assad committed no crimes, and, unlike Leila, Safie did not commit adultery willingly—she was kidnapped and enslaved. Reynolds's poem was sensuous, colorful, exotic, rhythmical, exciting, and sentimental. Without expending anything like the effort required for *The Giaour,* readers could revel in many Byronic effects with no twinges of conscience from sinful ingredients.

Byron's praise of the manuscript and his permission to dedicate *Safie* to him had led to the publication of Reynolds's first book. When Reynolds sent him the presentation copy, Byron was again generous in his response. On 20 February 1814 he wrote in his journal:

Answered—or, rather, acknowledged—the receipt of young Reynolds's Poem, Safie. The lad is clever, but much of his thoughts are borrowed,—*whence,* the Reviewers may find out. I hate discouraging a young one; and I think,—though wild, and more oriental than he would be, had he seen the scenes where he has placed his tale,—that he has much talent, and, certainly, fire enough.[25]

Byron was impressed with his young imitator, and the letter referred to in the journal showed that he sought to draw upon his own experience to guide him:

The poem itself, as the work of a young man, is highly creditable to your talents, and promises better for future efforts than any which I can now recollect. Whether you intend to pursue your poetical career, I do not know, and can have no right to inquire—but, in whatever channel your abilities are directed, I think it will be your own fault if they do not eventually lead to distinction. . . .

The first thing a young writer must expect, and yet can least of all suffer, is criticism—I did not bear it—a few years, and many changes, have since passed over my head, and my reflections on that subject are attended with regret. I find, on dispassionate comparison, my own revenge more than the provocation warranted—it is true, I was young—that might be an excuse to those I attacked—but to *me* it is none: the best reply to all objections is to write better—and if your enemies will not then do you justice, the world will. On the other hand, you should not be discouraged—to be opposed, is not to be vanquished, though a timid mind is apt to mistake every scratch for a mortal wound. There is a saying of Dr. Johnson's, which it is as well to remember, that "No man was ever written down except by himself." I sincerely hope that you will meet with as few obstacles as your self can desire—but if you should, you will find that they are to be *stepped* over; to *kick* them down, is the first resolve of a young and fiery spirit—a pleasant thing enough at the time—but not so afterwards: on this point I speak of a man's *own* reflections—what others think or say, is a *secondary* consideration,—at least, it has been so with me, but will not answer as a general maxim: he who would make his way in the world, must let the world believe that it made it for him, and accommodate himself to the minutest observance of its regulations.[26]

Byron did even more than furnish this carefully considered advice. Either by letter or at a personal meeting—Reynolds shared with Byron a vegetable dinner at this time[27]—Reynolds expressed his fear of reviewers. On 28 February 1814, Byron wrote Francis Hodgson:

> There is a youngster—and a clever one, named Reynolds, who has just published a poem called "Safie," published by Cawthorne. He is in the most natural and fearful apprehension of the Reviewers—and as you and I both know by experience the effect of such things upon a *young* mind, I wish *you* would take his production into dissection and do it *gently. I* cannot, because it is inscribed to me; but I assure you this is not my motive for wishing him to be tenderly entreated, but because I know the misery, at his time of life, of untoward remarks upon first appearance.[28]

If Byron told Reynolds of this appeal to Hodgson, Reynolds would have been pleased, because he had enjoyed Hodgson's poem *Lady Jane Grey.*

The reviewers treated *Safie* tolerably well. The *British Critic,* the *Anti-Jacobin Review,* and the *Critical Review* had attacked *The Giaour* and *The Bride of Abydos,* and they maintained consistency by being largely unfavorable to Byron's disciple.[29] But despite their strictures, they recognized talent in the young poet and were not unkind. Francis Hodgson, whose notice the *Monthly Review* did not print until seven months after Byron's request, was perhaps not quite so gentle as Byron expected.[30] He thought that in the main Reynolds had imitated Byron's faults rather than his merits, and he attacked what he considered ineffective rhythms and faulty rhymes. But he balanced his censure with warm praise of Reynolds's promise as a poet: "We discern traces of genius, of bold and nervous diction, of glowing but correct painting, of touches at once animated and pathetic, in this little poem; which convince us that Mr. Reynolds is capable of doing much better, if he had chosen a subject and style less exclusively imitative."[31]

Reynolds continued to participate in the Zetosophian Society during the excitement of his meetings with Byron and the publication of his first book. In the spring of 1814 the members decided to publish some of their essays and poems in a new quarterly magazine, the *Inquirer,* modeled on Leigh Hunt's now defunct *Reflector* and published by John Martin.[32] A moving force in the magazine, Reynolds owned a share and managed the poetical department. In the first issue in May he published an essay "On the Character of Hamlet" and two poems, "A Paraphrase of Catullus's Address to his Vessell" and "Stanzas to *,*, ******" (" 'Tis past;—the dream of life is o'er").[33] His critique of Hamlet had probably first been read as a paper to the Zetosophian Society, as had his close friend Benjamin Bailey's "Knowledge and Wisdom Distinguished" and William Squibb's familiar essay "On the Advantages of a Foggy Day" and his satire on pedantic literary criticism, "Critical Remarks on Epicoelegiac Poetry." Reynolds asked Dovaston particularly for a judgment of the essay by Bailey, who was so close a friend that he read Dovaston's letters to him.[34] Reynolds's friend Frank Squibb wrote "Political Retrospect," a survey of political events and foreign affairs during the year. Charles Wentworth Dilke, clerk in the Navy Pay Office and Reynolds's lifelong friend, was the only nonmember of the Zetosophian Society to contribute to the first issue; he wrote "A Sketch of the Rise and Progress of Dramatic Literature in this Country," an excellent account revealing that at the age of twenty-five he was already a scrupulous scholar and a learned critic.[35]

Reynolds had reason to be pleased with the first number. Dovaston, who had criticized much of his earlier work, praised the issue generally and his essay on Hamlet particularly.[36] At Reynolds's request Dovaston submitted an essay "On the Perversion of Language," which was published in the second issue.[37] Leigh Hunt, by now Reynolds's personal friend, thought highly of the first number.[38]

Reynolds planned an essay on poetry for the second issue in September, but did not complete it by the deadline.[39] He published only "Sappho's Address to the Evening Star," which he had copied into a letter to Dovaston a year earlier.[40] One hopes that a lack of submissions to choose from accounted for the weakness of the other verse that he allowed to be printed. He approved two badly sentimental pieces by Stanley and one by Seymour, and an epigram by Seymour so feeble that John Martin was moved to write in the margin of his copy, "Bad as this is, I believe it to be by Seymour."[41] The article by Dilke on the contemporary drama, as well as one on the same subject in the third and last issue, was competent journalism, but less satisfying than the scholarly essay in the first issue. Despite two rather lively essays by William Squibb, the second issue did not realize Reynolds's hope for improvement over the first. Reynolds's only contribution to the third and last issue was "The Song of a Spanish Lover to his Mistress," pleasing in its melody and pictures, but not especially memorable.[42] Then, as John Martin recorded, "a deadly feud arose amongst its members" and both the Zetosophian Society and the *Inquirer* died.[43]

Reynolds did not publish his best poetry of 1814 in the *Inquirer*. On 19 July he was "engaged on another poem"; by 30 July *The Eden of Imagination* was in the press; and it had been printed by 23 August when he left London for his annual vacation.[44] Leigh Hunt's *The Feast of the Poets,* recently reprinted from the *Reflector* in revised form as a book, had turned Reynolds's attention from Byron to Wordsworth. After mentioning his new poem to Dovaston, Reynolds proceeded to praise Wordsworth—an association of ideas had led him from the new poem in which he delighted to its source. Still feeling himself a novice despite the high praise heaped upon *Safie,* Reynolds chose for imitation not work like *Tintern Abbey,* which he already regarded as Wordsworth's greatest poetry, but Wordsworth's apprentice work, *An Evening Walk,* a somewhat rare volume of which he was proud to own a copy.[45] The versification and techniques of *The Eden* were markedly similar to Wordsworth's late eighteenth-century neoclassicism: written in the closed pentameter couplet, it abounded with personification (Imagination, Fancy, Hope), periphrasis (a fish is the "speckled inmate of the waters," birds are "a feathery throng"), and poetic diction (lave, rill, pleasing prospect).

Like *An Evening Walk, The Eden* was discursive. As Wordsworth shifted in time from noon to sunset to night to dawn, so Reynolds shifted from twilight to daytime to morning to night. As Wordsworth shifted his view from one section to another of the scene in the Lake District—from a "General Sketch" to a "Noontide Retreat" to a "Mountain-farm" to a "Slate quarry"—so Reynolds shifted his view from the bay to his "Mossy seat" to the "rough-hewn bridge" to his cot to the arbor and to his "sparry grot." Both Wordsworth and Reynolds described a "rill." Wordsworth has a cascade; Reynolds a waterfall. Wordsworth's "secret bridge" was matched by Reynolds's "rough-hewn bridge." Not nearly so imitative of Wordsworth, despite these parallels, as he had been of Byron in *Safie,* Reynolds nevertheless made *The Eden* the same kind of loosely organized topographical poem as *An Evening Walk.*

Reynolds enjoyed writing *The Eden* more than anything he had written before that time; in fact for no other poem in his entire career did he express such unqualified pleasure and satisfaction.[46]

This poem is successful in its own right because Reynolds shares with the reader his own delight in the imagined scene. The effect is somewhat similar to that of John Pomfret's *The Choice,* a favorite of Leigh Hunt's: one revels in a succession of sensuous pleasures presented in a leisurely and subdued way. The morning stroll is characteristic of its relaxed sensuousness:

> In the fresh morning, when the summer sky
> Beams blue and cloudless to the wakeful eye;—
> Forth from my cot I'll saunter to the fields,
> And revel midst the joys which nature yields,—
> Roam down the hedge where honeysuckle grows,
> Where sweet in wildness springs the blushing rose;—
> Or idly stray along the grove's green side,
> Where poppies hang the head in gaudy pride,
> To hear the black-bird pour his morning song,
> Midst the light chirping of a feathery throng.[47]

The book was printed by 23 August 1814, but Reynolds and his publishers, James Cawthorn and John Martin who had also published *Safie* and Hunt's *The Feast of the Poets* in book form, delayed publication for a few months until the season was more propitious.[48] The instant it was printed, however, Reynolds sent the first copy to Exeter to Eliza Powell Drewe, clearly the "maiden of my bosom" introduced into the poem to sing the love song, "The Lights in the Summer-house Brightly Were Burning."[49] She sang the song as she played upon the "lovely lute," just as she sang and played for his pleasure in several later love lyrics addressed to her. His courtship had already progressed so far that he had "received an earnest invitation to spend a week or two" in Devonshire, though other concerns prevented him from accepting at this time.[50]

After the reconciliation of Reynolds and Dovaston, there was no sign of any further friction; all Reynolds's letters to him were warm and friendly, as well as confident and assured—he no longer wrote as an adolescent to a mentor, but as one equal to another. He dedicated *The Eden* to Dovaston and sent him a copy along with a cordial letter requesting his judgment.[51] Grateful for the compliment, Dovaston replied promptly. Like most people, he was sensitive that his name be given correctly, and especially in a dedication. Reynolds had evidently never seen John Freeman Milward Dovaston written out entire; he depended upon his ear and the result was Milwood for Milward. Dovaston hastened to express his shock that he had been "misnomered,"[52] and he was scrupulous, if not pedantic, in objecting to what was probably an uncorrected typographical error: *Amicitae* for *Amicitiae* in a footnote quotation. He thought that Reynolds should have included their adored Henry Kirke White in his account of the books on the shelf in the cot (Reynolds explained that his plan limited him to the three greatest dead English poets—Shakespeare, Milton, and Spenser—and living contemporaries only), and he believed that the poem should have been greatly expanded.[53] As always, he was candid in finding fault.

But with the poem as a whole, Dovaston was very pleased, deeply impressed, and no doubt a little surprised; some of Reynolds's juvenile pieces had seemed promising, and *Safie* had been interesting, but he had not realized that Reynolds was capable of so satisfying a poem as *The Eden.* Reynolds's response showed how happy he was to have at last so much praise from his exacting and censorious friend: "The true end of Poetry is to please and by so much the more is a Poem worthy of existence—the more it conduces to the pleasure of its author, his friends or the world: I am become much wonder of my little ⟨sketch⟩ bantling since you admire its features and dress— Your admiration has placed it higher in mine—And I look upon it as a sort of link in our friendship's chain—which may make our affections faster & better."[54]

Benjamin Bailey's comments, though favorable, are perhaps not so enthusiastic as one would expect from the man who, along with James Rice, shared Reynolds's closest friendship at the time. "The very least that can be said of this is that it is a very beautiful little poem which may bring pleasing recollections to a town reader, and reflect, as in a mirror, scenes which are daily spread before the enraptured view of those whose happy lot it is to live embosomed in such delightful 'Edens' and who have in their own minds an Eden of Imagination to relish it."[55]

Only two periodicals reviewed *The Eden of Imagination,* the *Critical Review* and the *British Critic,* and both were largely unfavorable.[56] Reynolds must have been disappointed because he was so well satisfied with the poem that he apparently hoped for a second edition. He wrote in an interleaved copy 130 additional lines, which would have expanded the poem by more than one-third.[57] The additions, however, were all inferior to the published poem; they are so wordy and mediocre that they would have weakened the poem by diluting it.

The greatest satisfaction *The Eden* brought Reynolds came from Wordsworth himself. By the time he wrote *The Eden,* his admiration for Wordsworth equaled his earlier high regard for Byron. Though he shared the widespread reservations about the lowliness of Wordsworth's language and some of his rural subject matter, he realized that Wordsworth at his best was the finest poet of the age. He wrote Dovaston:

> Have you seen Wordsworth's Lyrical Ballads? There are certainly some of the most delightful & delicate ideas—some of the most deep & philosophical reflections in his Poetry. He is one of those rare Poets who write from actual Feeling & personal Observation. It is certainly to be lamented that Mr Wordsworth is known to the Generality of Readers only by his inferior works—by the weaknesses & peculiarities of his Genius:—They know nothing of his fine feelings & deep thoughtfulness and brilliant Imagination. I hope in a New Poem which he is about to publish [*The Excursion*], we shall find he has cast away all the small clouds from his Fancy & given us a work in his best manner   The chief fault in Mr Wordsworth is a love of speaking as Men in the humbler walks of Life speak:—He has mistaken puerility at times, for simplicity—and in the Preface to his Ballads holds up as a reason for this familiar tone of expression & unsoaring Style of Poetry—That Poetry & Prose are more intimately connected than is generally imagined. This, though it is apparently open to cavil, is literally true—in the same manner that simplicity is the very foundation of sublimity.[58]

Having imitated Wordsworth's apprentice work in *The Eden,* Reynolds was bold enough to send him a copy with an accompanying letter. By about 18 February 1815, he had received from Wordsworth "a very friendly letter" congratulating him on the love of nature revealed in the poem. He had reason to be elated, "and highly do I feel the honour of it."[59]

He had a busy year in 1814, working full time at the Amicable, attending weekly meetings of the Zetosophian Society, managing the poetry department of the *Inquirer,* and publishing two books. Somehow he also found time to write large sections of a second oriental romance, evidently planned to capitalize on his success with *Safie.* He selected and copied for Dovaston from a larger mass of verse no less than seventy-six lines "from different parts" of "A Tale."[60]

These extracts reveal only a little of the plot: the unnamed warrior speaker and his adored Zilia travel over the sea to join the speaker's brother Sahmed, who has been soured by the infidelity and later the death of his beloved. It is just as well that the second Eastern romance never saw print, since the extracts, presumably the best parts, show no poetic advance over *Safie.*

The name of the heroine is tantalizing. Zilia is a near anagram of the first name of the Devonshire girl whom Reynolds was already courting, Eliza Powell Drewe. When Benjamin Bailey borrowed the name Zilia from the manuscript to serve as a disguise for his would-be sweetheart, Thomasine Leigh, he most often spelled it as Reynolds did, Zilia, but in three places he spelled it Zelia, a perfect anagram for Eliza; the chances are that Bailey knew the real name from which it had been originally derived. We know Reynolds liked to play with an anagram of Eliza's name because years later in *The Garden of Florence* he devised another one for her, Azile. There can be little doubt that, like the "maiden of my bosom" in *The Eden of Imagination,* Zilia referred to Eliza Powell Drewe.

Eliza Powell Drewe was born in Exeter on 25 June 1793 and baptized at the Bow Meeting, Presbyterian, on 11 August 1793. A little more than a year older than Reynolds, she was the daughter of William Drewe (1766–11 November 1818) and Ann Powell Drewe (died 8 June 1844).[61] The other children were George Powell Drewe, born 14 November 1794; Lucy, born 13 February 1796; and a set of twins, William and Ann, born 2 August 1798.[62] William Drewe, Sr. was a prosperous wine merchant of South Street, whose generous contributions to charitable and patriotic causes were listed from time to time in the *Alfred, West of England Journal,* a newspaper published in Exeter.

Instead of accepting Eliza's invitation to visit her family in Exeter, Reynolds spent his September 1814 vacation "making a complete tour of most of the inland Counties."[63] It was a hectic trip, requiring so much traveling and moving in and out of inns that he scarcely had time to write to his mother. Near the close of his tour, he wrote Dovaston from Banbury, Oxfordshire that he had "seen some sweet scenery" which he hoped later to use for poetic purposes. On 29 September 1814 he returned to his post in London as a "compleat Cockney clerk."

CHAPTER 4

The *Champion* and *The Naiad*—
1815–1816

THE REYNOLDS FAMILY continued to live in the schoolmaster's quarters attached to the Lambeth Boys Parochial School through 1814. The *Gentleman's Magazine* published "The Hand," which came from Lambeth, in January 1815—another in Reynolds's long series of poems grieving for his dead sweetheart. With the children growing up—Jane, the oldest, was now an adult of twenty-two, and Charlotte, the youngest, was thirteen—the Reynolds family needed more space. The room Jane used as a studio to give piano lessons eliminated one bedroom. John was gregarious and hospitable, and the family enjoyed entertaining London relatives and friends and putting up friends from out-of-town. Cramped for space after six years in the renovated schoolhouse, they moved early in 1815 to 19 Lamb's Conduit Street, which was to be their home for the next three years. On 24 February 1815, Reynolds dated a letter to Leigh Hunt from that address for the first time.[1]

At this time "a party" tried to displace George Reynolds from his position as master of the Lambeth Boys Parochial School, and John was so much engaged in assisting his father in the matter that he was unable to write to Dovaston until his father's position was secured.[2] The family's move from the house attached to the school may have had some connection with the attempt to displace George, for the long-standing agreement had been that the master and his family live in the school complex, and the break with the practice may have brought objections. There is no evidence how long after 25 February 1815 George continued to serve as master of the school. Perhaps a later attempt in 1815 or 1816 to displace him succeeded, and he moved to new employment as one of the several writing masters at Christ's Hospital, where he was elected head writing master in May 1817.

Reynolds was very modest, even deprecating, about his next small pamphlet—he wrote Dovaston that at least *An Ode* on the overthrow of Napoleon was printed well. James Cawthorn and Reynolds's fellow Zetosophian John Martin had published his first two books jointly; John Martin published this third effort alone. Although following Byron's lead in publishing an ode on Napoleon's exile to Elba in 1814, Reynolds's poem resembled Byron's in little other than the occasion and the genre. Alone in his chamber at night, the distraught Napoleon gazed at a stagy train of eighteenth-century personifications: Terror, Anger, Love, Hope, Despair, and Hate. At the close, "The crown he wildly cast away," as the visions cried "Lost!" It is less surprising that only one copy has survived than it is that two contemporary periodicals thought it worthwhile to review it, one with more charity than it deserved.[3]

Reynolds's friendship with Dovaston faded away. There was no further quarrel; he simply stopped writing his former mentor after Dovaston answered his last letter of 25 February 1815 on 21 March. But his friendship with Rice and Bailey in London continued. Rice, troubled all his life by chronic illness, often traveled for his health to the south of England, where at Sidmouth on 26 June 1814 he had met the three Leigh sisters of Slade Hall, daughters of the widowed Mrs. William Leigh (née Sarah Pearse): Mary, Sarah and Thomasine.[4] The next day Bailey also met the Leighs, and a week later the Leigh girls attended a party at Rice's lodgings. With repeated visits to Sidmouth by Rice and Bailey during the next few months, the circle of sentimental "brothers" and "sisters" became very close, broadening to include the Leighs' cousin, Maria Pearse of nearby Honiton.

The precise relationship of Reynolds's sweetheart, Eliza Powell Drewe, to the Leigh girls is not now clear. She certainly became a close friend, as Willard B. Pope and Clayton E. Hudnall stated; she may have been a cousin as George L. Marsh once reported,[5] though he cited no evidence and I have been unable to locate a basis for the claim. Reynolds met Eliza well before Rice and Bailey met the Leighs. In those days of protracted courtships, he must have known her for months, if not years, before he would call her "maiden of my bosom" in *The Eden* in July 1814. She was related in some way to a London family close to the Reynoldses, perhaps either the Squibbs or the Butlers.[6]

Visiting the Leigh sisters and Maria Pearse at Slade Hall about a dozen times from 1814 to 1817, and meeting them once at Clifton near Bristol, Rice and Bailey established close bonds with all these "adopted sisters," to whom they supplied abundant verse and glowing prose celebrations of friendship. Bailey fell in love with the youngest, Thomasine, and waxed most sentimental about his adored "Zilia," but she never returned his love, and he came to realize that she was not just displaying maidenly modesty.

Two of the projects enjoyed by the group may give some of the flavor of their intimate association. In the spring of 1815, they planted six sweetbriars in the garden at Slade to commemorate their reunion and to represent their growing friendship. In that same spring, after reading and copying into commonplace books Wordsworth's "Poems on the Naming of Places," they made a walking tour of the coast, naming six rocks of the Dunscombe Cliffs for each of the group and adding a seventh "Union Rock" to symbolize their closeness.[7]

There is no evidence in the Leigh Browne-Lockyer Collection that Eliza Drewe visited Slade in the last half of 1814. In August she had sent Reynolds "an earnest invitation to spend a week or two" with her in Devonshire;[8] perhaps she hoped that they would spend part of the time with her family in Exeter and for the rest of the vacation join the Leighs and Rice at Slade—Rice was at Slade on 10 September 1814.[9] That is exactly what she and Reynolds did two years later in August 1816, including a meeting with Rice at Slade, when Reynolds finally accepted her invitation and visited her in Devonshire. But in 1814 Reynolds declined her invitation and instead spent his vacation on a tour of the inland counties. He was in love with Eliza, but not yet ready to get married.

To the Leighs and Maria Pearse, Bailey and Rice sang the praises of their London friend, the young published poet whose two 1814 volumes had made something of a name for him, and the ladies were so impressed that they welcomed any of his verses which they could secure for their commonplace books. By 25 March 1815, the record shows, Eliza Drewe had joined the group, though, as noted earlier, she may already have been acquainted with them. Hudnall inferred from the absence of any reference to her in the Leigh Browne-Lockyer Collection during the preceding months and from a poem by Bailey addressed to her that she was newly introduced to all of them at that time and that she had difficulty breaking into this "very dear circle of friends." The inference is improbable. Disappointed by her inability to introduce her prize, Reynolds, to the Leighs in the fall of 1814, she may have postponed visiting them. Bailey's poem, quoted by Hudnall, does not indicate that she was an outsider; instead it deals only with their personal relationship, imploring her not to misinterpret his light-hearted manner as a lack of solid affection:

> Oh! think not, though the rosy smile
>   Of levity may tinge my cheek,
> Opinion flutters on the style,
>   With which my playful tongue may speak!
>
> Oh think not thus! It is unkind
>   To wing my lightness with a dart:
> I *value* you for strength of mind,
>   But *love* you most for warmth of heart[10]

Though he delayed visiting their "adopted sisters" at Slade, Reynolds's warm friendship with Rice and Bailey continued unabated. When Rice and Bailey made an extended visit to the Leighs while he was bound to his desk at the Amicable office, he addressed a poem to Rice on 1 March 1815 which has little poetic merit, but is of biographical interest in revealing the strength of the bond between the two. The second of the six stanzas is typical of the whole:

> Then think of thy friend who is far from thy sight
> Who is happy when with thee and sad when away
> He would love to be near at the earliest light
> With the friend of his soul, o'er the mountain to stray[11]

He is "Beloved Rice" who has a "generous bosom" in Reynolds's sonnet "To James Rice on his birth-day," written on 18 August 1815.[12] Bailey expressed his love of Reynolds just as unreservedly on 9 September 1815 in "Stanzas Written on the birth day of my dear Friend John Hamilton Reynolds, when he came of age, and addressed to his family, he being absent":

> I would tell,
> Were not my heart too full to speak—
> Yes I would say how dear, how well
> I love him,—but my words are weak.[13]

By this time Bailey and Rice had long known all the members of the Reynolds family well. Reynolds was absent from London at the time of Bailey's poem on a month's vacation at Bradgate Park in Leicestershire.

His friendship with Leigh Hunt also grew. He visited Hunt, who was in prison for attacking the Prince Regent in the *Examiner,* borrowed Hunt's books, profiting from Hunt's annotations in them, and boasted to Dovaston of Hunt's approval of the *Inquirer,* which he and the other Zetosophians had tried to make resemble Hunt's *Reflector.* He knew of Hunt's plans for *The Descent of Liberty* months before it was published and for *The Story of Rimini* a year and a half before it was printed, and his praise of Hunt at this time was unqualified. "Of this Gentleman's Genius I entertain very ⟨h⟩ great ideas, and he certainly has the richest fancy (except My L^d. Byron & Moore) of any man living. . . . I know of no one, who, from his Intimacy with the Italian Poets and from his own brilliant (and if I may say) Italian Fancy, could throw into a Mask [*The Descent of Liberty*] so much of its real Poetry, airy sprightliness, delicate wit and Fanciful imagery."[14] When Reynolds received a presentation copy from Hunt of *The Descent of Liberty* accompanied by a friendly note, he was so "enraptured" that he sat up half the night to read the poem and to praise it in a letter to Hunt. After showing his pleasure with Reynolds's letter by acknowledging it in the notes to correspondents in the *Examiner,*[15] Hunt solicited a poem from him. Reynolds sent *The Fairies,* which Hunt told him he liked greatly,[16] but Hunt was unable to publish it in the *Examiner* because Napoleon's return from Elba barraged him with so many news reports that he had no space for a 130-line poem—he published no poetry at all for weeks and then only a few short poems before Waterloo. Reynolds's visit to Hunt and his family at 3 Maida Vale, Paddington, on 27 February 1815 showed that he entered Hunt's circle long before he or Hunt met Keats.

As a part owner of the *Inquirer* who was actively involved in the editing, Reynolds also knew Charles Wentworth Dilke, the regular theatrical critic for the magazine. Born on 8 December 1789, son of Charles Wentworth and Sarah Blewford Dilke,[17] Dilke was a Hampshire boy who attended Portsmouth Grammar School along with Charles Brown.[18] After studying at Cambridge,[19] he followed his father's lead and entered the Navy Pay Office. Before he was nineteen, he married the beautiful Maria Dover Walker from Yorkshire, who was even younger than he.[20] It is likely that he met the Reynolds family soon after his arrival in London, where he settled at 84 Newman Street, for in 1809 he contributed three guineas entitling him to be listed as one of the guardians of the Lambeth Female Asylum, where George Reynolds taught writing.[21] He did not join the Zetosophian Society—he is not included in Martin's list of members—perhaps because he was married and had a small child. All the other members about whom there is information were single. But the Zetosophian John Martin became his first publisher, just as he was Reynolds's; Martin published his continuation of Dodsley's collection of old plays in 1816, his first major scholarly project.

Reynolds's circle of friends was large, and because his wit and friendliness made him such good company, his friends were generous to him. In August 1815 recurring illness depressed him so much that the annual vacation already noted was especially welcome. Some "very kind friends," a married couple "pitying the maladies, mental and bodily" from which he suffered, persuaded him to accompany them on a month's vacation to Bradgate Park in Leicestershire. They traveled in a one-horse chaise, with Reynolds driving, to Leicester, where they met the gamekeeper Harry Adams, who led them on his horse through Anstey to Bradgate Park. Reynolds's married lady friend was a native of Leicestershire who had lived near Adams in her childhood, and it was she who had arranged for the month's stay in the cottage with Adams, his wife, and their numerous children. They enjoyed sitting in the parlor, talking with the Adamses about the earlier days at Bradgate Park and about its present earl. Reynolds spent some of his time lounging, reading, and meditating under the great oaks that arched the brook, where, still melancholy from his bodily ills and mental depression, he wrote "Stanzas Written Under an Oak That Grows in Bradgate Park," anticipating plaintively his own death and grave. The same painful-pleasing melancholy carried over to his meditations upon the ruined castle and its famous tragic occupant, Lady Jane Grey. After a time his spirits revived as he shifted from past to present and accompanied Harry Adams on his fishing and hunting expeditions through the park.[22]

Reynolds was still at Bradgate Park on his birthday, 9 September 1815 when Bailey sent the poem to his family; he returned to London late in September and resumed his close friendship with Bailey and Rice. In October and November 1815, Rice and Bailey wrote the Leigh sisters two letters from London that describe vividly the kind of life that they and Reynolds were living at the time. The three frequently spent their evenings together after Reynolds had finished his clerical work and Rice his legal duties. Rice wrote on 9 October 1815:

when the Evening closes in & we "stir the fire & wheel the sofa round and draw the curtain close" when "we retire the world shut out." Then it is that We Bailey Reynolds & myself in all the luxury of mental relaxation indulge our fancies our feelings & our humors, & without any of the prescriptions of form, ramble over the fields of imagination running after every butterfly subject that starts up before us.—You will of course suppose that *he* [Reynolds] is no stranger to our delightful & dear Sisterhood of Slade—but do not therefore for a moment think that we profane your names to those to whom you ought to be Strangers or in whose actual acquaintance we are not confident you would be pleased.—We have always some project on the carpet, some game ever afoot—Either Reynolds or Bailey have ever got the Muses Spur in their side that will not allow them rest or respite—& very sad things their productions *may* be for ought I know—but they give up pleasure & make us every now & then cry "excellent" & that serves our turn you Know as well as if they were better. Reynolds has made progress in a Tragedy that according to my own judgment (if it be not particularized) bids fair to stamp his name with very current reputation.—Within this week too we have bethought of us turning that delightful little tale of Louisa Venoni into an Opera for which it has ever seemed to me admirably suited—I have bargained to furnish the plot & some of the humour & Reynolds the serious & sentimental—or as a Satirist would quiz it, he is to be the Quack & I the merry Andrew of the Piece—no matter if these Our Plans never come to anything or change once a month like the Moon, like her too they serve to enliven our Nights whilst they *do* last.—[23]

A year later, in a theatrical review, Reynolds referred to the difficulties he had writing the tragedy; evidently it was never completed, nor was the planned opera based on Henry Mackenzie's *Louisa Venoni* ever written. On 24 November 1815 Bailey described their joint contributions to another work, not intended for publication, a poem to celebrate Sarah Leigh's birthday:

I told you in my letter of yesterday that we kept or were to keep your birthday at my rooms. . . . On the other side is our *playfulness of affection* [a poem]. Reynolds late in the Evening regretted that we had not sooner thought of writing a Poem on the occasion in *triplets* Each person writing a line. . . . I therefore immediately produced the paper, and wrote the first line. . . . They were all written in whirlwinds of laughing. For it was our delight so to change the thought of the person who wrote last as to puzzle him to convert it into anything like agreement or sense with his own, and then to laugh and make what noise we could to interrupt the unhappy artist who was doomed to scratch his head for a thought. . . . I wish you could see Reynolds whose lines are so superior in this little thing to ours—[24]

Unfortunately the triplets do not confirm at all clearly Bailey's claim of the superiority of Reynolds's lines. The first two are typical:

1.

Sarah! the wave that dances on the sea [Bailey]
Whose face reflects each summer beam like thee [Rice]
Hath all thy gladness, all thy melody. [R]

2.

Oh Thou! adopted sister—chosen friend! [Rice]
Awhile our hearts thy softer spirit lend— [Bailey]
And with our thoughts thy happy mildness blend. [R]

Close as this triumvirate was, they were too sociable to limit their friendships to a closed circle. Reynolds and Bailey met Benjamin Robert Haydon and lounged in his studio at 41 Great Marlborough Street during spare hours.[25] Before his vacation Reynolds had published two sonnets in the *Champion* on 13 July 1815. Perhaps it was through Haydon that he met the editor, John Scott. When Reynolds joined the staff of the *Champion* near the end of 1815, the newspaper was almost two years old. Well qualified as an editor by previous journalistic experience, Scott had conducted a weekly publication of his own called the *Censor* and edited an evening newspaper, the *Statesman*. After editing John Drakard's *Stamford News* for two years, he moved with that journal to London, where the first issue appeared on 10 January 1813 as *Drakard's Newspaper*. A year later Scott and Horace Smith bought the paper from Drakard and changed the name to the *Champion* on 2 January 1814.[26] After an unsatisfactory experience with George Soane as temporary editor from 27 August through 15 October 1815 while he was in Paris, Scott needed a capable and energetic young man like Reynolds to manage the theatrical reviews, many of the literary essays and reviews, and the original poetry. The paper had declined from the strong position it held when Hazlitt and Lamb contributed to it, and readers had protested.[27]

Reynolds had joined the staff of the *Champion* by 10 December 1815 when his "Mr. Wordsworth's Poetry" appeared in the literature section, signed with the initial R. His position with the *Champion* lasted until 28 December 1817. For the first five months Reynolds must have been hard pressed for time because he wrote for the paper in addition to his regular work at the Amicable office. His primary duty was theatrical reviewing, and for most of the issues during his connection with the paper he wrote notices which varied in length from half a column to a full quarto page. During the regular theatrical season from September through May, he reviewed performances of the two patent theaters, Drury Lane and Covent Garden. In the summer he reviewed productions at many of the smaller houses, though he ordinarily confined himself to the Haymarket, the New English Opera House, and the Italian Opera House.

In addition to dramatic criticism, Reynolds also contributed a large proportion of the literary reviews and original papers. Before Scott left for France in the summer of 1816, Reynolds wrote articles on Wordsworth, the Elizabethan and Jacobean dramatists, Chaucer, Milton, Akenside, the *Spectator,* an essay on egotism in literature, and a critique of most of the contemporary poets in the form of a dream vision. To the original poetry department, he was the largest single contributor, but the task was lighter because he had a large stock of poems already written upon which he could draw. Of his twenty-two poems published, five had been written long before they were printed, and two of the five were among the longest, *The Fairies* and "Reproach Me Not."[28] As manager of the original poetry section, he could also call on his friends for support: Bailey supplied a sonnet "To Milton" and Keats ensured that the newspaper would never be completely forgotten by providing four sonnets.[29] Charles Cowden Clarke sent one sonnet published on 21 April 1816, but it is probable he mailed it as an unknown correspondent, just as Keats mailed "To Solitude" to Hunt.[30]

Reynolds's poems published in the *Champion* before *The Naiad* volume of August 1816 include five irregular sonnets, which are capable verse, but pictorial rather than metaphorical. Three on Greece, prompted by the first two cantos of *Childe Harold,* contrast the sunny Greek landscape with the dark enslavement and invoke classical heroes to overthrow the Turkish tyranny. One to Wordsworth, in praising the older poet's healing power, sounds a little like Arnold, but the pictures and phrasing—"mountain solitude" and "distant waterfall"—are too expected to be satisfying. One feels Reynolds's love for *The Faerie Queene* in "To Spenser," but the promising diction of the first line, "Ye that have hearts vex'd with unquiet thought," fades into sentimental praise of the "mild, and beautiful, and bright." In "Stanzas Composed under an Oak," he is too sweetly gloomy in imagining his own grave, and "To Ella" is too vague to evoke any real sense of the love and heartbreak it mentions. All these poems can be pleasing if one is tolerant of their limitations, but they rise above competence only in occasional particulars.

Reynolds's first five months' work on the *Champion* built his confidence. The continuing responsibility differed from his earlier occasional contributions to Ackermann's *Repository,* the *Gentleman's Magazine,* and the *Ladies' Museum.* He had been prudent to continue with his clerical employment while participating in so risky a venture as the *Inquirer,* but he was now a regular staff member of a major periodical, the one that Wordsworth judged to provide the best journalistic prose of the day. Since he was earning money steadily and his prospects were bright, he resigned on 24 April 1816 as clerk at the Amicable insurance office, persuaded that he could support himself with his pen, either as a journalist or as a poet. His last book of poetry, *The Eden of Imagination* (the *Ode* had been only a pamphlet), had been very satisfying to his own judgment, and the revered Wordsworth had spoken well of it. Growing friendship with the extremely ambitious Haydon fired his own ambition. The time was ripe for an advance toward his great goal of becoming a genuine poet. He had high hopes for *The Naiad and Other Poems,* to be published, not by his old friend John Martin who had brought out his earlier work, but by the better-established firm of Taylor and Hessey.

Late in the summer of 1816 his work on *The Naiad* required so much of his time that he was hard pressed to supply his quota of material for the *Champion.* He wrote theatrical reviews and an essay on Milton from 23 June through 28 July, but with the beginning of August the quantity of his writing diminished greatly. For 4 August he wrote no theatrical review and printed only *The Fairies,* the substantial poem written a year and a half before, which he would also include in *The Naiad and Other Poems.* He filled "The Reader" department for that week with an article on Milton and Jeremy Taylor by his intimate friend Benjamin Bailey[, who was no doubt glad to assist in relieving some of the pressure on him]. In the following week he seems to have defaulted entirely, for he wrote neither theatrical review nor literary articles. The next week, 18 August, he wrote only a very brief theatrical review and called on another friend, Charles Brown, to substitute for him in "The Reader" with a long critical essay on *The Two Gentlemen of Verona.*[31] Reynolds had doubtless known Brown for years because of his long friendship with Brown's schoolmate Dilke, who had just built with Brown the double house they shared in Hampstead, Wentworth Place, where Keats later lived with Brown. Reynolds and Brown also had a mutual friend in John Martin, who had published the libretto of Brown's opera *Narensky* in 1814.

After finishing work on *The Naiad,* dedicated to Haydon, and leaving Taylor and Hessey to complete the process of publication, Reynolds wrote a letter to Wordsworth presenting him with a copy and requesting criticism. Late in the evening about 23 or 24 August, he hurried to Haydon, a personal friend of Wordsworth, and asked him to write an additional letter to accompany his own. But he found Haydon at home and so sleepy that Reynolds could only leave his letter to Wordsworth; however he was not sure Haydon understood what was wanted.

Shortly thereafter he left in high spirits for his six-weeks vacation visiting Eliza Powell Drewe, her family, and the Leigh sisters in Devonshire. On his arrival at the home of William Drewe, Sr., on South Street in Exeter, he wrote Haydon on 26 August to explain that in about a week Haydon would receive two copies of *The Naiad* and to ask that Haydon send Wordsworth one copy, along with the letter to Wordsworth he had left, and a covering letter to be written by Haydon smoothing the presentation and request for criticism. Often careless in such matters—Haydon delayed five weeks in sending Wordsworth Keats's "Great Spirits Now on Earth Are Sojourning"[32]—he was very slow in arranging to have Reynolds's book delivered to Wordsworth, who did not receive it until a few days before 28 November, three months after Haydon wrote Reynolds that he had sent it.[33]

An unusual assortment of influences converged to produce the title poem in the new volume. Reynolds had loved the old folk ballads since his Shrewsbury School days when he read, reread, and recited them to his schoolmates after they had gone to bed. He had enjoyed Scott's metrical romances and encouraged Dovaston's Scott-like expanded literary ballad, *Fitzgwarine*. He was very conscious of Wordsworth's *Lyrical Ballads* and of the high regard which Wordsworth had recently expressed for Percy's *Reliques* in "Essay Supplementary to the Preface" of *Poems* of 1815.[34] But *The Naiad* is more Coleridgean in spirit than Wordsworthian. Earlier in 1816 the magic of *Christabel* had caught the attention of the nation; Byron voiced the reaction of many readers when he called it a "singularly wild and original poem." Like many others, Reynolds mocked the mystification of the poem in his articles for the *Champion,* but his fascination with it shows through the mockery. He sought to combine beauty, the supernatural, and evil in his own literary ballad with a narrative quite different from Coleridge's. By this time he had taught himself to read Italian readily, and his interest in wildly fanciful and evil enchantresses was heightened by Renaissance Italian poetry, especially Tasso, from whose *Jerusalem Delivered* he drew his epigraph likening a beautiful and evil sea nymph to Homer's sirens.[35]

Struck by "The Mermaid of Galloway" in *Remains of Nithsdale and Galloway Romance,*[36] he was deceived by R. H. Cromek's claim in the preface that it was a genuine folk ballad. He did not know, though Cromek may have, that Allan Cuningham invented the entire volume with two small exceptions. The poem provided a vivid link between nature and the supernatural that Reynolds could turn to his own use. The analogue with Goethe's "The Fisherman," which he knew only through Madame de Staël's account, confirmed his belief that such a story deserved the attention of a genuine poet.

In his source a mermaid described the marvelous beauties under the surface of the river and seduced a fisherman into entering the river with her and drowning. Reynolds changed the beguiled fisherman to a medieval knight, Lord Hubert, and the mermaid to a naiad, added a page to warn his master of the danger and a bride, Angeline, to grieve after his mysterious death. The story was simple, as a ballad should be; it was what Reynolds shadowed forth through the slender thread of narrative that counted.

The Naiad cannot be read as a straightforward allegory; its merit is that it resists a simple interpretation. The tale remains a tale, and its implications are allowed to lurk tantalizingly under the surface. It doubtless did not influence any Keats poem directly, but Reynolds's ambivalence toward romance even before he met Keats can be clarified by discussing it in terms of some of Keats's best poems. Lord Hubert resembles the knight-at-arms who is fascinated, lured, and finally seduced by the power of romance—the magic of the dream which provides bliss but also steals him away from the stolid earth of everyday experience. The Naiad is like La Belle Dame, the *femme fatale,* the enchantress whose witchery draws the hero into ecstasy that is illusory and short-lived. She is beautiful, sensuous, and magically appealing, but also cold and cruel. The nightingale's dream world of imagination draws the poet to the brink of death; the Naiad's song of magic romance goes further and draws Lord Hubert to his death by drowning. Romance is fascinating, beautiful, and glorious, but it is also in a sense life-denying. The final episode leading to Angeline's embrace of the ghost-corpse, which Wordsworth would have excised, is integral to the poem. The lovely nature description, the sensuous depiction of the Naiad, and the entrancing siren song made the reader feel strongly the compelling appeal of romance. Like the "desolate town" and "cold pastoral," Angeline's embrace of the drowned corpse doubles back on the earlier, largely favorable, presentation. It goes further than *Grecian Urn* and makes the reader feel the chilling terror of the death that immersion in romance can lead to. This is not to say that Wordsworth was not right to find much that is weak in the final episode. Reynolds could not resist the temptation to milk every ounce of sentimental pathos from the bride-widow's grief and death of a broken heart. The final passage should have been pared down, but the climactic embrace was indispensable.

For the rest of the slim volume (it has only 63 pages), Reynolds had to write only three new poems, for he had written two of the others, "Margaret" and *The Fairies,* early in 1815. The two lyrics, both called "Stanzas"—"When first I lov'd, my heart was young" and "Thou art not lost—thy spirit giveth"—and both celebrating his dead first sweetheart, are complementary. The first describes their happy love while she was alive, and the second insists that her adored image lives on for him even after death. The second was said to be "From the Italian" when he printed it in the *Champion*[37] shortly before he published it in *The Naiad,* but it seems probable that he was disguising his personal emotion, since no Italian original has turned up. If it were a translation, he would have been even more likely to label it as such in *The Naiad* to protect himself from a charge of plagiarism, and he did not. The first lyric is a little better than the second because of the controlled tone with which the successful courtship is presented; the second protests so emphatically with its feminine rhymes throughout that it sounds somewhat strained. The flowing rhythms and sentimental imagery of both please immediately in an effortless way, but they are relatively less satisfying than two other poems on his dead sweetheart, "Lines: Can a Rosy Lip or a Sparkling Eye" (assuming that it hints at her) or "Reproach Me Not" (quoted in full below).

In "Margaret," the first version of which had been prompted by a Welsh beauty he saw on a tour of Wales with Dovaston in 1812, he aimed at the chaste simplicity and delicate melody of Wordsworth's Lucy poems and hit his targets remarkably. Instead of the ballad stanza of alternating iambic tetrameter and trimeter used in four of the Lucy poems, he chose the ballad stanza of three lines of iambic tetrameter followed by a line of iambic trimeter used in three of Wordsworth's Joyous Spring poems. He followed the *abab* rhyme used in four of the Lucy poems and widely by Wordsworth elsewhere.

Controlling the elegiac tone carefully, he did not have Margaret die, as Lucy did. Since he wrote so many poems on his dead sweetheart, and since he was so often lugubrious in other poems, it is surprising that for once he mustered the restraint not to have her die. He developed the mingled sweetness and sadness of the speaker's recollection of an irrecoverable past of innocent love all the more poignantly by underplaying it.

Imitative though the poem is, it shows firm craftsmanship. It is strange that Wordsworth did not comment on it; he criticized only *The Naiad* in his letter to Reynolds. It is even stranger that a poem of such merit should have been entirely forgotten over the years. It is a success that deserves quotation in full:

1.

The maid I well remember now,
    Though time hath travell'd since we met;
She liv'd beneath a mountain's brow,
    The youthful Margaret!

2.

She was the spirit of the place,
    With eye so wild, and cheek so fair;
Her form so playful in its grace,
    Mock'd her own mountain air.

3.

The rustic dress became her well,—
    How dear to trace its beauty now!
And rich the natural ringlets fell
    O'er her delightful brow.

4.

There was a music in her speech,
    That gave the heart a soft delight;
Like murmuring waves that kiss the beach
    On a still Summer night.

5.

With looks and language innocent,
    She won the heart of Memory;
Which oft in busy scenes hath sent
    Thoughts to her silently.

6.

Her home I saw at day's decline;
    It was in sooth a lovely spot;
And fair the starry jessamine
    Wreath'd o'er the little cot.

7.

I lov'd the loud brook's sparkling haste,
    I lov'd the fields and mountains green;
And her whose fairy presence graced
    The wildness of the scene.

8.

Oh, should my feet in future days
    Wander again beside the stream

That by her lonely cottage plays,
　My heart would pause and dream:—

9.
'Twould dream of hours for ever gone,
　Of hours which never more can be;
Yet she who like a spirit shone,
　Would brighten memory.

10.
Though wild is life's tempestuous gale,
　May she escape the stormy hour;
And, like the violet of the vale,
　Live an unbroken flower!

11.
Oft shall I turn me to the past,
　And muse upon the hour I met
With her, whose form such brightness cast,—
　The youthful Margaret![38]

Reynolds reworked the poem painstakingly from the original version he sent to Dovaston in February 1815. He strove successfully for simplicity, purity, and understatement. For example, he had written "The lightsome Margaret" as the last lines of the first and last stanzas, but realizing that the unusual "lightsome" called too much attention to itself, he toned it down to "youthful." He also tightened up the syntax without sacrificing simplicity: in the second stanza he changed "Her form was playful in its grace / As her own mountain air" to "Her form so playful in its grace / Mock'd her own mountain air." He improved the poem markedly by revising the loose first draft.

The plot of "A Tale" is simple. Meeting a somber woman in a graveyard at night, the speaker asks why she is in such a place at such a time and why she is so downcast. Responding to his sympathy, she relates her tragedy. After a rustic courtship, she had fallen in love with a young man, and they had dreamed of a simple but rosy domestic future, but on the night before their wedding day she saw him burned to death in a fire that destroyed his cottage. Ever since she has been haunted by waking visions and nightmares of the fatal moment when the floor crashed and her lover burned. The poem closes with the speaker's pronouncement that the only consolation he can give her is to share her grief.

Reynolds selected the eight-line stanza Wordsworth used for "Goody Blake and Harry Gill," but he gave his poem the mournful tone and dialogue form of other Wordsworth poems like "Her Eyes Are Wild," "The Last of the Flock," and "The Sailor's Mother." As Wordsworth sometimes did, he combined grimness and pathos. The poem is sentimental, but hardly more so than Wordsworth in many similar poems.

"A Tale" is not so satisfying as "Margaret" in part because Reynolds remained content to develop pathos without any of the psychological or moral ingredients that add interest to some comparable poems by Wordsworth like "Her Eyes Are Wild," "The Last of the Flock," and "Alice Fell." Reynolds's epigraph from "Hart-Leap Well" is inexact as applied to his own poem: "a simple song to thinking hearts" (l. 100). If Wordsworth had written "a simple song to *feeling* hearts," the line would have applied. Perhaps more importantly, "A Tale" is less satisfying than "Margaret" because the models imitated are less valuable than the Lucy poems whose tone is imitated in "Margaret." Even if Reynolds's "A Tale" is as good as "The Sailor's Mother," it still is not worth much.

In *The Fairies,* also published in the *Champion* shortly before the book went to press,[39] the speaker on a moonlit night by a placid lake has a vision of delicate fairies, who sail in lily-cups, fly up to the clouds where they sing in chorus, and finally descend to prepare a flowery bed for their queen before vanishing. It is thoroughly fanciful and sensuous, a word-painting of a vision, appropriately set in octosyllabic couplets (varied by a few triplets) to give it a tripping, lilting rhythm. Evidently not intended to make any deep impression, it succeeds well enough in closing the volume with a change of tone to high-spirited reveling in romance. Whether one responds to this kind of abandon to fairyland depends on one's temperament: it was probably this piece as much as the title poem that led William Beckford to scribble "ineffably silly" in his copy of the book.

Although *The Eden of Imagination* was Wordsworthian and two of the poems in *The Naiad: A Tale with Other Poems* were Wordsworthian, the latter volume nevertheless represented a change for Reynolds. *The Eden* was thoroughly late eighteenth-century neoclassical, a good poem in the old mode, just as *An Evening Walk* had been. As a beginner, Reynolds settled for imitating Wordsworth's apprentice work. In the later volume he more ambitiously sought to follow two segments of Wordsworth's mature and central work. And *The Naiad* was both Coleridgean in general spirit and at the same time original to a degree in developing an ambivalent attitude toward romance. That he published the book anonymously seems to indicate some remaining tentativeness, a measure of uncertainty about the quality of his poetry, but he sought to advance beyond his earlier apprentice poetry and for a time was optimistic about the results. Slender though the volume was, he hoped that the powerful *Edinburgh Review* would criticize it.[40]

Though the *Edinburgh* ignored him, Reynolds was widely reviewed by eight other periodicals.[41] He knew the reviewing ropes and was never backward about promoting works in which he was interested. As noted earlier, he had conducted a campaign to have Dovaston's *Fitzgwarine* reviewed; later he exerted every effort to have Keats treated favorably, and he asked Keats to have Hunt review his *Peter Bell* in the *Examiner*. It is very likely that he encouraged the wide reviewing of *The Naiad*.

Although the reviewers included considerable criticism along with praise, on the whole the reaction was favorable. The *Critical Review* charged him with artificiality and with an undue attention to particular details that distracted from the overall design, but concluded: "The author of 'The Naiad' . . . displays so much talent, that we hope to see him affix his name to something of higher aim in its subject, and greater originality in its style."[42] The writer in the *Eclectic Review* attacked what he judged a dangerous tendency among contemporary poets to corrupt poetic language by taking liberties with current usage: "We meet with the following phrases in 'The Naiad': 'Then *come thee*,' 'and *come thee*': 'shook' for 'shaken': 'now speak me outright'; 'to *list* the answer that he pray'd'; 'passingly sweet'; to 'glance up to' a person; 'now fair fall thy lip'; 'they rode *them* on'; 'dare not *to* kiss'; etc."[43] Most of these examples are archaisms, so that the charge seems largely unjustified in view of Reynolds's avowed intention to imitate the style of the old ballads. Despite this sharp objection, however, even the *Eclectic* saw promise in the new poet.

Gratifying as the public appraisal was on balance, it was less important to Reynolds than one private judgment he had solicited. Wordsworth, who had congratulated him on *The Eden,* now disapproved:

A few days ago I received a Parcel through the hands of Messrs. Long-man containing your Poem the Naiad, etc. and a Letter, accompanying it, for both which marks of your attention you will accept my cordial thanks. Your Poem is composed with elegance and in a style that accords with the subject; but my opinion on this point might have been of more value if I had seen the Scottish Ballad on which your work is founded. You do me the honour of asking me to find fault in order that you may profit by my remarks. . . . I will not scruple to say that your Poem would have told more upon me, if it had been shorter. How uncere-moniously not to say ungraciously do I strike home! But I am justified to my own mind from a persuasion that it was better to put the objection in this abrupt way, than to introduce it by an accompanying compliment which, however well merited, would have stood in the way of the effect which I aim at—your Reformation. Your Fancy is too luxuriant, and riots too much upon its own creations. Can you endure to be told by one whom you are so kind as to say you respect that in his judgment your poem would be better without the first 57 lines (not condemned for their own sakes), and without the last 146, which nevertheless have much to recommend them. The Basis is too narrow for the super-structure; and to me it would have been more striking barely to have hinted at the deserted Fair One and to have left it to the Imagination of the Reader to dispose of her as he liked. Her fate dwelt upon at such length requires of the reader a sympathy which cannot be furnished without taking the Nymph from the unfathomable abyss of the cerulean waters and beginning afresh upon gross Terra Firma. I may be wrong but I speak as I felt, and the most profitable criticism is the record of sensations, provided the person affected be under no partial influence.[44]

The criticism was honest and intended to be helpful. Reynolds was not so thin-skinned as to be unable to accept such strictures. Several years before when Dovaston suspected that he had hurt Reynolds with adverse comments on his poetry, he replied that he was not hurt at all, that such a reaction would be unreasonable since he had asked for objective criticism and received it.[45] He continued to be as high in his praise of Wordsworth in the articles he wrote for the *Champion* after he received the letter as he had been before. Some have thought that he nursed a grudge because of the letter and vented his spleen in *Peter Bell* three years later because of resentment over the letter. That inference oversimplifies. Memory of the letter undoubt-edly played a part in enhancing his delight in writing the satire. He must have been human enough to enjoy the reversal of roles in the fault-finding process, but clear perceptions of Wordsworth's shortcomings as both poet and person were stronger motivations than personal revenge. Reynolds was not a vindictive man.

Reynolds did not read Wordsworth's strictures until months after his six-weeks vacation. With the completed book behind him, he was in high spirits, despite a cold caught on the coach, when he arrived in Exeter and settled down in the Drewe home.[46] His letter to Haydon of 26 August bubbled with friendship for Haydon, delight in the countryside, and optimism about his own prospects. During the first week in Exeter, he attended the theater and sent to the *Champion*'s theatrical columns what was more a personal essay than a review. He expected that he would benefit from his stay in the country as much as the *Spectator*, whose papers from Sir Roger de Coverley's estate he judged the best part of the work. Like the tallow-chandler in Dr. Johnson's *Idler* who could not stay away from his former work after retirement, Reynolds was drawn to the local theater, which he was predisposed to like because Edmund Kean had made his start there before coming to London. He was not disappointed in the comfortable and pretty theater; though the audience numbered less than thirty, the provincial acting company was so energetic, versatile, and uninhibited as to be a little humorous. Two of the actors he thought good enough for the London stage.[47]

After a week with the Drewes, Reynolds and Eliza traveled to Sidmouth, arriving on 31 August, for a twelve-day visit with Mary, Sarah, and Thomasine Leigh, Maria Pearse, and James Rice, who came down from London to share the visit. Reynolds's happiness was unbounded. He was surrounded by an audience of admiring young women: for over two years Rice and Bailey had been singing his praises to the Leigh sisters and their cousin. Notes in their commonplace books after his handwriting indicate their attitude toward the long-awaited hero: "J. H. Reynolds—his hand."[48] His pleasure was the greater because Rice was there. The beauty of the countryside exceeded all his expectations, and, most of all, he and Eliza were in love. When he recalled the experience a year later in a letter to Mary Leigh, he was still glowing:

What a fine hour was that in your room with Eliza, Maria & yourself!—Do you remember it?—I have not forgotten a single slope, brake, or tree, which feasted my eyes when I was sojourning at your green, romantic & sea-crowned home. There was that delightful walk on the mellow Autumn evening, under the young trees, to the cliff!—There was the Sea "whispering eternally on desolate shores"!—There was the ruin, with its ivied window, and silent story of decay! There was the blessed sky, with its wide look of peace, and the calm smile on its face!—But "above all," there was the company of Eliza & yourself. I know not how it is, Mary, but that evening is sweeter to me apparently in recollection. It seems something hallowed by memory. I remember all—Eliza with her handkerchief over [her] head, by my side,—& you, with yr. brow "bared to the elements."[49]

At the center of the stage, he read to the company from *Henry IV, Part I* and from Hazlitt's essays.[50] Alone together under a purple beech tree, Eliza sang to him and moved him to celebrate the scene in a poem that he mailed to the *Champion*.[51] The natural beauty and strong emotion were lodged firmly in his mind so that a year later he could recall them "in tranquillity" and produce one of his finest poems, *Devon.*

On 11 September he and Eliza left Slade Hall and returned to Exeter for three more weeks of happiness. Haydon's letters awaited him—it is a mark of their warm friendship that Haydon had written him more than once in this short time—and he replied in buoyant spirits. He had promised Mary Leigh that he would visit Slade again, but some time before his return to London he wrote to thank her for her hospitality and to apologize for being unable to keep his promise this autumn.[52] He hoped that they would renew the friendship in some future summer and described his plans for reading Shakespeare and Milton together and walking once again through the beautiful countryside at Slade.

In the more than three weeks remaining at Exeter, Eliza delighted in showing him all her favorite scenic spots around the city, especially the lovely little valley of Ide, two and a quarter miles southwest of Exeter, which he celebrated in "Lines to a Valley," not published until 1821 in *The Garden of Florence*. In the little village (the population was still only 757 in 1968), the trees furnished seclusion by blotting out the ancient city, and he felt completely free from the pressures of London duties, "dull acquaintance," and "heavy strangers." His love for Eliza and his happiness shine through the serene content of the pleasant poem. On 23 September he, Eliza, and a friend walked along the banks of the River Exe in the moonlight, and on his return to the Drewe home he set down in his commonplace book "A Romantic Walk with Two Friends," which he later expanded into an essay for the *Champion*.[53]

During this vacation and for a year and a half afterward, Reynolds's poetic ambition was at its height. Either at Slade or Exeter, he conceived the idea for his most serious long poem, *The Romance of Youth*. The preface to the poem, when finally published in 1821, stated, "The plan of this poem came suddenly on the Author's mind some few years back, at a time when he was passing his hours in a most romantic part of the country,—and when all his feelings were devoted to poetry. At that time it was to him 'a dream and a glory.' "[54] He probably began the poem immediately in Devon, while he still had abundant leisure, and he finished most of the only canto he wrote by the end of the year. Since Reynolds has usually been remembered, when he has been remembered at all, for the sonnets in which he renounced the muse (and indeed they are among his best short poems), four rather good stanzas written close to this time are worth quoting to strike a balance and show his early confidence:

He [the young poet] look'd up to the sky, which quickly threw
A life into his mind. The stars were light,
Sprinkling the skiey fields with heavenly dew,
Or gemming well the raven hair of night:
From earth he sent his spirit on its flight,
To dream, wandering amidst them; and there came
A thought to him, that as those orbs were bright,
Brighter in darkness,—he might be the same,
And in a gloomy age make starlight of his name.

And glorious is the fate of him who rears
His name as a proud column on the earth,—
Round which the withering tempest of long years
Lingers, yet leaves it strong as at its birth.
It keeps high splendour. Never is there dearth
Of those who bend to it as glory's goal;
To thousands it gives elevated worth,
And points the pride of spirit. 'Mid the roll
Of dangerous times it stands, the landmark of the soul.

"My heart, all youthful, hath one passion towering
O'er all the other passions—'tis for Fame!
Whatever storms around my head be lowering,
Still be endurance high,—and hope the same.
It is the diet of my heart—the aim
Of my full spirit—and let others lie
The while the rust of time creeps o'er their name,

Wearing it from the world for aye,—while I
So consecrate my name, that it shall never die.

Were it not glorious at one vigorous bound
To spring, all life, upon the wings of Time,
And never more to touch the soiling ground,
But float, for ever, and through every clime,
The wonder of all lands? Oh, flight sublime!
Give me but this,—and I will throw this form
Back to its fellow earth, that cannot climb:
What matters that the body glut the worm,
So as the spirit flies proud o'er each worldly storm!"[55]

CHAPTER 5

The *Champion*—1816–1817

REYNOLDS'S better poetry, including that published in the *Champion* and in the volume *The Naiad,* has already been discussed. Before beginning an account of his friendship with Keats, it will be well to consider what Reynolds's prose in the *Champion* reveals about his reading, critical views, and intellect. When he joined the staff of the weekly newspaper in December 1815, he could read Latin and Italian, and he had taught himself a little Greek. His wide reading in English literature in the five years after he left St. Paul's School, done in the evenings after work between dinner and midnight, was systematic and thorough enough to prepare him to be an informed critic.

His knowledge of English literature began with Chaucer, whose most striking achievement, he believed, was vividness in describing external nature: "A leaf is described by him so clearly, that its crispness and glossy greenness come directly before the sight."[1] He valued especially Chaucer's ability to portray "internal feelings as connected with external nature"; instead of merely observing a landscape, the reader caught the mood and entered into the feelings of the author. Chaucer's most characteristic mood was happiness, and descriptions of the morning, colored by that mood, he found particularly appealing: "Chaucer is the clear and breathing Poet of the months of April and May—of morning—of meadows, and birds and their harbours. . . . Chaucer delights to be up and out, before the sun—while the stars are coldly light in the cold white sky—while the trees are still, and the waters are looking through the silent air to heaven, and the dew is twinkling, and all the world seems wrapt in cheerful and quiet thought."

He praised Chaucer's subtlety in bringing characters to life; a veiled reference to the Friar's conduct, for example, struck off the essence of his character in two brief lines:

> He had ymade ful many a marriage,
> Of young women at his owen coste.

Although he found that Chaucer's low characters had more "pure bold strength" than those of any other writer, the tales of romance impressed him more than the fabliaux. He praised lavishly the magnificent vestments and the marvels of "The Squire's Tale." He found Chaucer's versification harmonious and praised his ability to fit the sound to the sense. Far from taking Chaucer's apparent simplicity at face value, he saw both the humor and the artistry of it.

He was especially pleased, as was Keats, with "The Flower and the Leaf," mistakenly attributed to Chaucer at the time. His favorite passage was the celebration of the nightingale, a subject which always made him "feel a kindness" toward any poet who treated it. Chaucer's two faults he judged to be grossness of language and a lack of selectivity.

He greatly admired all the major Elizabethan and Jacobean dramatists, but he literally worshiped Shakespeare. Reynolds frequently used religious terms to express the extent of his devotion, on one occasion describing Shakespeare as the "divinity of the world of imagination."[2] In a review of a contemporary play, he carried the analogy further:

For our own parts, liberal and tolerant as we are in our sentiments on ordinary occasions, we must confess ourselves bigots of the right Spanish breed in matters of this kind.—Were we exalted to the Papal Chair of criticism (and critics possess the same attribute of infallibility with his holiness) we should certainly pronounce against these heresies in taste, the same sentence that our holy brother used in religious differences of opinion, only reversing the *order* of the punishment—we would have them *damned here* and trust their being *burnt hereafter.*—Since however we live in so tolerant an age, that it would be in vain for us to preach up persecution against the whole sect of these dissenters from the Shakespearian Orthodoxy, it would be unjust to attack one for the offences of the whole.[3]

He was joking in part, but the reference to "Shakespearian Orthodoxy" was revealing. Such an attitude virtually precluded adverse criticism. "We feel that criticism has no right to purse its little brow in the presence of Shakespeare. He has to our belief very few imperfections,—and perhaps these might vanish from our minds, if *we* had the *perfection* properly to scan them." Consequently, the only value judgment he could make was to determine the degree of praise to be bestowed upon each of Shakespeare's works. After discussing the limitations of the historical plays, he declared: "We hate to say a word against a word of Shakespeare's,—and we can only do so by comparing himself with himself."[4]

Like Coleridge, Schlegel, and Hazlitt, Reynolds concentrated on psychological analyses of the characters. Since he considered Shakespeare the foremost "anatomist of the human heart," he felt that the critic's primary duty lay in interpreting personalities and motives. He insisted repeatedly that the characters in the plays were real people, and not merely "the idle coinage of the Poet's brain."[5] Although this device was a common Romantic method of paying tribute to Shakespeare's genius, few other critics approached the extreme to which Reynolds took it. Almost all his discussions of Shakespeare have some variation of his statement that "Macbeth, and Lear, and Othello are real beings."[6] Arguing from this premise, he eventually arrived at the strange conclusion that Shakespeare lost control over the characters after he created them.[7]

Since he was primarily interested in psychological interpretation of Shakespeare's characters, he had little use for most of the earlier critics, who "preyed only on the expressions of Shakespeare, and wholly disregarded his spirit and feeling" with their "little questionings of words and phrases . . . petty cavillings about black-letter books, or worn-out and worthless customs."[8] The only two critics whom he considered worthy of the subject were Schlegel and Hazlitt. He did not know Coleridge's similar criticism because none of Coleridge's lectures delivered before 1818 were published until 1849 and later. He regarded Schlegel's lectures, which he read in the translation of John Black, as the first significant criticism of Shakespeare.[9]

An even greater influence on his Shakespearean criticism was Hazlitt, his idol as a periodical essayist, whom he knew personally at least by 2 June 1816, when he wrote of him, "We also know one writer of the present day, who delights his readers with the most able and ingenious speculations, and who is never so eloquent as when he speaks of his own feelings. He then seems to rise above this earth, and to float in an air and in a light of his own:—his youth comes back upon him. His heart lives in a vision. He talks the purest poetry."[10] Reynolds saw Hazlitt often and for long periods of time, as we know from his glowing account of Hazlitt in the letter to Mary Leigh of 28 April 1817.[11] The two had much in common. Both had spent their early years in Shropshire, Reynolds in Shrewsbury and Hazlitt in nearby Wem. Both were theatrical and literary reviewers and essayists, and both supported themselves by their journalism—Hazlitt, indeed, wrote occasionally for the *Champion*. Because of their shared interests and because of Reynolds's charming personality and lively conversation, they became fast friends, Hazlitt offering a sympathetic and very high appraisal of Reynolds's ability and Reynolds becoming Hazlitt's disciple in literary matters. From Hazlitt Reynolds derived many of his most cherished ideas; he imitated his style, quoted him often, repeated his quotations from the old poets, and adopted his critical terms and catch phrases.[12] He seldom called Hazlitt by name in the *Champion*, but the reader of his essays soon learns to identify Hazlitt with almost any anonymous reference to a gifted writer of prose. Hazlitt is "an able writer," "a great authority in these matters," and "the critic of the *Times*."[13]

When Hazlitt's *Characters of Shakespeare's Plays* appeared in 1817, Reynolds reviewed it at length in two installments and paid Hazlitt the highest possible tribute: "This is the only work ever written on Shakespeare, that can be deemed worthy of Shakespeare;—some remarks in Schlegel's German lectures only excepted. Now this is a sweeping assertion,—and yet it is true." He described his personal reaction to the book: "The work before us is one, of all others, which we longed to see written,—and now it is come we must make the most of it." His description of it as "a sort of mental biography of Shakespeare's characters" would have been equally applicable to his own Shakespearean criticism. He included large extracts accompanied by praise, and in only one case did he express a reservation about Hazlitt's treatment of his subject. The essay on Hamlet did not quite live up to his expectations, but he absolved Hazlitt of any blame by declaring that the subject was too sublime for even the greatest of critics.[14]

Another contemporary critic who influenced Reynolds's Shakespearean criticism was Charles Lamb, whose "Theatralia, No. 1. On Garrick and Acting; and the Plays of Shakespeare, considered with reference to their fitness for Stage Representation" (the title as Reynolds read it instead of the more familiar one given it in Lamb's *Works* of 1818), Reynolds read in the fourth and last number of Hunt's *Reflector* of 1812. He studied that short-lived periodical carefully, sent Dovaston copies of it, patterned the *Inquirer* on it, and copied one article from it before sending Dovaston the issue.[15] He did not say which one he copied, but it may well have been the most famous one in the magazine, in which Lamb argued that Shakespeare cannot be represented adequately on the stage. Reynolds never mentioned Lamb by name, perhaps because he did not know who wrote the anonymous article, but he echoed it clearly:

> We wished the other evening, at the theatre, for the presence of three friends [Mary Leigh, Eliza Drewe, and probably James Rice], to whom we had been lately reading the first part of *Henry the 4th*—and to whom we had been also asserting that Shakspeare's plays suffered in the representation. They would, we feel assured, have been convinced of the truth of our assertion,—for the performance of this admirable play made wondrous havoc with the wit, and spirit, and poetry, which are so excellent and evident on a perusal. We do not much like to see Shakspeare tortured on the stage:—what has he done to deserve it?[16]

Although the review including this passage was Reynolds's fullest exposition of the argument that Shakespeare's plays cannot be represented satisfactorily on stage, the idea was almost always present in his mind when he reviewed the contemporary productions of Shakespeare. On 14 December 1817, for example, he began a review of *Hamlet,* "What has Hamlet done, that he should be held up to mockery on an unfeeling stage, and all his utmost and most passionate sensations turned into pageants and the shews of grief?"[17]

Less overawed than in his criticism of Shakespeare, Reynolds was a judicious critic of Ben Jonson. Examining the traditional charge that Jonson's pedantry had overpowered his imagination, he admitted that the criticism had an element of truth, but he argued that the old generalization required qualification: *The Alchemist* and *Volpone* showed "a richness of character, added to a conversational humour, that cannot be surpassed."[18] He quoted several richly imaginative passages from Jonson's plays and masques to substantiate his claim. One such passage from *The Sad Shepherd,* in which an old shepherd instructs Robin Hood's followers in the art of finding witches, shows his early love of the Robin Hood legend, which later led him to write the two fine sonnets that he sent to Keats. Another quotation from *The Alchemist,* Sir Epicure Mammon's extravagant description of the exotic foods on which he planned to feast after he discovered the secret of alchemy (II, ii, 72–87), is typical of the richly sensuous poetry that he found especially appealing. He quoted the same passage with similar praise in a later article for the *Scots Magazine.*[19]

Though he was never able to achieve a comparable richness in his own verse, his admiration of it prepared him to appreciate Keats.

In an essay devoted entirely to Jonson, he used as a point of departure a statement by John Aikin in *Vocal Poetry* that the exquisite gem from *The Silent Woman,* "Still to be neat, still to be drest," was "one of the few productions of this once celebrated author, which by their singular elegance and neatness, form a striking contrast to the prevalent coarseness of his tedious effusions."[20] Such an assertion, said Reynolds, could prove only one of two things: Dr. Aikin's ignorance of Jonson's works or a total lack of taste. He readily admitted that many passages in the comedies were indelicate, but he found it difficult to believe that a critic could find "singular elegance and neatness" a rare quality in Jonson. In his earlier essay he had discounted the customary charge that Jonson's pedantry and love of polish had stifled his imagination, but he considered that overstatement more tolerable than Dr. Aikin's general censure of coarseness. Quoting William Cartwright's remark that Jonson polished until "the file would not make *smooth* but wear,"[21] he regretted that too often the bold and vigorous in Jonson was also bare and naked. Nevertheless, he felt that in an unusually large number of poems Jonson had struck the perfect balance between imagination and restraint to produce incomparable classic lyrics. Passing over "Drink to me only with thine eyes" and the lyrics in *The Sad Shepherd,* which he supposed were already well known to his readers, he selected for quotation several beautiful, but less familiar lyrics from *The Gipsies Metamorphosed* and *The Forest and Underwoods.* In conclusion he declared that any composer might bring honor to himself by setting Jonson's lyrics to music, though in most cases because of the excellent modulation of the verse, music would be superfluous.

Reynolds's analyses and judgments of the other Elizabethan dramatists, who he thought occasionally approached Shakespeare and Jonson, need not be particularized. Contemporary revivals of Massinger and Beaumont and Fletcher provided opportunities for thoughtful studies at some length. In his second theatrical review, he recommended that John Ford be revived,[22] and, when his recommendation went unheeded, he devoted his greatest attention to his favorite Ford in the second essay "On the Early English Dramatists."[23] Marlowe, Marston, and Dekker he discussed generally and briefly.

Reynolds was either indifferent to, or contemptuous of, the revivals of the tragedies of the Restoration and eighteenth century like those of Thomas Southerne and Nicholas Rowe, but he had a high regard for the comedy. Congreve and Farquhar, Goldsmith and Sheridan, he used frequently in his theatrical reviews as models of wit to contrast with the dull writers of his own day. John Gay's *The Beggar's Opera* was one of the first plays that he saw as a boy, and it remained a favorite throughout his life. He referred to it more often than to any other work except the plays of Shakespeare. Very much interested in boxing, he filled his essays with figures of speech based on the sport. Since boxing was illegal in his time, the participants and many of their followers were a part of the underworld. The lives of these people, which he later depicted in *The Fancy,* fascinated him, and the scenes in *The Beggar's Opera* often reminded him of them.

Dramatists received most of Reynolds's attention because of his position as theatrical critic, but he also criticized nondramatic poets in the literature section of the newspaper. During his connection with the *Champion,* he and Benjamin Bailey engaged in friendly rivalry over the relative merits of Spenser and Milton. Reynolds championed Spenser; Bailey, Milton. Each wrote a sonnet on his idol for the *Champion,*[24] and Reynolds addressed another sonnet to Bailey in which he said, "Milton hath your heart,—and Spenser mine."[25] Though Reynolds did not write a separate essay on Spenser, he frequently praised Spenser's rich sensuousness. Reynolds's part in the argument, however, was more the exercise of ingenuity than the expression of firm conviction. Though partial to Spenser, he never failed to recognize the sublimity of Milton, often coupling Milton with Shakespeare and on one occasion paying Milton the highest tribute: he said that he had met with only three or four intelligent readers who did not think Milton as great a genius as Shakespeare.[26]

On two occasions Reynolds published comprehensive essays evaluating many of the poets of the period. To the miscellanea department of 7 April 1816, he contributed "The Pilgrimage of Living Poets to the Stream of Castaly."[27] Pretending to be apprehensive about his boldness in passing judgment on the successful poets of the day, Reynolds introduced the printed essay with an apology for his own limitations: "I am one of those unfortunate youths to whom the Muse has glanced a sparkling of her light,—one of those who pant for distinction, but have not within them that immortal power which alone can command it. There are many,—some, Sir, may be known to you,—who feel keenly and earnestly the eloquence of heart and mind in others, but who cannot, from some inability or unobtrusiveness, clearly express their own thoughts and feelings." When he published this passage, the twenty-two-year-old Reynolds had written a large amount of verse, but was uncertain as to whether he was destined to become a genuine poet. The disclaimer of ability, however, must not be taken entirely at face value. He admired Chaucer, and there are several indications that he followed the pattern of Chaucer's dream visions in this essay. As we have seen, he admired Chaucer's irony in pretending to be a simple person; he was fond of "my wit is shorte, ye may well understand."[28] A repetition of the pose later in the essay sounds even more Chaucerian than the introduction: "I have a great desire to attempt giving publicity to my dream, but I have before told you how limited are my powers of expression;—so I must rely upon your goodness, in receiving the crude description, or not." The expression of modesty was largely a pleasant Chaucerian convention, for he knew perfectly well that the *Champion* would print the article. He had been a regular member of the staff for over four months.

In the body of the essay, Reynolds pretended that he walked forth one evening to the side of a brook, where he sat down to read one of the old poets. Falling into a deep sleep, he dreamed that, while walking through a romantic valley, he met a beautiful female figure who was the guardian of the stream of Castaly. The Spirit explained that, because of Reynolds's love of her favorite Spenser, she would allow him to see the annual procession of living poets who came to obtain water from the Castalian stream. The treatment of a selection of them will show the nature of the satire. The first was a melancholy figure bearing a Grecian urn, whom Reynolds recognized from his look of nobility as Lord Byron. After shedding tears, which purified the water into which they fell, he declared that he would preserve his portion untouched for several years. He had hardly finished speaking, however, before he allowed several drops to fall carelessly to the ground. The second poet, whose breastplate and rough plaid contrasted strangely with his dress shoes and silk stockings, proved to be Walter Scott. Although the old helmet in which he collected his portion was very shallow, the water received a pleasant sparkle from the warlike metal shining through it. Scott announced that he had already arranged to dispose of his share on advantageous terms. Southey, whose brow was encircled by a wreath of faded laurel, appeared bewildered and could hardly find his way to the stream of inspiration. Though chanting the praises of kings and courts, he dropped several poems which were opposite in tone from those he was singing. After scooping up only a little of the water in his gold vessel, he mounted his horse and rode off at an uneven pace toward St. James's.

Walking toward the stream together, Coleridge, Lamb, and Lloyd (the close friend who had published with them) conversed about the beauties of nature, its peaceful associations, and the purity of the domestic affections. The conversation turning to poetry, Lamb and Lloyd spoke simply, but Coleridge soon became confused by the abstruseness of his own observations. When he mentioned his plan of writing a metaphysical poem in a hundred books, Lamb remarked that he would prefer one of Coleridge's fine sonnets to all the wanderings of his mind. Reynolds directed the most effective satire of the piece against Coleridge:

Lamb and Lloyd dipped in a bright but rather shallow part of the stream;—Coleridge went to the depths, where he might have caught the purest water, had he not unfortunately clouded it with the sand which he himself disturbed at bottom. Lamb and Lloyd stated that they should take their porringers home and share their contents with the amiable and simple hearts dwelling there;—Coleridge was not positive as to the use to which he should apply his portion of the stream, till he had ascertained what were the physical reasons for the sand's propensity to mount and curl itself in water.

His praise of Leigh Hunt was warm and friendly: "Next came Hunt, with a rich fanciful goblet in his hand, finely enamelled with Italian landscapes; he held the cup to his breast as he approached, and his eyes sparkled with frank delight. After catching a wave, in which a sun-beam seemed freshly melted, he intimated that he should water hearts-ease and many favourite flowers with it. The sky appeared of a deep blue as he was retiring." Though he found no fault with Hunt's work, he did not place him among the first order of poets, complimenting him for gracefulness and geniality rather than more serious qualities.

With the entrance of the last poet, the tone of familiarity with

which he had treated the other contemporaries vanished. Wordsworth appeared almost like a god:

> Last came a calm and majestic figure moving serenely towards the
> stream. . . . It was Wordsworth! In his hand he held a vase of pure
> chrystal,—and, when he had reached the brink of the stream, the wave
> proudly swelled itself into his cup:—at this moment the sunny air above
> his brow, became embodied,—and the glowing and lightsome Spirit shone
> into being, and dropt a garland on his forehead;—sounds etherial swelled,
> and trembled, and revelled in the air,—and forms of light played in and
> out of sight,—and all around seemed like a living world of breathing po-
> etry. Wordsworth bent with reverence over the vase, and declared that
> the waters he had obtained should be the refreshment of his soul;—he
> then raised his countenance,—which had become illumined from the wave
> over which he had bowed,—and retired with a calm dignity.

Reynolds found some faults with Wordsworth later, but he never
doubted that along with Keats he was the preeminent poet of the age.

After he had observed the procession of poets to the true Castalian
stream, Reynolds noticed another brook nearby where the poetasters
were splashing around like a flock of gabbling geese. William Hayley, John Wilson, and Amos Cottle were among the group who mistakenly believed that they were drawing the genuine water of inspiration from the false stream. Most foolish of all was William Lisle
Bowles, who "laboriously engaged in filling fourteen nutshells."
Bowles improved the joke by taking umbrage and writing an indignant letter to the *Champion* proclaiming the merit of his sonnets.[29]

Reynolds's second comprehensive appraisal of the contemporary
poets appeared in "Boswell's Visit."[30] He was well prepared for his
work as a critic for the *Champion* by a close reading of the periodical
essayists of the preceding century, including Johnson's *Idler*. His
greatest interest in Johnson, however, was in the man and critic as
seen in Boswell's *Life of Johnson*. In an essay on egotism in literature, he had written, "Dr. Johnson was a thorough egotist: his mis-
givings—his asperities—his downright, *adamant* assertions—his weighty
reasonings—his charitable kindnesses—were all egotistical. He was,
however, on the whole, a melon of human nature,—for under a rough
outside he had the very kindliest feelings at heart."[31] In his second
comprehensive article on contemporary poets, he devised a clever

anachronism in which Dr. Johnson and other members of the Literary Club judged the poets of the early nineteenth century.

In "Boswell's Visit," Reynolds described himself returning home weary after the theater to prepare his review of the play, only to find that the printer's devil had called to warn him that copy was due the next morning. Worrying for some time about the deadline, he fell asleep and dreamed that James Boswell visited him and solved his problem. Boswell presented him with a record of the conversation of Dr. Johnson, Edmund Burke, and Sir Joshua Reynolds at the Literary Club, which had continued to meet in the shades after the death of the members, and Reynolds pretended that he transcribed the paper from memory after awakening. Those with strong interests in both the Johnson circle and Romantic poetry can hardly fail to be pleased by Reynolds's success in re-creating in an unexpected way minor disagreements between Johnson and Boswell, Johnson's lofty abstractions and balanced sentence structure, and his dogmatic assertion. The critical judgments of George Crabbe, Samuel Rogers, Robert Southey, and Walter Scott in the first installment follow logically and amusingly from Johnson's literary principles and tastes.

Reynolds devoted most of the second installment to Coleridge, Byron, and Wordsworth. The frame he had chosen proved most suitable for criticism of Coleridge: the common sense of the imaginary Dr. Johnson was ideal for satirizing metaphysics and mystification. Boswell began the discussion.

I stepped forward and asked the Doctor what he thought of Coleridge.

Johnson—"Why Sir, I think him a strange fellow."

Boswell—"But do you think him a better metaphysician than a poet?"

Johnson—"Sir, it is impossible to separate his fancy from his ponderous logic. He has made negus of his poetry and his metaphysical prose. I have read some of his early poems with pleasure, because they were written before he had bewildered himself with the intricacies of philosophy. He is very rich in the good gold of feeling,—but he hoards it up. Two or three of his Odes are lofty."

Boswell—"But have you read his Christabel, Sir?"

Johnson—"I have Sir—and it is a very dull enigma. He has put nonsense into fine words, and made her proud. I do not like to be puzzled to no purpose:—and it is a downright insolence in Mr. Coleridge to pester us with his two incomprehensible women. Sir, Geraldine is not to be made out:—she may be Joanna Southcote for all I know. Then what can be said of the dreams. They are arrant stuff. If Coleridge annoys us with more, the world will wish him a dreamless sleep. Sir, he might as well kick you."

Burke—"His politics appear to be very changeable."

Johnson—"Yes Sir, but he seems to be wise in his late opinion on that head."

Sir Joshua—"I think his description of the shadow of pleasure's dome floating midway on the waves of a river, gives you a grand idea of the size of the structure. It seems to me very picturesque."

Johnson—"But, Sir, I can make nothing of the dream. Any man may say an occasional good thing, but that will not embalm his eternal follies. He talks of a *sunny* dome, with caves of *ice;*—Sir, such a building could not exist. Fancy turns away with disgust from such an absurdity."

Boswell—"Lord Byron has spoken well of the poems, Doctor."

Johnson—"Sir, if he chuses to say a silly thing, I am not bound to abide by it. He may write an eulogy on Idiotcy, but I shall be bold to deem him mad, Sir, he may write ten yards of complimentary prose, or ten inches of insane poetry, if he likes; and I will neither read the first, nor admire the last. Let us hear no more of Coleridge."

Despite his objection to Byron's praise of Coleridge, the imaginary Dr. Johnson's opinion of Byron was generally favorable. He preferred *Childe Harold* to his other work because of its serious tone and intellectual content, but he found its hero almost as objectionable morally as the leading characters of Byron's Eastern romances. He declared the Giaour, Lara, and the Corsair to be black villains. Though he considered the descriptions of the natural landscapes pleasing, he thought Byron unwise to devote so much attention to scenery, since men and the affairs of society were more interesting and valuable subjects.

Although Reynolds had the fictitious Johnson express great admiration for Wordsworth, the criticism is brief and general. Dr. Johnson wished that he might write the life of "the glorious poet," and he compared the tone of his poetry to Milton's. In this case Reynolds probably saw that if Dr. Johnson's principles were applied to Wordsworth's poetry strictly, the resulting appraisal would have fallen short of his own high conception of the poet's genius. Consequently, he avoided the difficulty by treating Wordsworth briefly.

Except for the two general articles just discussed, Reynolds's criticism of the contemporary poets was scattered throughout the *Champion* in literary articles, reviews, and theatrical notices. His criticism there of Wordsworth is significant enough to merit detailed consideration.

As we have seen, Reynolds early in life recognized Wordsworth as the greatest poet of the age. His friendship with Haydon and contact with John Scott, editor of the *Champion,* confirmed his commitment. Haydon had been a friend of Wordsworth's for years, and Scott knew him personally and corresponded with him regularly from 14 May 1815 through 19 June 1816. Reynolds looked forward to *The Excursion* as a great philosophical poem in which Wordsworth would put behind him the simplicities that limited some of his earlier work,[32] and he valued the work so highly when it appeared that he wrote a guide to assist readers in their progress through its loosely arranged and uneven attractions.[33]

His earliest prose contribution to the *Champion* was an epistolary essay entitled "Mr. Wordsworth's Poetry."[34] The subject, he wrote, was of the utmost importance to the literary world, for the very character of the age would depend to a large extent on its reception of Wordsworth's poetry. In intellectual content he found Wordsworth's work comparable to that of Milton and Jeremy Taylor. He admitted that Wordsworth lacked the popular appeal of many of his contemporaries, having neither the haughty melancholy and troubled spirit of Byron, the melodious fancy of Moore, nor the "gentlemanly prettinesses" and touches of antiquity of Walter Scott. Nevertheless, Reynolds believed, his descriptions of nature mingled with philosophy would continue to live after the fame of the others had receded. In discussing genre, Reynolds distinguished between the true and artificial pastoral. He considered the pastorals of the eighteenth century coldly conventional with little intellectual and no emotional appeal. As an example, he cited Shenstone, who in his opinion deserved the sharp criticism of Gray and Johnson, since he "would make us believe that the fields are for ever green, the sheep for ever feeding, and that the shepherds have nothing to do but to make love and play on a pipe." With the publication of *Lyrical Ballads,* Wordsworth had begun a revolution against the artificial system. Though strongly opposed by many, his innovations had been welcomed from the first by a few intelligent readers, and they had gained further support through the years. Pleased to find that Wordsworth was aware of the extent of his own powers, Reynolds closed with a quotation from the "Essay Supplementary" to the preface of *Poems* of

1815, in which Wordsworth declared his conviction that his work was destined to endure.

In the issue of 18 February 1816, Reynolds continued his praise with his sonnet "To Wordsworth," a graceful but conventional and undistinguished poetic tribute. He mentioned the solace and gratification which he had received from Wordsworth's poetry and wished that the beauties of nature might continue to inspire him. Wordsworth was mildly pleased by the poem, though he showed no curiosity about the author. After mentioning the *Champion* in a letter to John Scott dated four days after the issue in which Reynolds's sonnet appeared, Wordsworth wrote, "Thank you for the verses—I have the satisfaction of not infrequently receiving tributes of the same kind. What numbers must find their way to your namesake! and to the 'bold bad bard Baron B.' "[35]

In subsequent articles, Reynolds referred to Wordsworth's poetry frequently. In a theatrical review, for instance, a discussion of stage pastorals led to a comment on Wordsworth's descriptions of nature.[36] The affected simplicity of the actors and the obvious artificiality of the scenery made "a rural opera" ridiculous. The beauties of nature, he contended, could be portrayed most successfully in poetry. The two authors who had been best able to describe the woods and the fields were Chaucer and Wordsworth: Chaucer delighted the reader with his freshness and spontaneity, while Wordsworth cast a different kind of charm over his descriptions by introducing reflections and moral philosophy.

After his return from Exeter in early October 1816, Reynolds wrote two essays in which he included his most extensive appraisal of Wordsworth's genius. Wordsworth published his *Thanksgiving Ode* on the victory at Waterloo earlier in the year, and the *Champion* was late in reviewing it. In the first article, "Popular Poetry—Periodical Criticism, & c" on 13 October 1816, Reynolds explained that he would have noticed the poem earlier except for "personal circumstances of interruption," a reference to his six-weeks vacation in Devonshire.[37] He devoted the first article to a discussion of general principles that were to serve as an introduction to the specific criticism of the second essay. For his major thesis he returned to "Essay Supplementary" to the preface to *Poems* of 1815, quoted in his first article on Wordsworth, and selected a passage in which Wordsworth maintained that new poetry should not be judged by its popularity. Reynolds agreed that inferior poets were likely to have a wider appeal because their work required very little of the reader. In developing the idea, he pointed out that the general advance in education had altered conditions for the poet. During earlier periods, the number of readers had been small, but those who could read were well prepared to appreciate poetry of the highest order. The number of readers had increased greatly in his own day, but their learning was so superficial that they were incapable of judging properly. Progress was also a mixed blessing in other respects: "Modern improvements are excellent things,—as every one who has lately bought stoves or dining tables must know: but we have the convenient in lieu of the romantic." Country houses, shooting-boxes, curricles, and gigs had been acquired at the expense of old moated castles and coaches and six.

Another unfortunate concomitant of the advance of society, Reynolds maintained, was that the proper relation between poetry and criticism had been reversed. In earlier times the poet had preceded the critic, and the critic had derived his principles from great poetry. In his own age the reviewers were violating the natural order by attempting to prescribe for poets. The rules might be applied correctly to minor poets, but they could not possibly have any bearing on the productions of an original genius, whose work must be, by definition, an exception to the general rule. Yet Reynolds did not attack all contemporary criticism indiscriminately; he admitted that the *Edinburgh Review* had done much toward developing the public taste, and he showed considerable respect for its editor Francis Jeffrey's judgment. Despite his attack on Wordsworth, Reynolds believed that Jeffrey himself appreciated the true nature of Wordsworth's genius.

In Reynolds's opinion, however, the *Edinburgh* was an exception to the poor quality of the contemporary periodicals, which had reduced criticism to "giving rules by the observance of which Mr. Higgins may write well to his correspondents, and his wife may deliver her opinion like a sensible woman at a tea table." With cant phrases and pert remarks the journalists were attacking works of real genius because they were incapable of understanding them. Unable to comprehend larger meanings, they selected petty faults in lines and phrases and applied "dictionary interpretations to the imagination's abstractions." Furthermore, they were inconsistent in their condemnation of lowly details, for they ridiculed Wordsworth's Wanderer as a Scotch pedlar, while they overlooked the fact that Spenser had made his "lovely ladie" ride upon a "lowly asse." According to Reynolds, one of the greatest offenders was the *Quarterly Review,* which he admonished, "To him, for instance, who favoured the public with the egregious criticism of *The Tale of Rimini* that appeared in the *Quarterly!* What would they say to the phrase in the second line that follows?

> 'The noble hart, that harbours vertuous thought,
> And is *with child* of glorious great intent.' "[38]

How dare small-minded critics object to what they call lowly details when Spenser had used the simple bodily image of pregnancy for his powerful line.

The danger of such criticism as that in the *Quarterly,* Reynolds believed, was its tendency to draw poets down to the level of critics. Since the great majority of readers in fashionable society were only superficially educated, they relied upon the periodicals for their critical opinions. Hence, there was strong pressure upon any poet who wanted monetary or social success to conform to the standard of the critics.

In the second article, entitled "Wordsworth's Thanksgiving Ode," Reynolds returned to his principal theme of the preceding week: "Mr. Wordsworth . . . is not a popular poet:—we are very sure he is an admired one; and as to popularity, though it is a desirable thing for any weekly newspaper, yet we do not know that it is absolutely necessary for the Cartoons or the Samson Agonistes."[39] That Wordsworth's poem was occasional seemed of little importance to Reynolds, for he maintained that Wordsworth was never dependent on his subject. The chief reason for Wordsworth's success lay in his depiction of his own imagination, no matter what the subject. After quoting the opening stanza of Wordsworth's ode, Reynolds indulged in transparent mystification: without mentioning the author or title, he included a long passage from *Samson Agonistes* and declared it was by an earlier author who had been just as unpopular as Wordsworth. He apologized with mock seriousness for inserting such "tedious" lines and pretended to fear that the publisher of the paper would object when he found that they had been included. Then, shifting his ground, he promised that if any reader could admit the sublimity of the extract by the unnamed author, and at the same time deny any merit to Wordsworth's ode, he would renounce all pretensions to criticism.

By praising Wordsworth, Reynolds was running counter to a strong current of literary opinion even as late as 1816. He reported that a lady had written from Edinburgh to ask whether he really believed that Wordsworth had ever written anything as fine as Campbell's *The Pleasures of Hope*. He admitted, moreover, that some of his friends did not agree with him. One had been puzzled about Wordsworth's meaning, and another had asked sarcastically whether Harry Gill's teeth were still chattering. Despite these objections, Reynolds was firmly convinced that Wordsworth was the great poet of the age—he had barely met Keats. The only reservation in his praise of the *Thanksgiving Ode* was to its reactionary political tone. Although he joined Wordsworth in rejoicing over the victory at Waterloo, he was not nearly so satisfied with conditions in England. He took exception, though somewhat cautiously, to Wordsworth's "excess of saintly rapture" in having the angels welcome the hideous defeat of the French and declared that his own political opinion was closer to that which Wordsworth had held earlier in life than to that which he professed in the *Thanksgiving Ode*.

Reynolds's error of judgment in overvaluing the *Thanksgiving Ode,* which posterity has forgotten, undercuts these two essays for the twentieth-century reader. But despite the serious error, much that is valuable remains in the two critiques, for though he was wrong about the particular poem, he was right about Wordsworth.

CHAPTER 6

Friendship with Keats—1816–1817

ARLY IN OCTOBER 1816, Reynolds returned home from his vacation in Devonshire to 19 Lamb's Conduit Street, where the family had been living for more than a year and a half. Shortly thereafter the most momentous event of his life occurred: he met Keats at Leigh Hunt's cottage in the Vale of Health in Hampstead.[1] Reynolds had been Hunt's friend since 19 July 1814 and had visited Hunt several times since February 1815;[2] he knew well most of Hunt's circle. A warm friend of Haydon, Reynolds had welcomed Haydon into his home to meet his sisters.[3] Reynolds had known Hazlitt well since before 2 June 1816 when he reported being enraptured by Hazlitt's animated talk, and he knew Horace Smith as part owner of the *Champion* and fellow contributor to it. Reynolds probably met Charles Cowden Clarke for the first time in Keats's company; when they met, they had one small subject of common interest—a sonnet of Clarke's that Reynolds had published in the *Champion* on 21 April 1816.[4] After Clarke introduced Keats to Hunt in mid-October 1816 and Keats presented Hunt with a sheaf of his selected poems, Reynolds was no doubt one of the friends among whom Hunt circulated the work for judgment.[5]

After being introduced at Hunt's house, Reynolds and Keats soon met again despite their busy schedules. Reynolds dined with Haydon and Keats at Haydon's temporary home in Hampstead on Sunday, 20 October 1816, and again with Keats at Hunt's house on another evening in October.[6] By the latter occasion the two were already friends, for when Keats wrote the sonnet "On Leaving Some Friends at an Early Hour"; Reynolds was one of those friends mentioned in the title. Hunt began immediately to think of Keats and Reynolds as a pair of aspiring young poets; on 3 November he promised in the *Examiner* to publish "Chapman's Homer" and selections from *The Naiad* at "the earliest opportunity."

Keats and Reynolds had much in common. Both had middle-class backgrounds and were about the same age—Reynolds a year older than Keats. Both had left school to enter pedestrian vocations: Reynolds spent six years as an insurance clerk and Keats five years of apprenticeship to become an apothecary-surgeon. Reynolds had just renounced his first vocation several months before to make his way in the literary and journalistic worlds; in a few months Keats was to leave the apothecary's trade to take a similar risk. Both had just returned from vacations at the sea where they had been writing and moving toward a greater commitment to poetry. They were close in their religious and political views. Reynolds was mildly, but good-naturedly, skeptical and on guard against authoritarianism in the established church—in later life he declared his Unitarian conviction openly; Keats was a firm religious skeptic. Both were liberal in politics; while not so extreme as the admired Hazlitt, they consistently opposed autocratic rule and at the same time were certain that they were patriotic Englishmen. Reynolds wrote for liberal and moderate periodicals and opposed the Tory leaders and press on many occasions; Keats's letters show his unvarying support of civil liberties and liberal politics. To be sure, there was a difference. Reynolds had been very precocious, while Keats had not. Reynolds had been writing verse since he was nine years old at Shrewsbury School, and he had published three books, a pamphlet (the *Ode* on the overthrow of Napoleon), and a large number of verses in periodicals. Keats, on the other hand, had been writing verse for less than two years and had published only the sonnet "To Solitude." But that difference did not matter. Reynolds's greater experience was more than balanced by Keats's greater potential, which Reynolds sensed quickly.

Keats did not visit the Reynolds home at 19 Lamb's Conduit Street before 6 November 1816; if he had done so, he would have met the ever-present Bailey, who left on that date for Oxford.[7] On the evening of 21 November, Haydon visited the Reynolds-family home and showed Reynolds Keats's sonnet "Great Spirits now on earth are sojourning," celebrating Haydon along with Wordsworth and Hunt, which Keats had written after spending an evening with Haydon. Later that evening Reynolds's own sonnet "To Haydon" sprang into his mind and he set it down.[8] This is the first of many poetic interactions between Keats and Reynolds; sometimes, as here, Keats wrote a poem, and Reynolds responded; at other times Reynolds wrote a poem, and Keats responded. In this instance, Reynolds followed Keats's pattern closely: Keats spent an evening with Haydon and mailed him a sonnet the next day; Reynolds spent an evening with Haydon and mailed him a sonnet the next day. Reynolds did not try, however, to imitate Keats's sonnet: unlike Keats, he focused his poem entirely on Haydon. Reynolds saw the merit of Keats's sonnet and asked Haydon to tell Keats how much it pleased him. Reynolds's sonnet, which he published immediately in the *Champion* (24 November 1816), was merely respectable. At this time Haydon and Reynolds were still more intimate with each other than either was with Keats. Keats addressed Haydon in both his letters as "My dear Sir"; Reynolds addressed him as "My Dear Haydon." And Reynolds still referred to Keats as "Mr Keats."

On 1 December 1816 Hunt kept his promise of a month earlier and published "Chapman's Homer" and a selection from *The Naiad* in the *Examiner*; indeed, he did more, for in "Young Poets" he recommended Shelley, Reynolds, and Keats to the public as those most likely to lead "the new school of poetry" away from "the French one that has prevailed among us since the time of Charles the 2nd." Hunt treated the three poets according to the order in which he had met them: first, Shelley, whom he had met in 1812; second, Reynolds, whom he had met in 1814; and last, Keats, whom he had met in October 1816. Hunt could not be blamed for mistaking Reynolds's middle name—calling him John Henry Reynolds—because *Safie* and *The Eden* had been published under the name J. H. Reynolds, *The Naiad* was anonymous, Reynolds signed his correspondence to Hunt J. H. Reynolds, and customarily last names only were used at social gatherings. If quotations are counted, Hunt gave more space to Reynolds than to the other two, but he did note small faults in Reynolds and not in the others: "The author's style is too artificial, though he is evidently an admirer of Mr. Wordsworth. Like all young poets too, properly so called, his love of detail is too overwrought and indiscriminate; but still he is a young poet, and only wants a still closer attention to things as opposed to the seduction of words, to realize all that he promises. His nature seems very true and amiable."[9]

Reynolds showed his gratitude for Hunt's notice by responding immediately with praise of Hunt in a sonnet on *The Story of Remini,* published in the *Champion* a week later.[10] It was one of Reynolds's middle sonnets, not among his best, but about as good as Keats's sonnet on the same subject written in early March 1817. Reynolds's poem was airier, with " 'dapper elves . . . Dancing delightedly," without the earthiness of Keats's "Where robins hop," but the bounciness of Keats's phrase was hardly successful. Perhaps Keats had Reynolds's sonnet in the back of his mind because the structures were similar: Reynolds's is "Ye who do love to hear. . . Ye, who would hear" turn to Hunt's *Rimini,* while Keats's is "Who loves to peer. . . . Who loves to linger" let him turn to Hunt's *Rimini.* Not to be outdone in gratitude, Hunt replied, still mistaking Reynolds's middle name, with "To John Henry Reynolds, on his lines upon the Story of Rimini," not published until *Foliage* of 1818, by which time he had corrected the name.[11] Reynolds also took a copy of Hunt's personal sonnet to Keats of 1 December 1816, " 'Tis well you think me truly one of those," and kept it until he inserted it two years later in the *Alfred, West of England Journal* as "Leigh Hunt's *Sonnet Addressed to John Keats, Author of Endymion.*[12]

About 15 December—a Sunday, the day when Haydon most often had friends visiting him—Reynolds met Keats at 41 Great Marlborough Street, and Keats invited him to a party on the evening of 17 December at the Keatses' place at 76 Cheapside. That Tuesday Reynolds spent the evening with Keats, Charles Cowden Clarke, and Joseph Severn and probably met Keats's two brothers for the first time. Struck by Keats's potential poetic genius and drawn irresistibly to his intense and warm, friendly personality, Reynolds wrote Bailey at Oxford describing his new friend in glowing terms. Shortly thereafter Reynolds introduced Keats—and either at the same time or soon after, George and Tom—to his family in their hospitable home at 19 Lamb's Conduit Street, where the Keatses were welcomed for frequent visits.[13]

Throughout the excitement of his early friendship with Keats, Reynolds continued to work steadily on the poem which he hoped would be a real advance, *The Romance of Youth,* devised and probably begun while he was on vacation. During the Christmas season Reynolds attended the pantomimes at Drury Lane and Covent Garden, wrote a review of them as well as writing "A Song: To Albion" for the *Champion* of 29 December, and either left at the *Champion* office or later mailed from the country a second theatrical notice for 5 January 1817 in which he used the idea of pantomime as a springboard for a fanciful satire on Castlereagh, the Tory foreign minister. He and Rice then left for Slade Hall, Sidmouth, for a New Year's vacation with the Leigh family and Eliza Drewe. As he had the previous autumn, Reynolds read from Shakespeare to the assembled company, this time from *Macbeth,* provided them with his short prose guide to *The Excursion,* and copied into their commonplace books five complete stanzas of *The Romance of Youth* (nos. 30, 31, 35, 92, and 93) and two incomplete ones.[14]

Reynolds had probably completed a first draft of the first canto (all he ever wrote) by this time, for the canto contains only 104 stanzas, and stanzas 92 and 93, which he copied, lead directly into the close. The two partial stanzas, which he did not complete and publish, show that he did some revising and polishing. He later added at least one passage, stanzas 82–84, in which he remarks that he is writing in May; almost certainly it was the spring of 1817 or 1818 since in the preface to the 1821 published poem he makes a point of not having revised the work after finishing it several years earlier. He may have taken the word "sandal-shoon" (p. 92) from the last stanza of *Childe Harold,* Canto IV, after the publication of Byron's poem in the spring of 1818, but it is possible that Reynolds borrowed the word independently, just as Byron did, from ballads and other old poetry where it commonly appeared as the mark of a pilgrim.

There are signs that Reynolds, by writing so substantial a poem as *The Romance of Youth,* was attempting to become recognized as a serious poet. A few brief passages of uncertainty about his chance for success qualify the four stanzas (quoted on pp. 78–79) celebrating fame and expressing his longing for it; on the whole, however, the tone of the poem is one of considerable confidence and assurance. It was chiefly this poem, which he called Reynolds's "richest and most interesting work," that Oliver Elton had in mind when he wrote "it would be hard to name any unregarded writer of that age in whom the poetic *will* is stronger and more genuine."[15] Reynolds chose the Spenserian stanza for the work because, as he said in the preface written in 1821, "it is the richest and most capable of variety in the language."[16] For years it had been the kind of verse he admired most; on 24 May 1813 he wrote Dovaston, "If I were to recommend any style for you to pursue, it would be the *Spenserian;*—The stanza is particularly harmonious,—The Sense may with ease be *compleated* in every Stanza,—the double Rhyme in the middle is very sweet,— The Alexandrine winds up the whole with great force and Beauty,—

no poet has ever failed in it yet.”[17] He had not used it often in the profuse number of verses that he wrote with facility and often in haste. He reserved it for passages about which he really cared: the ten-stanza introduction to *Safie*—the best part of that weak poem— and “Sappho’s Address to the Evening Star,” which he had revised thoroughly, making additions and accepting some of Dovaston’s recommended changes before he finally published it in the *Inquirer*.

“One or two intelligent friends” to whom he showed the manuscript said that the plan of the poem reminded them of James Beattie’s *The Minstrel*. Reynolds, however, denied he even thought of Beattie when he wrote it and pointed out correctly that after the opening, the further development of the poem bears no resemblance to *The Minstrel*.[18]

Reynolds’s young hero, living alone with his mother in a rural cottage, indulged in romantic dreaming, wandered through the woods entranced by nature’s beauties, fell gravely ill, revived at the coming of summer, and found consolation in the classical myths of Psyche and Cupid and Diana and Endymion. Restored to health, he again visited the woods alone to view the trees, the brook, the lake, a pair of swans, colorful birds, fish, and butterflies. One evening by the lake after reading from a book of fairy stories and recalling other fairy stories that had enraptured him, he saw a bright company of “spanlong” fairies flow from the lake to the flowery bank. They played on honeysuckle trumpets, drank dew wine from a crystal goblet, and conjured up with a magic wand “ivory tables” stored with “dainties rare” (p. 67). “Drunken with th’ excess of wonder” (p. 69), the boy heard the fairies sing a song greeting their fairy queen. Drawn across the lake in a curved shell by two tiny swans, the fairy queen landed; the boy ambiguously reached the height of his ecstasy and at the same time felt the sadness of his earthly limitations. The fairy queen warned him of the suffering he would endure when he entered the “poisonous world” of mature experience (p. 77). The fairy scene vanishing, the boy poured forth his soul in ambitious longing for immortal fame.

Two years passed, and the boy conferred with an older friend and mentor, one who was cold and stern with others but not with him, who scorned religion and the idea of life after death, and who was intent on radical “change/In human practices” (p. 84). The older friend urged him to leave youthful innocence, to develop his potential genius, and to explore "metaphysic labyrinths" (p. 86). He praised the youth and promised that if he developed his mind in the world of experience, he would receive great praise from "learned men in cities of the wise" (p. 86). Excited by the prospect of the challenging world of experience, the youth slept and had a chilling vision of a tall, gaunt female whose "shadowy dress" and hair partially concealed her "sunken cheeks" and pallid lips. "His blood ran in coldness to his heart" as the majestic figure warned him of the "bitterness and fear" (p. 88) he must suffer if he moved into the active world. The recollection of that unearthly shape and "dooming lip" (p. 90) haunted him for days and eradicated all his former sense of the blithe gaiety of the fairies. He left his pastoral world and set out for the busy world of strife and pain.

Clearly much of the supposedly realistic part of this story is fictitious: Reynolds had not lived in a country cottage alone with his mother, and he was not without father and sisters. But he drew some elements from experience: he had twice been so gravely ill that his parents feared his death, he had delighted in the beauties of nature, and he had loved the notion of fairies with a consuming passion. Even more significantly, the older friend and mentor was William Hazlitt. The combination of generally saturnine temperament, agnosticism, radical politics, mastery of metaphysics, and high opinion of Reynolds's talent identifies Hazlitt beyond question.[19]

The relation of three passages in *The Romance of Youth* to Keats's poetry is reasonably clear. Reynolds probably wrote most of the canto except stanzas 82–84 before January 1817. If he did make further additions later, he made them before the autumn of 1818, because his preface connects the writing of the poem with the period of his thorough commitment to poetry "some few years back" (p. 32). His advertisement says in effect that he did not rewrite any of the earlier poems before publishing them: "Many of the poems in this little volume, indeed the greater part of them, have been written for some years, and I very much fear that age has not improved them" (p. xi).

Therefore, the passage describing the "ivory tables" stored with "dainties rare" is not, as some have thought, a pale echo of Porphyro's feast prepared for Madeline,[20] but an anticipation of Keats and possibly an influence on him. Even if one rejects a direct influence by Reynolds on Keats, it is worthwhile to consider Reynolds's three stanzas as an example of the love of sensuousness that Reynolds shared with his co-scribbler, Keats:

> A wand was waved through the charmed air,
> And up there rose a very costly throng
> Of ivory tables, stored with dainties rare,
> At sight of which e'en dieted men might long:
> They rose amid strange minstrelsy and song,—
> And there was pheasant from enchanted wood,
> And swan from fairy stream,—and these among,
> Were chalices of Eastern dew—wine brew'd
> By pearly hands in far Arabian solitude.
>
> And golden berries, steep'd in cream, were soon
> Brought there from stores in Asian palaces;
> And from the lonely Mountains of the Moon,
> From which swarth Afric's serpent-river frees
> Its wily head,—fish, stranger than the seas
> Hold in their deep green wastes, to the bright feast
> Were brought in coral dishes by streak'd bees;
> And fruit, the very loveliest and the least,
> Came from young spangled trees in gardens of the East.
>
> There was good store of sweet and sheening cherries,
> Gather'd from trees that under water grew
> In mystic orchards,—and the best wood-berries
> That blush in scarlet ripeness through the dew,—
> And tiny plums, round, and of blooming blue,—
> And golden apples of a fairy size,—
> And glossy nuts, the which brown squirrels drew,
> Eying them longingly with sly dark eyes,
> And stealing when they could a little hazel prize.[21]

Features that Reynolds's passage and Keats's (too familiar to need quotation) have in common are the Spenserian stanza, exotic Eastern sources for the viands, and the repetition of six words: tables (Keats has table), dainties, plums, apples, dishes, and golden. The Eastern sources suggest the possibility of influence, but that is hardly convincing because two poets independently could think of the East to add an exotic twist. The six repeated words mean next to nothing, because a passage as long as Reynolds's would by chance include four words and two fruits later used by Keats. Keats had read Reynolds's passage some six months before he wrote *The Eve of St.*

Agnes, and a general recollection of it may have reinforced his own impulse to create the sensuous, but Keats echoed few, if any, details.

It is difficult to be fair to Reynolds because one has been spoiled by Keats's superb condensation. Reynolds's sensuousness has a cumulative effect in the manner of his master Spenser, as he presents the wealth of details in leisurely fashion through the three stanzas. Instead of Keats's compressed catalogue, we have a relaxed, though concrete and varied catalogue of the sort that Reynolds admired so much in the speech of Sir Epicure Mammon in Ben Jonson's *The Alchemist*. Though Keats far surpassed him, Reynolds was certainly in good company with Spenser and Jonson.

A second passage that preceded and, in this case, clearly influenced one of Keats's was Reynolds's account of the "shadow of a woman," the tall, gaunt, visionary female who spoke oracular truth to the young poet, so like Keats's "Majestic shadow" Moneta in *The Fall of Hyperion:*

> and one night, late,
> A strange and dreary vision did arise:
> That in the forest deep he lay with musing eyes;

> That when he lifted them,—before him stood
> A figure tall, and in a shadowy dress:
> It was as some lone spirit of the wood,
> With eyes all dim, and fixed with distress,—
> And sunken cheeks,—and lips of pallidness,—
> Standing with folded arms, and floating hair,
> The shadow of a woman!—but a tress
> Was sometimes lifted by the gusty air,
> And now the waved robe a heaving breast did bare.

> He gazed—his hand paused on a turning leaf,
> And his blood ran in coldness to his heart:—
> He gazed—but still his eyes felt no relief;
> For that dim lonely form would not depart:
> It stood—as prison'd there by mystic art,
> Looking upon him steadily;—he tried
> To utter speech, but not a word would start
> From his weak lips—his very feelings died,
> As he beheld that spirit of melancholy pride![22]

Having read Reynolds's account, Keats echoed it, either consciously
or unconsciously:

> Then the tall shade in drooping linens veil'd
> Spake out, so much more earnest, that her breath
> Stirr'd the thin folds of gauze that drooping hung
>
> . . . .
>
> I had no words to answer; for my tongue,
> Useless, could find about its roofed home
> No syllable of a fit majesty
> To make rejoinder to Moneta's mourn.
>
> . . . .
>
> But yet I had a terror of her robes,
> And chiefly of the veils, that from her brow
> Hung pale, and curtain'd her in mysteries
> That made my heart too small to hold its blood.
> This saw that Goddess, and with sacred hand
> Parted the veils. Then saw I a wan face,
> Not pin'd by human sorrows, but bright blanch'd
> By an immortal sickness which kills not.[23]

Both female shadows are supernatural admonishers; both are tall;
both wear flowing robes; both have faces at first concealed (Reynolds's by hair, Keats's by veils) and then revealed; and both faces
show sickness and suffering. Both Reynolds's poet and Keats's are
terrified by the encounters; both at one time struggle to speak to the
shades, but cannot (though of course Keats's poet does speak to Moneta at other times); and both feel the intense terror in their very
blood. Such a pattern of correspondences could not be chance. Keats
read Reynolds's poem about the development of a poet from innocence to maturity and adapted its most striking image for his own
purpose in his poem about the development of a poet from dreamer
to poet of greatest stature.

     Again, Keats's extraordinary intensity in presenting Moneta and
his poet's reaction to her makes difficult a just assessment of Reynolds's lesser achievement. But if we can succeed in separating Keats's
mastery from Reynolds's passage, we can see that Reynolds is unusually successful in his own way. Just as he used Angeline's embrace of
Lord Hubert's corpse-ghost for shock in *The Naiad,* he startles the
reader, who has watched fairies prance and dance for ninety-three

Spenserian stanzas, with grimness, mystery, and terror, rather well condensed into a few stanzas. And the drear vision is more than just rhetoric; it makes the reader feel upon his pulses some of the harshness and bitterness that inevitably accompany entry into the world of experience.

A third passage in *The Romance of Youth* may have exerted some small influence on the imagery and diction of *Ode to a Nightingale*. The fairies' song equated stars and fays, "Elves are stars, and stars are fays" (p. 71), and linked the fairy queen by simile with the moon:

> our queen
> . . . . brings with her
> A crowning presence for our night:—
> So with dress of silver light,
> And motion that no silence mars,
> The Moon glides in among the stars.
>
> (P. 72)

Reynolds attached the words "cluster" (p. 70) and "clustering" (p. 76) to his fays. It may not be mere coincidence that Keats later wrote:

> And haply the Queen-Moon is on her throne,
> Cluster'd around by all her starry Fays.
>
> (Ll. 36–37)[24]

On Reynolds's return to London from Devonshire, where he had copied stanzas of *The Romance of Youth* into the Leighs' commonplace books, his friendship with Keats prospered as much as his love affair with Eliza Drewe. He took supper with Keats and Shelley at Hunt's on 5 February 1817.[25] After reading Keats's sonnet written in Clarke's Chaucer, Reynolds wrote on 27 February "Sonnet—to Keats On reading his Sonnet written in Chaucer," a better sonnet than the one by Keats that had prompted it. His deep satisfaction on finding that Keats shared his enthusiasm for *The Flower and the Leaf*, which everyone at the time thought Chaucer's, moved Reynolds to one of his better efforts. The last line of the central section is fine:

> Thy genius weaves
> Songs that shall make the age be nature-led
> And win that coronal for thy young head
> Which Time's strange hand of freshness ne'er bereaves.[26]

No one should forget the quickness with which Reynolds recognized Keats's genius and his readiness to proclaim it. By this time he had seen the sheaf of Keats's verses circulated by Hunt the last October, several sonnets including "Chapman's Homer," and possibly some of the manuscript poems Keats was sorting out and preparing for publication in *Poems* of 1817. Shelley advised Keats to delay publication, but Reynolds did not.

On Saturday, 1 March, he was not present at the exchange of laurel and ivy crowns by Hunt and Keats, an act that later grated on Keats because of its frivolous presumption. It is possible, as Keats's biographers have conjectured, that Reynolds's sisters dropped in at Hunt's after the crowning. The only evidence is that Keats copied into the volume of *Poems* he gave Reynolds his two sonnets on the occasion: the inference would seem to be that he copied "To the Ladies Who Saw Me Crown'd" because Reynolds's sisters would be especially interested, having been there. It is possible that Jane and Marianne were there, but the conjecture is unlikely; a better reason that Keats copied the sonnets, including "To Some Ladies," would be that Keats knew Reynolds wanted copies of all his verse. Keats's reaction against the crowning did not set in immediately. Reynolds had just said two days before, in the sonnet prompted by Keats's sonnet on *The Flower and the Leaf*, that Keats deserved a "coronal" for his "young head," and Keats would want to show him that he had received one.

Though Keats, Reynolds, and Haydon were all sociable creatures who saw a great many people, they became something of a triumvirate in February and March 1817, spending much of their time together in Keats's rooms at 76 Cheapside, at Haydon's studio at 41 Great Marlborough Street, and in the Reynolds home at 19 Lamb's Conduit Street. Reynolds visited Keats on 27 February, when he read Keats's sonnet on *The Flower and the Leaf* in Clarke's Chaucer. Either on Saturday, 1 March, before Keats went to Hunt's for the laurel-crowning, or more likely on Sunday, 2 March, Haydon, Keats, and probably Reynolds went to the British Museum to view the Elgin marbles. On Monday night, 3 March, Reynolds visited Haydon in his studio, along with Keats and Clarke. Some time later, probably in the same week, Keats visited Reynolds in the evening at home, and Haydon joined them later.[27]

During this period Keats must have given Reynolds a presentation copy of *Poems;* he could not have done so before 2 March because Keats copied the laurel-crowning sonnets and the Elgin marbles sonnets into the volume. And he probably delivered the book to Reynolds at Haydon's studio on Monday evening, 3 March—an occasion that seems to have been a celebration of the official publication day. After arranging to have the publishers, the Olliers, send Bailey a copy at Oxford, Reynolds, who had been eagerly awaiting the opportunity to review *Poems,* published his review proudly in the next *Champion* of Sunday, 9 March.[28]

In the review he proclaimed Keats's superiority over nearly all contemporary poets. The "power and passion" of Byron, the "playful and elegant fancy" of Moore, the "correctness" of Rogers, and the "sublimity and pathos" of Campbell were favorite subjects in literary society, he said, but Keats was likely to eclipse them all. He did not mention Wordsworth in the first part of the review but had his poetry in mind when he wrote that Keats looked "at natural objects with his mind, as Shakespeare and Chaucer did,—and not merely with his eye as nearly all modern poets do"; the "nearly" excepted Wordsworth, whom Reynolds had praised repeatedly for projecting his own thoughts and feelings into his depictions of nature. Reynolds also implied a comparison with Wordsworth when he wrote: "He relies directly and wholly on nature. He marries poesy to genuine simplicity. He makes her artless,—yet abstains carefully from giving her an uncomely homeliness:—that is, he shows he can be familiar with nature, yet perfectly strange to the habits of common life." Despite occasional "uncomely homeliness," Wordsworth had been Reynolds's idol among contemporary poets; now Reynolds bestowed the same kind of praise upon Keats that he formerly had reserved for Wordsworth. He implied that Keats was potentially Wordsworth's peer without Wordsworth's limitation, but he did not modify his extremely high valuation of Wordsworth, which he now extended also to Keats.

In view of Reynolds's earlier sharp criticism of the mystification in *Christabel* and "Kubla Khan," we can assume that he referred to Coleridge when he wrote: "Again, though Mr. Keats' poetry is remarkably abstracted, it is never out of reach of the mind; there are one or two established writers of this day who think that mystery is the soul of poetry—that artlessness is a vice—and that nothing can be graceful that is not metaphysical." The other writer may well have been Byron, whom a *Champion* reviewer, probably Reynolds, had accused of imitating Coleridge in the dream poems included in *The Prisoner of Chillon and Other Poems.*[29]

The remainder of Reynolds's review of Keats included large extracts with enthusiastic praise for each. His favorite single poem in the volume was *Sleep and Poetry,* which he thought "the most powerful and the most perfect," and he considered the sonnets second only to those of Milton and Wordsworth in the whole range of English poetry. In his opinion the three poems addressed to ladies ("To Some Ladies," "On Receiving a Curious Shell," and "Hadst thou liv'd in days of old") and "To Hope" were very much inferior to the others, but he called attention to Keats's explanation in the prefatory note that they had been written at an earlier period. He saw as defects occasional lapses into faulty measure, excessive use of compound epithets, and a tendency toward too lavishly embellished descriptions. At the close, Reynolds included the two Elgin Marbles sonnets Keats had copied into Reynolds's volume of *Poems.*

No one can now fail to see that Reynolds's praise of the 1817 *Poems* was inflated. To mention only the most obvious example, he claimed that the collection of sonnets in the book equaled the best in English poetry, excepting Milton and Wordsworth, but not excepting Shakespeare. Not even the most avid Keatsian would agree that aside from "Chapman's Homer," more than two or three of the other sixteen sonnets are among the greatest in the language. And yet Reynolds should be forgiven his enthusiastic admiration. Though his friendship with Keats played a part, Reynolds saw in Keats the potential for a new Shakespeare and felt it his duty both to encourage Keats and to startle the public into attention.

Reynolds certainly achieved his first intention. Keats was not just gratified, but deeply moved to have a promising poet with ambition of his own and a practicing critic of several years' standing lavish praise on work about which he was uncertain, especially after Shelley had advised him not to publish. The evening before the review appeared Keats had accompanied Reynolds to Drury Lane for the opening of a new tragedy, C. R. Maturin's *Manuel,* reviewed by Reynolds in the *Champion* of the next week. On Sunday evening, 9 March, Reynolds sent Keats by personal messenger a copy of the *Champion* containing the review of *Poems* along with a note asking whether the time he suggested for their next meeting would be satisfactory.[30] While Reynolds's messenger waited for his reply, Keats read the welcome review and poured out his gratitude hurriedly: "Your kindness affects me so sensibly that I can merely put down a few mono-sentences—Your Criticism only makes me extremely anxious that I sho^d not deceive you. It's the finest thing by God—as Hazlitt wo^d say However I hope I may not deceive you—"[31]

Another friend of Keats, George Felton Mathew, was not so well pleased. Keats had spent much time with Mathew and his sisters in 1815, but later drifted away from their circle. In a review of Keats's *Poems* in the *European Magazine,* Mathew rebuked Reynolds: "we cannot, as another critic has injudiciously attempted, roll the names of Byron, Moore, Campbell, and Rogers, into the milky way of literature, because Keats is pouring out his splendours in the Orient." As Dorothy Hewlett first suggested, part of Mathew's irritation can be charged to jealousy of Keats's new friend. Mathew would have had no more difficulty in learning who wrote the *Champion* review than the writer in the *Anti-Gallican Monitor,* who reported Reynolds's name.[32]

By 9 March 1817 the expansion of Reynolds and Keats's friendship to include Reynolds's sisters and Keats's brothers was well established.[33] Gentle, unselfish, active Jane, now twenty-six, was Reynolds's favorite. Her central interest was music—playing the piano, singing, and presumably continuing to give music lessons. In a peculiar reversal Reynolds alluded to his pleasure in her singing by denying that the fictitious young poet in *The Romance of Youth* had any sister:

> no sister young
> To woo and win, far surer than another,
> His nature from its dreams, and with sweet tongue
> To scatter silver sounds his listening thoughts among.
>
> (P. 37)

Jane had a sense of humor, as a poem Bailey addressed to her some time from 1814 through 1817 revealed. He gave the poem to Maria Pearse, cousin of the Leigh sisters, explaining:

An amiable young lady of my acquaintance, Miss Reynolds, who had been very dangerously ill, jocularly asked me to write such a poem as I would have done had her disease unhappily proved fatal. I therefore wrote the following:

Elegy
On the death of a young Lady.
Ah me! when Angelina's cheek grew pale
When o'er her frame a deathly chillness crept
The doleful news came sighing on the gale—
Behind a cloud the Sun in sadness wept.[34]

Bailey continued his mock-lugubrious elegy through six stanzas. Along with the courtesy title without Christian name normally used for the eldest daughter, Bailey's explanation of a phrase, "soul of harmony," identified the Miss Reynolds as Jane, the expert musician; "The young Lady had an exquisite taste both for Music and Poetry particularly the former in which she was exceedingly skillful."

Marianne, now twenty, was the beautiful sister: five years before, Rylance had likened her to a Greek goddess and Dilke later praised her beauty. She was quiet, patient, decorous, and firm in character— she made her own decisions and abided by the consequences. Nothing is known of the appearance and temperaments at this time of eighteen-year-old Eliza and fifteen-year-old Charlotte unless the picture of Eliza half-a-dozen years earlier chasing the cat pell-mell through the house means something. George Keats at twenty was friendly and dependable, though as yet unsuccessful in establishing himself financially; his favorite Reynolds was Marianne, who was his own age. Tom Keats at seventeen, though not robust and fated to die young, was good-humored. All the indications are that for the first year the Keats brothers and Reynolds sisters enjoyed each other's company thoroughly. In March when Jane presented Keats with a Tassie gem depicting the drowning Leander, he showed his appreciation by writing for her the sonnet, "On a Leander Which Miss Reynolds, My Kind Friend, Gave Me."[35]

By 17 March 1817, when Keats mentioned Maria Dilke for the first time,[36] the Keats brothers had extended their friendship to Charles Wentworth Dilke and his wife, long-time close friends of the Reynolds family. The two families were so intimate that the Reynolds girls not only visited the Dilkes in Hampstead; they also visited Dilke's sister, Mrs. Letitia Snook, in Bedhampton. Since the Keatses knew the Dilkes while they were living at 76 Cheapside, they must have met when the Dilkes were also guests in the bustling house at 19 Lamb's Conduit Street.

From the same address Keats wrote his first letter to the publishing firm of John Taylor and James Augustus Hessey.[37] They had invited him to some kind of meeting, either business or social, and he had to decline the "kindness" because he was leaving town. Reynolds played a large part in detaching Keats from his first publishers, the dissatisfied Olliers, to the steady, helpful, and generous Taylor and Hessey. This firm had published *The Naiad* at a financial loss, but was later to publish *Peter Bell* and *The Fancy* profitably. Reynolds was close friends with Taylor and Hessey from 1818 through 1823—a friendship that may well have grown out of their business relationship. Hessey later spoke of the many hours they enjoyed in the Reynolds house in Little Britain;[38] it would have been unlike Charlotte Reynolds and her son not to have invited them before 1818 to 19 Lamb's Conduit Street.

Since James Rice came so often to the Reynolds home, Keats must have met him there, although he did not mention Rice until 17 April 1817. Keats would have met before long other former Zetosophians, Reynolds's close friends William and Frank Squibb, though he did not mention them until almost a year later.[39] He would have encountered John Martin, Reynolds's early publisher as well as fellow Zetosophian, and lately Dilke's publisher—Martin had published Dilke's collection of old plays in 1816 and would later publish more of Dilke's work.

Though Reynolds's health was not as bad as Rice's, he suffered so often from recurring illnesses that one wonders how he could write so much for the *Champion*. In the spring of 1817 illness struck again. It was not serious on 17 March when Keats, who was also indisposed, tried to cheer him up by laughingly adapting Falstaff's speech and punning on their shared nickname, "But right Jack Health—honest Jack Health, true Jack Health—banish health and banish all the world."[40] He probably heard Reynolds called Jack fairly often at Lamb's Conduit Street—his mother, Dovaston, and Reynolds himself had used the nickname often—but he applied it to himself here in jest, since his brothers and friends seem not to have addressed him that way. After the mild onset, Reynolds's affliction worsened and hung on for a month to six weeks. In *Epistle to* ———— [Eliza Drewe] dated May 1817, Reynolds called it "long departing sickness" and spoke of having recovered only recently.[41]

But he could not have been confined to his bed long, for Keats did not realize how troublesome his illness became. After leaving for the

Isle of Wight on 14 April to start *Endymion,* Keats wrote his brothers from Southampton the next day, reporting that he thought of
them, Haydon, and Reynolds constantly—already Reynolds was growing almost as close to Keats as his brothers were, though Keats did
not yet call Reynolds brother as he did later. Expecting George,
Tom, and Reynolds to meet convivially at Haydon's, Keats joked
that his ghost would appear at the gathering and asked either George
or Tom to take his part in the trio—singing or playing a concert on
imaginary musical instruments—a standard part of their social occasions.[42]

Soon after arriving at Carisbrooke on the Isle of Wight, Keats, in
buoyant spirits, wrote Reynolds describing the scenery, his lodgings,
and most excitedly of all the sea, on which he had just written the
splendid sonnet that he copied into the letter. Keats had been startled
to open Spenser by chance to a passage that applied directly to his
high endeavor:

> The noble Heart that harbors vertuous thought,
> And is with Child of glorious great intent,
> Can never rest, until it forth have brought
> Th' eternal Brood of Glory excellent—[43]

Not only did Keats think that fate was guiding him, but he knew
that the passage was one of Reynolds's favorites. Possibly he had even
read the article of the preceding October where Reynolds had given
the first two lines a prominent place.

Keats thought of Reynolds as a brother poet and almost as a member of the family; he called him Jack a second time and directed him
to have Haydon make a sketch of him, George, and Tom. Keats felt
so close to the Reynolds sisters and Maria Dilke, who had promised
and then failed to supply cups, a basket, and some books to bring
with him that he indulged in a cryptic joke: "Will you have the
goodness to do this? Borrow a Botanical Dictionary—turn to the
words Laurel and Prunus show the explanations to your sisters and
Mrs Dilk and without more ado let them send me the Cups Basket
and Books they trifled and put off and off while I was in Town."
Jack Stillinger solved the riddle by explaining that Keats had in
mind a dictionary "in which the laurel ('Daphne') is described as
having no cup and the prunus as having petals 'fixed to the cup by
claws.' "[44] Some readers, however, may profit from further explana-

tion: the laurel is the poet Keats, the plum[s] (*prunus* is so close to prunes that it misleads) are the Reynolds girls and Maria Dilke. The plums, sensuously appealing and delicious, but not so high in the scale as the laurel, should be dutiful and serviceable and provide the laurel with the things that they promised.

In London with his absent friend on his mind, Reynolds adapted the last line of "How Many Bards Gild the Lapses of Time" as "Most pleasing music, and not wild uproar" in a theatrical review of 20 April.[45] On Thursday, 24 April, Hazlitt spent the evening with him at 19 Lamb's Conduit Street and stayed until three o'clock the next morning, hypnotizing him as always with eloquent discussion of poetry and charming him with flashes of wit and gaiety.[46] Bailey, who because of the death of a friend had come down from Oxford to London before Keats left on 14 April, had met Keats and had Reynolds's earlier glowing accounts in letters confirmed by the man himself.[47] Bailey stayed on through 27 April, when Reynolds passed the evening at Rice's in friendly conversation with Bailey, Rice, and Eliza Drewe's brother George, who was on a visit to London from Exeter. Meanwhile, Eliza and Anne Drewe were visiting with the Leighs at Sidmouth. Probably the meeting with George and the reminder of the Leighs nagged at Reynolds's conscience because he had not written Mary Leigh since he, along with Eliza and Rice, had enjoyed the Leighs' hospitality in January. Contrite because of his neglect, he wrote a long essay of a letter, combining discussion of Shakespeare and Spenser, a brief but lively account of his evening with Bailey, Rice, and George Drewe, one of the best recorded eulogies of Hazlitt, and a nostalgic recollection of one of the happiest times in his life—his vacation the preceding autumn with Eliza and Mary. With Keats still on his mind, he quoted from "On the Sea," sent to him ten days before.[48]

At this time he published in the *Champion* a poem that he had written before 25 December 1816, "Reproach Me Not," the best of all his many poems on his dead sweetheart. Since he did not include it in *The Garden of Florence,* and it is therefore not available in Donald Reiman's reprint of that book, it must be quoted entire:

REPROACH ME NOT

1

Oh! gentle shade—reproach me not,
For hours of mirth too late gone by;

Thy loveliness is ne'er forgot
  However wild the revelry.
For o'er the silent goblet thou
  Art still remember'd—and a cloud
Comes o'er my heart, and o'er my brow;
  And I am lone, while all are loud.

2

Reproach me not—Reproach me not—
  For mingling in the noisy scene;
Mine is indeed a gloomy lot
  To think of joys which but have been:
To meditate on woes, which yet
  Must haunt my life, and speed my fall,
Some minds would struggle to forget,
  But mine would fain remember all.

3

I think on thee—I think and sigh
  Though thoughts are sad, and sighs are vain,
There's something in thy memory,
  That gives a loveliness to pain:—
But yet, Ah! gentle shade, forgive
  The faults this wretched breast hath known;
Had fate allow'd thee but to live,
  Those shadowing faults had ne'er been shewn.

4

Thy friends are fading from my sight,
  But from my mind they ne'er depart;
They leave behind them in their flight,
  Their images upon my heart:—
And better 'twere that all should go
  From this dark world;—since thou art gone;
I need no friend to share my woe—
  I love to weep apart—alone.

5

Thy picture! it is life—health—love—
  To gaze upon that eye—that cheek—
Those lips which ev'n in fancy move—
  Which fancy teaches even to speak.
Oh! I have hung so long at night,
  O'er thy still 'semblance, charmed from pain,

That I have thought the living light
Came beaming from those eyes again.

6

At my dark heart thy image glows,
In life and light divinely fair,
Youth sketch'd the form, when free from woe[s],
And faithful memory placed it there:
In revelry 'tis still with me,
In loneliness 'tis ne'er forgot—
My heart beat[s] still the same to thee:—
Reproach me not—Reproach me not.[49]

Inevitably some will say, "If that is the best, spare me the others."
Critical self-consciousness is likely to make us defensive with a poem
so thoroughly Byronic. Byron's Thyrza poems, Reynolds's favorites
among Byron's short pieces, lie behind this poem and most of his
others about his dead sweetheart in general tone. Like the rest of his
innocent contemporaries, he would have been shocked if he had
known that Byron's poems expressed homosexual love. Reynolds
adapted "Reproach Me Not" from Byron's "Remind Me Not," but
borrowed little else from that poem besides the title. He borrowed
the stanza, a little of the diction ("gentle shade," "goblet," and "semblance"), and the picture of the bereaved man engaging in convivial
pleasures from Byron's "If Sometimes in the Haunts of Men,"[50] but
gave the poem his own pattern of development. It is dramatic, perhaps even theatrical, and it is swinging in its rhythm; nevertheless,
his deep emotion, tempered by the passage of time, shines through.

Expecting that Reynolds would visit him at Carisbrooke, Keats
looked forward to reading each other's verses in his favorite spot
near the castle, but he stayed only a week, and Reynolds's bad health
made him decide against the trip. Recovering his health in a few
weeks, Reynolds made instead a longer trip. At the close of his letter
to Taylor and Hessey of 16 May 1817, Keats wrote, "[I] think Reynolds will like his trip—I have some idea of seeing the Continent
some time in the summer."[51] Circumstantial evidence and a later remark by Keats argue that Reynolds did make a trip to Paris to con-
fer with John Scott, who had been living there since before 5 August
1816,[52] about the future of the *Champion* and his own future with it.

The *Champion* was undergoing a drastic change from the 1814–16
period when John Scott and Horace Smith owned shares. Horace

Smith wrote that the *Champion* "did not prove a very thriving concern, and in 1816, the whole was sold to Mr. J. Clayton Jennings [error for Jennyns], who had been Fiscal at Demerara and Essequibo [for Essequebo], in which capacity he considered himself to have been aggrieved by the tyrants of Downing-street; and wanting some weapon wherewith he might blow the foreign secretary to atoms, he purchased *The Champion* for the accomplishment of his benevolent purpose."[53]

While Scott was in England, the editorial position of the paper had been moderate to liberal, but from 27 January to 20 July 1817 its course was very erratic. In the leading editorial of 27 January, "The Meeting Y'Cleped Reform," the paper veered to the right with a strong denunciation of the reformers Henry Hunt and William Cobbett. On 30 March it turned again toward the left with an editorial, "Wat Tyler," attacking Southey for attempting to have his play suppressed. Though Scott remained nominally both publisher and editor, it is difficult to believe that he exercised close control over editorial policy during this period; he probably supplied only the articles on Continental affairs, which appeared regularly, and left the management of the paper to others.

J. Clayton Jennyns's resignation as fiscal was accepted on 30 September 1816, but his blasts against the ministry did not begin in the *Champion* until 4 May 1817. After buying the paper late in 1816, Jennyns delayed half a year in presenting his case. Jennyns's dispute with the ministry was a combination of personal pique at having failed to get a promotion from second to first fiscal and a dispute about slavery. While he was serving as an official in the West Indies, a number of missionaries in favor of abolition caused unrest among the slaves. When the white residents objected, Jennyns agreed that the missionaries should be restrained and appealed to his superiors. The government failed to take any action, and Jennyns resigned in protest. On 4 May 1817 he began his editorial attack on the government and his defense of West Indian slavery.

One can infer that when Reynolds learned on 4 May 1817 that Jennyns would dominate editorial policy with his narrow West Indian interest and his championing of slavery, he questioned whether he ought to remain on the staff. He decided to go to Paris to consult with John Scott, still nominally the editor; Keats learned of his intention and commented on it twelve days later on 16 May. Reynolds probably made the trip between 25 May and 8 June, since he wrote nothing for the *Champion* of 1 June. After conferring with Scott, he returned to London and worked out some kind of agreement with the new proprietor that would allow him to continue on the staff for another seven months.[54]

The *Champion* announced a new editorial policy on 20 July 1817 (p. 225) and repeated the announcement the next week: After apologizing for the reactionary opinions published in the paper during the early part of the year, the writer declared that the *Champion*'s "columns have been consecrated to the interests of freedom and humanity." He admitted a great esteem for other opponents of the administration, but denied any connection with other liberal periodicals. He accepted Jennyns's special interest by expressing particular concern for the white inhabitants of the West Indies. A week after the article first appeared, a new notice, "Printed and published by R. D. Richards," replaced the old notice, "Printed and published by John Scott." Jennyns had engaged a new editor who wished to make his political position clear as he began his new duties. The *Champion* remained consistently liberal for the rest of the year except for Jennyns's articles against the abolitionists. The redefinition of liberal policy doubtless reassured Reynolds and assisted in securing his master Hazlitt's third series of articles, beginning on 31 August 1817 with "On the Effects of War and Taxes."[55]

At first glance it may seem unusual that Reynolds and Hazlitt temporized on slavery: they did not defend it, but they remained quiet while the newspaper for which they wrote defended it. But one should remember that politics was tangled on the subject of slavery. Not the reformers, but William Wilberforce and the Tory Evangelicals, Reynolds's and Hazlitt's opponents, led the fight against slavery. Neither Reynolds nor Keats ever wrote a word about slavery; it was simply not their particular concern. George Keats showed that a political liberal could readily accept slavery. He owned slaves in Kentucky and joked about them to that zealous Godwinian Dilke, expecting that Dilke would enjoy his jokes, as Dilke no doubt did.

Reynolds and Keats returned home from their travels about the same time in early June. Keats visited the Reynoldses soon afterward—he posted a letter to Taylor and Hessey from Lamb's Conduit Street on 10 June 1817.[56] It seems likely that Reynolds read the first book of *Endymion* and that he valued especially the "Hymn to

Pan," which the next year he probably induced Hazlitt to print in the *Yellow Dwarf* before the registered publication of *Endymion.* This summer was the rosiest period of Reynolds's and Keats's friendship: they spent many days together, wandering over Hampstead Heath and reading from the facsimile folio edition of Shakespeare that Keats had acquired.[57] Impressed by Keats's rich appreciation of Shakespeare, Reynolds alluded to it in his review of Hazlitt's *Characters:* "We have heard it remarked by a friend, who *reads* Shakespeare,—and *really* to read Shakespeare, is 'to be one man picked out of ten thousand,'—that he was always correct in his costume of language."[58]

It is fitting that in this time of happy companionship with Keats, Reynolds wrote his finest poem—*Devon*—first published in the *Champion* of 27 July 1817.[59] It is Wordsworthian in many ways and is about the same length as its great model; 164 lines of blank verse for *Devon* as compared with the 159 in *Tintern Abbey.* The work shows how a poet can follow Wordsworth's lead in making memorable poetry from "emotion recollected in tranquillity." It succeeds in what Reynolds had been praising as Wordsworth's central achievement for years, the projecting of the poet's own thoughts and feelings into natural description. Though its tone is effectively modulated, as a whole it falls between the tone of his favorite of Coleridge's conversation poems, *The Nightingale,* and the tone of Wordsworth's *Tintern Abbey;* it is more impassioned than Coleridge, but shows less burning ardor than Wordsworth. Though Reynolds follows Wordsworth, the reader hears Reynolds's voice and shares his emotions.

In crowded London in the summer, Reynolds recalled first the dreariness of the winter scene in Devon when he visited in January and then contrasted that sullen scene with the golden autumn before it when his own elated spirit had merged with hill, wood, and sea spread out around the Sid. Human companionship of Eliza Drewe and Mary Leigh (probably, though the second friend may have been Rice) enhanced the beauty of the scene and his appreciation of it. The sun and sea became twin symbols of majestic nature linked to the highest human aspirations. Reynolds controlled and modulated the tone admirably: the poem rises and falls from surges of passion to descents into calm content. Although there is a danger that quotations may not satisfactorily represent the modulations of tone in this firmly crafted poem, two passages will suggest something of the range. First the excitement of vigorous recall:

> Hark! hear ye not?
> The streamlet in that dell is not at rest,—
> 'Tis muttering something to the drowsy wood.
> Once, how adown the brambles wild I broke,
> To trace the hidden murmurer: How oft,
> In solitary hours, the lonely sound
> Of that obscure and melancholy stream
> Comes blending with my thoughts!
> Now upward winding,
> I rise above the trees, and look upon
> A sea of wood, with all its billowy leaves
> Rolling in heavy sunshine,—and one field,
> Like a green island, pleasant and at rest.—
> Thou madcap bird! thy sudden gush of song,
> Pour'd out through amber leaves, hath startled me
> Into a wild delight:—thou sing'st, and then
> Spreadest thy wings, as though it were thy wish
> To chase the giddy song.

Then the final fading subsidence of memories as he returns reluctantly to the city:

> But now my fancies do in part subside,
> And set realities come o'er me; now
> The visionary scenes have fleeted from me,
> And left me lonely in this populous city.
> The mind hath, like the sea, its swells and sinkings,
> Its turbulence, its tremblings, and its sleep;
> Sway'd by the very temper of the elements.
> No bird sings now its rash enchanting lay
> In my startled ear; no green and careless wave
> Vexeth the indolent pebble on the beach;
> No solitary bee rocks the wild-flower,
> Or hangs upon the air with drowsy humming;
> No rustling of gold leaves is heard; no song
> Framed by the moist lips of the pilgrim brook:—
> All these are quiet now, or only heard
> Like mellow'd murmurings of the distant sea.[60]

The report Richard Woodhouse heard that *Devon* was Reynolds's best poetry was correct;[61] the poem showed decidedly that Reynolds was maturing as a poet. Not only was the poem better than anything Reynolds had written before, it was better than anything in Keats's *Poems* of 1817 except "Chapman's Homer," "How Many Bards," and a few passages in *Sleep and Poetry*. Keats knew Reynolds's ability as a poet far better than the critics of the last 160 years. Never condescending to Reynolds, though like Reynolds he recognized his own greater genius, Keats always treated Reynolds as a fellow craftsman capable of writing poetry of a high order. *Devon* shows that he had reason to.

The *Champion* published a curious letter in the original poetry department on 3 August 1817. Addressed to the editor and signed Pierre, it contained the following passage: "I have seen some lines in your paper, occasionally signed J.H.R. which have pleased me much. I think that the writer (whoever he is) can furnish something much better than your favorite Mr. Keats, whom my perverseness of taste forbids me to admire. I cannot understand this circumstance altogether, as in *every other* instance I have felt the beauty of your selections in poetry."[62] One wonders whether Reynolds, who usually managed the department, knew that the letter was to be printed. Perhaps the illness which became serious three weeks later had already begun, and he could do no more work for the newspaper than send in his theatrical review for that week. He wrote nothing at all for the paper the next week. Two weeks later Pierre received an answer in the original poetry department: "The following sonnet ["On the Sea"] is from the pen of Mr. Keats. It is quite sufficient, we think, to justify all the praise we have given him,—and to prove to our correspondent Pierre, his superiority over any other poetical writer in the *Champion.*—J.H.R. would be the first to acknowledge this himself."[63] Despite the impersonal third-person reference, Reynolds himself perhaps wrote the notice, because it had been he who praised Keats superlatively, and he was back at work that week, for in the theatrical review he quoted "shadows of sweet sounds" from Keats's unpublished "Unfelt, Unheard, Unseen."

In addition to Keats, Reynolds saw much of Rice and John Martin this August. Martin had recently returned from a tour of the Lake District and had stories to tell about the Wordsworth country.[64] Haydon, who had been away in his native Devonshire and had written Keats from there, on his return to London invited Reynolds, along with Keats, to attend one of their old festive sessions at his studio. Keats, who was at 19 Lamb's Conduit Street when Haydon's letter arrived, explained to Haydon that Reynolds was "very unwell" with "distressing Symptoms" and it was better that he had declined to attend because carousing would have been dangerous to his health. Keats's letter sounds as if Haydon had been a little miffed at Reynolds for declining to attend because of no "spare time" and that Keats was preventing misunderstanding.[65] Rollins dated Keats's letter to Haydon as 21 or 28 August. Probably 21 August was correct because around that date Reynolds was so unwell as to be unable to write his theatrical review; Hazlitt had to substitute for him as theatrical critic for the *Champion* of 24 August.[66] By 31 August Reynolds resumed his theatrical reviewing.

As a result of George Reynolds's election as head writing master at Christ's Hospital in May 1817, the Reynolds family were given the privilege of living in one of the large master's houses in Little Britain near the school. But with five children and all the belongings they had accumulated in the two and a half years they lived at 19 Lamb's Conduit Street, it was no easy matter for George and Charlotte to move, and they delayed many months. Furthermore, it was difficult to move after late August with Jane and Marianne gone on an extended visit with a friend at Little Hampton and with Dilke's sister in Bedhampton. Thus the Reynoldses now had two houses—the one in which they lived at 19 Lamb's Conduit Street and the one into which they planned to move in Little Britain. Bailey, who was in London during August and as usual spending much of his time at the Reynoldses', developed a warm friendship with Keats. He invited Keats to stay with him at Oxford to continue his work on *Endymion*. Probably to show Bailey and Keats the new house, since they would be at Oxford after the planned move, the Reynoldses invited them to a repast in Little Britain, where they ate biscuits.[67]

Before Bailey and Keats left London, the Reynoldses told them the family would move shortly to Little Britain. When Keats at Oxford wrote Jane at Little Hampton on 14 September, therefore, he sent his "Rememberences to little Britain."[68] On 27 September, he addressed his letter to Reynolds to Little Britain, Christ's Hospital.[69] By the next time he wrote Reynolds from Burford Bridge his error had been corrected, and he addressed the letter correctly to Lamb's Conduit Street, but he mocked the confusion caused by the Reynoldses' procrastination in moving, adding a note below the old address, "Give my love to both houses—hinc atque illinc."[70] Reynolds would catch the allusion to *Romeo and Juliet*, "A plague o' both your houses," and understand that Keats was both amused and a little exasperated. The common Latin idiom, appearing not only in the Virgil passage cited by Rollins, but in Livy, Cicero, and others, means "on this side and on that," in one part of London and in another.

The bantering letters Keats wrote while at Oxford to Jane and Marianne Reynolds, flowering delightfully from the small seed of the laurel-prunus joke of the past spring, show how intimate his friendship had become. They are his "dear friends," and he closes one, "Your affectionate Brother."[71] His saying "A Letter from John the other day was a chief Happiness to me" makes later readers regret that Keats did not save Reynolds's letters so that we would have both sides of the correspondence.

As Reynolds's friendship with Keats grew warmer, his attitude toward Leigh Hunt shifted, as did Keats's, from earlier unqualified friendliness to a growing realization of Hunt's weaknesses. Long after Keats's death, Charles Cowden Clarke noted, "Reynolds poisoned him against Hunt—who never varied towards Keats."[72] That was only partially true: Reynolds and Haydon both pointed out Hunt's faults and limitations, but they merely confirmed what Keats saw for himself. On 10 September 1817 Reynolds met Hunt in the pit at Drury Lane, where one had gone to review for the *Champion* and the other for the *Examiner*. When he told Hunt that Keats was progressing toward the completion of four thousand lines of *Endymion*, Hunt replied possessively, "Ah! . . . had it not been for me they would have been 7000!"[73] Haydon had warned that Hunt jealously wanted to preserve the idea that Keats was his protégé, and now Hunt's statement confirmed Haydon's assertion. Reynolds wrote Keats at Oxford of the incident, whereupon Keats conjured up an image of the scene in the theater, "I think I see you and Hunt meeting in the Pit," and launched into combined disparagement and praise of Hunt.[74]

The one letter from Keats to Reynolds from Oxford that has survived, aside from the three stanzas of clever doggerel that Woodhouse extracted from another letter, shows both openly and by implication the closeness of Keats' and Reynolds's bond. Reynolds had charged Keats with owing him a letter, and Keats replied with a mocking attack on all duns. He proceeded to satirize a methodical and arithmetical approach to nature: "I have not time to elucidate the forms and shapes of the grass and trees; for, rot it! I forgot to bring my mathematical case with me; which unfortunately contained my triangular Prism so that the hues of the grass cannot be dissected for you."[75] He knew either from reading Reynolds's "The Arithmetic of Poetry" in the *Champion* of 16 February 1817 or from conversation that one of Reynolds's favorite satirical targets was an arithmetical and scientific approach to nature, a topic that Reynolds was to ridicule again in the pseudo–*Peter Bell*.[76]

At Bailey's Keats discovered a neglected seventeenth-century poet, Katherine Philips, whom Bailey knew as a friend of his favorite Jeremy Taylor.[77] It was not only the quality of her fine poem that caused Keats to quote it to Reynolds in full, it was also the subject— a close bond between two friends of the same sex who are separated from each other. Keats too was now separated from Reynolds, and by quoting the poem he rejoiced implicitly in the closeness of their friendship without becoming openly sentimental. He underlined one line in the poem, not italicized in the original: "If I have any Bravery, / *'Tis cause I have so much of thee.*"[78] Keats was no doubt thinking about how much Reynolds's unswerving support meant to him in his development as a poet. From poems such as "On Seeing the Elgin Marbles," we know how much he was awed and shaken by his own poetic ambition. He needed all the bravery he could muster, and Reynolds's friendship was a vital element in strengthening his growing confidence. After quoting the Philips poem, Keats wrote, "Believe me, my Dear Reynolds, one of my chief layings-up is the pleasure I shall have in showing it [the third book of *Endymion*] to you."[79]

Bailey wrote on the doublings of Keats's letter what was more on his mind than poetry: "we are two beings in the bosom of dark and stormy waters, my Friend we *have been* rather—for I am flung upon a desart shore atter much tossing:—*You* are yet on the waters:—may you be wafted to a quiet and sunny harbour! . . . I have more to tell you of my own affairs, than yours."[80] Bailey had been courting Thomasine Leigh fruitlessly, and something had happened since he last discussed his love with Reynolds: he was wrecked on a "desart shore" because he had learned that Thomasine Leigh was engaged to Lt. John Carslake of the Royal Navy—they were married in a little more than a month, on 28 October 1817.[81] Bailey knew that, unlike him, Reynolds was still afloat in his courtship of Eliza Drewe and had every reason to hope that he would be "wafted" to the "sunny harbour" of marriage.

On 6 October, the day after he returned from Oxford, Keats stopped in at the Reynoldses' to find Reynolds and his mother not at home; he therefore left the parcel Bailey had sent by him with Jane and Marianne.[82] He reported to Bailey on Jane's health from time to time; she remained ill for weeks. The next day, while Keats was at Charles Brown's, Reynolds came in, and the two were so glad to see each other that they spent the whole day together, Reynolds walking back home in the cold night. The next day Reynolds dined with Keats and his brothers at Brown's.[83] Reynolds read the third book of *Endymion,* which Keats had been eager to bring him, and echoed it later in the *Champion.*[84]

On Saturday, 25 October, Reynolds almost certainly attended the first meeting of the Saturday Club, though Keats did not mention his name.[85] Rice was the moving force of the club, and the two other named members were Reynolds and Keats, but the club probably included also Reynolds's friends William and Frank Squibb, Rice's relative and old friend of the Reynoldses Frank Fladgate, and John Martin. They were all young men, Rice at twenty-five and William Squibb about twenty-six the oldest, and all except Keats were middle-class working men who enjoyed unbending on Saturday after the week's labors. They drank wine, played cards, rolled dice, and caroused generally.[86] They had their own racy slang for sexual adventures and dissipation; as Keats explained to his brothers, "I have had a great deal of pleasant time with Rice lately, and am getting initiated into a little Cant—they call dr[i]nking deep dying scarlet, and when you breathe in your wartering they bid you cry hem and play it off—they call good Wine a pretty tipple, and call getting a Child knocking out an apple, stopping at a Tave[r]n they call hanging out."[87] They were so pleased with the raucous camaraderie that they agreed to meet every Saturday for as long as they could foresee.[88]

In October Reynolds was not distracted by this recreation from his work for the *Champion* or his other writing. As Keats's request from Oxford that he send a few stanzas shows, Reynolds was still writing poetry; and he was writing a story in the form of letters, which has not survived.[89] Bailey, who corresponded with him and with Jane Reynolds as well as with Keats, was much on his mind. The Reynoldses at one time expected Bailey to come down for Christmas, and Reynolds, Keats, and Rice considered visiting Bailey to hear him preach his first sermon, but neither plan materialized.[90]

Concerned about his financial future, Reynolds now took a decisive step that would affect the course of his life. Without a recognized journalist like John Scott in control, the *Champion* no longer seemed a good prospect. Reynolds needed a reliable vocation to earn a steady income, and the law seemed suitable. He had done much more pedestrian work as an insurance clerk, and that job had been bearable, and had left him with time to pursue his literary interests. Keats could continue to devote himself entirely to poetry, but Keats had some independent resources, and he did not. He could hardly ask Eliza Drewe to wait forever if he did not have some plan to establish himself financially. Rice's example showed that a man could have a satisfying life as a solicitor, and, most of all, Rice wanted him to enter the law. Generous Rice paid the fee of £110, found him a place in the office of his relative Francis Fladgate along with the Reynoldses' old friend, Fladgate's son Frank, and promised to take Reynolds in as a partner when Rice succeeded to his father's business. At the time Reynolds thought he might assure his worldly maintenance without sacrificing entirely his devotion to poetry. He signed the articles in the office of Francis Fladgate, Sr., on 3 November 1817.[91]

Making the crucial decision and getting settled in his new vocation interfered temporarily with his work for the *Champion*. Though he sent in a review of Coleridge's *Zapolya* for 16 November, he missed two weeks of theatrical reviewing. He resumed as dramatic reviewer on 30 November, but the chore was not to last long.

When Keats made plans to leave for Burford Bridge to finish *Endymion* in the country, Reynolds and his family persuaded him to stay a day longer in London to meet a friend of Bailey's, Jonathan Henry Christie—a close friend of John Gibson Lockhart, editor of the Tory journal *Blackwood's*. More than just courtesy to Bailey's friend was involved; Reynolds sought to protect Keats's public image. He had seen the *Blackwood's* article savaging Hunt with Keats's name also in bold letters, and he knew from years of experience how politics and personal influence operated in journalism. He hoped he might prevent unfair Tory treatment of Keats by the intercession of Christie. The meeting seemed promising; the company talked of ghosts; and Keats impressed Christie by reciting from his favorite Chatterton.[92] Rice and Martin were also there. Martin's presence was probably no accident; as a practical publisher, he would be tolerant of political differences, inclined to discount them, and useful in smoothing them over. When Reynolds's effort failed, and *Blackwood's* attacked Keats, as well as Hunt and Hazlitt, Martin at first "found excuses for Blackwood," evidently counseling that they be thick-skinned and pass off the attacks as broad joking.[93] At the time of the meeting Reynolds had thought that his plan was working: Christie liked Keats, reported favorably on him to Lockhart, and was asked by Lockhart on 27 January 1818 "to write a little review of him."[94] But Lockhart printed no review and later changed his mind disastrously.

In an exchange of favors in December, Reynolds revised lightly the manuscript of *Endymion*. Toward the close of his life, on 30 December 1846, he wrote R. M. Milnes that he would show him the early "M.S. of Endymion—I had little to do in revising."[95] That initial light revision had to have been done in December because Reynolds was in Exeter through the first part of January 1818, and Keats began his own revision—profiting from Reynolds's small changes—about 6 January while Reynolds was still in Exeter.[96] Keats returned the favor by substituting as theatrical critic for the review of Edmund Kean in the *Champion* of 21 December. Reynolds wrote his last review for the 28 December edition; after having Keats substitute a second time for 4 January, he relinquished his post at the *Champion* to his old friend Charles Dilke.

CHAPTER 7

Home in Little Britain—
January–August 1818

IN NOVEMBER 1817 Keats's bond with Jane and Marianne Reynolds began to loosen when he thought they had hurt Rice's feelings by objecting to his joking with their mother. It is hard to believe they were sharp with Rice, but even a hint of unexpected caution may have been enough to deflate Rice's customary high spirits. This was a small matter which Keats explained openly to Reynolds himself.[1]

Before he visited the Reynoldses on 24 December 1817, Keats wrote an unfavorable comment about the Reynolds sisters to George and Tom, which can only be inferred because John Jeffrey excised it from his transcript—the only surviving copy of the letter. The context, however, suggests Keats's objection. After expressing his dislike of the kind of wit and mannerism shown at a dinner with the Smith brothers, Thomas Hill, John Kingston, and Edward Dubois, Keats wrote just before the passage censored by Jeffrey: "I know such like acquaintance will never do for me & yet I am going to Reynolds, on wednesday." He apparently accused the Reynolds sisters also of mannerism and fashionable affectation. The second charge Keats leveled so obscurely in the excised passage that he had to explain it in his next letter of 5 January 1818: "as for George I must immediately, now I think of it, correct a little misconception of a part of my last Letter. The Miss Reynolds have never said one word against me about you, or by any means endeavoured to lessen you in my estimation. That is not what I refered to: but the manner and thoughts which I knew they internally had towards you—time will show." Maurice Buxton Forman explained the twisted clause accurately: Keats meant "to assure his brothers that the Misses Reynolds had not said anything *to* him *against* George."[2] One might add that his twisted wording reveals that he would take any attack on his brother to be an attack on himself.

There is indirect circumstantial evidence that the Reynolds sisters did not much like George. Bailey wrote R. M. Milnes many years later of George: "there appeared a want of refinement, & generally of intellectual endowments, immeasurably inferior to John. *Nor, if I remember, was he a great favorite with the poet's friends.*"[3] There is evidence that Reynolds and Dilke *did* like George. The friends who did not probably included the Reynolds sisters, with whom Bailey was in frequent communication. Bailey did not much like him either, and they undoubtedly told each other about their reservations. Robert Gittings's inference that the Reynolds women were displeased because George looked elsewhere for a wife, though possible, is more speculative and less likely than this view.[4] Bailey's low opinion of George Keats developed before 3 September 1817, earlier than George's courtship of Georgiana Wylie,[5] because after that date Bailey and George never met. The Reynolds sisters would not speak openly of their reservations about George to Keats, but he was sensitive enough to infer their attitude. There is also reason to believe that Bailey and the Reynolds sisters disapproved of Tom's gambling away a rather large sum of money in Paris,[6] but Keats did not deduce that.

Although Keats had cooled a little toward the Reynolds sisters since he wrote the effervescent letters to Jane and Marianne from Oxford, he remained on friendly terms with them. By January 1818 the Reynolds family had at last moved from 19 Lamb's Conduit Street to the more spacious master's house in Little Britain at Christ's Hospital, where they were to remain at least until George Reynolds's retirement in 1835. The new house had a large drawing room, with folding doors evidently leading into the dining room, a sofa, chairs, tables with antique china teapots, a piano, and a fireplace.[7] Keats and his circle of friends continued to spend as much time in this house as they had in the old one. A poem showing how relaxed he was with the family was the mock-bellicose sonnet "To Mrs. Reynolds' Cat," written on 16 January 1818.[8] Later in the Reynolds house he wrote the sonnet "Spenser, a Jealous Honourer of Thine" and gave it to Reynolds's sister Eliza on 4 February 1818.

In 1817, for the first time in many years, Reynolds had not taken a long vacation in the late summer and early fall—and he was not to omit that vacation again for several years to come. He had corresponded with Eliza Drewe, of course, though the only letter that has been preserved is the verse epistle of May 1817, published with that date in *The Garden of Florence*. His courtship had progressed smoothly, but he must have been impatient to see her and to explain in person his new career in the law. Persuading Keats to write the theatrical reviews for him for the *Champion* of 4 January 1818, he took some time off from Fladgate's law office and went down to Exeter to see her in early January. About 8 January he returned to London to face an uproar.[9]

Reynolds's relations with Haydon had declined from the intimacy they had shared from 1815 through the spring of 1817, the spring when he, Haydon, and Keats had been a triumvirate. Haydon had been a little miffed in the summer when Reynolds declined to attend one of their traditional parties because of lack of spare time. The Charles Cripps affair made matters worse. At Haydon's invitation, Bailey and Keats started arrangements to have Cripps, a young Oxford painter, study with Haydon, spending much time and effort negotiating with Cripps and raising money for him by solicitation. Haydon then turned cool toward the project that he himself had started and wrote Bailey a cold letter that hurt him. Although Bailey's letters to Reynolds on the subject have not survived, we can be sure that Bailey protested to Reynolds just as quickly and vehemently as he did to Keats. Bailey and Reynolds had been the closest of friends since 1812, and Bailey understood the closeness of Reynolds to Haydon. By 22 November Reynolds was deeply troubled about the matter, and his resentment against Haydon was growing. Keats tried to calm him down. "Why don't you, as I do, look unconcerned at what may be called more particularly Heart-vexations? They never surprize me—lord! a man should have the fine point of his soul taken off to become fit for this world."[10] Keats succeeded only in postponing an open break between Reynolds and Haydon.

Reynolds's failure to attend the Immortal Dinner on 28 December 1817, so dear to Haydon's heart, caused an explosion. Glorying in the opportunity to present Wordsworth as guest of honor, with Lamb and Keats as the other chief guests, Haydon could not tolerate any ruffling of his triumph. He invited Reynolds; Reynolds neither attended, nor sent any notice giving a reason why he would not attend. Haydon sent Reynolds a sharp note and then cooling somewhat, a second note which he thought one of palliation. Reynolds did not see either of these notes until he returned from Exeter about

8 January 1818. He was offended by them, taking the second note to be an aggravation rather than a softening. Because of Haydon's long history of high-handedness about appointments and other obligations, Reynolds could not brook Haydon's explosion. When it came to sarcasm, Reynolds could always give better than he received; he was second only to his idol Hazlitt in that department. Reynolds replied to Haydon with "one of the most cutting" letters Keats had ever seen, blasting him for all his faults and weaknesses. Reynolds consulted closely with Keats during the quarrel, showing him both Haydon's letters and his own. Though Keats thought Reynolds should have been more tolerant, he conceded that Reynolds was "on the right side of the question." Between 13 and 19 January Haydon sent Reynolds a sharp reply, and the friendship was at an end.[11]

Wishing to preserve his friendships both with Haydon and Reynolds, Keats trod softly in the wake of the quarrel. On 10 January Keats wrote to excuse himself from visiting Haydon because on that evening he had to attend the Saturday Club, which Reynolds would attend as well. Keats was careful to send the excuse because of Haydon's reaction when Reynolds failed to do so. Inferring Keats's reason for sending the excuse so punctiliously, Haydon wrote defensively as a result of his quarrel with Reynolds, "now you know my peculiar feelings in wishing to have a notice when you cannot keep an engagement with me; there can never be as long as we live any ground of dispute between us."[12]

Keats saw from the beginning that Haydon and Reynolds had very different personalities: "I have an affection for them both for reasons almost opposite."[13] Normally Reynolds was merry, gregarious, and vivacious with a flashing wit; dedicated to the highest ideal of poetic art, he was modest about his own ability to achieve it. Haydon, on the other hand, was earnest, self-absorbed, and ponderous of intellect to the point of being bearlike, without the slightest doubt that he was one of the world's greatest painters. There was no lightness to Haydon; even his recreations he pursued with the "fury" that he so often connected with his work. In their three-year friendship, opposites had complemented each other, but the break was too sharp for Keats to succeed in his long-range hope of bringing them back together again. The pain was no doubt great for both of them because of the background of earlier strong affection.

Unfortunately in Exeter at the time, Reynolds missed the bois-
terous party at George Reddell's, where Keats met his outspoken
young friend George Squibb for the first time and heard the learned
discussion of the word "cunt" after Squibb boldly said the word flat
out. Like the many members of the Saturday Club, Reynolds would
have enjoyed Rice's puns and the other bawdiness.[14] Keats's erotic
letter to him of 31 January indicates Reynolds's responsiveness to
that kind of ribaldry. Intending to write Reynolds "a serious poetical
letter," Keats was distracted "by a mere muslin Handkerchief"
neatly pinned over the bust of a buxom girl into writing the "Song
on the Maidenheads." Reynolds was his fellow poet, whom in rol-
licking "Hence Burgundy, Claret & Port" he invited to follow him
in being intoxicated and inspired by the bright outdoor scenery.[15]

Seeing Keats very often through late January and early February,
Reynolds continued to write both verse and prose. Word that he had
left the *Champion* and might be available for other periodicals circulated quickly. He did not resign until after 4 January when Keats
substituted for him as theatrical critic; before 24 January Archibald
Constable had already offered him ten guineas a sheet.[16] Probably
Hazlitt, who had long written for Constable's publications, the *Edinburgh Review* and the *Scots Magazine,* recommended him for the
Scots Magazine, as he did later for the *Edinburgh Review*. It was an
attractive offer; it is surprising that he did not take advantage of it
for almost a year.

Some time after Reynolds entered the law on 3 November 1817
and before Byron published *Beppo* in February 1818, Reynolds
wrote his comic fragment, *The Fields of Tothill*. When he included
the piece in *The Fancy* in 1820, he credited the Whistlecrafts' (i.e.,
John Hookham Frere's) *The Monks and the Giants* with the ottava
rima and the comic digressions and stated that it was written before
Beppo appeared.[17] As he said in the introduction (p. 52), he probably
wrote and then omitted several stanzas after number 17 that satirized
prominent persons of the day; he retained only the lightest of mockery of Moore and Southey. He may or may not have written two
other cantos, as he claimed, and refrained from publishing them
until he had tested public reaction to the first canto. The claim may
have been merely a part of the elaborate hoax that he was editing
posthumously the works of Peter Corcoran. The poem showed Reynolds wondering how he ever became involved in the complex rou-

tine of the law[18] and continuing to doubt his ability as a serious poet. He was resigned to reducing his ambition to that of popular rhymester:

> I long to be a writer of the rhyme;
> And since men may be Poets, and not know it,
> Why may not I be fit for the soft crime
> Of linking language with the view to show it.
> I do not make a fuss about *"all time,"*
> Give me to be the fleeting darling Poet,
> That simmers on the pot of life, and then
> Is skimmed away with other scum of men.[19]

Reynolds announced that he had no plan at all for the poem, but would follow wherever the spirit led him. Outdoing Frere with his digressions, he provided no plot at all other than the promise that it would concern the love affair of Bessy Abberfield.[20] A few stanzas depicted the voluptuous beauty of Bessy, and a few others her suitors, but in fifty-three stanzas he never mentioned who her lover was to be. From his childhood Reynolds had loved to write essays, and this work was a meandering essay in verse. With only the slight idea that the poem was to be about a place frequented by the Fancy and an account of their sports and practices, Reynolds wrote whatever came to mind. The poem does reflect his mercurial personality and it is an interesting anticipation of Byron, but it was doomed to be forgotten because, good as it is, it does not measure up to any passage of comparable length in *Don Juan*. And it is relatively less successful than the dedication of *The Garden of Florence*, where Reynolds caught some of the spirit of *Don Juan* after reading the first two cantos.

Since the comic verse offered no immediate prospect of remuneration, Reynolds turned to prose. Instead of accepting Constable's offer to write for the *Scots Magazine*, he began writing before 31 January a series of articles for John Hunt's new liberal weekly, *The Yellow Dwarf*, to which Hazlitt was the leading contributor. The three articles on popular preachers entitled "Pulpit Oratory" appeared in the 7, 14, and 28 February issues, all signed Caius.[21] Reynolds wrote the first article before 31 January, for on that date Keats referred to him as Caius in "Hence Burgundy, Claret, and Port."[22] Reynolds adopted the pseudonym, used only for this series, from Dr. Caius, the enemy of the priest Sir Hugh Evans, in *The Merry*

Wives of Windsor. He wrote the second article only a few days before it appeared on 14 February, because in it he referred to an incident he observed at Hazlitt's fifth lecture on 10 February.

Late in life Reynolds offended people with his outspoken Unitarianism,[23] but in his youth he restrained the public expression of his religious views. As *The Romance of Youth* reveals, he had been swayed by Hazlitt's agnosticism and regretted the loss of his childhood faith.[24] He did not wish to offend unnecessarily his family and friends; his mother and father were Anglicans with a dislike for dissent; his long-time close friend Bailey was of course a staunch Christian preparing for the priesthood; and other friends like Taylor, Hessey, and Woodhouse were firm Christians. Since he loved the tradition of the Church and the charity and human brotherhood for which it stood, he could write without hypocrisy: "We are far from being among those who do not love the Established Church; we only hold ourselves against those who abuse it, under the cloak of petitioning for its safety."[25] He took a prudent anticlerical stance; he did not express straightforwardly his belief in Christianity.

The incident that incited Reynolds to write the three articles was a speech delivered to both houses of Parliament proposing an appropriation for building a number of new churches. The church authorities argued that the increase in population made the buildings that were available inadequate. But Reynolds suspected the real reason was that the Methodists and other dissenters had made such great inroads into the membership of the established church that the higher clergy, awakened at last from their lethargy, had decided to retaliate by awing the people with imposing new structures: "It is proposed to build high towers, from which the orthodox-keepers may shout and halloo the scared herd back within the national pale of established Christianity."[26]

Reynolds did not include all Anglican clergymen in his attack; his praise of the devout, self-sacrificing priests he had known was a glowing tribute to the highest ideal of human conduct. Without mentioning the name, he cited Bailey as a specific example:

We know at this moment of one who is about to enter holy orders, with a heart pure for the truth, and a mind ardent and strong and just. If he has any failings, they are such as bind us closer to him. He is destitute of selfishness, loves his God, and feels for all mankind. His youth has been tried with heaped up sorrows,—afflictions have been rained upon his nature: yet he is still strong, for his mind was sinewy enough to endure the weight of misery, depression, and falsehood, which fate, in its spite of superior mortality, piled upon it. He is still young; but ere his days are told, we look to see his name placed with the best, and of a kin with the noblest.[27]

As his ideal, Reynolds chose Parson Adams, emphasizing the short-comings of contemporary preachers by contrast with Adams's simplicity, devotion, and unselfishness. Unlike Parson Adams, a large proportion of the clergy of his day were infected with laziness, avarice, pride, and hypocrisy. In an introduction to the series, Reynolds sketched the various kinds of clergymen who are as vivid and memorable as the best of the seventeenth-century characters. Perhaps the best example is his portrait of the typical rector:

There is the snug Doctor in Divinity, who raises his tythes and lowers his voice in proportion, Sunday after Sunday,—who puts his name and his guinea down on the books of the Religious Tract Society, and gives away the Bible which he has not time to explain,—who feeds at great tables, and talks sweet things over his tea,—who pays a tythe of his income to his Curate for preaching two sermons in a week, gabbling prayers oftener, christening children, churching women, catching colds at buryings, and speaking well of the Rector in all companies. . . . he calls us his flock, but he cares not if the wolf take us day by day, and by twos and threes, so that he be not disturbed after his dinner. He calls us his brethren; but meet him, ponderously pondering and pacing through the street, taking with his well-fed wig and broad black skirts "ample room and verge enough," and then call him brother, or expect him to call you or treat you as a brother, and see how he will act.[28]

Reynolds's portraits of the "Sycophant Curate" and "High Evangelical" were also sharp and effective, the latter exciting his indignation especially for Reynolds was a political liberal and had no love for the emotionalism of the Methodists. He felt that William Wilberforce and his followers were a cross between two of the most objectionable groups possible: they were Methodists in everything except name, and they were conservatives in politics.

Reynolds objected principally to the reactionary political views of the contemporary clergy, who, he believed, used the pulpit as a means of quieting the just resentment of the people against an oppressive government. Because of their ambition and avarice, the clergy had allowed themselves to become dupes of the Tory leaders.

Since the bishops in the House of Lords could always be counted on to vote with the government, Reynolds proposed sarcastically that they be relieved of the trouble of attending the sessions by authorizing substitutes, who might serve the purpose just as well by voting exactly as the lord of the treasury directed them. The ridiculous length to which most of the clergy would go from fear of losing favor with men of influence was epitomized, Reynolds felt, by a young curate of Twickenham, who thought it necessary to advertise in the *Times* that "he was not the person mentioned in the list of those who had given alms as enemies of Arbitrary Imprisonment. There was no such stuff in his thoughts. He disclaimed all such dangerous charity and opinions."[29]

Reynolds chose for his first specific attack the Reverend Daniel Wilson of the Chapel According to St. John in Bedford Row, who whipped his congregation to the highest emotional pitch by alternating maudlin sentiments with terrible descriptions of hell. Yet Wilson himself was coldly calculating in striving for effect. He preached without manuscript, for he sought not to reason with his flock, but to arouse their passions, progressing from a clerical whine in his sentimental passages to a simulated frenzy in his threats of hell-fire and damnation.

Threats of punishment as an inducement to good conduct Reynolds found especially objectionable, for he believed unselfishness to be the very basis of virtue. Influenced by Hazlitt's *Principles of Human Action,* as Keats was, he believed that any virtue worthy of the name must be "disinterested," a word he used often, as Keats did.[30] Yet Reynolds almost despaired of convincing the mass of people that they should be guided by reason instead of emotion. He cited as an example of the hopelessness of the task an incident during one of Hazlitt's lectures on the English poets:

They like to have their passions appealed to, and detest and shrink from all attacks upon their reason. It is this innate love of ignorance that has made faith so powerful in the world,—so great an ingredient in all religious things. We witnessed a curious instance of this enjoyment, at hearing of the ignorance of their fellow creatures, in a set of people assembled at a lecture the other evening. The Lecturer read the following lines, among others of Cowper's:—

> Just knows, and knows no more, her Bible true,
> A truth the brilliant Frenchman never knew.

And his audience instantaneously burst into a joyous applause at the Frenchman's ignorance.[31]

The second specific target of Reynolds's satire was the Reverend Henry G. White, one of the preachers at the Lambeth Female Asylum, where George Reynolds still taught writing part time. Using just as many oratorical tricks as Wilson, White was even more obviously insincere. Some time earlier he had sought public notice by writing prefaces to a series of printed speeches and by publishing a reply to a review of one of his sermons in the *Gentleman's Magazine*. Then, professing a lack of eloquence and a delicate modesty, he submitted the manuscript of a sermon to the *European Magazine* with the apology that his parishioners had pressed him to publish.

Reynolds's satires in "Pulpit Oratory" were "capital articles" when Keats read them, and their irony still makes them fine reading even though the targets of the attacks have become nothing but forgotten names. About this time Reynolds also wrote five sonnets that approached the quality of the very best that he ever produced, "Were This a Feather from an Eagle's Wing" in *The Fancy*. It was probably at the London Coffee House, where Keats attended a dance shortly before 19 January 1818,[32] that Keats wrote "Lines on the Mermaid Tavern." When he mentioned the event, he promised to tell his brothers about it in a future letter. That letter has not survived, but a late-nineteenth-century American magazine preserved an account of it.[33] Horace Smith and Horace Twiss also attended. After Keats recited the poem, according to Keats, "Reynolds, Dilke, and others were pleased with this beyond any thing I ever did."[34]

In his letter to Reynolds of 31 January 1818, Keats asked for a "refreshment," meaning verse, in Reynolds's reply. Taking his cue from Keats's reference to Robin Hood in "Lines on the Mermaid Tavern," Reynolds wrote two of his Robin Hood sonnets and enclosed them in his letter, also requesting a copy of "Mermaid Tavern," which he admired. Reynolds punned upon Keats's word *refreshment*, being refreshed, by using the slightly different sense of the plural *refreshments:* his Robin Hood sonnets were something to eat, nuts and filberts. It is clear from Keats's remark that Reynolds wrote modestly—that he did not know whether the nuts were worth cracking or not. The sonnet form was responsible for the metaphor: Reynolds had associated sonnets with nuts since on 7 April 1816 he had mocked William Lisle Bowles's sonnets in "The Pilgrimage of the Living Poets to the Stream of Castaly" by depicting Bowles as "laboriously engaged in filling fourteen nut-shells," and Bowles had enriched the joke by referring the nutshells in his egotistical reply.[35] Both Reynolds and Keats liked filberts: when Keats described "A filbert hedge" in *I Stood Tiptoe* (l. 35), Reynolds was so pleased that he referred to it in his review of *Poems* of 1817.[36] The two knew that catkins often grow around filbert trees.[37]

Association of ideas was at work in Keats's letter: filberts look like acorns. Keats jumped quickly from Reynolds's metaphor of the sonnets as filberts to acorns to the pigs that commonly eat acorns to squirrels that eat filberts to his own metaphor of his *Robin Hood* verses as catkins.[38] Keats delighted in this kind of mental acrobatics, and he was doubly delighted to be able to share his antics with so witty and sensitive a person as Reynolds.

Keats judged the two of Reynolds's Robin Hood sonnets favorably, "About the nuts being worth cracking, all I can say is that where there are a throng of delightful Images ready drawn simplicity is the only thing."[39] As with the successful underwriting in the earlier "Margaret," Reynolds restrained the diction and phrasing carefully and at the same time provided abundant sharp and concrete pictures: "loose-slung bugle," "belt and bow," "pheasant," "horn of ivory mouth," and "silver Can," to select a few examples. Both sonnets are colorful, lively, and striking, but not equal in merit. Keats was right to prefer the first because of its witty condensed metaphor, "No arrow found,—foil'd of its antler'd food," and to relegate the other to second place because of the facile sentiment of "tender and true" applied to Maid Marian. Reynolds profited from the criticism and changed the phrase to "young as the dew" when he published it. The first sonnet impressed Hazlitt so greatly with its "spirit of outlawry" and its balladlike briskness that he read it at the end of his lecture "On Burns, and the Old English Ballads" on 17 February. It deserved that public recognition:

> The trees in Sherwood forest are old and good,—
> The grass beneath them now is dimly green;
> Are they deserted all? Is no young mien
> With loose-slung bugle met within the wood:
> No arrow found,—foil'd of its antler'd food,—

Struck in the oak's rude side? Is there nought seen,
To mark the revelries which there have been,—
In the sweet days of merry Robin Hood?

Go there, with Summer, and with evening,—go
In the soft shadows like some wandering man,—
And thou shalt far amid the forest know
The archer men in green, with belt and bow,
Feasting on pheasant, river-fowl, and swan,
With Robin at their head, and Marian.[40]

Pleased by Keats's praise and Hazlitt's honor, Reynolds decided to dedicate the sonnets to Eliza Drewe, wrote a third about equal in merit to the others, "To E——, With the Foregoing Sonnets," and printed them in the *Yellow Dwarf* on 21 February.[41] The sonnets deserve the favorable reputation they have enjoyed, though John Masefield exaggerated a little when he ranked them above that gem of a sonnet in *The Fancy*, "Were This a Feather from an Eagle's Wing": "His short poems are the best; and the very best of them are the three 'Robin Hood' sonnets."[42]

On 8 February Reynolds wrote a fourth superior sonnet, "Sweet Poets of The Gentle Antique Line," worthy of being read along with the even better sonnet it prompted from Keats, "Blue!—'Tis the Life of Heaven." Having long loved the dark hair and dark eyes of Eliza Drewe, Reynolds sought to immortalize them at the expense of the blonde and blue-eyed beauties more commonly celebrated by poets. His love of Eliza combined with his love of poetic fame to make the poem burn with an ardor that is more than sentimental; the two parallels between earlier poets and himself and the two kinds of feminine beauty provide firm, yet unobtrusive structure. Keats's rebuttal, however, is even richer in the intricacy with which he developed the various blues, from the majestic heaven to the humble blue bell. It is a mystery why weak sonnets like "On the Flower and the Leaf" should be often reprinted and "Blue! 'Tis the Life of Heaven" never.

The fifth sonnet to flower within this brief two weeks was "Farewell to the Muses," written on 14 February in the copy of Shakespeare that Reynolds later gave Keats. Reynolds might well have printed it in *The Fancy* along with his best sonnet on the same subject; probably he did not because it lacks the hint of comic lightness that made "Were This a Feather from an Eagle's Wing" fit the tone of the mock-autobiography. Since "Farewell to the Muses" has seldom been printed, it should be quoted in full:

> I have no chill despondence that I am
> Self banished from those rolls of honoring men
> That keep a temperate eye on airy Fame
> And write songs to her with a golden pen.
> I do not wail because the Muses keep
> Their secrets on the top of Helicon
> Nor do I in my wayward moments weep
> That from my youth Romance is past and gone
> My boat is trimmed—my sail is set—And I
> Shall coast the shallows of the tide of Time
> And rest me happily—where others lie
> Who pass oblivious days. No feelings climb
> Ambitiously within me. Sweet Farewell
> Be to those Nymphs that on the old Hill dwell.

Though it is a Shakespearean sonnet, the rolling negatives of the octave give it a resonance that shows he learned his lesson well from Milton and Wordsworth. The simple metaphor of the boat fits easily with the note of humility that runs throughout.

Reynolds loved to laugh at prolonged goodbyes: at the "more last words of Mr. Baxter," the seventeenth-century preacher who could not quit printing farewells; at Sarah Siddons for retiring and returning and retiring and returning; and at himself for failing to break cleanly and leave a social gathering. Keats told a story of how he dawdled and dawdled with his leave-taking from a group of friends until he finally tucked his coattails between his legs like a cowering dog and slunk away with mock sheepishness.[43] If his cherished dream to become a serious poet had not been so close to his heart, he might have laughed at the disclaimers of ability and renunciations of poetic ambition that he repeated for many years.

On Valentine's Day 1818 he had not really abandoned all intention to write serious poetry, for at that very time he and Keats were planning to collaborate on a collection of poems. He had long reveled in collections of stories like *Vikrama's Adventures, The Arabian Nights,* and of course *The Canterbury Tales.* He had bought a Boccaccio to send to Dovaston as early as 4 September 1813—it must have been the *Decameron.*[44] He had turned especially to Italian literature during his early friendship with Hunt and had taught himself to read some Italian. Probably both he and Keats attended Hazlitt's lecture on 3 February when Hazlitt said, after praising Dryden's modernizations of Chaucer and Boccaccio, "I should think that a translation of some of the other serious tales in Boccaccio and Chaucer, as that of Isabella, the Falcon, of Constance, the Prioress's Tale, and others, if executed with taste and spirit, could not fail to succeed in the present day."[45] Their master had spoken. Reynolds proposed that they modernize in verse some of Boccaccio's tales; we know that Reynolds made the initial proposal from Woodhouse's note to Keats's *Isabella,* "Written at Teignmouth in the Spring of 1818 at the suggestion of J.H.R."[46] He recommended that Keats take *Isabella,* a tale Hazlitt had named, and he chose, either at this time or later, two other serious stories.

The importance of Reynolds in prompting poems from Keats and in suggesting subjects to him was matched by Reynolds's value as a contributor and responsive listener during the development of Keats's critical thinking. One should not forget that both Reynolds and Keats were taught by Hazlitt, that Reynolds enrolled before Keats, and that Hazlitt treated Reynolds with more favor than he did Keats. Furthermore, Wordsworth's letter on *The Naiad* and Reynolds's pseudo–*Peter Bell* should not obscure the fact that despite his perception of shortcomings in the man and poet, Reynolds always had the highest regard for Wordsworth as the greatest of the first generation of Romantics. In the critical section of Keats's letter to Reynolds of 3 February attacking the egotism and pettiness of moderns like Wordsworth and Hunt as contrasted with the objectivity and expansiveness of the Elizabethans, Keats wrote all the more freely and fervently because he knew that Reynolds was receptive. Reynolds had distinguished between the objectivity of Shakespeare and the subjectivity of other poets as early as 2 June 1816 in an essay "On Egotism in Literature."[47] He had stressed the extreme degree of Wordsworth's egotism, though at the time he thought that the poetic result justified it. Now, along with Keats, Reynolds was prepared to modify his earlier unqualified praise. In the letter to Reynolds of 19 February, where, as Robert Gittings justly said, "Keats's philosophy of Negative Capability finds its most characteristic and perfect expression,"[48] Keats wrote in a relaxed fashion to a sympathetic friend who he could be sure shared his views.

Reynolds's major poetic plan for the spring of 1818 was the joint

poet. It was not the book but the inscription that Hazlitt, Reynolds, and Keats valued. Rollins did not fully realize how close Hazlitt and Reynolds were at this time. Nothing is more likely than that Hazlitt would have visited Reynolds in his illness and brought the book along to show him the inscription. Reynolds would naturally pass on this praise of their shared mentor in his long letter replying to Keats's letter of 27 April. The closeness of the date argues not against, but for, identifying the present as Thomas Moore's; Reynolds was reporting the latest news to Keats.

Rollins noted that "Hazlitt disliked and disparaged Moore," but that dislike did not develop until later. Less than a year after this incident, Hazlitt praised Moore highly. Reynolds had seen Moore at the theater a year earlier on 22 May 1817 and written favorably of him.[65]

While he convalesced at the Butlers' in late April, little three-year-old Fanny Butler lifted his spirits at the close of his long illness. Still in some pain, he watched the blonde, blue-eyed child frolic about on the carpet and listened to her happy prattling. She gave him so much solace that he tried to capture the spirit of her beauty and gaiety in a poem, "To F—— B——. Aged Three Years."[66] Using a quotation from Wordsworth's "Characteristics of a Child Three Years Old" as a point of departure, he chose tripping octosyllabic couplets as a more appropriate rhythm to re-create childish happiness than Wordsworth's blank verse. Hunt saw the merit of these pleasant verses and published them in the *Examiner* of 14 June 1818.[67]

About the time Keats returned to London, Reynolds perhaps nudged Hazlitt or John Hunt to publish the *Hymn to Pan* in the *Yellow Dwarf* of 9 May to arouse interest in *Endymion* before its officially registered publication date of 19 May. Reynolds and Keats probably spent some time on Hampstead Heath reading together Keats's recently acquired black-letter Chaucer, as Keats had expected in Teignmouth, but both had much less free time than the summer before. Now, spending weekdays in Fladgate's office, Reynolds had only weekends, and Keats was busy with George's approaching marriage and with preparations for his own trip to Scotland. Reynolds bounced back from his illness: on 25 May Keats noted, "Reynolds has been getting much better," and by 10 June he could report, "Reynolds is getting I may say robust—his illness has been of service to him—like eny one just recovered he is high-spirited."[68]

Reynolds's recovered high spirits no doubt made him a lively guest at George Keats's party for his new wife, Georgiana Wylie Keats, on 18 June, which Keats and John Taylor also attended.[69] Reynolds's mother opposed George taking young Georgiana to the American frontier, but hardly because she resented losing him as a son-in-law, as Gittings suggested.[70] She wondered that Mrs. Wylie did not object to such a large and dangerous separation; she would not have wanted George to take one of her daughters to the primitive American West. In fact, one of Keats's reactions resembled hers: George is going to America, and Tom is dying, as if one were about as bad as the other.[71] And, as previously noted, it is probable that the Reynolds sisters did not especially like George. They were polite and friendly, as we know from George's visiting Little Britain often while Keats was in Teignmouth with Tom, but it is unlikely that they thought of him as a possible husband.

Keats left so hastily for Liverpool with George and Georgiana that at the last minute he had to ask John Taylor to cut out a few words in his hand to be pasted into the presentation copy of *Endymion* for Mrs. Reynolds, a makeshift for which he later apologized.[72] While he and Charles Brown were on their tour of the north, the Reynoldses kept in touch with poor Tom Keats, now alone at 1 Well Walk except for the Bentleys, from whom the Keatses rented, and the Dilkes close by. Tom sent all Keats's letters to the Reynoldses, who made them available to other friends like John Taylor who wished to read them.[73] Soon after reading Keats's first letter to Tom, Reynolds wrote Keats that Bailey planned to go to Cumberland, in case Keats might like to write or visit him on the return from Scotland, and to ask Keats to send him an account of the trip. Replying on 11–13 July, Keats declined to describe a second time what he had already described to Tom in three letters,[74] because Reynolds or Tom or both had informed him that Tom was sending his letters to Reynolds. Instead, he reported what had happened recently in the Burns country.

A reference to Burns's marriage led Keats to a discussion of Reynolds's forthcoming marriage to Eliza Drewe, which sounds like a reaction to a report in Reynolds's letter of a formal engagement. Keats must have known about Reynolds's courtship since they first became close friends, but now the matter was settled. Keats had spoken to him against marriage, but now that he had made the commitment, Keats wished him happiness: "upon my soul, I have been getting more and more close to you every day, ever since I knew you, and now one of the first pleasures I look to is your happy Marriage."[75]

Still extremely close to John Hamilton, Keats had drawn away from the Reynolds women in June before he left on the walking tour. He wrote Bailey from Scotland on 18 July 1818, "I am sorry you are grieved at my not continuing my visits to little Britain—yet I think I have as far as a Man can do who has Books to read to [and] subjects to think upon—for that reason I have been no where else except to Wentworth place so nigh at hand."[76] After calling at Little Britain at Bailey's request on 26 May,[77] in his last letter of 10 June Keats had not mentioned Jane and Marianne at all, and Bailey had probably complained. Keats insisted that he did visit Little Britain, but at the same time revealed growing dissatisfaction with the sisters. He did not blame them openly, but blamed himself for having evil thoughts about them when he was with them. It was not their fault but his that they did not measure up to the exaggerated ideal he had set for women when he was a boy. He tried to be tactful because he knew that Bailey's regard for them was undiminished.[78] But the strain showed; he was already feeling without admitting it a reaction against their sentiment which he revealed openly to George and Georgiana several months later.

Jane and Marianne Reynolds were charmed by Keats and had welcomed his feeling that he was as close to them as a brother. Keats was a very lovable man with an extraordinary character, and it is understandable that many readers of his letters have supposed that Jane or Marianne would have fallen in love with him if he had given either of them the chance. No one would be surprised if some new evidence turned up to show that one or the other of them did love him as more than a brother, but, as facts now stand, there is not a shred of evidence that either of them was romantically interested in him or that Charlotte Reynolds looked at him as a possible son-in-law. The stereotype from Jane Austen's *Pride and Prejudice* has slipped into too many biographies of Keats. Like Mrs. Bennet, Charlotte Reynolds had many daughters, whom it is certainly safe to assume she wanted happily married. Aside from that and the fact that she liked to talk (but knew it and tried to keep her chattering under control), she was in other respects the reverse of Mrs. Bennet. She was intelligent, literate, and thoughtfully loving toward her children. There is no evidence at all to support the idea that she looked possessively at the young men around her as possible husbands for her daughters.

Keats's biographers have always looked at this matter too one-sidedly; Keats's record is all we have, and it is natural for a reader to identify automatically with the person from whose point of view an experience is recounted. Keats's letters to Jane and Marianne from Oxford had encouraged them to be as unreserved and frivolously sentimental as possible. They are hardly to be faulted if their sentimental expressions lacked the wit to keep them from gushing. They are not to be blamed much, nor is Keats. What happened is a common occurrence. We all enjoy intimacy, and then, when it has run its course, tire of it.

Keats returned to London on 18 August, but he probably stayed in Hampstead because Tom was very ill; and he still had the sore throat that brought him home, now compounded by a toothache. Only a few days thereafter Reynolds made a business trip to Brighton, the coach overturned near Horsemonger Jail, and though he was not "materially hurt," he may have been shaken. Keats did not see Reynolds after the accident, for on 1 September he replied to Jane's report of it, "I am glad John is not hurt, but gone save into Devonshire."[79]

CHAPTER 8

Exeter and London—
September–December 1818

O N 28 AUGUST Reynolds left for his six-weeks vacation, arriving safely the next day in Exeter.[1] Free from the work in Fladgate's law office that he usually disliked, he was very happy in the
assured love of Eliza Drewe, now that they were formally engaged.
Perhaps at this time he saw the domestic scene at the Drewes' that
he later described in the sonnet published in *The Garden of Florence*;[2] the sonnet must have been written before 11 November 1818
because it mentioned Eliza's father, who died on that date. Eliza and
Reynolds must have sat around the fireside, read Shakespeare, and
conversed amiably with her sisters and "placid sire." Reynolds sent
word of his great joy to his family, who reported to Keats that he was
"almost over happy," and he wrote Keats directly that things were
"going on gloriously."[3]

In contrast with Reynolds's serene happiness, Keats wrote in the
same letter of 22(?) September that "the shape of a woman" had
"haunted" him. He described her sensuously to George and Georgiana. "She is not a Cleopatra; but she is at least a Charmian. She
has a rich eastern look; she has fine eyes and fine manners. When
she comes into a room she makes an impression the same as the
Beauty of a Leopardess."[4] She was Reynolds's cousin Jane Cox, who
appealed strongly to Keats and who caused his displeasure with the
Reynolds sisters. After praising her effusively when she first came to
Little Britain following a dispute with her grandfather, the sisters
had veered around, found fault with her, and considered her a flirt.
Keats's report makes Jane and Marianne sound jealous and spiteful,
but again we have only the one-sided account—under the spell of
Jane Cox, Keats can hardly be regarded as objective. We cannot
know what Jane Cox's character really was, nor whether Jane and
Marianne, who saw much more of her than Keats did, had rational
grounds for disapproval. Reynolds had not seen Jane Cox because

he had been in Exeter since 29 August, but his family must have written him about her. Keats tactfully said so little about her that it is doubtful whether Reynolds could identify her when he received the letter.

Keats also remarked briefly on his sort throat, which he thought an aftereffect of the gonorrhea contracted a year before: "I am confined by ⟨Saturday's⟩ Sawrey's mandate in the house now, and have as yet only gone out in fear of the damp night—You know what an undangerous matter it is. I shall soon be quite recovered."[5] Reynolds had known all along about Keats's gonorrhea; no member of the Saturday Club would regard it as a matter for severe moral condemnation, but more likely for joking at the expense of the victim in the manner of Boswell's acquaintance who, on Boswell's being confined to his quarters, consoled him with the thought that he could catch up on his reading, giving a new twist to the old saying, "He who runs can read."

Shortly after Reynolds left London, Jane Reynolds, evidently acting on instructions from her brother, told Keats warmly and emotionally that Reynolds would write him a special letter. Keats's reaction to her promise shows that without revealing its contents she had conveyed the idea that it would be more than an ordinary letter, "I shall be in great expectation of his Letter—but the promise of it in so anxious and friendly a way I prize more than a hundred."[6] It seems likely that the Reynolds family in council had discussed Tom's severe illness and the strain on Keats of nursing him and had resolved to make some unusual offer of assistance. Jane radiated her pleasure over the decision, but kept quiet about its nature because her brother was the proper one to make the offer. Reynolds surprisingly delayed about three weeks in writing, but he did make the offer in his letter of about 20 September. Whatever the offer was, Keats's response makes it clear that it was unselfish and that he was moved. "Your offer I shall remember as though it had even now taken place in fact—I think it cannot be." The offer was probably some special service that the Reynolds women volunteered—Keats wrote George three weeks later that they had been "very kind."[7] If so, perhaps Keats declined because seven months earlier when Reynolds was ill, Keats thought that the presence of the Reynolds women around a patient was more a hindrance than a help.

Two weeks later Reynolds provided a different kind of service. He contributed to an Exeter newspaper, the *Alfred, West of England Journal and General Advertiser,* on 6 October 1818 a review of *Endymion* entitled "The Quarterly Review—Mr. Keats," reprinted by Hunt in the *Examiner.*[8] Reynolds preserved a fictitious stance throughout the article—a pretense that he was a stranger to Keats, a rural resident of Devonshire who had been attracted to *Endymion* by the very passages quoted by the *Quarterly* in condemnation, and whose subsequent reading of the entire poem had left him appalled at the unfairness of the *Quarterly*'s treatment.

Reynolds's experience as a liberal journalist had familiarized him with the effects of political prejudice on the criticism of contemporary authors. His own remarks in the *Champion* on Southey and Coleridge had almost always been colored by partisan feeling. He had already attacked the *Quarterly Review* in "Popular Poetry—Periodical Criticism, & c"; its editor, William Gifford, in "Boswell's Visit"; and a leading contributor, John Wilson Croker, in a theatrical notice.[9] Consequently, in his defense of Keats he was quick to attribute a political motive to his old opponents. Understanding the Tory hostility to Leigh Hunt, he argued that the *Quarterly* had damned *Endymion* simply because the *Examiner* had praised its author. He did not know who wrote the review in the *Quarterly;* at first he implied that he strongly suspected Gifford, but later accused Gifford only of sanctioning it. He managed to hit the real author, Croker, however, by firing a general blast at three chief contributors: Croker, George Canning, and John Barrow.

In a second section of the article, adopting the same method he had used in his review of Keats's *Poems* of 1817, Reynolds compared Keats's work with that of the leading contemporary poets. In the comparison with Byron, Reynolds used as a basis for judgment his old idea of the effect of egotism on literature, which he had first introduced before he met Keats in another essay in the *Champion.*[10] He admitted that Byron's poetry was striking, but denied him a place among the first order of poets because of his egotism. On the other hand, he considered Keats a poet of the highest rank because his work revealed "none of this egotism—this daring selfishness, which is a stain on the noble robe of poesy," and because Keats did not "obtrude his person before you" in his poetry. Reynolds's attitude toward Wordsworth had changed, and he now for the first time censured Wordsworth's egotism sharply. His comment that "Wordsworth might have safely cleared the rapids in the stream of time, but he lost himself looking at his own image in the waters" indicates that he shared Keats's strong reaction against Wordsworth's egotism. Keats must have been pleased to see in print, as well as to know from Reynolds's letters and conversation, that Reynolds shared his view on the egotistical sublime, as Keats labeled Wordsworthian self-centeredness.

Reynolds felt that Keats had no real rival among the other poets of the period; neither Coleridge, Southey, Moore, Campbell, nor Rogers could offer a serious challenge. While he admitted that Keats had "not yet perfected anything," he argued that *Endymion* evinced "more natural power than any other work of the day." To support his claim, he included a number of fine extracts from the poem.

Nowhere in the review did Reynolds mention *Blackwood's Edinburgh Magazine,* against which we know he was at least as much incensed as against the *Quarterly,* for on 14 October he wrote to Keats of "the ignorant malevolence of cold lying Scotchmen and stupid Englishmen."[11] The *Quarterly,* however, was by far the more influential magazine in 1818, and anyone intent on protecting the reputation and sale of Keats's book would have been likely to direct his attention to it. Despite its political bias, the *Quarterly* offered reasoned criticism and guided many lesser periodicals and a large number of readers by its critical decisions. *Blackwood's,* on the other hand, though increasing in popularity at the time, was widely known to be both malicious and frivolous. Reynolds probably decided not to dignify such an abominable personal attack with a serious reply.

As a final move in his support of Keats before his departure from Exeter, Reynolds copied, probably from his own manuscript book, Hunt's "Sonnet to Keats," and left it with R. Cullum, editor of the *Alfred,* for publication the next week, 13 October. Although Hunt wrote the sonnet on 1 December 1816, Reynolds gave it a new anachronistic title to suit his purpose, "Sonnet Addressed to John Keats, Author of Endymion." Returning by way of Bath, where Reynolds called upon several people to whom Hessey had given him letters of introduction, he arrived in London by 13 October.[12]

When Reynolds returned home, he found that his mother had been ill, but was recovering.[13] During a visit with Keats at Well Walk on 13 October, they discussed their project of publishing jointly a volume of tales from Boccaccio that Reynolds had first proposed in February. Reynolds had probably already read the manuscript of *Isabella* during the six weeks Keats was in London before the Scottish tour. While at Teignmouth, Keats intended to make a copy, at first expecting that George would take it to Reynolds;[14] when George did not come to Teignmouth and Keats returned to London, Keats probably lent Reynolds an early version of the poem to read. In April Keats had urged Reynolds to wait many months after his recovery from illness to begin his tales from Boccaccio;[15] now those months had passed. What was to be done? Reynolds took the manuscript of *Isabella* home with him to read again before making his decision.

Fresh from writing his reply to the *Quarterly* in the *Alfred,* Reynolds decided that Keats should provide an even better reply to the attacks on *Endymion* by publishing immediately what all of Keats's friends judged to be one of his very best poems, *Isabella.* If Keats waited for Reynolds to write his poems from Boccaccio, the best time to strike against the Tory critics with the most effectual answer would be lost. It would be selfish of him to hold Keats to the original plan. Furthermore, with his vacation over he must now devote much of his time and attention to the law. Therefore on 14 October he wrote his only letter to Keats that has been preserved, reporting his decision in memorable passages like "cold lying Scotchmen and stupid Englishmen"; "Men do not set their muscles, and strain their sinews to break a straw"; and "Do *you* get Fame,—and I shall have it in being your affectionate and steady friend."[16]

Keats remaining much on his mind, Reynolds visited him again on Sunday, 25 October; and probably about this time Reynolds wrote his "Sonnet on a Picture of a Lady," drawing on Keats's poem for the sestet.[17] He also continued his close friendships with Taylor, Hessey, and Woodhouse. He promised Taylor and Hessey that he would review their publication, Morris Birkbeck's *Letters from Illinois,* but he seems not to have kept his promise.[18] Because Reynolds was so close to Keats, Woodhouse wanted to use him to get a copy of the pseudonymous P. Fenbank sonnet that had accompanied a gift of £25 to Keats.

Keats surely did not tell Reynolds for some time about his meeting with Mrs. Isabella Jones—a woman who had succeeded in retaining his friendship after declining his amorous advances—because she asked Keats to continue their relationship without its being known to their common acquaintance.[19] She had been at a social gathering with Reynolds and George Keats; if she saw them both on the same occasion, of course it would have had to have been before 22 June 1818 when George started out for America, and probably it would have been at a time when Keats was away from London, most likely late May or early June 1818.

Shortly before 24 November Keats described to Rice how he had unintentionally annoyed Reynolds by attributing to him motives of self-interest. Reynolds had said, "Keats I shall go and see Severn this Week," and quickly without thinking that the visit might be merely one of friendship, Keats replied, "Ah . . . You want him to take your Portrait." On another occasion Reynolds asked, "Keats . . . When will you come to town again?" And Keats, remembering that he had recently asked to borrow manuscripts of poetry to copy, replied unthinkingly in such a way as to imply that there was an ulterior motive behind the question, "I will . . . let you have the Mss next week."[20] Though Reynolds flushed the first time and looked angry the second, his irritations were only momentary; his friendship was too firm to be disturbed by slightly comic misunderstandings. Shortly thereafter Keats delivered to Reynolds the promised manuscripts including *The Fall of Hyperion,* I, 1–326, and Reynolds had his youngest sister, Charlotte, copy them into his commonplace book before returning them.[21]

By late November 1818 Reynolds was considering publishing another book of his poetry. In the two years since *The Naiad,* he had accumulated many sonnets and poems of medium length including his best, *Devon,* which he had copied into a book of manuscripts also containing poems by Keats and Hunt. Expecting that Taylor might continue as his publisher as well as Keats's, Reynolds gave Taylor the book of manuscripts, perhaps asking for advice on the desirability of publishing and on selecting from those available. Taylor passed on the book to Woodhouse, who was much more interested in the poems by Keats that Reynolds had copied than he was in Reynolds's poems, but he did approve mildly of some of Reynolds's sonnets, and he liked the parts of *Devon* that he sampled. He had saved *Devon* until the last (and then ironically had insufficient time for it) because he had heard it was the best and understood, probably from Reynolds, that it would certainly be one of those selected for publication in book form. He did not know that it had been published sixteen months before in the *Champion.*[22]

Reynolds's discussions with Taylor were doubtless only preliminary. His last book, *The Naiad*, had been short, only sixty-three pages. He would need more for his next venture than just the short and medium-length poems in the manuscript book. He had the first canto of *The Romance of Youth* in 104 Spenserian stanzas, but for some reason he could not bring himself to write the planned second canto to complete it. Instead, he turned to the tales from Boccaccio. He had released Keats from the earlier agreement to publish jointly, but, since Keats had not taken his advice to publish *Isabella* separately, perhaps he thought he might still collaborate with Keats on a volume. But with or without Keats he needed substantial poems if he were to publish. He probably began *The Garden of Florence* and *The Lady of Provence* at this time or soon after; he had certainly finished them before 9 September 1819, his twenty-fifth birthday, because he said in the dedication, which he must have written after the poems, that he was writing when he was "twenty-four, / And *upwards*."[23] Reynolds's italicizing *upwards* points to the spring of 1819 as the time of completion, but he may have begun them at the close of 1818.

Perhaps Reynolds's success with his critical prose at this time gave him confidence to revive the poetic ambition that had been the great dream of his life. Keats did not need to embellish his laconic remark on 11 December 1818, "Reynolds is well—he has become an edinburgh Reviewer," for everyone knew the prestige attached to a contributor to the most powerful journal in the land.[24] Hazlitt had used his good offices with Francis Jeffrey to have him review *Letters from the Hon. Horace Walpole to George Montagu, Esq. from the Year 1736, to the Year 1770*.[25] Not surprisingly this review has been mistakenly attributed to Hazlitt since the middle of the nineteenth century because Reynolds's prose was as close to his master Hazlitt's as he could make it. The most interesting part of the review now is an implied tribute to the superb letters Reynolds had been receiving from Keats for about two years:

A poet, in his private letters, seldom thinks it necessary to keep up the farce of feeling: but casts off the trickery of sentiment, and glides into the unaffected wit, or sobers quietly into the honest man. By his published works, we know that an author becomes a "Sir John with all Europe;" and it can only be by his letters that we discover him to be "Jack with his brothers and sisters, and John with his familiars." This it is that makes the private letters of a literary person so generally entertaining. He is glad to escape from the austerity of composition, and the orthodoxy of thought; and feels a relief in easy speculations or ludicrous expressions.[26]

Although Reynolds proceeded to cite Gray and Cowper as examples of poets who wrote valuable letters, he must also have had in the back of his mind his priceless letters from Keats.

Reynolds's enthusiastic recommendation that all such valuable letters be published hinted at what he must have known when he wrote it, that Dilke was working on a greatly expanded edition of Walpole's letters. In addition to *Letters from the Hon. Horace Walpole to George Montagu,* which Reynolds reviewed in the *Edinburgh,* Martin also published *Letters from the Hon. Horace Walpole, to the Rev. W. Cole, and others* in 1818. His next project was to publish all the letters of Walpole known at the time in a collected edition. He engaged Dilke to combine all the letters from the Mary Berry edition of 1798[27] with the letters Martin had published for the first time in his two volumes in 1818.

On 3 January 1819 Keats wrote George and Georgiana, "I have been dining with Dilke to day—He is up to his Ears in Walpole's letters."[28] Further facts confirm Dilke's editing of Walpole's letters. On 4 March 1820 Keats wrote Dilke, "You certainly should have been at Martin's dinner for making an index is surely as dull work as engraving."[29] Martin had given a dinner for engravers in his employ and not asked Dilke, who was hard at work on the index for the collection of Walpole's letters. Three months later in June, after Dilke had completed the index, Rodwell and Martin joined with Colburn to publish *Private Correspondence of Horace Walpole, Earl of Orford* in four volumes.[30]

A part of Keats's assessment of Dilke, "Dilke was a Man who cannot feel he has a personal identity unless he has made up his Mind about every thing," echoed Reynolds's assessment of Horace Walpole in the *Edinburgh Review:* "We do not think he [Hogarth] was mad [as Walpole had called him]:—But the self-idolatry of fanciful persons [like Walpole] often exhibits similar symptoms. A man of limited genius, accustomed to contemplate his own conceptions, has long settled his ideas as to every thing, and every other person existing in the world."[31] In working on Walpole's letters, Dilke had become like Walpole, so that Keats transferred Reynolds's judgment of Walpole to Dilke himself.

Reynolds's step up to the *Edinburgh* in December 1818 was no doubt a source of satisfaction to the family at Christmas, but Keats—grieving over the recent death of Tom on 1 December—marred their pleasure with his confusion about where to spend Christmas day. He must have ruffled Charlotte Reynolds and embarrassed her son by his peculiar behavior. When Keats visited Little Britain on 14 (?) December, Mrs. Reynolds received the impression that he had no invitation for Christmas and let him know that he would be welcome there. Keats's contorted letter makes the situation cloudy. Apparently too embarrassed to decline while there, the next day he had to write to excuse himself as best he could. He had accepted another invitation (from Mrs. Brawne, though he did not tell Mrs. Reynolds that) with the understanding that he would come only on the slight chance that he was still in London. He had accepted the previous invitation rather thoughtlessly because at the time he thought it very likely he would be away in the country visiting Dilke's relatives. But the timing of his visit to the country had changed, he would be in London, and he had to accept the prior invitation. It probably did not placate Charlotte's feelings that Keats closed the letter by reaffirming his old friendship. He had managed the affair so awkwardly that she had to be at least a little displeased.

During the brief remainder of December 1818, Keats came less often to Little Britain to avoid the boredom he now suffered there. But Reynolds did see Keats elsewhere, telling him that he had dined at Horace Twiss's about 26 December with the actors John Liston and Charles Kemble.[32] Although it is undated, Reynolds's note among the Twiss papers in the Bodleian is probably his acceptance of the invitation, "I believe your note is for to day—I shall have great pleasure in making one at the proper hour."[33]

Immediately thereafter Reynolds was called away to Exeter so suddenly that he had to borrow a warm coat from John Taylor to make the trip in the winter weather.[34] Eliza Drewe and he had been saddened before by the untimely death of her father on 11 November, reported in the *Alfred* as follows: "On Wednesday, after a short illness, Mr. William Drewe, of this city, wine-merchant, aged 52 years.— As a husband, father, and friend, he was an example of affection, tenderness and truth.—Indefatigable in business, in which his conduct was invariably marked by strict honor and integrity. His loss will be long and severely felt by his afflicted family, and deeply lamented by his numerous friends and acquaintance."[35] Although there is no record of it, one would think that Reynolds went to Exeter to comfort Eliza and attend the funeral at the Mint Meeting on 17 November.

Now there was a second and more unexpected shock: on Christmas day Eliza's young brother George, with whom Reynolds had mixed socially in London as well as in Exeter, died suddenly. Again the *Alfred* reported:

Died—Friday morning last, in the 24th year of his age, in a fit of apoplexy, Mr. George Drewe, son of the late much-respected Mr. Drewe, of this city, wine and spirit-merchant, whose demise was noticed in the Alfred, of the 17th ult. The affectionate disposition and truly pleasing manners of this excellent young man, endeared him greatly to his relations, friends, and a large circle of respectable acquaintance, whose distress is augmented by the consideration of his sudden and melancholy decease, affording another proof of the instability of human happiness and life.—He had breakfasted with his friends, in apparent good health, and returned to his room to dress, where he was, a short time after, discovered a corpse![36]

Fortunately, despite the double tragedy, the widow Ann Drewe and her daughters, Eliza Powell now twenty-five, Lucy at twenty-two, and Ann at twenty, were not without steady support from within the family. Another son, William, Jr., who was Ann's twin, took over his father's wine business and continued to prosper with it until the time of his mother's death on 8 June 1844, when he was her sole executor. William postponed marriage until 31 October 1829;[37] one can infer that he provided his mother and sisters stable support and protection.

CHAPTER 9

Popular Success—1819

ARCHIBALD CONSTABLE's approach to the two periodicals he
published differed; he did not interfere with the editing of the
celebrated *Edinburgh Review*—Hazlitt had to intercede directly with
Francis Jeffrey to place Reynolds's review of Walpole's letters there.
But Constable took an active hand in assisting his editor, the Reverend Robert Morehead, with the management of the *Scots Magazine,*
now losing ground to its competitor, the scurrilous but exciting
Blackwood's. Constable had tried to recruit Reynolds as a promising
new author for his magazine in January 1818. At the end of the year
Reynolds belatedly accepted the offer and at the same time showed
his gratitude to Hazlitt for the favor of placing him in the *Edinburgh* by reviewing the first five of Hazlitt's eight *Lectures on the
English Comic Writers* for the *Scots Magazine* of December 1818 and
January and February 1819. Since Taylor and Hessey did not publish the lectures until April 1819,[1] Reynolds must have used a manuscript supplied by Hazlitt for the frequent quotations contain many
differences from the printed text. Reynolds did not, as Robert Gittings
shows Keats did, use the extracts from the lectures printed in the *Examiner.*[2] Hazlitt had written the lectures at Winterslow between
June and October 1818, and he delivered them at the Surrey Institution from the first Tuesday of November (3 November) through
the first Tuesday of January (5 January 1819).

One feature of this long and enthusiastic review is especially note-
worthy. Reynolds disagreed for the first time with a major critical
thesis of Hazlitt's: that Shakespeare's comedies were greatly inferior
to his tragedies and that Shakespeare showed less comic genius than
Rabelais, Cervantes, Molière, Congreve, and Vanbrugh. Reynolds
dismissed this heresy against the "Shakespearian orthodoxy" and argued that the entire collection of Shakespeare's plays was "a harmony
of humanity," from which no part might be rejected.

When Reynolds came to the periodical essayists in the third and
last installment, he remembered that he had already written an arti-

cle on the *Spectator* for the *Champion* and decided to save himself the trouble of writing another critique. With only a few changes in words and phrases, he included in its entirety the earlier essay describing Sir Roger de Coverley and his circle of friends. Though shady, such reprinting was not without precedent: on several occasions Hazlitt had transferred long passages from old essays to new articles. Although Reynolds reviewed only five of Hazlitt's eight lectures, he broke off the review without noticing the last three lectures. One might suspect that someone detected his deception, if it were not for the fact that he again reprinted old material as if it were new in two later articles for the magazine.

Reynolds's reputation as a journalist rose to such a height that William Blackwood went to surprising lengths to seduce him away from his liberal friends. Blackwood sought him out: Keats reported that "Blackwood wanted very much to see him—the scotch cannot manage by themselves at all—they want imagination." John Gibson Lockhart flattered him by praising him above Hazlitt: "The only enlivening things in it [Constable's *Scots Magazine*] are a few articles now and then by Hazlitt, and a few better still by a gay writer of the name of Reynolds. . . . Mr. Reynolds, however, is certainly a very promising writer, and might surely do better things than copying the Cockneys." Blackwood's ally in the enemy camp, Peter George Patmore, brought to a climax this campaign to make Reynolds abandon his friends and turn his coat; on 7 April 1819 he wrote Blackwood: "I dined with Reynolds a few days ago—and talked with him about writing for you—but, as I expected, from his friendship with Hunt and Hazlitt, he has a feeling about the Magazine which prevents him—otherwise I know he would like to do so—for I was pleased to find that he didn't scruple to speak very highly of the general talent with which the work is conducted. He was very much pleased with the liberal offer you made him—to choose his subject and name his own terms."[3]

Reynolds's acquaintance with J. H. Christie, Lockhart's closest friend, played a part in this attempt to secure Reynolds's pen for the Tory cause. Later when Sir Walter Scott and Lockhart were looking for an editor for a new Tory magazine, Lockhart asked Christie for advice, and Christie replied that he could think of no one except Reynolds. In the light of Reynolds's financial need and Blackwood's startling offer to name his own terms, it was very much to his credit that he resisted all advances and remained just as determined as Keats not to "Mortgage [his] Brain to Blackwood."[4]

Reynolds and Keats did not see each other for over a month because Reynolds was in Exeter from shortly after Christmas 1818 until 16 January 1819 and Keats was away in Chichester and Bedhampton from 18 or 19 January to 1 or 2 February. Keats wrote on 14 February, "I see very little of Reynolds."[5] His dislike for the Reynolds sisters increased; on 2 January he wrote, "I shall beg leave to decline going again to Redall's or Butlers or any Squad where a fine feature cannot be mustered among them all."[6] He would have been certain to meet the Reynolds girls at a party at the Butlers.[7] At Reddell's, though Keats probably had Reddell's ugly nieces chiefly in mind, he might also have encountered Jane and Marianne. Keats's lively account of the party at Reddell's a year before described the scene only after all the unnamed ladies had left the room. Reynolds had been at Exeter at the time, but with Rice, Bailey, Frank Fladgate, and the three Squibbs attending, it would be surprising if Jane and Marianne were not among the ladies who left the gentlemen to their wine. Over a month after Keats mentioned Reddell's, when Jane and Marianne visited the Dilkes next door to Keats for a few days around 14 February, Keats found them "very dull."[8]

His account on 19 February of the break between Bailey and the Reynoldses reveals most fully his unfavorable attitude toward the Reynolds females. A richly gossipy story, it seemed all the spicier to him because he did not get it directly from the Reynoldses—he was not supposed to know anything about it. He reported to George and Georgiana of Bailey's being rejected by Thomasine Leigh and his courtship of Marianne Reynolds and Miss Martin. On the central point Keats was very clear: though teased by her mother and Jane, Marianne had been very upright in the affair—she liked Bailey like a brother and not a husband, and she had never given him any reason to think otherwise.[9]

Keats was misleading about both Bailey and the Reynoldses. Not hearing of Marianne's rejection of Bailey until months after it occurred—he had stopped writing Bailey on 22 July 1818—he gave the impression that Bailey turned much more swiftly from woman to woman than he really did. Marianne had probably rejected Bailey by September 1818. The Reynoldses did not tell Keats, but he sensed that the relationship of the family with Bailey had changed when he wrote Dilke, "I think he [Bailey] is not quite so much spoken of in Little Brittain."[10]

Then, said Keats, Bailey turned immediately to Miss Martin, but added quickly that he really knew nothing about that affair. As Maurice Buxton Forman and Robert Gittings have suggested, that part of the gossip may have been a mistake, for Miss Martin married another man named Bailey.[11] After Miss Martin, Bailey turned swiftly, according to Keats's impression, to Hamilton Gleig, driven by a sexual impulse like that of a plowman. Hamilton Gleig was the daughter of Bishop Gleig of Stirling, not far from Carlisle where Bailey had his curacy, and the sister of Bailey's Oxford roommate, George R. Gleig. Apparently to assure his prospective father-in-law that he had no prior commitment to another woman, he showed him Marianne's letters and asked her to return the letters he had written her, presumably as a sign of the finality of the break between them. Leaving no doubt as to his severing the friendship with Marianne, he wrote her mother some very abrupt letters. With the way clear, he became formally engaged to Hamilton Gleig.

Keats had heard that Rice had studied the matter carefully and cut off his old friendship with Bailey entirely. But Keats had not seen Rice and did not know his reasons. Gittings can hardly be right in supposing that the loss of Bailey's £3,000 marriage settlement disturbed Rice,[12] because there was no possibility of Marianne's securing it after she rejected Bailey. Marianne was consistent and firm; she did not love Bailey and would not marry him. According to Dilke, she had a strong character; she would not change her mind. There must then have been other reasons for Rice's disapproval. The idea that Rice and the Reynoldses disapproved of Bailey's marrying outside the Reynolds family is not borne out by the evidence. They might well have accepted the marriage and continued the friendship. What was shocking was Bailey's disregard of their feelings. Showing Marianne's letters to Bishop Gleig, besides violating the privacy of an old friendship, implied that Bailey had to prove she had rejected him, that she did not know her own mind, and that she might expect him to continue the courtship.

Already sensitive because of Thomasine Leigh's refusal, Bailey's ego was bruised by Marianne's rejection, and he was in no mood to spare the Reynoldses' feelings. His request that Marianne return his letters and his abrupt letters to Mrs. Reynolds show that he had expected a break. Rice understood that neither the Reynoldses nor he could continue the old friendship in the face of such behavior. In fairness to Bailey one can sympathize with his hurt feelings when he confused Marianne's close friendship with love; he would have had to be a saint to blame himself entirely for the error and not be angry with the Reynoldses.[13]

Keats's gibe that the whole affair served the Reynolds women right showed how far his antipathy toward them had gone by this time. His account of how they had praised Bailey at every turn— mention teapot and out came "noble" Bailey—is amusing, but less than fair because he had himself praised Bailey just as extravagantly and repeatedly before Bailey revealed that he was human after all.

After his conduct, Bailey could never again be on the same intimate terms with the family. Reynolds must have been as indignant as Rice over the callous treatment of his sister and mother, but the scars of the quarrel faded with time. When Bailey came down to London in 1820, Reynolds met him and talked with him.[14]

No longer practically a member of the Reynolds family, as in 1817 and 1818, Keats now stayed away from Little Britain. He could still show an interest in the family as on 13 March 1819 when he wrote his sister Fanny, "Mrs Reynolds has had a sick house; but they are all well now,"[15] but that was little more than politeness. He still saw Reynolds away from the house occasionally as when he, Reynolds, and Rice dined with the Dilkes on 20 February on the pheasant that Isabella Jones had given him. On that occasion, in the company of his fellow lawyer Rice, Reynolds was more likely to talk about his legal concerns than he would have been alone with Keats. Keats may have felt a little left out of Reynolds and Rice's conversation about the law.[16] A month later Keats wrote George and Georgiana, "I have not seen Reynolds Rice or any of our set lately— Reynolds is completely limed in the law: he is not only reconcil'd to it but hobbyhorses upon it."[17]

Keats fell into mental depression in the early spring of 1819, understandable with all the pressures upon him, but he could still revive the high spirits of 1817 and the festive good cheer of the Saturday Club. About 10 April, Reynolds attended a claret feast at Brown's, along with Keats, Dilke, Martin, and others, where they "all got a little tipsy—but pleasantly so."[18] Keats described the time as "some little while ago" before he wrote on 16 April, and the tenth was a Saturday, a likely time for workingmen Reynolds, Dilke, and Martin to carouse. On 13 April Reynolds met Keats at a gathering at Sawrey's, and Keats's comment showed that Reynolds's charm still operated: "I went to a rout at Sawrey's—it was made pleasant by Reynolds being there, and our getting into conversation with one of the most beautiful Girls I ever saw."[19]

Along with Taylor, Hessey, and Woodhouse, Reynolds still believed that Keats would follow his recommendation of the preceding fall and publish *Isabella* separately. On 12 January he wished to see a sketch for the poem that William Hilton planned, and on 9 March Woodhouse sent Taylor, along with an unexplained lost letter from Reynolds, a definition of basil, bearing in some way on the expected publication of the poem.[20] Steadfast in his confidence that the new poem would prove Keats's greatness, Reynolds made his own last effort at serious poetic achievement by completing the two poems from Boccaccio earlier planned for joint publication.

Keats having taken *Isabella* (Day 4, Novel 5 of the *Decameron*), Reynolds, not caring for the other tale recommended by Hazlitt, the *Falcon* (Day 5, Novel 9), chose instead two other tales from Day 4, Novel 7 and Novel 9. In the first, entitled *The Garden of Florence,* Pasquino and Simona, a simple worker in wool, fell in love and appointed a special meeting in a garden in the city. Pasquino ate a leaf of sage and died; Simona was charged with murder; the judge and spectators returned to the scene of the death for clarification; Simona demonstrated by eating another sage leaf and died immediately; and at the judge's order attendants dug up the sage bush and found a poisonous toad who had infected it.

Reynolds imitated his original tale even more loosely than Keats had done with *Isabella*. Reynolds changed the heroine's name from Simona to Simonida, promoted Pasquino from servant of a woolmonger to a merchant, eliminated the sexual consummation, substituting instead a meeting between Simonida's father and Pasquino and permission to visit the garden, and omitted a pair of accompanying lovers in the garden, the two vengeful friends of Pasquino's who appeared after his death, and the gross swelling of the corpses.

Reynolds either removed or toned down elements that he considered coarse in Boccaccio. Passages in Keats's letters to him, such as the "Song on the Maidenheads," suggest that privately Reynolds was just as frank about illicit sex as any other member of the Saturday Club, but his public depiction of romantic love was prim to the point of prudishness. The domestic scene where Pasquino met Simonida's father, who virtually gave his blessing, strained tritely and unnecessarily to insure the morality of the love affair. Reynolds's heroine was unbelievably pure—instead of inventing a pious lie to manage the assignation as Boccaccio's heroine had, she first attended a religious function and then proceeded with her father's approval to the garden.

Like Keats's other friends, Reynolds overrated *Isabella* as one of Keats's greatest poems, so Reynolds was very conscious of it as he wrote his own poem. Like Keats with Isabella, he lingered over the beauty and innocence of Simonida, protracting the account of the developing love as she carded and spun the wool brought by Pasquino. But Reynolds, unlike Keats, included no comic twists to relieve the sentiment, such as Lorenzo's excessive timidity that brought Isabella to press the suit to conclusion with her inviting look and tone; Reynolds's sentiment is pure and unalloyed. Of the few faint verbal echoes, only one is significant, and that because of the difference between Keats and Reynolds. Keats's repeated "All close they met again" (ll. 81, 83) at least hints at sexual consummation. Reynolds writes "They met all innocence" (p. 7), going out of his way to stress the purity of their love, since Boccaccio's original implied sexual consummation, "the one soliciting and the other delighting to be solicited, it befell that, he growing bolder than of his wont and she laying aside much of the timidity and shamefastness she was used to feel, they gave themselves up with a common accord to mutual pleasures."[21]

Reynolds missed his chance to balance the sentiment with some intellectual complication. He hinted at a theme with an ironic line not in Boccaccio:

> A bed of sage was near them as they walk'd,
> (Fit plant to match with that of which they talk'd!)[22]

He could have enriched the poem by continuing the theme of opposition between unthinking love and the knowledge signified by sage, but he left it as an undeveloped hint, and the sage remains merely a plant in the rest of the poem as in Boccaccio. The only real check on the sentiment is the briskness of the heroic couplets, which, as Oliver Elton saw long ago, "are nearer to the firm, Dryden-like music of *Lamia* than to the weaker measures of *Endymion*."[23]

Despite all the limitations, a reader who can bring himself to suspend sophistication and enter into the spirit of *The Garden of Florence* can derive pleasure from the simple sentiment and the controlled pathos of the double tragedy. Reynolds put his heart into the poem, and he did not fail entirely. It is surprising that the poem did not win more favor in the sentimental age that adored *Isabella*.

In the second tale, *The Ladye of Provence,* Virgillisi, his wife, and Gardastagno, were all fast friends. Gardastagno became enamored of his friend's wife, who was so aroused that she allowed him to continue the exciting intrigue. Learning of the disloyalty, Virgillisi killed Gardastagno, cut out his heart, and had his cook serve it as a great delicacy to his unknowing wife. When she discovered the recipe for the dish, she leaped from the castle window to her death.

Reynolds had substituted Virgillisi from another tale (Day 3, Novel 5), because Boccaccio's original name, Rossiglioni, was not accommodating to blank-verse meter, as Reynolds explained in the advertisement (p. xiii) when he finally published the poem. But he made few other significant changes. He named Virgillisi's wife Indreana and added a wife for Gardastagno, who grieved at her husband's disloyalty and death. Unable to bring himself to adopt Boccaccio's adultery, Reynolds made a small but damaging alteration. In the original, Boccaccio's wife had said in effect, "If I have been unfaithful, you should have killed me." Reynolds shifted that conditional clause to have Indreana protest that she had not been physically unfaithful, but had lusted only in her heart. Reynolds doubtless intended to heighten the pathos of Indreana's tragedy by preserving her technical virtue, but he lost more than he gained by making himself look squeamish.

Nevertheless, Reynolds was a little more successful in *The Ladye of Provence* than in *The Garden of Florence* because he did not give way entirely to emotion. He played the stark grimness of the plot against the plaintive pathos to create a kind of quizzical irony. Two small near-puns reveal that he strove consciously for that curious effect. After the murder and the setting of the plan for unwitting cannibalism, Indreana's question and Virgillisi's reaction are grotesquely comic:

"The air blows chilly—did not Gardastagno
Promise that he would sup with us to-night?"
Virgillisi smiled.

(P. 168)

And so does the reader at the thought that Gardastagno will not be the eater, but the eaten. Reynolds also played with the idea that Indreana and Gardastagno had exchanged hearts in their disloyal love and that she became his living tomb:

In marble silence sat she,—tears alone
In bitter plenteousness ran down her cheeks,
And fell upon the white tomb of her heart.

(P. 170)

As Ian Jack suggested, the young Browning might well have written this poem.[24]

When Reynolds finished the two tales from Boccaccio, probably by late spring and certainly by the summer of 1819, he wrote the dedication to Eliza—spelling her name backwards as Azile—and planned a collection of poems to include also *The Romance of Youth*. He wrote the dedication after the publication in July of the first two cantos of *Don Juan*, which he echoed, and before his twenty-fifth birthday on 9 September 1819, for he noted that it was written by a "gentleman of twenty-four, / And *upwards*" (p. vii). The theme of the dedication was Eliza's disapproval which intensified as the dedication proceeded: Eliza had chidden him for writing verse (p. vi), entreated him to write no more (p. vii), and finally forbidden him poetry (p. viii). Because he loved her devotedly, he accepted her command and renounced his muse with this final harvest of his happy years committed to poetry. In Byronic ottava rima he caught the tone perfectly of Byron's rapid alternation of sentiment and devil-may-care nonchalance in the just-published first two cantos of *Don Juan*. He echoed a couplet from the Haidée idyll,

He was her own, her ocean-treasure, cast
Like a rich wreck—her first love, and her last

(II, clxxiii)

giving it a different twist,

I give a sigh (a trifle) to times past;—
These are my latest verses, and my last.

(P. viii)

He shifted amusingly the rhythm and diction from Haidée's love of Juan to his love of his relinquished muse.

Though not matching Byron's "intellectual-hen peck'd you all," Reynolds's comic feminine rhymes were clever enough: "increases-leases" and "vexations-relations." His puns were prizes: "idol Muse" (p. vi), meaning both *idol* and *idle* to show his adoration and his streak of frivolity, and "But thy advice is law" (p. viii), meaning both that her advice had the force of law and that she advised him to spend all his time practicing law. And best of all was the culminating paradox unlike anything in Byron. Eliza was poetry, and she therefore unwittingly forbade herself:

> I wish the world could know how young and bright
> Thou art whose voice forbids me poesy;
> And how thy cheek, June-born [it was 25 June], doth take delight
> In marring thy sweet caution:—oh! to me
> Thine eye is lustrous with the Muse's light,
> And that which thou forbiddest is in thee:—
> 'Tis as the lily in some magic hour
> Should speak, and warn the heart against a flower.
>
> (P. viii, stanza 6)

Eliza wanted Reynolds to establish himself financially so that they could be married; she did not want to wait forever, though, as it happened, she very nearly did. The tone of the dedication warned against seeing Eliza as a villain who robbed the world of a promising minor poet. Eliza loved poetry; almost every time Reynolds visited her they read poetry together, and she and her family read Shakespeare among themselves. Reynolds could hardly wait to send her the first copy of *The Eden of Imagination,* and he addressed poem after poem to her, including this dedication. His renunciation of poetry did not come solely because she ordered it. His own doubt about his chance for success, responding to her warning, was the determining factor:

> And can I shun the voice that I adore,
> The voice that hath an echo in my heart?
>
> (P. vii, stanza 5)

In fine fettle when he finished the two imitations of Boccaccio, Reynolds was in a perfect frame of mind to write his masterpiece. For almost three years he had nursed the treasured ambition to become a serious poet, and he had done his best, but he now believed that his best was not enough, and he accepted what he considered the hard fact. Indeed, the gaiety of the dedication that followed shortly after the writing of the two poems suggests that he was not only resigned, but a little relieved at being freed from his mission. But if he lacked Keatsian richness and intellectual complexity and the full measure of Wordsworthian resonance, even in *Devon,* he had a remarkable wit that would enable him to produce a small work outside the range of either of his greater contemporaries.

The London newspapers printed an advertisement early in April 1819 that "in a few days will be published, Peter Bell, a Tale in Verse, by William Wordsworth, Esq." The few days stretched to weeks, giving Reynolds his opportunity. Keats described the genesis of the anticipatory parody:

Wordsworth is going to publish a Poem called Peter Bell—what a perverse fellow it is! Why wilt he talk about Peter Bells—I was told not to tell—but to you it will not be tellings—Reynolds hearing that said Peter Bell was coming out, took it into his head to write a skit upon it call'd Peter Bell. He did it as soon as thought on it is to be published this morning, and comes out before the real Peter Bell, with this admirable motto from the "Bold stroke for a wife' " 'I am the real Simon Pure' "[25]

One Fitzhopkins, an acquaintance of Reynolds and fellow member of the Garrick Club, added a few details after Reynolds's death:

I knew Reynolds, and often talked to him about *Peter Bell.* Wordsworth's poem had been advertised, but its publication was from time to time put off. Some literary men were guessing at the cause of this delay, and one said, "Wordsworth is keeping it back to elaborate." "Elaborate!" said Reynolds, "I'll see if I can't get one out before him." He set to work that afternoon, and sent his poems to the printer the next evening. I think it was about a fortnight before Wordsworth's. Reynolds was a great admirer of Wordsworth, and though rather averse to continuous exertion, had read through all *The Excursion.* Up to the publication of *Peter Bell,* they were literary friends and occasionally exchanged letters. The joke annoyed Wordsworth, who gave up the acquaintance.[26]

Despite the lapse of years and the secondhand nature of the account, Fitzhopkins's story rings true. He recalled correctly the two-week interval between Reynolds's poem and Wordsworth's, and he was right about the correspondence—Reynolds wrote Wordsworth at least two letters and received two from him. Keats may have been among the literary men; if not, Reynolds told him soon afterward, because he knew the motto.

Although the parody deserves its lasting recognition, most readers probably agree with Coleridge that the prose is better than the verse. Imitating the inflated and pompous tone of much of Wordsworth's prose, Reynolds, through absurd exaggeration, ridiculed Wordsworth's defects: his egotism, his complacent Toryism, his eccentric dwelling on the lowly, and his redundancy. Reynolds controlled the irony admirably, not mentioning Shakespeare by name, but depending on the reader's knowledge of a quotation to reveal the conceit of the pseudo-Wordsworth's declaring him to be "a poet, scarcely inferior to myself,"[27] and allowing the incongruous shift from Wordsworth's pose of serene objectivity to the heated denunciation of Francis Jeffrey to secure its effect dramatically without any unnecessary guidance. The numerous notes are fine too: "See my story of the Leech-gatherer, the finest poem in the world,—except this."[28] In the "Supplementary Essay," mocking Wordsworth's practice of piling up appendixes and supplements on prefaces, Reynolds for the most part allowed Wordsworth to satirize himself by quoting a long passage of complacent self-congratulation from "Essay Supplementary to the Preface" of *Poems* of 1815.

Among Reynolds's satirical targets in the poem were Wordsworth's eccentricity in going to the dregs of society for subjects, his tedious minuteness, his redundancy, and his sentimental approach to nature's lowliest creatures—as pseudo-Wordsworth, Reynolds claimed that even fleas feel a "moral joy." The loose framework of the poem was formed by Peter Bell's relationship to many of the subjects of *Lyrical Ballads:* Betty Foy was his aunt, Simon Lee his nephew, Alice Fell his niece—and most of the characters lived in his region and were connected with him in some way. But many of Peter's relatives and neighbors were dead, and he wandered through the graveyard at night, pondering over their tombs, until at the climax he arrived at the tomb of the poet himself:

> And tears are thick with Peter Bell,
> Yet still he sees one blessed tomb;
> Tow'rds it he creeps with spectacles,
> And bending on his leather knees,
> He reads the *Lake*iest Poet's doom.

> The letters printed are by fate,
> The death they say was suicide;
> He reads—"Here lieth W.W.
> Who never more will trouble you, trouble you:"
> The old man smokes who 'tis that died.[29]

Had Reynolds seen a proof or a prepublication copy of Wordsworth's *Peter Bell* before he wrote his parody? Willard B. Pope thought so because Wordsworth mentioned in his dedication to Southey that the poem was on the verge of passing from its minority, and Reynolds noted in his preface that Wordsworth began his "simple system of natural narrative" twenty-one years ago.[30] But that was probably mere chance, for Reynolds did not say that *Peter Bell* was twenty-one years old, only that the poems in the original *Lyrical Ballads* were. Any Wordsworthian would be acutely conscious of the importance of the date 1798.

Sara Hutchinson believed that the author of the parody had seen Wordsworth's *Peter Bell:* "Some People attribute [the spurious *Peter Bell*] to H. Smith . . . but I believe it is Hazlitt (tho W^m says H. could *not* write anything so foolish) because there are some expressions & rhymes, in the extracts which we have seen, that occur *only in Peter Bell* which Hazlitt saw many years ago."[31] She was understandably led astray in her inference that the author of the parody must have read Wordsworth's original. The expression "Jove" appeared in both, but in different senses, and the word is common. The only two repeated rhymes at all unusual are Wordsworth's *able, table* (ll. 173–74) paralleled by Reynolds's *table, able* (stanza 8, p. 12) and Wordsworth's *taper, paper* (ll. 748–49) followed by Reynolds's *paper, taper* (stanza 8, p. 12). In a poem as long as Wordsworth's *Peter Bell,* sheer chance would account for two such similarities of rhyme, inverted as both are. But Sara Hutchinson did not read all Reynolds's parody, only extracts in some review, and these similar rhymes seemed more important because she could not know that the rest of the parody contained no other examples.

What probably influenced her more than the rhyme words, however, was the striking similarity of rhyme patterns. Wordsworth's stanza was consistently *abccb,* iambic tetrameter, with a last-line variation to iambic trimeter in many stanzas. In Reynolds, thirty of the forty-two stanzas had the identical *abccb;* all but one (the first stanza) of the others had *abcbc,* Reynolds varying the last lines of many stanzas of both kinds by dropping a syllable instead of Wordsworth's foot. Of all the hundreds of poems Wordsworth had written, only one, *The Idiot Boy,* had the same stanza as *Peter Bell.* Laws of probability virtually rule out Reynolds's striking on that stanza pattern by chance. But he would not have had to read Wordsworth's *Peter Bell* to learn its stanza pattern. If Hazlitt happened to be one of the "literary men" mentioned by Fitzhopkins, he could have told Reynolds that the stanza was the same as that curious one used in *The Idiot Boy.* If not Hazlitt, any of Reynolds's numerous publisher friends who had talked with someone at Longmans, Wordsworth's publisher, could have told him what the stanza was. Reynolds probably did not see a copy of Wordsworth's *Peter Bell* before he wrote his parody.

The advertisement of the spurious *Peter Bell* surprised Coleridge, who wrote immediately on 16 April 1819 to ask whether it was the poem that Wordsworth had kept in manuscript for so long. Taylor and Hessey replied promptly and carefully:

We enclose the little work which has occasioned you so much perplexity, and we trust that when you have looked it over we shall still retain your good opinion.

It was written by a sincere admirer of Mr. Wordsworth's poetry, by a person who has been his advocate in every place where he found an opportunity of expressing an opinion on the subject, and we really think that when the original poem is published, he will feel all that intense regard for its beauties which distinguishes the true lover of Mr. Wordsworth's poetry. The immediate cause of his writing this burlesque imitation of the "Idiot Boy" was the announcement of a new poem with so untimely a title as that of "Peter Bell." He thought that all Mr. Wordsworth's excellencies might be displayed in some work which should be free from those ridiculous associations which vulgar names give rise to, and as a Friend he felt vexed that unnecessary obstacles were thus again thrown in the way of Mr. Wordsworth's poetry.

You do not know the author, nor are we at liberty to mention his name. There was no *malice prepense* in the undertaking, we can assure you, for we happen to know that it was written in five hours after he first thought of such a thing, and it was printed in as many more. He never heard a line of the original poem, nor did he know that it was in existence till he saw the name in the advertisement.

We are placed in a situation which enables us to see the effect of these peculiarities which this writer wishes Mr. Wordsworth to renounce, and we must say that they grieve his friends, gladden his adversaries, and are the chief, if not the only, impediments to the favorable reception of his poems among all classes of readers.[32]

The only disingenuous part of this scrupulously accurate letter was the claim that Reynolds had written a burlesque imitation of *The Idiot Boy.* Reynolds mocked Betty Foy and Susan Gale no more than he did all the other characters in *Lyrical Ballads;* he chose the unique stanza from *The Idiot Boy;* Taylor and Hessey must have known that he did so because he knew Wordsworth had used the same stanza for *Peter Bell;* and they protected Reynolds from a charge of ferreting out information about Wordsworth's poem by telling less than the whole truth. Satisfied that the satire was completely fair, Coleridge enjoyed it thoroughly and believed that he would have laughed as heartily if he had been the target.[33]

Wordsworth did not laugh, though he profited from the raucous reception of his book, the derisive publicity carrying the genuine *Peter Bell* into three editions within a month. Edmund Gosse's rumor, said to be from the time, that Wordsworth, eagerly awaiting his own *Peter Bell,* was startled to receive Reynolds's parody in the mail instead, is unreliable because Sara Hutchinson reported no copy of Reynolds's poem available in the house.[34] Wordsworth denounced all detractors of his *Peter Bell,* including the unknown Reynolds and all reviewers who kept the joke alive for months, by firing off a sonnet "On the Detraction Which Followed the Publication of a Certain Poem," avowedly imitating Milton's tone in "A Book Was Writ of Late Called Tetrachordon." The egotism of his citation of Milton damaged further an already weak sonnet, which argued defensively that it was no worse to write about a sinful potter than about sinful outlaws like Robin Hood, Rob Roy, and Tam O'Shanter.

Reynolds's parody was his greatest success both in satirical merit and popular appeal; it went to a second edition within two weeks and a third in May or June.[35] Reviewers in at least thirteen newspapers and magazines helped keep public interest alive, many of them pretending to be unable to determine which of the two poems was Wordsworth's.[36] The most famous reviewer was Keats; when Reynolds asked him to induce Hunt to print a review, he complied by writing the review for the *Examiner* himself. He took essentially the same tack publicly that Taylor and Hessey had taken privately in their letter to Coleridge. He stressed the truth, from which some later readers of the parody have been distracted by the very success of the satire, that Reynolds was a profound admirer of Wordsworth's genius who sought only to ridicule elements that diminished that genius: "The more he may love the sad embroidery of the Excursion; the more he will hate the coarse Samplers of Betty Foy and Alice Fell."[37]

As George Marsh suggested, Reynolds himself probably reviewed his own parody in the Exeter newspaper, the *Alfred,* to which he had been accustomed to contribute occasionally.[38] The reviewer explained that the parody satirized only Wordsworth's "infantine follies," which he feared would never cease. With mock patience he told how Wordsworth had brought out a series of Betty Foys, Stephen Hills, Reginald Shores, and Harry Gills until he had exhausted the tolerance of his readers. When the year 1819 saw the advertisement of yet another such hero, "some wag who thoroughly understood the Lake Poet's mode of *doing* poems and prefaces" had decided to chastise him.[39]

Shelley followed Reynolds's lead in what he called "the antenatal Peter" by producing *Peter Bell the Third.* Byron was delighted, unwittingly paying Reynolds tribute when he wrote Thomas Moore, "Did you write the lively quiz on Peter Bell? It has wit enough to be yours, and almost too much to be any body else's now going."[40] Byron appended a caustic handwritten epilogue in his copy of Wordsworth's *Peter Bell* and added further derision in *Don Juan.*[41]

Another author sought to capitalize on Reynolds's success with the mock *Peter Bell* by publishing a burlesque *Benjamin the Waggoner* later in the summer; he was not Reynolds, as some have too quickly assumed, because he knew the inner workings of *Blackwood's Magazine* and he was dull, verbose, and pedantic.[42] Reynolds probably did not write yet another sequel, *The Dead Asses,* though George L. Marsh thought it might possibly be his.[43]

In the spring and early summer of 1819, Reynolds continued his warm friendship with Keats, though now that Keats seldom called at Little Britain, they met only from time to time elsewhere. On 17 April, he, Keats, Rice, and Martin attended a musical play at Covent Garden, Daniel Terry's adaptation of *The Heart of Midlothian.*[44] Two days later he, Taylor, and Woodhouse visited Keats and Brown; they started playing cards at nine in the evening, but the weather became so bad that they were unable to leave and continued to play all night.[45] Perhaps it was this May or June, shortly after he wrote *Ode to a Nightingale,* that Keats gave Reynolds the original manuscript, knowing that the friend who prized all poems on nightingales could not fail to treasure the greatest of them all.[46] In addition to these nonvocational interests, Reynolds continued to attend to the law, studying French as an aid in dealing with some clients and amusing Keats by joking about how cheap his lessons were.[47] Rice had business connections in Calais, and Reynolds was no doubt looking forward to the time when he would complete his service with Fladgate and join Rice as a partner.[48]

On 27 June at the invitation of Rice, who was again ill and needed rest in a quiet place away from the pressures of the city, Keats and Rice left for the Isle of Wight, settling in at Shanklin on the next day. Keats had told Reynolds that because of financial pressure he was considering a return to medicine, possibly even accepting a position as a surgeon aboard an East Indian ship; Reynolds had advised against any such sacrifice of poetic genius, urging Keats to continue to write poetry and to publish. On 11 July Keats wrote that he knew Reynolds would be glad to hear he had diligently completed the first act of *Otho* and the first part of *Lamia.* His fondness for Reynolds remained unaltered, "I know you have my good at heart as much as a Brother."[49] Reynolds replied soon with a letter that has been lost except for the sentences Keats quoted for George and Georgiana, "I am glad to hear you are getting on so well with your writings. I hope you are not neglecting the revision of your Poems for the press: from which I expect more than you do."[50]

Otho the Great was a potboiler; Keats and Brown knew that the theater was the place for literary men in need to earn money quickly with a workmanlike production. Also realizing that truth and always needing money, Reynolds too turned to the stage for popular success and profit. He could do so without any pangs of conscience because, with the completion of the two tales from Boccaccio, Reynolds had abandoned the writing of serious poetry, though he still planned to publish a collection of his best work, hoping that a favorable reception might change his mind.

Samuel James Arnold, manager of the English Opera House, arranged to have Reynolds write the musical entertainment *One, Two, Three, Four, Five; By Advertisement* as the first performance of the mimic John Reeve.[51] For the father—Old Coupleton who came from

Shropshire to London with his daughter Sophy—Reynolds probably drew on his childhood memories of rural eccentrics or on his visits to Dovaston. Wishing to see his daughter Sophy settled, but rejecting the amateur actor Harry Alias, whom she had chosen, Old Coupleton advertised in the newspapers for a husband. With the cooperation of Sophy, Harry Alias secured revenge for the violation of delicacy by answering the advertisement in four different disguises: Sir Peter Teazle, with Reeve imitating the comic actor Farren who had played that part in Sheridan's *The School for Scandal;* Dr. Endall, with Reeve imitating Harley; Sam Dabbs, the doctor's assistant, with Reeve imitating Munden; and the actor Buskin, with Reeve shifting his imitations to four famous actors, Mathews, Kemble, Kean, and Liston. These appearances so bewildered Old Coupleton that he was glad to accept Harry Alias as a future son-in-law when Harry revealed the deception.

Though like most farces it seems shallow when read in cold print, its lively puns, its comic use of Shakespeare, and its bustling stage business complemented Reeve's mimicry to make it a great success that ran for fifty nights beginning on 17 July. Soon it was printed from the acting copy with an introduction by Daniel George and an engraving from a drawing by Robert Cruikshank in the theater.[52] Its favorable reception was not soon forgotten; the Bath theater revived it on 21 May 1825.[53]

The popularity of the farce, presumably boosting Reynolds's ego and filling his pocketbook, started him writing for the theater, the high points of which were recorded: the prologue to James Sheridan Knowles's *Virginius, Gil Blas,* two more pieces for Fanny Kelly, the best of Charles Mathews's monologues, and another farce in 1838. Dilke, whose own farce *Loveless* was not accepted by Covent Garden in 1818,[54] was glad to write Keats of their friend's good fortune.[55] Reynolds recognized it, however, as ephemeral popular success. Like much of his later theatrical work, it was close to ghostwriting; the actor, not the author, took most of the plaudits. In his last years he did not bother to mention his plays in the list of his works sent to R. M. Milnes, and after his death Dilke omitted them from the account of his achievements.[56]

In the late spring and summer of 1819, Reynolds's light successes with *Peter Bell* and *One, Two, Three, Four, Five* coincided with Keats's enduring successes with some of the greatest poetry in the language from *Ode to Psyche* through *Lamia*. But by late summer their moods were very different. Reynolds was lighthearted because he had received public recognition and money for his work and because he was looking forward to his annual six-weeks vacation. Keats, on the other hand, was gloomy because he was beset by so many personal and financial problems and because he had been working hard for months almost without respite. His letter to Reynolds of 24 August showed how tired and melancholy he was. Having just written Rice why he and Brown left Shanklin and how they liked Winchester, Keats asked Reynolds to learn these matters from Rice so that he would not have to expend the effort to repeat. Quietly, though darkly confident that he could write great poetry, he disdained any compromise of his genius to become a popular writer.[57] It was a mark of the closeness of their friendship that Keats could attack popular success at the time Reynolds enjoyed it without fearing that Reynolds would misunderstand and suspect some personal envy. Reynolds had long shared Keats's view that the genuine poet should be above popularity; he had turned his hand to popular successes only after he had relinquished his dedication to poetry. As he had become accustomed to do, he passed Keats's letter on to Woodhouse and Taylor.[58]

Before Reynolds left on his annual fall vacation, Woodhouse invited him to spend some of the time with him at his father's house in Bath. Leaving about 31 August,[59] Reynolds took his sisters with him to visit with Eliza Drewe and her family. When Keats hurried to London because of bad news from George and spent six hours with Woodhouse,[60] Woodhouse told him of Reynolds's plan. Keats therefore addressed his letter of 21 September to Reynolds in Bath, before Reynolds had arrived, and referred to the presence of Reynolds's sisters in Exeter.[61] Woodhouse wrote Reynolds on 22 September to tell him that he had arrived in Bath and to give him notice that he should come.[62] Reynolds left his sisters in Exeter, planning to return to escort them back to London.

In a much better frame of mind than when he wrote Reynolds his last moody letter, Keats described in his letter of 21 September the small local events of Winchester in a relaxed and jocular way. Though Keats was alone, the cool autumn weather had lifted his spirits, and he described the landscape that inspired *To Autumn* in prose worthy of the great poem. Reporting that he had abandoned

Hyperion, he thought at first he would copy out passages, marking phrases that were unduly artful and others that were "the true voice of feeling," but found that he could not make the distinction and copied no poetry. He apologized for writing in a "scraplike way," meaning his rapid skipping about through disparate topics, but he realized that Reynolds knew his disposition well enough to understand that his moods and interests shifted quickly. Knowing that Reynolds would return from Bath to Exeter, he recommended that he see Babbicomb, which he thought one of the finest sights in Devonshire. He closed with a tactful remark about Reynolds's sisters, hoping that they would pick up the charming Devonshire pronunciation.[63]

Reynolds also figured in Keats's letter to Woodhouse of 21, 22 September because Keats knew that the two close friends would "interread" each other's letters. Both Reynolds and Woodhouse had urged him to publish *Isabella,* but he demurred because his opinion had changed on the poem that was the favorite of most of his friends. Knowing Reynolds's fondness for fairies, he recommended de la Motte-Fouqué's *Undine,* as well as the novels of the American Charles Brockden Brown, of which they had often heard Hazlitt speak favorably.[64]

Now pressed to earn money to assist George and to establish himself financially so that he could marry Fanny Brawne, Keats had Reynolds very much in mind as a man who had supported himself by journalism and miscellaneous writing for a year and a half before he entered the law and who had continued to earn appreciable sums after his entry. In the letter to Woodhouse of 21, 22 September, Keats declared that he would take lodgings in Westminster, seek Hazlitt's advice about the market, and secure employment with the periodicals.[65] Because Hazlitt had assisted Reynolds's journalistic career, Keats believed Hazlitt would do him the same favor. In his letter to Brown of 22 September, Keats cited Reynolds specifically as one who could support himself with his pen if he were not in the law, and he repeated the example of Reynolds in his letter to Dilke of the same day.[66] Keats planned to start with theatricals, no doubt recalling his brief substitution as drama critic for Reynolds on the *Champion.* He had no love for the *Edinburgh Review,* because he thought it cowardly for completely ignoring *Endymion* after the Tory attacks, but he would not be delicate. Hazlitt had arranged a

place for Reynolds there and might also for him.[67] Journalistic work
need not prevent him from writing poetry in his spare time any more
than it had Reynolds, who had produced enough creditable poetry to
fill a sizable volume during the time that he wrote for the *Champion*
and the *Yellow Dwarf*. It is ironic that fate forced Keats to plan so
intensely to imitate Reynolds, who realized clearly the difference
between Keats's genius and his great talent.

Keats did not pursue his plan because his health failed, but Reynolds resumed periodical writing in October 1819 in Constable's *Scots
Magazine* with "Boswell Redivivus, a Dream," a thorough revision
of one of his best essays in the *Champion*.[68] He altered the prose and
added comments on many authors not mentioned in the first version: Rousseau, Rabelais, Gibbon, Fielding, Goldsmith, Congreve,
Voltaire, Milton, Jeremy Taylor, and Izaak Walton. He deleted a
slighting reference to Horace Twiss, whom he had met socially after
writing the first version and did not now wish to offend. He stiffened
his strictures on William Gifford, whom he held responsible for the
attack on Keats in the *Quarterly Review*. "He is a whipper-in of a
whole pack of writers" became "He is a whipper-in of a whole pack
of *hungry* writers." "He writes *little* poems to pretty women" became "He writes *lying* poems to pretty women." And he added a
sentence, "He lashes others into agony, and himself into madness."[69]

The small change in the section on Wordsworth confirmed what
Taylor and Hessey had written Coleridge when they published
Reynolds's *Peter Bell,* that despite Reynolds's objection to some
faults he remained a staunch admirer of Wordsworth as the greatest
of the first generation of Romantic poets. In the first version Reynolds had the fictitious Dr. Johnson praise Wordsworth highly and
wish to write his life; he repeated the same passage in the revised
version with one addition: "As I [Boswell] was desirous of putting
in a word in this interesting conversation, I declared my opinion,
that many of this poet's performances were childish and insipid.
Johnson, 'So they are, Sir, but then he redeems himself manfully in
many solemn lines. Peter Bell is a simple business; but then it has
had its castigation.' "[70]

Archibald Constable had been enthusiastic about Reynolds's ability as a prose writer ever since he first offered him ten guineas a
sheet to write for the *Scots Magazine* in January 1818. After the long
hiatus of seven months following Reynolds's last contribution in

February 1819, Constable was extremely pleased to have such an excellent article as "Boswell Redivivus, A Dream," apparently unaware that it had been published before in an earlier version. When he came down to London in November 1819, he met with Reynolds and they signed a contract to publish a book of prose, leaving Reynolds completely free as to its nature and paying him an advance of £80.[71] Although Reynolds kept alive for almost two years the possibility that he would write the book, he never wrote it, much to the annoyance of Constable, who showed extraordinary patience.

After his vacation in Exeter and Bath, Reynolds moved from the family home in Little Britain to 18 Portland Street, Poland Street, near Rice's place at 50 Poland Street.[72] Now twenty-five, Reynolds no doubt wanted more independence, and he could afford his own quarters after his successes with *Peter Bell* and the farce and Constable's advance of £80. Though Reynolds had not completed his term of preparation in Fladgate's law office, it is likely he arranged to assist Rice with his legal work. In December 1819 Rice was very busy on an important case, the successful completion of which led to his advancement. Whether or not Reynolds assisted, he knew all about the case and reported events to Keats from time to time.[73] About the time of Reynolds's move, Keats wrote George, "Our Set still continue separate as we get older, each follows with more precision the bent of his own Mind," mentioning Brown, Rice, Reynolds, Dilke, and Severn as members of the old set.[74] Two of the set, Rice and Reynolds, moved separately from the others, but together in the law. The closeness of Reynolds to Keats and of Rice to Keats should not obscure the fact that the strongest bond was between Rice and Reynolds.

Some time in December Reynolds returned to Bath, perhaps at a second invitation from Woodhouse or possibly on legal business of the sort that took him to Brighton in August 1818. He told Archibald Constable that he would be out of town in December, and the poem "Winter. Bath" in the first number of the *London Magazine* shows where he went.[75] A rondeau of the sort that Keats grew partial to in "Lines on the Mermaid Tavern" and "Bards of Passion," its thirty-six lines place it between the twenty-six of the former and the forty of the latter. Set in tripping octosyllabic couplets, it is also slightly reminiscent of Burns with its repeated references to "bougies" and its effective contrast between the cheerful hearth scene and the "social hours" inside and the "driving sleet" and "chilling winds" outside. The ironically lofty address to the season is perhaps the best part of this lightly pleasing poem:

> Hail! winter, hail! and let my prayer
> Through the loud storm arrest thine ear:
> Propitious solstice to my mirth
> That piles my flaming cheerful hearth—
> Leave the rude Scythian to his thaw,
> Leave spring and summer for the Spa:
> At Bath for ever fix thy reign,
> Nor to thy Alps return again!

On Christmas day Brown dined at Dilke's with Keats and challenged his host to a contest in writing fairy stories. Reynolds, Keats, Rice, and Taylor were appointed judges, and the prize was a beefsteak dinner. Later, at a dinner at Taylor's, the judges unanimously awarded the decision to Dilke, and on 22 January 1820 the competitors and the judges enjoyed the beefsteak dinner at Brown's expense at Dilke's place on Great Smith Street.[76]

CHAPTER 10

Keats's Illness and *The Fancy*— January–June 1820

A**FTER BIDDING FAREWELL** to his muse in the dedication to the collection of poems written during his friendship with Keats— the period when he devoted his best effort to achieving lasting fame— Reynolds no longer wrote the same kind of serious poetry. But he planned to publish those poems under the title of *The Garden of Florence and Other Poems* to test whether a favorable reception by public and critics might change his mind. Early in January 1820, when Keats anticipated publishing, Reynolds also began seeking a publisher.

Since Reynolds's friendship with John Taylor, James Hessey, and Richard Woodhouse was very close, it is surprising that Taylor and Hessey did not publish his book promptly in 1820, as they had published *The Naiad* in 1816. Apparently Taylor and Hessey would not have been unwilling to publish Reynolds's book if he had pressed them, but they were uncertain and perhaps reluctant. Woodhouse enjoyed Reynolds's company immensely (like almost everyone else) and delighted in his popular successes, but he by no means saw Reynolds as a second Shakespeare, as he did Keats. Taylor, who assumed more responsibility for such decisions than Hessey, had reservations even about Keats; he certainly must have had stronger reservations about Reynolds. The firm had lost some money on the slim book, *The Naiad,* and more on the lengthy *Endymion.* They were willing to sustain some losses for the sake of the prestige of publishing significant poets, but there was a limit. They had just published John Clare after the expenditure of much time, energy, and money, and they were determined to vindicate the judgment of everyone in the Keats circle by publishing Keats. One can understand why they were in no hurry to publish Reynolds, creditable though his poetry was.

Early in January 1820, instead of the book of prose stipulated by his contract, Reynolds sent Constable the manuscript of "The Garden of Florence and Other Poems," offering the opportunity to publish, but explaining that he need not press because another publisher would be willing to issue it in case the prestigious Constable and Company should not be interested. The other unnamed publisher was probably Taylor and Hessey. Though Constable was extremely conciliatory and might even have been willing to publish it as a way to ensure Reynolds's continued services if Reynolds had insisted, he was decidedly uninterested in publishing Reynolds's or almost anyone else's poetry:

> We have every wish to do your will as to this said favorite—but to be honest, as I told you before we have a hor[r]or at poetry, and decline it at all hands, except where the author pays the paper and print—and this resolution arises from experience—no one poem that we have published having done any [good?] saving Walter Scott—the public are gorged with Poetry—and the trade will not look at it we therefore return your M.S. with this—but when we do this we are happy you have another channel for it—as the disappointment will not be so great.[1]

Constable also urged Reynolds to start sending immediately as much prose as he could to the *Scots Magazine*.

About the same time Horace Smith, negotiating for John Scott, did his best to secure Reynolds's services on a regular basis for the new *London Magazine*. Smith wrote Scott, "I am very intimate with Reynolds . . . & if his professional occupations will allow him I have no doubt he would cheerfully become a Contributor on the terms you mention. or accept, the dramatic department should it not be otherwise appropriated. . . . I hope that we shall shortly have the pleasure of asking you to meet Reynolds, when you might arrange plans for the benefit of the London Mag."[2] But Scott did not meet Reynolds; the dramatic department was otherwise appropriated by a more powerful pen, William Hazlitt's; and Reynolds was content for a time to submit only the poem, "Winter. Bath" to the *London*.

Reynolds and his sisters were just as sociable as ever during the sudden reappearance of George Keats in London from 9 through 28 January 1820. Attending a dance at the Dilkes along with Keats and the newly arrived George, the Reynolds sisters came in for Keats's sharpest criticism: "the Miss Reynolds I am affraid to speak to for fear of some sickly reiteration of Phrase or Sentiment. When they were at the dance the other night I tried manfully to sit near and talk to them, but to not purpose, and if I had 't would have been to no purpose still—My question or observation must have been an old one, and the rejoinder very antique indeed."[3]

Keats's feelings had changed from warm affection in 1817 to dislike in 1820, but to understand his attitude, two factors should be kept in mind. Keats, in a terrible mental depression, had been attacking not just the Reynolds women but everyone else he mentioned—Hunt, Haydon, and Dilke. And he was straining to console Georgiana by proving that English society was just as bad as the American of which she had complained. In his dismal state of mind, all social conversation seemed unavoidably clichéd and stale; even his remarks would have been hackneyed, if he had actually made any. The degree to which Keats projected his own inner misery onto others is indicated by the fact that he said almost nothing to the Reynolds sisters and they had no chance to utter "sickly reiteration of Phrase or Sentiment." There must have been some triteness and sentiment in Jane and Marianne, but Keats's dark mood exaggerated them out of all proportion in this passage.

On Sunday, 16 January when Reynolds and Rice were not at work, Keats brought together some of the old set for a party, from which the guest of honor, George, was called away to Haslam's. This occasion prompted Keats's comparative assessment of his three close friends, Rice, Reynolds, and Richards, "three witty people all distinct in their excellence."[4] "Reynolds the playfullest" agrees with Keats's other accounts and with Woodhouse's, Clare's, and Hood's accounts. Reynolds "makes you laugh and not think" does not agree exactly with Reynolds's printed satire, but does agree with Clare's depiction of his good-natured joking. "I enjoy the second" is part of the reason that Keats spent so much time with him; most others also enjoyed his company: Dovaston, Rylance, all the Keats circle, and later Clare, Hood, Barham, and Thackeray. Reynolds's being inspired "by Mercury" agrees with the sudden production of *Peter Bell* and in general with the rapidity with which he wrote such different kinds of material, but this was only a part of him—he also had a measure of steadiness. Despite intermittent problems with self-discipline, he wrote abundantly for many periodicals and for a time—until about 1825—managed his legal business with moderate success. That Reynolds was slovenly in his dress we learn only from this comment. That Reynolds spoke "alegretto," or rather rapidly, fits his mother's account of his speech patterns and Clare's and Hood's descriptions of his conversation at the *London Magazine* dinners. Keats's description of Reynolds as being "Tom cribean" is disparaging compared with Rice's "Swiftian," and Richards's "Shandean," but it is fair. The name came from Thomas Moore's political satire, *Tom Crib's Memorial to Congress,* for which he borrowed the name of a real boxer; the work was topical and transitory, and much of Reynolds's comic work had a topical and transitory quality, as in *Peter Bell* and *The Fancy.* Keats was no doubt prompted to compare Reynolds with Moore because Reynolds had told him that he planned to follow up Moore's success with *Tom Crib* by writing his own different kind of book about boxing, *The Fancy.*

As mentioned earlier, Reynolds dined at Dilke's on 22 January 1820 with Keats, Brown, Rice, Taylor, and probably Thomas Richards and George on the beefsteak paid for by Brown. And he doubtless saw Keats and George at other times not recorded because he asked George to send him an American edition of *Waverley* and George asked Keats to apologize to Reynolds for leaving in such haste that he could not shake his hand goodbye.[5]

Tragedy soon followed George's departure; Keats hemorrhaged dangerously on 3 February. Three days later Mrs. Reynolds called on him,[6] and a week after his mother's visit Reynolds also called on a free Sunday, though he was so tired that Keats regretted not having asked him to stay longer and have lunch. In a letter to Rice the next day, 14 February, Keats asked Rice to tell Reynolds that he would like a letter from him.[7] Shortly after hearing the request indirectly through Rice, Reynolds wrote Keats and received in reply Keats's twenty-first and last surviving letter to him. Keats's letter reveals that Reynolds had complained of a cold, offered to lend him books, and promised to write comic footnotes to *The Cap and Bells.*

Reynolds provided only two of the notes, one merely a brief quotation from the *Spectator* and the other not very amusing.[8] In the second note, to the passage in which Elfinan ordered Hum, son of Cham, to find a way to bring him his beloved Bertha Pearl, Reynolds wrote, "Cham is said to have been the inventor of magic. Lucy learnt this from Bayle's Dictionary and had copied a long Latin note from that work." Possibly Gittings was correct in inferring that Reynolds intended to satirize Lucy Vaughan Lloyd, the pretended authoress, as a bluestocking by implying that the note was in Latin because it was indecent and that she copied it without realizing its indecency.[9] It is not known when Reynolds wrote the notes; perhaps he jotted them down as a beginning during his visit on 13 February and they were the best he could manage in his fatigue. He may also have agreed to supply further notes on similar Sundays and holidays and may have repeated the promise in his letter to Keats.

Reynolds also told Keats that he planned to travel to Brussels, probably a business trip that took him away from London for no more than a week. Hyder Rollins was puzzled by Keats's, "You will not meet with so much to hate at Brussels as at Paris,"[10] wondering whether Keats had visited Brussels and Paris. Instead, Keats referred to Reynolds's earlier trip to Paris some time from 25 May 1817 to 8 June 1817. Reynolds had disliked Paris, and told Keats of his dislike. Although Keats had probably not been to Brussels, he had informed himself about the city when on 14 February 1819 he and Brown planned to travel there.[11] He could therefore predict a more pleasant second trip abroad for Reynolds than the first had been. Still viewing Reynolds and himself as brother poets, he regretted that he was not well enough to paraphrase Horace's ode on Virgil's voyage to celebrate Reynolds's trip.[12] Keats's conjecturally dated letter to Fanny Brawne of March (?) 1820 reveals that Reynolds continued to visit Keats in his illness: "Perhaps Reynolds or some other of my friends may come towards evening."[13]

Living in his own quarters at 18 Portland Street, Poland Street, Reynolds spent much time at the family home in Little Britain, where on 14 March 1820 he wrote John Scott that he had changed his mind about being a regular contributor to the *London Magazine*. When Horace Smith had first made him the offer, Reynolds had feared he would not have sufficient time, but now he sent Scott an article "of a light kind" that might be printed in two parts. Sick of the dull *Scots Magazine,* he sought to publish instead in the *London,* but in case the article should not win approval he asked Scott to return it to him so that he could submit it to Constable's editor as a second choice. Glad to have him, Scott printed it entire; "A Literary Gem. Original Dramas, by James Plumtre" was mildly

amusing mockery of some woefully bad plays by a simple coun-
tryman.[14]

But Reynolds had little time to write for the magazines, for he
devoted most of his available time during the first six months of
1820 to *The Fancy,* published by Taylor and Hessey in June 1820.
Keats probably knew about the plan as early as 16 January when he
compared Reynolds with Tom Crib;[15] both Moore's and Reynolds's
books are about boxing, although Reynolds's volume contains other
poems as well, but no other work by Reynolds would have prompted
Keats to make the comparison. Keats had no doubt read poems written earlier and included in the volume like *The Fields of Tothill*
and perhaps a few small pieces, but Reynolds wrote much of the
book after Keats's remark. Over two pages of the mock biography of
Peter Corcoran—a real boxer who had fought successfully until 1776
when he threw a fight and fell into disgrace—could not have been
written before 6 April because they were based on a letter of that
date from Nan Woodhouse to her brother Richard.[16] Woodhouse
had sent Nan a copy of the "Sonnet on the Nonpareil" (Jack Randall) just before that date, and Reynolds wrote "Lines to the Brum-
magem Youth" after the boxing match between Philip Samson and
Belasco in the spring.

The longest poem in the work, *King Tims the First: An American
Tragedy,* Reynolds wrote in April or afterward. While George Keats
was in London in January, Reynolds asked him on his return to
America to send him "a copy of the small American edition of
Waverley and Guy Mannering, to present to a young lady who,
strange to say, read books, and wore pockets."[17] Sailing from Liverpool on 1 February, George could hardly have reached America and
sent the book before 1 March, and Reynolds could not have received
it before 1 April.[18] However, the invented introduction to *King
Tims* by the fictitious Peter Corcoran includes the account of *Waverley* being sent from America and is dated 1819—but the date is a
fiction. Pretending to edit the work of the deceased Corcoran, Reynolds had to set the date when Corcoran supposedly wrote it sometime before *The Fancy* was published in June 1820.

The popular success of Moore's *Tom Crib's Memorial to Congress*
(1819) probably suggested the idea of *The Fancy.* Both books have
introductory prose sections followed by poems. Both borrow the

names of real boxers, though Reynolds borrowed only the name; there are no further similarities between his fictitious amateur boxer and the real professional. In other respects Reynolds did not follow Moore's lead. Moore's prose introduction was a mock-pedantic history of boxing from the ancients to the moderns; his poems were chiefly anecdotes of boxing, many sprinkled with political satire. Reynolds's prose introduction was an invented history of his hero, and only a few of the poems dealt with boxing, the others ranging from polar exploration to nostalgic recollection of his school days.

Drawing often on his own experiences, Reynolds sketched specific details in the manner of a genuine biographer. Born at Shrewsbury of frugal Irish parents who saved enough for his education, Peter Corcoran attended Shrewsbury School, where his inclinations toward wildness developed early. He broke rules, pilfered orchards, swore, fought, and stole out at night to swim and fish in the Severn. Though guided by a kindly tutor, he paid slight attention to his lessons, instead exercising his wit with smart remarks and verses. When he proceeded to Oxford, his childish faults worsened to dangerous drinking and gaming. Enamored of Kate, a friend's sister he met on a visit to London, he left Oxford without a degree and began less than halfhearted study of the law at Gray's Inn. He spent most of his time writing superficial verses for the magazines and for his sweetheart, whose influence restrained his unruliness. But when Kate left for a visit in the country, Peter threw himself recklessly into the world of the Fancy—boxing for sport, attending prize fights, financing boxers, and carousing until all hours at pugilistic taverns. When he wrote Kate a letter filled with boxing slang, she denounced him indignantly for his low pursuits, and he compounded his offense by responding with a jocular letter bristling with boxing puns. On Kate's return, Peter reformed temporarily, but soon drifted back to the Fancy, finally offending her beyond hope of pardon by appearing before her with two black eyes. When Kate rejected all his pleas for forgiveness, he sank into despair and died.

Peter Corcoran was Reynolds himself in a great many particulars: his birth date, his birthplace, his school, his tutor, his precocity, his profession, his admonishing sweetheart, his wit, his rapid writing, his renunciation of his muse, his interest in sports, and his conviviality. But some fictions set Peter apart from the author: Reynolds entered Shrewsbury School at nine, not seven; his mother was not a "rather illiterate woman"; he did not attend a university; and of course he did not lose either his self-control or his fiancée.

The irony achieved by the clash between the unnamed editor's moral disapproval and the reader's understanding that Reynolds's real purpose was to celebrate shady sports, made the introductory biography the best part of the book. The editor was a kind of colloquial Dr. Johnson (whom he quoted twice), mixing moralizing with sympathy as he presented the exemplum from which young men should learn. Like Dr. Johnson too, he was free with his adverse literary judgments: "There are some lines extant on the event; but they are not good."[19] The final assessment of Corcoran's style was a simplified version of Johnsonian balance: "His style of writing is not good; it is too broken, irresolute, and rugged,—and is too anxious in its search after smart expressions to be continuous or elevated in its substance. . . . He wrote with great rapidity, when he could bring himself to write at all; but he more often commenced than concluded works; and it was a common case for him, to plan and open a new piece at night which was neglected or forgotten in the morning."[20]

The biography included the finest sonnet Reynolds ever wrote, presented as the first of two examples of Corcoran's relinquishing poetic aspiration:

> Were this a feather from an eagle's wing,
> And thou, my tablet white! a marble tile
> Taken from ancient Jove's majestic pile,—
> And might I dip my feather in some spring,
> Adown Mount Ida, thread-like wandering:—
> And were my thoughts brought from some starry isle
> In heaven's blue sea,—I then might with a smile
> Write down a hymn to Fame, and proudly sing!
> But I am mortal; and I cannot write
> Aught that may foil the fatal wing of Time.
> Silent, I look to Fame: I cannot climb
> To where her temple is—Not mine the might:—
> I have some glimmering of what is sublime—
> But, ah! it is a most inconstant light.

Wistfulness and resignation temper Reynolds's sadness (Peter is Reynolds for the moment) at giving up his great dream of becoming a poet of the first order. The comic twist prevents any hint of bathos;

he is laughing a little at having taken himself so seriously. The classical references and personifications add solidity and weight, while at the same time they are managed with such a light touch that they blend with the flowing colloquial rhythm. The sonnet is a minor masterpiece which ought not to be neglected.

Reynolds veered sharply away from the deftness of the sonnet to the broadest of farce in the longest poem in the collection following the biography, *King Tims the First: an American Tragedy*. In the editor's introduction to the musical playlet, he had himself and his own *Peter Bell* in mind when he charged that Peter Corcoran's claim that an American wrote the "tragedy" could not be trusted because Peter "was fond of inflicting the glory of his little productions on the names of his acquaintance, or his favourite authors."[21] Peter Corcoran's introduction reported solemnly that he had asked a friend to send him from America copies of American editions of *Waverley* and *Guy Mannering* and that his friend had bought the books, wrapped them in loose sheets of paper he found in his backwoods hut, and sent them to London. To his surprise Peter found *King Tims the First* written on the wrappers. Neither his American correspondent nor he could identify the author, but he suggested either Morris Birkbeck or Richard Flower, prominent British settlers who both published letters from America. He proved that it could not be any of twelve English poets running from Byron to William Lisle Bowles by demonstrating that it lacked the salient features of each: for two examples, "Coleridge would have left it unfinished, or *gloomed* it with metaphysical lore:—Wordsworth, the man 'not ungently made,' would have turned it to a preparatory school for the brain's poor children, and put a pedlar into it, to talk a linsey-woolsey philosophy in uninhabited woods."[22]

The plot of the play was as simple as the other elements were extravagant. Tims, formerly a butcher on Dowgate hill, had brought his wife, his son, and an undertaker named Hatband to a backwoods settlement in Illinois, where at the time of the play a bankrupt, Mr. Jenkinsop, and his wife and daughter Jemima joined them. After longing for a man, even an Indian, Jemima loved the son Anthony Tims and he her. King Tims and Jenkinsop, thinking that they were deceiving each other, began illicit love affairs with each other's wives. Tims discovered the planned infidelity of his wife, murdered Jenkinsop and the two wives, and committed suicide. The play fit the title of the book only in part; the shady characters had been on the fringe of the Fancy before they left London, especially Tony Tims who had reveled in dog fights, bull-baiting, boxing, rowing matches, and gambling.[23]

Filled with puns, pompous posturing, grotesque mortuary humor, absurd romantic speeches, comic songs, and copious mock-pedantic footnotes, the musical playlet has something like Burns's wild abandon in *The Jolly Beggars,* but differs from Burns's cantata which has an underpinning of stark realism—one never for a moment supposes that Reynolds's clowns are real people. Reynolds labored to exploit every comic resource, and the strain shows, but after a century and a half it remains a laughable burlesque.

Next in the volume came *The Fields of Tothill,* a poem that treated almost every aspect of the Fancy. Of the remaining ten short poems, all but two, "When Lilies Lie Uneasily at Rest" and "Stanzas on Revisiting Shrewsbury," were comic. Reynolds reserved for last place the best of the short pieces, "What Is Life?" a miniature counterpart in verse to Hazlitt's "The Fight." In skipping octosyllabic couplets, cleverly rhymed and sprinkled with slang, he recounted step by step all his activities on the day of the fight: rising at dawn, dressing sportively, taking a gig from the livery stable, racing to Moulsey Hurst, viewing the spirited crowd, and focusing at the close on the statuesque boxer about to begin "the Fight!" He was mostly serious in expressing his intense enthusiasm for boxing and all that surrounded it; it was life's greatest good, life itself in emotional fulfillment. And yet, as in Hazlitt, one senses that Reynolds felt, and expected the reader to see, the irony of an intellectual's being swept away by so flashy and earthy a sport. It was the sense of mental unbending that made the colorful spectacle especially gratifying.

Periodicals hailed the success of *The Fancy* as enthusiastically as Reynolds could have hoped, ranking it "with the first of humourous and satirical productions."[24] The only dissent came from Gold's *London Magazine,* which included it in a general attack (not a review) on all pugilistic literature, and Reynolds could discount that attack because Gold's *London* was known to be biased in its competition with Baldwin's *London,* with which Reynolds was loosely associated at the time. Reynolds's authorship of the anonymous book was not a well-kept secret. Francis Jeffrey knew soon after publication that

Reynolds wrote it. Reynolds's reply of 13 July 1820 to a lost letter from Jeffrey reveals that Jeffrey had agreed to consider an article on it in the *Edinburgh Review,* probably by one of Reynolds's friends: "The Fancy article you shall receive in time certainly,—by the 12th."[25] But the review did not appear in the *Edinburgh;* either the friend did not send it, or Jeffrey decided not to print it.

The *Blackwood's* group knew that Reynolds was the author[26] and continued their efforts to befriend him with a surprisingly long review of a dozen pages. The reviewer, probably Lockhart who had heard favorable reports of Reynolds from both J. H. Christie and P. G. Patmore, entered completely into the spirit of the hoax, pretending that Peter Corcoran had been a real person, claiming that he had once planned to edit Corcoran himself, and valuing especially the entertaining "Stanzas Written during a Voyage in Search of a North-West Passage, and Addressed to a Northern Princess" because of "having it in the author's own hand-writing."[27]

Reynolds and Woodhouse were delighted with the *Blackwood's* review, the latter wondering, "Where the d——ce could the Scotsman have purloined so much wit & humour from?"[28] Bryan Waller Procter's favorable review in the *London* seemed "a very tame one in comparison," though Reynolds was highly pleased by Procter's praise of "Where Lilies Lie Uneasily at Rest" as "very sweetly written notwithstanding the Editor's note." Reynolds had said in the note that "It only wants a meaning to be a perfect sonnet."[29] On 4 July Reynolds wrote Taylor, "What say you to Blackwood?—Is it not clever and apt.—I am & have been really amused with it."[30]

The hoax Reynolds and Woodhouse perpetrated on Woodhouse's sister Nan heightened Reynolds's amusement. Woodhouse had written Nan, exulting at length in the glories of attending boxing bouts and enclosing a copy of Reynolds's "Sonnet on the Nonpareil" (Jack Randall). Amazed and indignant, Nan protested in her reply against both Woodhouse's enthusiasm for the vulgar sport and the sonnet.[31] Introducing much of the letter into *The Fancy* as one of Kate's to Peter Corcoran, Reynolds quoted closely, changing only words and phrases here and there. When the book came out in June, Eliza Drewe, who was in on the secret and was visiting Nan in Bath, "had much amusement in making malicious enquiries, & hearing [Woodhouse's] sister wonder how her letter could have got into the Book." Keeping Nan in the dark, Eliza wrote Reynolds an account of her

part in the trick, which he read to Woodhouse. Trying to prolong
the joke through one more step, Woodhouse urged Taylor, who had
recently arrived in Bath, to show Nan *Blackwood's* review, continuing the pretense that Corcoran had been a real person who was a
friend of Woodhouse's.[32]

Delighted as he was by the *Blackwood's* review, Reynolds was
pleased in a different way by the *New Monthly's* recommendation
that he not "deprive the world of the pure gratification which it
would receive from his deeper and gentler effusions."[33] Such words
kept alive the hopes he still retained for the serious poetry he had
written during his years of association with Keats.

Woodhouse expected that *The Fancy* would go to a second edition, and Reynolds evidently shared that expectation, for he made a
number of minor changes in the copy he presented to his mother,
but it did not.[34] Next to *Peter Bell,* however, it has received the most
attention from later generations. Edmund Gosse discussed it favorably in *Gossip in a Library,*[35] and later John Masefield edited a reprint with an introduction.[36]

While engaged on *The Fancy,* Reynolds took a little time off to
write an amusing prologue to James Sheridan Knowles's *Virginius,*
first performed at Covent Garden on 17 May 1820 and published
in numerous editions, some crediting the prologue erroneously to
T. Reynolds, though many editions and Macready's *Reminiscences*
assign it correctly to J. H. Reynolds.[37] In thirty-eight lines of brisk
heroic couplets, he enlivened the conventional appeal for the audience to approve the author's efforts by having the actress speaking
the prologue champion women's loquacity and enter into a mild
battle of the sexes with the male actors.

Keats's worsening illness had saddened Reynolds during the first
half of 1820, but it had not so clouded his outlook as to prevent
popular successes in the less ambitious kind of writing to which he
was to turn increasingly in subsequent years.

CHAPTER 11

The *Lamia* Volume
and Fanny Brawne—
June–December 1820

B USY AS REYNOLDS WAS with his legal work and his own writing, his concern for Keats continued during the spring and summer of 1820. Keats was reluctant to publish the fragmentary *Hyperion* along with all the other completed poems in *Lamia, Isabella, the Eve of St. Agnes, and Other Poems*. After Taylor and Woodhouse insisted, he wrote opposite the editorial headnote in one of the presentation copies, "This is none of my doing—I was ill at the time."[1] Shortly before the publication of the *Lamia* volume in early July, Keats considered publishing it, or perhaps part of it, "with a work of Leigh Hunt"—probably the *Indicator*—where Keats did publish other poems not included in the *Lamia* volume such as *La Belle Dame*, "As Hermes Once," and an extract from *The Cap and Bells*. When Reynolds learned of Keats's intention, he wrote him "a letter of remonstrance . . . against the printing the marvellous fragment of Hyperion with a work of Leigh Hunt."[2] Realizing how detrimental Keats's association with Hunt had been to the public reception of his first two volumes and determined to do everything in his power to assist Keats in securing proper recognition for the third, Reynolds succeeded in persuading Keats against linking the epic fragment with Hunt's name. His opinion of Hunt personally had sunk to its lowest, as his diatribe against Hunt to Taylor a little later disclosed, but Reynolds had not changed his own liberal politics, for he "longed to get him free from being a Political adherent to a good, though then dangerous Side for a young Poet."[3]

As the time approached for the publication of Keats's *Lamia* volume in the first days of July, Reynolds mounted an energetic campaign to have the book favorably reviewed. Before it was officially published, he wrote a review and sent it to William Jerdan, who

printed only extracts from the book, and not the review, in the
Literary Gazette. Reynolds was disgusted with "the damn'd Literary
Gazette," but later he repressed his anger and was polite to Jerdan,
telling him that he could do whatever he wanted with the review,
"Even unto the feeding of the fire!"[4]

In correspondence with Francis Jeffrey about his own renewed
writing for the *Edinburgh Review,* which did not materialize, Reynolds suggested that Jeffrey review the *Lamia* volume. When Jeffrey
asked for further information about Keats, Reynolds answered in a
fashion calculated to encourage the review:

> Mr. Keats is young—22 I should think. He was educated for a Surgeon,
> but has been foolish enough to abandon his profession and trust to his
> books and a very trifling income left by his Father. He is an orphan. His
> health is now in the worst state, for as his medical man tells me he is in
> a decided consumption, of which malady his mother & Brother died. He
> is advised—nay ordered—to go to Italy; but in such a state it is a hopeless
> doom. Owing to Leigh Hunt's fatal patronage, Keats' name and fate have
> been joined with his in the Quarterly and Blackwoods magazine. By his
> friends he is very much beloved; and I know of no one who with such
> talents is so unaffected and sincere, or who with rich personal abuse, as
> he has suffered, could be so cheerful & so firm. His politics are strong
> against the Quarterly Review. I do not, my dear sir, at all ask you to
> review his book, unless you are disposed to do it, from reading it, as it
> were a book put into your hands by a Stranger.[5]

Keats was twenty-four, not twenty-two; with only the general impression that Keats was younger than he, Reynolds set his age back
as far as he honestly could to make his poetic achievement seem
the more remarkable and to evoke sympathy for so young a man beset by political enemies. Not only the Tories, but many moderate
Whigs—John Scott, for example—were not enamored of Leigh Hunt,
and Reynolds expected that Jeffrey would understand Keats's mis-
fortune in being linked to him. He inferred mistakenly that Keats's
"trifling income" came from his father because Keats had not explained, and Reynolds had never inquired. He called Keats "foolish" for abandoning his profession, but in so doing he made it clear
to Jeffrey that Keats needed the favorable review. He not only indicated that Keats agreed with Jeffrey in politics, but called attention
to the unfair attacks in the *Quarterly* and *Blackwood's* so that Jeffrey
would be inclined to defend him from their common political oppo-

nents. His last remark, that he would not have Jeffrey review Keats except impartially, was both strategic and safe; it might have been counterproductive to press too hard, and he was confident that an objective critic could not fail to be impressed by Keats's masterpieces.

John Taylor was optimistic that Reynolds had succeeded in convincing Jeffrey and counted on the favorable review in the *Edinburgh* to improve sales so that he might advance the money for Keats's trip to Italy. On 10 August 1820, he wrote his father, "They [poems in the *Lamia* volume] do *not sell very well,* but I rather think the Edinburgh Review will give them a lift, whatever the Quarterly may do. On the strength of this we must rest our Defence for advancing him so much as will carry him to Rome & back again, for he has no one else to look to, now his Brother George has borrowed all his remaining Money, & taken it to America."[6] Jeffrey published his laudatory review in the issue dated August.[7] but it probably did not reach readers until a month or so later, since the *Edinburgh* was notoriously late. Following Reynolds's erroneous estimate he called Keats "a very young man."

Reynolds encouraged only indirectly the reviews of *Endymion* and the *Lamia* volume in the *Scots Magazine* for August and October by influencing Jeffrey to review Keats favorably in the *Edinburgh*. Jeffrey's decision to review Keats was all the stimulus Robert Morehead needed to notice him also in Constable's other publication. Reynolds did not write the two-part review, though he must have welcomed its praise. Constable did not mention any request for a review of Keats in his letter to Reynolds of 21 August, in which he did refer to Reynolds's "Living Authors, A Dream," published in the same issue as the review. The review does not have one dash in it except for the few that introduce long quotations. Reynolds, however, used the dash more heavily than any other writer; he was incapable of writing seven pages of prose without a single dash used to separate clauses or phrases. Furthermore, the author of the review was a Scot, for he wrote "The picture of Thea, *in* p. 147, is very beautiful," a Scotticism that Reynolds could not have written.[8]

Reynolds continued to support Keats loyally despite friction caused by the Reynolds family's disapproval of Fanny Brawne. In fairness to the Reynoldses, it must be stressed that Fanny Brawne did have faults which other clear-sighted people like Keats, George Keats, Brown, Charles Dilke, and William Dilke also saw. Keats attracted Fanny as soon as she met him; she later reproached him for waiting so long to return her affection.[9] Presumably she wished to put her best foot forward when she was with Keats, and yet Keats found her "silly, fashionable and strange" and "ignorant—monstrous in her behaviour flying out in all directions, calling people such names—that I was forced lately to make use of the term *Minx*."[10] The Reynoldses had been friends with the Dilkes for a long time, perhaps a decade, and they visited in each other's houses from time to time. At the Dilkes' the Reynoldses had ample opportunity to see Fanny for what she was, both when Keats was present and when he was not. If she was "monstrous" when Keats was there, she must have been even worse when he was not; since the others were not in love with her, there was no reason for them to excuse her conduct. Years earlier Charlotte Reynolds had written Dovaston that she hated the idea of a sensible man marrying a fool; it seemed to her that Keats was in danger of marrying just such a person, who was both "silly" and "ignorant."

Although George Keats did not approach Fanny with complete objectivity, because persons he very much respected, probably the Reynoldses and Charles Dilke, warned him "that she was an artful bad hearted Girl,"[11] he did see her for himself during three weeks of January 1820, and his testimony deserves attention. He saw in her a "want of affection for her Sister and respect for her Mother."[12] The appearance of lack of affection for a younger sister may not have mattered much because it is common for the oldest child to take the younger children for granted, but the lack of respect for the widowed mother striving to preserve her family must have galled Charlotte Reynolds and Jane and Marianne, who appreciated their own mother's firm and loving care.

Everyone but Robert Gittings has agreed that William Dilke spoke the truth when he said that his elder brother Charles also disapproved of Fanny.[13] Later Dilke was Fanny's friend and assisted her with the management of her finances, but that did not mean that while Keats was alive Dilke approved morally of her character or conduct. Jane Reynolds had the lowest possible opinion of Fanny in 1820, and yet she later became the good friend with whom Fanny and her husband stayed for an extended period when they first went to Germany. After his ambiguous behavior toward Fanny, Brown too thought that she had "many faults."[14]

All Keats's biographers have inferred that jealousy motivated the Reynolds women's dislike of Fanny and that their unreasoned antipathy swayed John Hamilton Reynolds in his sharp attacks on her. But as it has been noted earlier, there is no evidence that Charlotte looked possessively upon Keats as a prospective son-in-law or that Jane or Marianne was amorously interested in him. It is not fact that jealousy was involved, but inference. Keats was their brother's close friend and (they thought) their close friend, a wonderful person who deserved better than what all the evidence at the time revealed Fanny Brawne to be. Along with other members of the Keats circle, they were mistaken in not perceiving in Fanny staunchness and loyalty. But Fanny's behavior, not their malice, should be blamed for their failure to understand.

The Reynoldses' disapproval of Fanny can be clearly documented. Early in July 1820 Miss Reynolds, probably Jane, wrote Maria Dilke, "I hear that Keats is going to Rome, which must please all his friends on every account. . . . and absence may probably weaken, if not break off, a connexion that has been a most unhappy one for him."[15] On 21 September, after Keats had left for Italy, Reynolds wrote Taylor, "I cannot now but hold a hope of his refreshed health, which I confess his residence in England greatly discouraged, particularly as he was haunted by one or two heartless and *demented* people whose opinions and conduct could not but silently influence the bearings of his Thoughts & hopes. Absence from the poor idle Thing of woman-kind, to whom he has so unaccountably attached himself, will not be an ill thing."[16]

What happened between Keats and the Reynoldses in their heated disagreement over Fanny Brawne must be inferred from reading behind the lines of Keats's letters, with the lack of certainty that inevitably accompanies such inference. In his letter to Fanny Brawne of June (?) 1820, Keats made it very clear that he knew the Reynoldses, and probably also the Dilkes, were disparaging and mocking Fanny, and his bitterness suggests that he was prepared to do something about it:

My friends laugh at you! I know some of them—when I know them all I shall never think of them again as friends or even acquaintance. My friends have behaved well to me in every instance but one, and there they have b[e]come tattlers, and inquisitors into my conduct: spying upon a secret I would rather die than share it with any body's confidence. For this I cannot wish them well, I care not to see any of them again. If I am the Theme, I will not be the Friend of idle Gossips. Good gods what a shame it is our Loves should be so put into the microscope of a Coterie. Their laughs should not affect you (I may perhaps give you reasons some day for these laughs, for I suspect a few people to hate me well enough, *for reasons I know of,* who have pretended a great friendship for me) when in competition with one, who if he never should see you again would make you the saint of his memory—These Laughers, who do not like you, who envy you for your Beauty, who would have God-bless'd-me from you for ever: who were plying me with disencouragements with respect to you eternally. People are revengeful—do not mind them—do nothing but love me—[17]

Some time in mid-June 1820, when Keats was living alone at 2 Wesleyan Place, Kentish Town, he did tell his friends to stop their unwelcome interference in his love life, and he was so blunt that he believed he had hurt the Reynoldses' feelings. After the quarrel was over and he had calmed down, Keats remembered all the unselfish kindness and friendship they had shown him over the years, and he decided he should apologize. Although Brown omitted the name, the circumstantial evidence is so strong that it is almost certain Keats referred to Reynolds when he wrote Brown about 21 June 1820: "When you hear or see XXXXXX it is probable you will hear some complaints against me, which this notice is not intended to forestall. The fact is I did behave badly; but it is to be attributed to my health, spirits, and the disadvantageous ground I stand on in society. I would go and accommodate matters, if I were not too weary of the world. I know that they are more happy and comfortable than I am; therefore why should I trouble myself about it?"[18]

Rollins noted that "Bodurtha and Pope suggest Bailey, and add that Keats's bad behavior may concern the disapproval he felt about Bailey's sudden marriage." But that cannot be right because Keats could not possibly in his physical condition "go and accommodate matters" all the way to Carlisle, where Bailey lived. He could, however, manage to go from Kentish Town to Little Britain, since he was able to go to town at this time for other reasons. Aside from Reynolds, the only other reasonable candidate for the six X's would be Dilke; Brown was closer to Dilke than to Reynolds and would certainly expect to hear from him or see him. But it was not Dilke because Dilke very probably had been referred to earlier in the letter by three and four X's. In Brown's "Life of Keats," there are two certain references to Dilke, which are represented by four X's and three X's.[19] Brown did not use more than four X's to represent so short a name as Dilke. On the other hand, in the certain instance when he referred to Reynolds, he did use six X's for the longer name.[20] There can be little doubt that it was the Reynoldses to whom Keats felt he owed an apology.

It is probable that Keats continued to regret his attack on his old friends for meddling in his love affair, and that Reynolds is the name omitted in his last letter to Brown from Rome (though this time Brown used only five X's): "I have not written to XXXXX yet, which he must think very neglectful; being anxious to send him a good account of my health, I have delayed it from week to week. If I recover, I will do all in my power to correct the mistakes made during sickness; and if I should not, all my faults will be forgiven."[21]

Keats was right. Reynolds did not change his opinion of Fanny Brawne during Keats's lifetime, as his blistering reference to her in the letter to Taylor showed, but neither he nor his family ever gave the slightest hint of any ruffled feelings after Keats's death. After a number of years and closer acquaintance, Jane Reynolds Hood changed her opinion of Fanny and became a good friend. The Hoods and the Lindos (Fanny's husband Louis later changed the name to Lindon) met often and cordially as members of the Dilke circle; the Lindos carried a parcel and letters to the Hoods in Germany; Jane and Fanny exchanged letters; Fanny visited Jane in Germany; and Fanny wrote for *Hood's Magazine*.[22]

Reynolds did not stay in London to join Taylor, Woodhouse, and others in seeing Keats off on the trip to Italy. He had had a busy summer, some of his time devoted to advancing Keats's reputation, and he looked forward to the long vacation from the end of August through September that he had always taken from 1812 through 1819 with the exception of 1817. It was not just his own pleasure that he would have sacrificed if he had canceled his vacation; Eliza Drewe had come to count on it—they had spent his vacation together in Devonshire in 1816, 1818, and 1819—and they had special plans for this year. After 12 August Keats was staying at the Brawnes', and, if Reynolds had stayed in London to visit him, his strong disapproval of Fanny Brawne would have caused friction, which was the last thing Keats needed. At the time Reynolds left London on 1 September,[23] no decision had been made as to when Keats would sail for Italy. He knew Keats could not spend another winter in England, as he reported to Francis Jeffrey, but for all he knew Keats might leave in October when he would have returned from his vacation. When Taylor wrote him immediately after Keats's departure on 17 September, he was gratified, but also surprised that the deed had been done so swiftly. "I do not know when I have been more gratified at the receipt of a letter than now, for you give me the best of news, full to the brim, that Keats is positively off for a better Lungland.— There is no half-measure information of expected departure or promised amendment,—but smack you come down upon me with the *Ultimatum* to Sir John. Your Alphabet commences at Z. Your Letter is in *finals* only."[24]

His wish that he could have been present along with Taylor, Woodhouse, and the others to say farewell bore no more than a trace of self-reproach, if any. He still loved Keats, "If ever I wished well to man, I wish well to *him!*"[25] He and his family had done all they could for Keats. The decline in intimacy between Keats and the others in his family had been Keats's doing, not his or his family's. There had been no possibility of the Reynoldses' nursing him during his last seven months in England; if they had invited him to Little Britain, he would have refused. Powerless to care for Keats himself, Reynolds was even grateful to the Brawnes for taking him into their home during the most trying time. "You scarcely tell me enough, I fancy, of the Brawnes, or whether Keats said anything of *them* before he left. They have been really attentive to him, which we should not forget."[26] Like others, he had some reservations about Severn's fitness as a traveling companion, but he had visited Severn along with Keats so often that he knew the pleasure Keats took in Severn's company would compensate in some measure for any problems caused by Severn's weakness.

When Reynolds heard during the summer that the managers of the Lambeth Female Asylum, where George Reynolds had served part time as writing master for fifteen years, were planning to cut his father's annual salary from £50 to £30 as an economy measure, John Reynolds on 4 July 1820 asked John Taylor to write Lord Radstock, a member of the board, to oppose the reduction if careful inquiry showed it to be unwarranted. Considerate of his father's feelings and uncertain whether Taylor would agree to help, Reynolds said nothing to his father of his effort.[27] He was evidently successful in preventing the reduction, for the salary of the writing master remained £50 in subsequent years.[28]

In his own work that always supplemented his legal vocation, Reynolds was a beehive of activity this summer, but he planned more writing than he could accomplish. He wrote little of the prose tales for Constable, and he did not publish either the criticism of the comic drama in conjunction with B. W. Procter's treatment of the tragic or the review of Hazlitt that he proposed to Jeffrey for the *Edinburgh*. He hoped to do some kind of writing for Henry Brougham, possibly legal or political, but there is no evidence that Brougham engaged him. His hesitant request for an advance of £40 or £50 on work to be done for the *Edinburgh* indicated that he continued to need money.[29]

Following up the success of *The Fancy*, he wrote for the *London Magazine* a two-part article, "The Jewels of the Book," describing sports and shady underworld characters.[30] Bestowing jocular praise on Pierce Egan's *Sporting Anecdotes*, he selected several characters from it to describe half sympathetically and half satirically. Always a sports enthusiast, he expanded Egan's sketches by drawing upon his own knowledge of boxing, bowling, and cricket. He praised particularly the well-known boxer John Jackson and a fighting dog named Street-walker. By chance he mentioned that he found the recently published *Memoirs* of R. L. Edgeworth very dull.[31]

In the same issue as the first part of "The Jewels of the Book," John Scott in "Lion's Head"—a regular department devoted to editorial comment on the affairs of the magazine—started a good-natured quarrel with Reynolds about his judgment of Edgeworth's *Memoirs*. Scott had reviewed the book favorably in May[32] and took issue with Reynolds's disparagement of it:

We have now, however, an account of another sort to settle with our *fanciful* contributor: Mr. Egan's encomiast: Mr. Jackson's admirer: the dealer in jewels: and what is still more to his credit in our eyes, the warmhearted friend of old Street-walker, the Bull-dog, whose promised Biography we long to receive. What astonishes us is, how any man, who has good taste enough to cherish these partialities, should not like Mr. Edgeworth's Memoirs, written by himself! . . . That he has not judged for himself in regard to it, we are sure, for there is no man whose taste we have a better opinion of. We are confident, for instance, that he thinks highly of Mr. Keats' last volume of poetry (which we mean to review in our next number), and that he regards the joke of electing one of Blackwood's Editors to be professor of moral Philosophy, as infinitely more laughable than anything that has ever appeared in the pages of that work. That such an one should undervalue the amusement furnished by Mr. Edgeworth's Memoirs is lamentable.[33]

Despite all the scurrilous abuse that John Wilson had written in *Blackwood's,* he had been elected Professor of Moral Philosophy at the University of Edinburgh earlier in 1820, and his new position made him an easy target for the satire of his opponents.

In September Reynolds began the second installment of his article by reiterating his earlier censure of Edgeworth's *Memoirs* and insisting that the book was ridiculously egotistical. He evidently enjoyed this paper warfare, for he argued his case with a merry spirit and closed with a humorous boast, "Therefore, right valiant Head! having given the return blow, and met thy defiance in the periodical ring, as becomes us,—we leave the public to decide whether we have *darkened thy daylights or not.*"[34] He referred to Keats's poetry twice: first in the account of the dog, "From this time, having got into high hands, the fame of Street-walker began to grow: it grew fifty times better than Isabella's potted basil, of which so much has been lately said." Later, in discussing the pleasures of driving out of town to attend sporting events, he quoted from *Ode to Fancy,* "Well does one of the best poets of the age say,—'Pleasure never is at home.' "[35]

Reynolds also showed that he agreed with the "Lion's Head" opinion of John Wilson, as well as with his estimate of Keats. Egan had told a comic story of an ass who wandered into a lady's library and ate several of her books. Reynolds pretended to have personal knowledge of this "singular circumstance" and added a number of details which he said were unknown to Egan. His list of books which only a stupid ass could devour included John Wilson's *The City of the Plague* and John Wilson Croker's *Battle of Talavera; The City of the Plague* was so bad that it disagreed with the ass. Reynolds's unrelenting attitude toward the Tory critics at this time showed a disinterested loyalty to his friends, for he had enjoyed the jocosely favorable treatment of *The Fancy* in *Blackwood's.*

Not content to let Reynolds have the last word in the dispute about Edgeworth's *Memoirs,* Scott replied crisply in "Lion's Head" in the same number of the *London:*

Lion's Head presents compliments to Fighting Dog's Biographer: flatters itself that it knows what is due to both parties in the dispute—a good contributor on one side, and an Oracular Letter-Box on the other. Indeed L.H. feels, very sensibly, the handsome manner in which F.D.B. has contrived to acknowledge his error, in appearing to maintain himself in the right. His objecting to Mr. Edgeworth, that, in writing his *own* Memoirs, he sometimes alludes to *himself,* is perhaps as elegant an artifice of this nature as has ever been practised.[36]

The September issue also included Reynolds's "Address Spoken, in the Character of the Comic Muse, by Miss Kelly."[37] After praising Fanny Kelly in his theatrical reviews in the *Champion,* Reynolds, as well as Lamb, became her friend and wrote these amusing verses for her to deliver on stage.

He still planned to write the book of prose tales in two volumes for which he had contracted with Constable in November 1819.[38] In response to his letter of 10 May 1820, Constable complained on 15 May that he was "at a loss indeed to imagine how you had managed to lose sight of your agreement," asked him to supply a title for listing in a prepublication catalogue, and pleaded with him to supply their London printer, Mr. Moyes, with manuscript copy. Reynolds wrote on 20 June to suggest as a title either "Tales of a Ferryman" or "The Sempstresses," neither of which Constable liked.[39] Reynolds wrote on 18 August to report that he had submitted some beginning copy to the printer and to ask that the publication date be postponed until the Christmas season. Delighted at what they thought was movement toward a profitable book at last, Constable and Company agreed to the postponement.[40]

Constable's editor of the *Scots Magazine,* the Reverend Robert Morehead, was even more pleased than his employer at the postponement of the book, for Reynolds also sent along with his letter of 18 August as a peace offering a fine article entitled "Living Authors, A Dream."[41] In it he incorporated most of an earlier essay from the *Champion,* "Pilgrimage of the Living Poets to the Stream of Castaly"; but "Living Authors" is not so much a revision as a new article based on the same idea as the old, with the first two-thirds consisting of a long introduction not in the earlier essay.[42] Recalling his last article, "Boswell Redivivus," which had been a dream vision, Reynolds requested permission to sleep in the columns of the magazine again. He pretended that after encountering Boswell in a dream, he made every effort to induce another vision, but without much success until recently. In explaining how he finally succeeded, he mentioned that he made a practice of seeking the society of literary people and observing their peculiarities of thought, manner, and person.

Among the literary men he had met, Reynolds continued, were Samuel Rogers and Lord Byron, with whom he had dined on different occasions. His tribute to Coleridge's eloquence was a pleasant change from his usual ridicule of the great poet, "I have heard, and thrilled while I hear[d] the round and rolling periods come from the mouth of the celebrated metaphysician and poet of the age, as from an ocean cavern,—grand—deep—eternal; or as from the sea itself." He objected once again to Wordsworth's haughtiness, comparing Haydon's portrait of him in *Christ's Entry into Jerusalem* with his usual demeanor in society and finding the former inappropriate, for he was "there bowed down with humility." Despite Wordsworth's egotism, however, Reynolds still believed that he was " 'a great personage,' and would be greater, if he did not think himself the greatest." His opinion of Lamb was more favorable, "The writer of John Woodvil I have known well, and commend me to him for the vigour of his judgment, the nicety of his taste, and the fine severity of his wit. He cuts with his tongue the tumours of men's minds. His discourse amongst that of other men 'sticks fiery off indeed.' He is a bright little man,—the stilletto of conversation."

Having indicated his familiarity with these eminent men of the age, Reynolds explained that he had made a habit not only of cultivating their acquaintance, but also of preserving his impressions of them in commonplace books "of a reasonable size, neatly bound, ordered after the method of the great Mr. Locke, to be had of two worthy booksellers, yclept Taylor and Hessey, 93 Fleet Street, price only 12s." We may be sure that he was not employing a convenient fiction, for in the *Champion* he had quoted from a commonplace book on one occasion and transcribed an entire article from one on another.[43] The only one of his commonplace books that has been preserved is at the Bristol Central Library; unfortunately the others have not survived.

In odd moments, Reynolds continued, he liked to thumb through the index of his commonplace book, select a name, and call up an image by reading his own account. Under the letter *O,* he selected

the name of Amelia Opie, novelist, poet, and the cousin of Richard
Woodhouse. She was "the pride of the Blues," and in her fashionable
circle the value of a book was determined by the name of the author
instead of the contents. If the book were by Hazlitt, it must be condemned instantly; but if the charming Henry Luttrell, whose *Advice
to Julia* had just appeared, were the author, it must be a very fine
book indeed. The mention of Hazlitt led Reynolds to pay his finest
tribute to his idol, as well as to record one of his personal peculiarities:

> But let me not here omit the society of one, whose mind is the store-
> house of all deep thoughts and proud imaginations. If his early hopes,
> from their very ardour, have been broken and frustrated, still the memory
> of those hopes sheds a melancholy thoughtfulness over his mind, and over
> his countenance, which awakens in others a fellow pensiveness. He is the
> first prose writer of the age, and yet of manners simple and modest as a
> child. The world, by repeated blows, has stricken him into patience. He
> has learned to *endure,* in a hard school. His keen, yet serious face, en-
> circled by its raven hair, has all the intellect and quiet power of one of
> Titian's portraits. His prose is lion-hearted, and lion-sinewed. His style
> of writing, however, it must be confessed, is very superior to his style of
> shaking hands. The first is all eagerness, intensity, and vigour; the last is
> cold, tame, and indecisive. He appears to abandon a bunch of melancholy
> fingers to your threatened squeeze, with some hope of their not coming
> to a shake. . . . I wish he would "palpably confirm his grasp" in future,
> that my own paw may not be disconcerted or lured into the same lifeless
> habits. But what has this to do with his strong and impressive writings?
> Nothing. Only I find it recorded in my observant book, and therefore I
> cannot choose but remember it. He is a good hearted man, as well as a
> fine minded one,—good hearted still, in spite of rude usage, and the de-
> spoiled poetry of his youthful hopes. May he yet see a happy sunset after
> all the boisterous gustiness of his morning.[44]

In a letter to Hunt of 21 April 1821, Hazlitt wrote that he did
not see Reynolds for a year and a half after securing him a place in
the *Edinburgh Review*.[45] In one of his irritable moods when he
wrote the letter, he implied that Reynolds had deserted him. By
the summer of 1820 the year and a half had elapsed, Reynolds was
seeing Hazlitt again, and his admiration for him was as great as before the interruption in their personal contact.

After paying high tribute to Hazlitt, Reynolds next explained how he managed to induce the dream. Late one evening he had read for hours in the collection of literary treasures in his commonplace book until he fell asleep and dreamed. At this point he inserted the earlier essay, "The Pilgrimage of Living Poets to the Stream of Castaly," in revised form; with a few exceptions he repeated the same criticism of the poets that had appeared in the *Champion,* but in some cases he brought his comments up to date by adding references to works that had been published after the first essay.

Under his pseudonym Peter Corcoran, he introduced a humorous comment on the decline of his own literary aspirations. When Peter Corcoran requested the water of inspiration, the spirit of the stream first discouraged him because he had become a lawyer and then dismissed him outright for making a bad pun. Other significant additions were contemptuous allusions to William Gifford and John Wilson Croker.

The most important omission was Leigh Hunt, whose poetry he had praised highly in the essay in the *Champion.* His attitude toward Hunt had changed drastically during the years after 1816: a month after this article appeared, he wrote John Taylor that one of the chief advantages of Keats's trip to Italy would be his separation from Hunt: "And who would not be banished from the vain and heartless eternity of Mr Leigh Hunt's indecent discoursings. I quite pity you the three days visits of that feeble man,—not on account of the ill-conditioned power of his tongue (for I could not wish him a more wholesome medicine than your own good sense)—but for the irksome, wearing consciousness of a disgusting presence, than which I know of nothing more dispiriting."[46]

In a postscript to the article, Reynolds wrote, "I have a third very good dream in my head," but a third dream never appeared in the magazine. A reader detected the incorporation of an old article into the new and charged him with misconduct. The October issue included this notice:

A Correspondent has brought a charge of Plagiarism against the writer of "Living Authors, A Dream," which appeared in one of our late Numbers. We have too high an opinion of that writer's originality to suppose that any other person ever dreamed his dream; but, like people who are fond of repeating their dreams, he may, for any thing we know to the contrary, have related it before. We wish, to put the matter out of doubt, that he would send us his third dream, without delay, and, if it is akin to the former, and has never been seen elsewhere, the accusation will be laid to rest.[47]

The correspondent had cited the first article in the *Champion,* and the editor realized at once what Reynolds had done, for Reynolds signed the first article with his initials. He valued Reynolds's services enough to overlook the matter, but he received no further contributions.

By the end of the summer of 1820, Reynolds had worked busily to finish his articles for the *London* and the *Scots Magazine* and to clear up all pressing legal business before he left on vacation. Writing to William Jerdan from Rice's place at 50 Poland Street, Reynolds declined a dinner invitation at Jerdan's with Procter and explained that he could not spare the time.[48] Having looked forward longingly to the vacation for six months—he described his anticipation and the vacation in some of the best prose he ever wrote in "Exmouth Wrestling"[49]—he took a hackney cab to Piccadilly, full of such exultation that he willingly overpaid the coachman who was shrewd enough to notice that Reynolds would not object. From Piccadilly he took the impressive Exeter coach, lording it, in his imagination, over the mere city-dwellers he passed as he watched the successive neighborhoods of London recede from his view. Arrived in Exeter, rumpled and weary after not sleeping for a night, but still happy, he both savored and laughed silently at the combination of affectionate and frivolous remarks from the Drewe family, probably including Eliza's mother and two sisters Lucy and Ann, as well as Eliza: "dear! what a very odd hat you have!" [surely from Eliza], "you are really grown, or you appear to be so!" "you are certainly thinner!" and most inane of all, "how natural your voice sounds."[50]

Eliza Drewe *induced* him—he liked that private pun on the parallel between her name and the Latin, and "Lion's Head" snapped it up when he submitted his article to the *London*—to join with her in renting a small brick house at nearby Exmouth on the seashore, other members of her family accompanying as companions and chaperones. There they were free to do nothing at all or whatever they pleased, gathering seashells as long as they had nothing to put them in and then losing interest immediately when he bought a basket to hold them. Looking idly out the window one morning after breakfast, he saw workmen building a ring and booths, and the servant-woman told him that they were preparing for a traditional set of Devon and Cornish wrestling matches. With Eliza no doubt accompanying him, he joined the country lads and lasses in watching the rural strong men compete. His happiness during the vacation at the close of a productive and successful year was marred only by his sorrow at Keats's tragic illness; as he gazed at the waves beating up on the seashore, a phrase from the poem Keats had written him when he was so ill in 1818, "an untumultuous fringe of silver foam" from the epistle "To J. H. Reynolds, Esq.," popped into his head and he quoted it in his essay in the *London,* though his readers could have no notion of where it came from or what it meant to him.[51] His and Keats's situations were reversed two years after Keats had written him the treasured poem during his dangerous illness.

After his vacation Reynolds waited anxiously in London, like other members of the Keats circle, for news of Keats in Italy. By 23 November he had heard of Keats's safe arrival in Naples, and by 5 December he planned to write to Keats.[52] He continued to meet socially with some of Keats's old friends; before 21 December he held a card party for "the batch of Brag players," including Brown and probably Rice and Martin, in his quarters at 18 Portland Street, Poland Street, where Brown was jubilant at winning £2.10.[53]

When Benjamin Bailey came down to London some time after Reynolds's vacation and before the end of the year, Reynolds did not allow any hard feelings from the Bailey-Marianne Reynolds quarrel to prevent him from meeting and talking with his and Keats's old friend. Reynolds told Bailey that in the bitterness of his fatal illness "poor Keats attributed his approaching end to the poisonous pen of Lockhart."[54] John Scott, who began his devastating attacks on Lockhart and *Blackwood's* in the November *London,* thought that Reynolds should have relieved him of the painful duty.[55]

But Scott's suggestion was little more than a passing thought; as editor of the *London* he was responsible for the decision to "abate a public nuisance," and it was better that he mount the attack with his own direct and forceful pen. Reynolds contented himself for the moment with a satirical thrust at John Wilson in the December issue of the *London.* After praising a young wrestler named Cann in "Exmouth Wrestling," he wrote: "Mr. Wilson, the Plague-Poet, and *Moral Professor,* is very fond of running about the Highlands, wrestling and leaping with the distillers of his favourite beverage whiskey. We wish he would try a fall with the younger Cann, for we cannot help thinking it would 'take the conceit out of him,' and better fit him for those serener pursuits, to which Blackwood's Magazine and the lecture-chair of Edinburgh particularly invite him."[56] "Plague-Poet" (alluding to Wilson's best-known poem *The City of the Plague*) and *"Moral Professor"* are both excellent puns: contemptuous and at the same time laughable from their ingenuity.

"Lion's Head," which had called Reynolds a good contributor two months earlier, announced "Exmouth Wrestling" in November as one of the major attractions of the next issue and described it as a "Rough Diamond" and a "clever paper."[57] With an easy and graceful style, wit, and a mingling of personal feeling with the scenes and incidents described, it is one of Reynolds's best familiar essays. Drawing freely from the Elizabethan chronicler John Stow and the eighteenth-century antiquary Joseph Strutt, Reynolds wrote a humorous survey of wrestling in England, spiced with quaint quotations and a woodcut from the eccentric Sir Thomas Parkyns's rare old pamphlet on the sport, to balance the earthiness of the account of the wrestling matches he attended.[58]

A former friend from the past, Ralph Rylance, began seeing Reynolds again occasionally in 1820. After his insanity and break with the Reynoldses in 1814, his derangement had continued off and on for years. The antiquarian John Britton wrote Dovaston on 5 October 1815 that he could not comply with Dovaston's request and "preserve an intimate acquaintance with him [Rylance]" because he was still "subject to occasional derangement." On 4 June 1816 Rylance wrote that medication for disease of the penis had thrown him into a long-lasting "merry madness." A Shropshire friend, Martha Yates, commented to Dovaston on Rylance's "dreadful malady" on 31 October 1816, and Maria Williams, a domestic servant from Shropshire, but working in London, who had been frustrated for years in her love of Dovaston, wrote on 18 February 1817 to acknowledge Dovaston's explanation of why Rylance had strangely stayed away from her for three years. Reynolds's letters to Dovaston stopped on 25 February 1815, and the two never resumed their friendship, though they may have met briefly to talk over old times in 1836. If Dovaston was very angry with Reynolds—sooner or later he quarreled with almost all his friends except Rylance—he did not make his anger known. Not knowing of Dovaston's break with the

Reynoldses, the wife of his London friend John Britton joked about his former friendship with Charlotte Reynolds as if it still continued.[59] Only two letters from Rylance to Dovaston are preserved from 1814 through 1819, but by 1820 Rylance began writing regularly again and continued the correspondence through 17 September 1828.[60] If Dovaston now was of little interest to Reynolds, Reynolds was out of favor with Dovaston, as Rylance's letters show.

In an undated letter apparently written in September 1820 when Reynolds was on vacation in Devonshire, though endorsed by Dovaston 5 December 1820 when he answered it, Rylance wrote:

Let me give you some tidings of our co-mate of other days John Reynolds. Months have flown since I saw him; but his friend Mitchell whom I spoke [to] t'other day tells me he is gone into Devonshire to be wived. The lady is prosperous and fair, and kind as fair, so the match is like to prove auspicious. Though yoked to law, he still woos the nine, and you may have seen announced in Constable's catalogue some tales in two volumes, which he is now writing, or should be, if the purblind imp Cupid have not plucked from his own wing a quill and given it him in hand to be used for more courtly purposes.

The letter showed how little Rylance knew of Reynolds, who now had little time for him. Rylance reported only the planned prose tales which he had seen announced in the catalogue; he did not know that Reynolds had written *Peter Bell* and *The Fancy,* or he would have mentioned them—later when he learned Reynolds's authorship of *The Fancy,* he sent Dovaston a copy. He misunderstood from Mitchell (not otherwise known) the purpose of Reynolds's visit to Devonshire; Reynolds did not marry Eliza for another two years. By 30 November Rylance was able to correct his error, "I saw Reynolds on Sonday: he is not yet married and he saith that event is not near at hand I found him over law papers; and from some lines of study in his face I opine that he still burns his midnight lamp to the muses. He is known to be deeply read in the Elizabethan poets."

CHAPTER 12

Brown's Hostility and
the Scott-Christie Duel—1821

B Y 1821 Reynolds presumably earned respectable sums from his legal work and supplemented that income with his writing; both Constable and the *London* paid ten guineas a sheet. But he found it more difficult to hold onto money than other bachelors like Rice and Woodhouse because he enjoyed living well and he helped his family by supplementing his father's income. After Reynolds's death Anne Skepper Procter wrote that she "looked at a little Copy of Gray's letters he gave me—in 1821—when he was so merry—so good—working so hard for his Mother & Sisters."[1]

Because of his limited resources, Reynolds's offer to contribute £50 towards Keats's expenses in Italy showed some generosity, though a misunderstanding about how he was to contribute the money prevented it from being used. About 24 January 1821 he wrote Taylor that he wanted Keats to draw upon him for £50. Knowing that Taylor managed the funds furnished Keats through the banker Torlonia in Rome, Reynolds expected that Taylor would add another £50 to the credit at Rome, for which he would repay Taylor when the money was claimed. Taylor misunderstood the manner in which Reynolds planned to make the money available and thought that Reynolds intended to enclose a draft for £50 in a letter mailed directly to Keats. On 6 February Taylor wrote Severn, "Reynolds sent £50 a fortnight since Did you receive it."[2] By 3 April he discovered his error and reported it to Severn, "Reynolds, I find, did not send the £50 after all. I did not know that till very lately; he wrote [to me of his] desire Keats would draw upon him for that sum."[3] Although it is true, as Rollins noted, that Reynolds "supplied none of the money that Taylor *used* to cover Keats's expenses in Italy,"[4] he should nevertheless be credited with the willingness to contribute. Unfortunately Reynolds's letter to Taylor has not survived so we cannot tell who was more responsible for the confusion in communication—Reynolds in the writing or Taylor in the reading. Taylor showed no sign of blaming Reynolds: after he discovered his error, he wrote straightforwardly that Reynolds had written that he wished to be drawn on for £50.

After Keats's death on 23 February 1821, Taylor's effort to write his biography strained relations between Taylor, Hessey, Woodhouse, Reynolds, and Rice on one side and Brown on the other. Taylor's motives were honorable. On 28 March, he wrote his brother James, "Perhaps you have not heard of the Death of poor Keats. He died 3 days before his defender Scott. This ought to be another Blow to the Hearts of those Blackwood's Men. I believe I shall try to write his Life—it is the wish of his Friends, and was Keats's wish also—in that Case I shall have Occasion to speak of the Treatment he has met with from the Race of Critics and Lampooners."[5] Keats had wished him to write the life, Keats's friends whom he saw often agreed that he should, he wished to vindicate Keats after the abuse of the Tory critics—all were laudable motives. If the book were to achieve his primary purposes, it would have to sell well and make money, but profit was not his primary motive. He advertised the planned book on 29 March in the *New Times* a little more than a month after Keats's death, "Speedily will be published, with Portrait, Memoirs and Remains of John Keats."

Brown's motives in impeding the book, which was never written, are difficult to fathom. Eccentric and stubborn as he was, he was an honest man, as Dilke wrote even after the two had become bitter enemies. He had loved Keats; Keats's letters from others, papers, and books were at his disposal; and he felt an obligation to ensure that Keats's memory be given the most favorable treatment. He suspected that Taylor's book would be a mere bookseller's job with profit as a large motive. When Reynolds applied to Brown on Taylor's behalf for Keats's papers, Brown would not give up any of them until he had exacted from Taylor the condition that he be permitted to read and approve the work before publication. After Taylor, with some reluctance, granted the condition, Brown gave him "the chief things," but withheld other materials.[6] The "chief things" were four manuscript books of poetry; Brown requested the return of them after copying on 24 July and 12 August 1821.[7] Brown did not lend Taylor letters and papers.

Reynolds had been Keats's closest friend for over two years, while

Brown had been merely one of many other friends. However, soon after Tom's death on 1 December 1818, Brown began spending much more time with Keats, because the two lived together for a year and a half. Brown was jealous of the part that Reynolds would play in Taylor's biography because Reynolds was very close to Taylor and Woodhouse, and he was not. Brown's jealousy grew to such a surprising degree that he wrote on 14 August 1821, "Reynolds is the secret spring; it is wished he should shine as the dear friend of poor Keats—(at least I suspect so)—when the fact is, he was no dear friend to Keats, nor did Keats think him so."[8] The statement is amazing to anyone who has read Keats's letters to Reynolds, but Brown had not read those letters. Instead, he must have had some other evidence that he exaggerated out of proportion.

Keats had allowed himself to believe temporarily, in the late spring or early summer of 1820, when his anger against the Reynoldses for their disapproval of Fanny Brawne had reached the boiling point, that Reynolds was not his friend. Reynolds was among those he meant when he wrote Fanny Brawne, "I suspect a few people to hate me well enough, *for reasons I know of,* who have pretended a great friendship for me."[9] Keats may well have given more specific details to Brown, which he left unexplained to Fanny, in a letter to Brown of 15 May 1820, from which Brown preserved only nine lines.[10] Later Keats regretted having given way to blind anger and wanted to patch things up with Reynolds, who he knew had always been his steadfast friend. Either this or similar evidence was probably available to Brown to feed his jealousy.

Brown may also have had whatever letters the Reynoldses wrote Keats in May and June 1820 when the disagreements about Fanny Brawne were at their worst. On 21 November 1821, Fanny Brawne wrote Fanny Keats, "Never be intimate with the Reynolds. . . . Every day I live I find out more of their malice against me."[11] Brown had under his control Keats's letters and papers, which he had not lent to Taylor along with the four manuscript books of poetry. Living in Hampstead near Fanny Brawne, Brown saw her often at this time; he was the likeliest source of revelations that she would certainly see as the Reynoldses' malice toward her. As Brown read and reread old letters, he would have either shown them to Fanny or told her about them.

Taylor's proposed biography was not the only reason Brown felt less friendly toward the Rice-Reynolds group. Rice disapproved of Brown's keeping his questionably legitimate child in the house with him, and Brown's resentment probably spilled over onto Reynolds.[12] If the Reynolds women did not gossip about Brown's keeping Carlino, with his mother, Abby, confined to her separate bed, they exercised more than mortal restraint.[13]

Reynolds's mind was on the Scott-Christie duel and the *London Magazine* as much as on Keats during 1821.[14] John Scott had no doubt told him of the depths of *Blackwood's* deceit and infamy that he had learned from John R. McCulloch, editor of the *Scotsman* newspaper, and others when he visited Edinburgh in the summer of 1820. Reynolds could not have failed to approve as Scott built his smashing attacks on *Blackwood's* through the November and December articles to the climax in January when he printed the name of the chief culprit in bold capitals, John Gibson Lockhart. Reynolds knew well all those involved on Scott's side in the impending duel: he had worked for Scott on the *Champion* in 1815 and 1816; he was intimate with Horace Smith, to use Smith's word; and he was on familiar terms with Peter George Patmore, Scott's assistant and like Reynolds himself a close friend of Hazlitt. He also knew Jonathan Henry Christie, Lockhart's best friend, whose influence he had tried unsuccessfully to use to prevent the *Blackwood's* attack on Keats.

Reynolds must have been both fascinated and concerned as Lockhart charged down from Edinburgh to London; as Scott consulted with Horace Smith, who disapproved of dueling and tried to pacify him; and as Scott insisted on the central moral issue and refused to fight unless Lockhart would deny having been editor of *Blackwood's*. Surely he was as appalled as Scott by Lockhart's brazen maneuvering: sending Scott a single printed copy of his final statement without the all-important denial that he had been an editor of *Blackwood's,* immediately thereafter printing in the *New Times* the same communications with an added paragraph to include the lying denial, claiming in the newspaper version that he had sent Scott the first copy of it, posting Scott as a coward and a poltroon, and departing for Edinburgh before Scott had a chance to read the newspaper version and accept the challenge once his moral condition had been met. Reynolds was close in the background when, after Christie insulted Scott in his last printed statement, Scott realized that a duel was probable as he sent Patmore to Christie on 16 February with two documents: a letter demanding "a disavowal of [Christie's] having intended to say anything disrespectful" and a challenge in case Christie should refuse it. To prepare for any eventuality, Scott entrusted to Reynolds two letters to be delivered in case of his death: one to his wife Caroline and the other to her brother Dominic Paul Colnaghi. Thinking also of his ally in Scotland and of his responsibility to the *London Magazine,* he directed Reynolds in case of the worst to write to John R. McCulloch and to the chief contributors to the *London.*

Scott, with Patmore as his second, and Christie, with James Traill as his second, fought the tragic duel by moonlight on 16 February, attended by the surgeon Thomas J. Pettigrew and his assistant William Morris, whom Patmore had engaged. As he had told Traill he would beforehand, Christie aimed wide of Scott on the first fire, but instead of firing up in the air or down at the ground he leveled his pistol in the general direction of Scott so that neither Scott nor Patmore could see that he had missed intentionally. After the first fire, during which Scott missed, Scott heard Traill say, "Now Mr. Christie, take your aim, and do not throw away your advantage as you did last time" and called out "What! did not Mr. Christie fire at me?"[15] Unfortunately Patmore understood from Traill only Christie's name and supposed mistakenly that Scott was answering a charge by Traill that he had fired too soon unfairly, "What! did not Mr. Christie fire at me! [just at the time I fired at him]." Not realizing that Christie had fired wide intentionally and thinking that he was doing his duty as a second by preventing a quarrel between his principal and the opponent's second, he refused to let Scott speak further and insisted on a second fire. Scott missed again, and Christie wounded Scott fatally in the abdomen. Scott lingered on in agony for ten days at Chalk Farm Tavern before he died on 27 February.

Patmore engaged Rice and Reynolds to represent him in his defense. Their first step was to spare Patmore from arrest by sending him to Calais, where he remained for several weeks under the name of P. G. Pitt. Reynolds, Rice, and a third young lawyer, who was a friend of Scott but not retained in the case (probably Thomas Noon Talfourd), attended the inquest held at Chalk Farm Tavern on 1 March before the coroner Thomas Sterling of Middlesex and his jury. When a member of the jury challenged their presence, Reynolds identified himself as a friend of Scott and a legal representative for a person involved, while Rice explained that he too had been retained.[16] When a member of the jury suggested that the names of the suspected participants be mentioned to refresh the memory of a witness, they objected and succeeded in preventing it.

The first day of the inquest began safely enough for Patmore, as well as for Christie and his second, James Traill. The carpenter Thomas Smith and the hostler James Ryan, who had helped to carry Scott to Chalk Farm Tavern where they had been employed, testified very minutely as to details, but pretended to a laughable ignorance of names. They identified men only by apparel—the man in the white coat, the man in the blue coat, the man in the red coat, but no, I believe it was plaid—in such a confusing way as to endanger no one. But later the landlord Hugh Watson, while posing no threat to Christie or Traill, implicated Patmore by name repeatedly. He recognized Patmore in the tavern after the duel because he had known him before; indeed he had known Patmore's father for twenty years. He reported that a pistol brought in after the duel was Patmore's, and that Peter Patmore, Sr., had offered a reward for the recovery of the pistols. All this was dangerous enough, but the real bombshell came when Dr. George Darling read the following memorandum, reporting Scott's account to him on the day after the duel:

"This ought not to have taken place: I suspect some great mismanagement: there was no occasion for a second fire." After a short pause, he proceeded—"All I required from Mr. Christie was, a declaration that he meant no reflection on my character: this he refused, and the meeting became inevitable. On the field Mr. Christie behaved well, and when all was ready for the first fire he called out—'Mr. Scott, you must not stand there; I see your head above the horizon; you give me an advantage': I believe he could have hit me then if he liked. After the pistols were re-loaded and every thing ready for a second fire, Mr. Trail called out—'Now, Mr. Christie, take your aim, and do not throw away your advantage as you did last time.' I called out immediately, 'What! did not Mr. Christie fire at me'? I was answered by Mr. Patmore, 'You must not speak: 'tis now of no use to talk; you have now nothing for it but firing.' The signal was immediately given; we fired; and I fell."[17]

When he made the statement to Dr. Darling, Scott did not realize that Patmore failed to understand that Christie had aimed wide on the first fire. Later, when a friend of Patmore's visited Scott, he dictated a second statement exonerating Patmore, but it was never made public. On the first day of the coroner's inquest, Dr. Darling's memorandum placed the whole weight of the blame for the second fatal fire upon Patmore, and public sentiment against him raged unabated for several weeks.

The second day of the inquest on 2 March went somewhat better for Patmore. To be sure, the surgeon Thomas J. Pettigrew revealed that Patmore had engaged him, and he placed Patmore on the field, but he also presented Patmore's case in the misunderstanding about the first fire. He described the altercation between the seconds after Scott was wounded when Patmore had insisted angrily to Traill that he knew nothing of Christie's firing wide on the first exchange. And he testified that Patmore had visited him after the duel to reaffirm his complete ignorance after the first fire that Christie had missed intentionally. Nevertheless, the jury delivered its verdict: "Wilful murder against Christie, Patmore, and Trail."[18]

Seeking to temper the effect of Dr. Darling's testimony on public sentiment, Rice inserted an advertisement in the *Morning Chronicle,* urging that people not be misled by partial evidence but that they wait for further developments to clear Patmore.[19] Reynolds pressed his desire to quiet public feeling rather too far when he attempted to postpone a notice in the *London Magazine* soliciting funds for Scott's family with the argument that it would be inflammatory, but fortunately for Caroline and the Scott children Robert Baldwin printed the notice despite Reynolds's objection.

Reynolds and Rice worried about the influence of public opinion on the jury, but they were even more concerned about the legal status of Darling's memorandum. It had been admitted at the inquest because of the rather flexible rules for evidence at the preliminary hearing, but it might be possible to bar it from the trial. The law held that the statement of a dying man was admissible only if he knew at the time he made it that death was imminent, the reason being that knowledge of approaching death substituted for an oath to ensure veracity. Reynolds succeeded admirably in developing this aspect of the case. He secured Caroline Scott's report that her husband had thought he would recover at the time he spoke to Dr. Darling. He won the same admission from Dr. Darling after telling him point-blank that Patmore's life was at stake. And he received corroboration from Dr. Guthrie, who had been most optimistic in the first few days after the wound.

Caroline Scott presented a serious problem. At first she refused to see Rice, who was a stranger to her, but Reynolds managed to see her readily, since she had known him a long time as a friend of her husband. Reynolds also made tactful and effective use of their mutual friend, Mrs. Basil Montagu, to persuade her to cooperate fully. The problem was not that she was reluctant to shield Patmore; her friendship remained very warm, and she wished him to emerge from the affair with his reputation unblemished. She discounted Dr. Darling's testimony strongly; Scott could not have said it, or, if he had, he was delirious. She blamed Traill bitterly for not stopping the duel after the first fire, and she resented the great reputation which Christie had won. She was more than willing to testify to clear Patmore and blast Traill, but the problem for Patmore's attorneys was whether to let her testify.

At a conference of legal authorities retained for counsel on 21 March, John Adolphus and a Mr. Curwood decided against calling Caroline Scott as a witness because of the emotional effect her appearance might have on the jury. The appearance of the widow on the stand might press the jury to convict all the defendants as an example against the evil of dueling. We can infer the strategy recommended by Reynolds and Rice from Reynolds's and Caroline Scott's letters to Patmore and from the newspaper accounts of the trials. They would concentrate on barring Dr. Darling's evidence from the trial; in this they could hope for cooperation from Christie's and Traill's attorneys. Although the Darling memorandum represented Christie and Traill favorably, it also placed them on the field and described their participation in a duel. Admitting it virtually guaranteed as a minimum a verdict of manslaughter for all three defendants. On the other hand, if there were no clear identification of Christie and Traill, they might be acquitted. Reynolds and Rice evidently advised holding Caroline Scott in reserve: not to use her if Darling's evidence were barred, but to call her to counter the Darling evidence if it should be admitted.

Rice and Reynolds worked thoroughly for Patmore's welfare. Rice attended to most of the practical details: arranging to send him a passport, referring him to an influential French friend at Calais in case of need, visiting his parents and his uncle, and effecting the assignment of his £10,000 estate to prevent forfeiture in case of conviction for manslaughter or worse. Reynolds tried unsuccessfully to negotiate an agreement with Mr. Minshull, magistrate at Bow Street, so that the police would not seek to arrest Patmore on his return if he agreed to surrender for the trial. Reynolds succeeded, however, in negotiating with Mr. Brown, the keeper of Newgate prison, who knew Rice well from earlier dealing, to ensure that Patmore's confinement would be as agreeable as possible if it were necessary. They explained the dangers frankly and left the final decision to Patmore on whether to risk return for trial.

Early in April Patmore returned secretly to London, communicating with Caroline Scott and conferring with his attorneys.[20] As the trial approached on 13 April, Reynolds, Rice, Adolphus, and Curwood faced a decision. They wanted to make whatever arrangements would guarantee Patmore the best chance for acquittal or light sentence, and they were not faced with hostility from any quarter. Scott's family had instigated the legal proceedings leading to the trial,[21] and Caroline Scott was extremely sympathetic toward Patmore. Reynolds had determined "that the feeling of the prosecutors is known to be . . . favourable."[22] In the light of subsequent events, it seems probable that Patmore's attorneys conferred with Christie's and Traill's attorneys to reach an agreement whereby the latter would not press for the admission of the Darling memorandum in exchange for a guarantee that Patmore would not surrender for the first trial. Christie's and Traill's attorneys could elicit from the surgeon Pettigrew all the evidence they needed: Christie's firing wide the first time, his remorse, his humane concern for the wounded Scott, and Scott's judgment that all had been fair and honorable. Pettigrew's testimony ensured that Christie and Traill would receive no more than a verdict of manslaughter, and the exclusion of Darling's memorandum might make possible an acquittal, for Pettigrew could not after the foggy-night view identify either Christie or Traill. But Pettigrew must identify his old acquaintance Patmore, and a conviction of Patmore would pose some danger to Christie and Traill, since a jury might wish to avoid the appearance of partisanship. The sensible solution would be an agreement by all parties to drop Darling's evidence and to have Patmore refrain from surrendering while Christie and Traill were tried.

The degree to which the first trial was arranged in advance must be speculative, but Patmore's reason for not surrendering is fact. An advertisement in the *Times* informed the public that Patmore refrained from surrendering, on the advice of counsel, to avoid the risk of endangering Christie and Traill.[23] Before the trial, Patmore moved from London to Witney, Oxfordshire, where he remained in hiding under the name of P. G. Preston.[24]

The first trial went off like clockwork on Friday, 13 April at 10:00 A.M. before Lord Chief Justice Abbott and Justice Park. The court was crowded with "persons of distinction," as Mr. Walfourd presented the case for the prosecution and Mr. Gurney the case for the defense. It would be impossible to find a more sympathetic prosecutor than Mr. Walfourd, who glowed with emotion for Christie and Traill:

It was difficult for him to find adequate language to convey any idea of the painful feelings with which he rose to state the evidence which he had to adduce in support of the indictment against the gentlemen at the bar. It was impossible for him, when he recollected the rank in society in which these gentlemen moved, and when he reflected upon the fatal consequences which might come to them upon this trial—it was, he repeated, impossible for him to behold this situation without emotion. The man, who standing there, could do so, must have firmer nerves than he possessed.[25]

This statement was from the *prosecutor*. The mild case he presented was exactly what one would expect after that maudlin preamble. He drew from Pettigrew all the evidence favorable to Christie including Christie's statement that he had fired wide, except that Pettigrew unfortunately forgot to add what he had reported at the coroner's inquest—that Christie had been forced to shoot Scott in self-defense. But the alert defense attorney, Mr. Gurney, immediately prodded his memory, and that too went into the record. The prosecutor then called Pettigrew's assistant Morris, Hugh Watson, and James Ryan to establish the order of events on the fatal night. None of them could identify Christie or Traill as participants on the field. Lawyers and participants alike were doubtless startled when Thomas Smith departed from the script to say, "The prisoner Traill was one of the gentlemen in the field," but no one heeded that truth which everyone knew, but agreed to ignore. The climax came when Dr. Darling testified. After he and Dr. Guthrie explained that Scott had not believed he was dying when he made the statement, the judges conferred for a few minutes at the bench and then pronounced the evidence inadmissible.

The defense offered only a long succession of character witnesses for the defendants, who were of course attired in deep mourning. Lord Chief Justice Abbott did everything he possibly could for the prisoners, at one time even indulging in a mental hand-spring with possibility, "It was possible, he said, that the real perpetrators of the crime might have escaped from the field before the arrival of Mr. Pettigrew, and that the prisoners at the bar might have appeared accidentally at the moment." No one could have been much surprised when the jury returned the verdict, "Not guilty."

According to Caroline Scott, Reynolds was chiefly responsible for representing Patmore's interests *in absentia* during the first trial.[26] She was present in court, but there was no occasion for her testimony since Dr. Darling's statement was barred and since Pettigrew had protected Patmore by mentioning the altercation between the seconds and by quoting Patmore's outburst, "Why was it not communicated to me—I knew nothing of it."

Rice was the solicitor chiefly responsible when Patmore eventually surrendered for the second trial on 8 June before Justice Bayley. Since Pettigrew was an old acquaintance of Patmore's who had been sympathetic toward him throughout the affair, it seems certain that what happened was planned as a neat legal maneuver. Both Pettigrew and Morris, who were the only witnesses able to identify Patmore as a participant on the field, refused to testify on the grounds that they might incriminate themselves. They were in no danger of prosecution, for the coroner's jury had specifically refused to indict Pettigrew after he explained that he had merely done his duty as a surgeon by responding to a call for professional service. The other witnesses repeated their testimony from the first trial. "Without the slightest hesitation," the jury reported its verdict, "Not guilty."[27]

Caroline Scott was strongly dissatisfied with the conduct of the case by Rice and Reynolds. She had wanted them to clear Patmore's name without a shadow of a doubt and at the same time to preserve her husband's character as stainless. One can infer from her letters to Patmore that she wished to testify herself. But surely Rice, Reynolds, and her other counsellors were wiser than she. Her testimony might well have influenced the juries emotionally and caused them to make an example of all three defendants. Moreover, lengthy and detailed justification of Patmore might have required at least some disparagement of Scott, and such an attack on the dead would have also been a risk. The acquittal of a man against whom the public had been incensed only a few weeks before was no small achievement.

CHAPTER 13

The *London Magazine*—1821-1825

BUSY AS HE WAS with the defense of Patmore, Reynolds, along with others, assisted the publisher Robert Baldwin in issuing the *London Magazine* from March through June 1821 after the death of John Scott.[1] Ralph Rylance, who saw Reynolds occasionally and no doubt learned of his influence with Baldwin, thought that he could place an article in the *London,* but he was mistaken and it did not appear. He was amused by one of Reynolds's jokes and reported it to Dovaston, "Appropos of the Georgian age: indulge me with reporting to you a joke of John Reynolds's this morning as touching thas [that] ⟨yes⟩ matter: the present favourite Georgian age is 56:—his ladies being required to be fat and six and fifty."[2]

Despite all his farewells to the muses and despite the fact that he had spent his time for the last several years on the law, on prose for the periodicals, and on comic productions, Reynolds had not relinquished entirely his small hope of becoming a serious poet. In May 1821 he finally published *The Garden of Florence and Other Poems* with John Warren. It is not known why he chose the otherwise unknown Warren to publish the book rather than Taylor and Hessey; perhaps Taylor and Hessey were unwilling to risk the financial gamble. After his first two books in 1814, he had published the next three anonymously; this time he compromised with the almost transparent pseudonym—John Hamilton. Most of the poems had been written years before, but the advertisement, or preface as we would say, was new, and in it he paid this brief but moving tribute two months after Keats's death:

The stories from Boccacio (The Garden of Florence, and The Ladye of Provence) were to have been associated with tales from the same source, intended to have been written by a friend;—but illness on his part, and distracting engagements on mine, prevented us from accomplishing our plan at the time; and Death now, to my deep sorrow, has frustrated it for ever!

He, who is gone, was one of the very kindest friends I possessed, and yet he was not kinder perhaps to me, than to others. His intense mind and powerful feeling would, I truly believe, have done the world some service, had his life been spared—but he was of too sensitive a nature—and thus he was destroyed! One story he completed, and that is to me now the most poetic poem in existence![3]

In the preface to the poem closest to his heart, *The Romance of Youth,* Reynolds held out the possibility that he might resume work as a serious poet if the public received the poem favorably, but even there the tone sounded pessimistic, "If this Canto be read,—the conclusion of it may follow: if it be disregarded, 'here the story ends.' And the Author will have reason to bless the alienation of mind that baffled its completion."[4]

Richard Woodhouse reviewed the volume with moderate favor in the *London*[5] and was perceptive enough to see the perfection of "Think of Me," which he quoted entire as beyond criticism:

> Go, where the water glideth gently ever,
> Glideth by meadows which the greenest be;—
> Go, listen to our own beloved river,
> And think of me!
>
> Wander in forests, where the small flower layeth
> Its fairy gem beside the giant tree;
> Listen the dim brook pining while it playeth,
> And think of me!
>
> Watch when the sky is silver pale at Even,
> And the wind grieveth in the lonely tree;
> Go out beneath the solitary heaven,
> And think of me!
>
> And when the moon riseth as she were dreaming,
> And treadeth with white feet the lulled sea;
> Go, silent as a star beneath her beaming,
> And think of me![6]

The poem became Reynolds's best-known lyric; it was parodied by Hood, set to music, and reprinted in a number of nineteenth-century anthologies.

Five other reviews were also favorable, two of them indeed urging him to continue writing poetry.[7] The *Gentleman's Magazine,* however, slashed him, concluding caustically, "Mr. Hamilton will have several steps to retrace before he ventures on a second effort; and we recommend to him an examination of Johnson's Dictionary, Lindley Murray's Grammar, and the common rules of versification."[8] And the *Scots Magazine* denounced scathingly and contemptuously the "silly imbecility" of the book with its "silly conceit and unpoetical rhyme."[9] The last attack so angered Reynolds that he protested to Constable, who explained that he had allowed the review to be published because he had not known that Reynolds was the author and that, if he had known, he would have suppressed it.[10] Constable noted later that before Reynolds protested he had learned accidentally of Reynolds's authorship by "the transmission of a Critique on it for the Edinburgh Review."[11] If the powerful *Edinburgh* had published the review, probably a favorable one by some friend like Procter or Talfourd, Reynolds might have changed his mind and continued with serious poetry, but Jeffrey did not print it, and Reynolds let his farewell to the muses stand. Constable, who had displayed Olympian patience with Reynolds's procrastination and failure to meet his contract, still hoped for a book, but at last began to show that there was a limit to even his tolerance: "We shall count on it by Xmas—but if not *then* ready, I can assure you we shall then have cause to complain and *shall complain*."[12] But displeased with Constable and no longer interested in the prose tales, Reynolds returned the £80 advance, and Constable released him from the contract.

Reynolds turned instead to spending what time he could spare from his legal work on assisting with the editing of the *London Magazine* and contributing to it more regularly and heavily than he had before. Taylor and Hessey bought the *London* from Baldwin, Cradock and Joy on 26 April 1821, but they did not begin publishing it until the July issue.[13] Reynolds was no doubt useful to his friend John Taylor in the transition; he assisted Baldwin with the May and June issues, contributing to the latter two humorous prose pieces. In "Letter from Mr. Humphrey Nixon," he pretended to be a simple, mindless resident of Exmouth quarreling with the outsider Reynolds's account of his village in "Exmouth Wrestling."[14] The comic non sequiturs and aimless drifting of Humphrey Nixon blended Sterne and Smollett with Reynolds's own fine ear for simple speech to show some skill in comic characterization. "Legal Lyrics" allowed him to exercise his wit by pretending to find poetry in dull legal language.[15]

One piece of Reynolds's well-meant assistance went awry. He introduced Ralph Rylance, who had long been a man of all work for publishers and was prepared to do any sort of pedestrian work for profit, to Taylor and Hessey, who suggested tentatively that they might pay him "two hundred guineas a year for reading the proof sheets, collecting and translating articles of literary intelligence from foreign Journals, and putting together the list of bankrupts and the Obituary."[16] Having introduced Rylance to Taylor and Hessey, Reynolds assumed that they would work out their own arrangement and intervened no further in the matter. When in June Rylance wrote Taylor and Hessey that he was prepared to perform his tasks, they replied that one of Robert Baldwin's conditions on the sale of the magazine would require postponement of Rylance's services. Taylor had agreed to continue to employ Baldwin's foreign translator and obituarian until Baldwin could find other work for him, and Baldwin had not yet succeeded. Rylance was unjustifiably annoyed that Reynolds had not taken an active hand in his employment and kept him informed. He was also irritated because Reynolds did not send him a copy of *The Garden of Florence* on publication, and his ruffled feelings probably contributed to the sharpness of his comments on the book in a later letter to Dovaston.[17]

John Taylor served as his own editor of the *London Magazine* from July 1821 through November 1824 with Reynolds and Thomas Hood as his "valuable coadjutors."[18] Reynolds and Hood rapidly became fast friends; they liked each other and shared a "partiality for the writings of each other."[19] For a time in the fall of 1821, Reynolds wrote the "Lion's Head," the jocular prefatory editorial section of the *London,* until he was replaced by Hood, who usually conducted that department during the rest of his most active connection with the magazine. They quickly became such close friends that Hessey extended Reynolds's pseudonym Peter Corcoran to both in writing to John Clare on 2 November 1821, "I hope you will like our old Friend Peter in his new Capacity of Shewman of the City *Lions* as the Curiosities of the great Capital are called—There is another Peter who resembles him so much as to be sometimes taken for his Brother, his name is Incog."[20]

On 6 December 1821 at one of the regular dinners given by Taylor and Hessey for the contributors at their quarters in 93 Fleet Street, Reynolds, Rice, and Lamb were "particularly lively and facetious," while Hood was no doubt as quiet and reserved as he usually was in company.[21] The next month Hood reported a dinner with "my ingenious and respected friend R. . . . I was delighted with his right merrie conceites, and the happy tone of his conversation; and I wished, which has since been realized, that the born friendship of that night might be of age in somewhat less than twenty-one years."[22] Years later Hood used Reynolds's *London* pseudonym Edward Herbert to describe his general demeanor at these dinners.

That smart active person opposite with a gamecock-looking head, and the hair combed smooth, fighter fashion, over his forehead—with one finger hooked round a glass of champagne, not that he requires it to inspirit him, for his wit bubbles up of itself—is our Edward Herbert, the Author of that true piece of Biography, the Life of Peter Corcoran. He is "good with both hands," like that Nonpareil Randall, at a comic verse or a serious stanza—smart at a repartee—sharp at a retort, and not averse to a bit of mischief. 'Twas he who gave the runaway ring at Wordsworth's Peter Bell. Generally, his jests, set off by a happy manner, are only ticklesome, but now and then they are sharp-flavoured,—like the sharpness of a pineapple.[23]

Another friend and regular guest, Bryan Waller Procter, confirmed that during these "very social and expansive hours" Reynolds's "good temper and vivacity were like condiments at a feast."[24]

Reynolds's contributions to the *London* while Taylor and Hessey owned it included the Edward Herbert papers; unsigned verses; the Ned Ward, Jr., verses; unsigned articles and book reviews; and most of the theatrical notices. Each of these categories deserves some attention, though they are of course unequal in their value.

Reynolds has always been best known for the Edward Herbert series. With Lamb's brilliant success as Elia before him as an example, Reynolds decided to use the pseudonym Edward Herbert when he agreed to serve as subeditor and to contribute heavily. The wrapper identified "Warwick Castle," given first place in the issue of July 1821, as written by Edward Herbert.[25] One of the best papers in the group, it is a regular essay and not in the epistolary form of most of the series—a form he struck upon almost by accident. For the August issue he capitalized on the great national interest in the panoply and pageantry of the coronation of George IV. In order to account for the loving detail with which he depicted the colorful costumes and elaborate rituals, he directed it primarily to a female audience who would revel in style and spectacle by framing it as a letter from a gentleman in town to a lady in the country, whom he identified as P——, who lived with her mother and sisters (as Eliza Drewe did with her widowed mother and two sisters). Probably unintentionally drawing on his own experience, he made Edward Herbert a lawyer by remarking on the difference between Westminster Hall when he was there a few weeks before on mundane legal business and the impressive national structure decked out for the state occasion. In all the later letters Herbert is not a lawyer, but an independent gentleman without vocation lately come to London. Even in the last Herbert letter which describes a trial, where making Herbert a lawyer would have accounted for his close knowledge of court procedure, Reynolds refrained from giving Herbert his vocation and maintained the fiction that Herbert was a layman.

John Taylor reported to his father that people said the August number was not only the best *London,* but the best issue of any magazine.[26] Though Lamb's "Imperfect Sympathies" and Hazlitt's "Table Talk" essay in the August issue were more solid literary achievements, Reynolds's coronation letter, lavishly written on a timely topic, also contributed to the favorable public response. Encouraged, Reynolds decided to continue the series in epistolary form. In September's "Lion's Head," in response to his inquiry, Reynolds received assurance that he might continue the letters as a series, though the question and answer were more advertising than real inquiry and reply because as subeditor in close contact with Taylor and Hood, Reynolds would already have received oral approval. He wrote the brief Herbert letter in the September "Lion's Head" as from the Albany, placing Herbert's residence in that fashionable hotel for bachelors.[27] In October Hood promised in "Lion's Head" that the second Herbert letter on Greenwich Hospital would appear in November and that the series would continue to describe unusual places in London.[28]

In November Reynolds set the frame for the remaining letters. Herbert, living at the Albany, would address letters either to P—— Powell (the maiden name of Eliza Drewe's mother and the middle name of both Eliza and her dead brother George) or to her younger brother Russell, depending upon whether the subject matter would appeal more to a young woman or a young man. In London Herbert would visit frequently with the family of the Mortons, consisting of husband, wife, and their adopted two nieces and a nephew. Setting the age of Mr. Morton at fifty-six, the same age as his father, suggests that Reynolds drew upon him for the main outline of the character, and the leading traits do not conflict with what we know of George Reynolds. Mr. Morton was hard-working, soft-spoken, and unobtrusive with a penchant for playing cards. He was, however, a middle-class merchant instead of a teacher. Mrs. Morton may have shown some features of Reynolds's mother: she was more intelligent and well-read than her husband, but devoted to him and determined to preserve the appearance of his superiority and her subordination to him. But Reynolds avoided any embarrassingly close identification by making her a number of years younger than Mr. Morton instead of four years older, as Charlotte Reynolds was.

Reynolds drew upon none of his sisters for the two Morton nieces. The tall, dark Prudence was a bluestocking who worshiped the theater and actors like a religion, lionized any poet she could capture, and automatically affected an unnatural literary attitude at any social gathering. By contrast, the petite, fair Agnes was gentle, kind, sensitive, and always herself. Young Tom Morton was an exaggeration of certain tendencies in Reynolds five years earlier, with his study of the law, his exuberance, his love of sports, and his craving for all kinds of experiences ranging from Lancelot Andrewes's sermons to the shady side of London life.

Having set the frame, Reynolds unexpectedly departed from it in the next Herbert paper, "Bradgate Park," signed E.H. for Edward Herbert, for it was not a letter, but a regular familiar essay. Reynolds had announced that the Herbert letters would describe out-of-the-way London scenes, and, since he wanted to write about the celebrated residence of Lady Jane Grey in Leicestershire, he dispensed with the epistolary framework. "Bradgate Park" resembled in subject and elegiac tone the first Herbert paper, "Warwick Castle," and equaled it in merit; surprisingly, the two best Herbert papers were not letters, though those who know the pseudonym think of the series as epistolary. In three later papers Reynolds returned to his plan and described the greenroom of a theater, the inside of a stagecoach, and a cockfight; in two others he loosened the framework, describing satirically an imaginary police office in Bow Street in one and addressing to the editor of the *London* a grim account of a trial for murder in Hertford in another. A Herbert "Letter on a

Peculiar Race of Men and Horses" was reported by Hood in "Lion's Head" as received, but was not printed.[29] There were nine papers in the Edward Herbert series. Reynolds's apparently erroneous numbering at one point probably showed that he considered "Warwick Castle" and "Bradgate Park" parts of the Herbert series: after numbering "The Cockpit Royal" five, he numbered "The Literary Police Office" eight, presumably to allow two numbers for the non-epistolary essays to which he had not assigned numbers earlier.

"Warwick Castle" mingled successfully the account of his visit to the medieval relic in the company of two unnamed young ladies who had also known Keats well (probably Reynolds's sisters), Romantic reverie over past chivalry, triggered by the castle and its fabled occupant Guy of Warwick, nostalgia for his lost childhood, and a moving lament for the dead Keats. During the visit in the spring of 1821 shortly after Keats's death, thoughts of his dead friend kept crowding into his mind. Gazing at the giant Greek vase given by Sir William Hamilton to the Warwick family, he saw a combination of beauty and underlying sadness that led to a comparison with Keats's "imaginary vase" and two quotations from *Ode on a Grecian Urn* (ll. 5 and 45–49), as well as a quotation from *Lamia* (II, 187–88). An unusual quietness in the castle made him the first to quote one of the finest similes in all English poetry, "As when, upon a tranced summer night" (*Hyperion*, I, 72–78). After these quotations, a portrait in the castle shifted his thought from the poetry to the dead poet and friend:

The picture that made the deepest impression on my mind, was one of Ignatius Loyola, a whole length, by Rubens;—but it was not the beauty of the colouring, or the name of the master, that worked this impression—it was the sweet and sainted expression of the features,—the lustrous resignation of the lifted eyes,—the placid virtue of the bald and passionless forehead; and, perhaps, I should not have felt all these so deeply, if they had not been recognized by others with me, as forming the perfect resemblance of a lost friend of ours.[30]

"Bradgate Park" again balanced present and past with Reynolds's vigorous prose at its best. He recalled how the beauty of the scene at the park and the friendliness of the deer-keeper and his family restored him to physical and mental health. As he surveyed the remains of the castle, he delighted in reconstructing it in his imagination as it had been when occupied by Lady Jane Grey and in describing his visions of tournaments, nobles, and Lady Jane herself. After quoting the memorable passage from *The Scholemaster* in which Ascham related how he found her reading Plato in the original Greek, he closed his tribute with seven graceful stanzas addressed "To Lady Jane Grey, at Bradgate."

"Greenwich Hospital" with its characterization of the Morton family was perhaps the best of the epistolary essays, followed by the moderately successful "The Green Room of a Theatre" and "The Cock-pit Royal," though Reynolds strained in making Tom Morton devil-may-care in "The Green Room" and he no doubt taxed the patience of some general readers by including excessive detail about cockfighting in "The Cock-pit Royal." "The Literary Police Office" was an amusing satire, but he was so cautious about wounding the feelings of his satirical targets that the piece was less effective than his earlier satires, "The Pilgrimage of the Living Poets," "Boswell's Visit," and *Peter Bell*. "The Inside of a Stagecoach" was a failure, as he seemed to realize when he virtually apologized for it in the next letter. After having Herbert complain about his illness in a seaside cottage for most of the essay, he lamely tacked on a dispirited account of a few dull passengers in the stagecoach that took him there.

Of the two occasional letters, sensuous and elaborate as "The Coronation" was, "A Pen and Ink Sketch of a Trial for Murder" was superior because it was more powerful. The murder of William Weare by John Thurtell in Gill's-hill-lane between London and Hertford on 24 October 1823 was one of the most sensational crimes of the period. Thurtell, believing that Weare had cheated him of £300, laid his plans carefully with an accomplice named Joseph Hunt, enticed his victim into the country by a promise of a weekend of hunting, and then shot, stabbed, and bludgeoned him to death. He attempted to dispose of the body by sinking it into a pond on the property of a second accomplice named Probert, but, fearing that it might be discovered in the shallow water, he transferred it to a second pond. After having scattered bloody clothes and weapons around the countryside in ineffectual efforts to conceal the crime, Thurtell and his confederates were apprehended.

Reynolds succeeded in making his account highly dramatic by bringing the courtroom scenes to life with telling details and by concentrating most of the attention on the central figure, the accused murderer. He depicted Thurtell as "one strong desperate man playing the hero of the tragic trial as at a play," and he heightened the tension progressively until the climax was reached in the defendant's final address to the jury, an appeal by a courageous combat veteran so persuasive that it planted unsettling doubts even after overwhelming evidence that he murdered Weare coldly and ferociously. Without minimizing the enormity of the crime, Reynolds evoked an uneasy respect for Thurtell's courage and composure during the trial and after the sentence of death was passed.

He concluded the article with a surprise ending like that of a modern detective story. Hunt, who denied being at the scene of the murder, was convicted of being an accomplice before the fact. Probert, a confederate who had turned state's evidence and had been charged only with being an accomplice after the fact, appeared throughout the article as a cowardly villain who had sacrificed Thurtell to save his own life. By a careful reexamination of the evidence, Reynolds showed the strong probability that both Hunt and Probert had lied to conceal that they had taken an active part in the crime from the beginning and had participated in the murder. Reynolds more than succeeded in his intention of making the account "interesting not only to the reader of this year, but to the reader of twenty years hence,"[31] for after more than a hundred and fifty years it is still interesting. It was, as Henry Crabb Robinson called it, "a masterly composition."[32]

When, on the publication of *The Garden of Florence* in 1821 there was no great demand for him to return to serious poetry, Reynolds continued writing the light verse that had succeeded so well in *Peter Bell* and *The Fancy*. In 1821 and 1822 he published six comic poems anonymously in the *London:* "The Champion's Farewell," "Faithless Sally Brown" (in collaboration with Hood), "A Bachelor's Soliloquy," "Don Giovanni the XVIII," *The Princess of Moonland,* and "Ode to a Sparrow."[33] With rapid rhythms and ingenious puns, they were exactly what he intended them to be, good magazine verse, but little more.

In 1823 and 1824 Reynolds found a new pseudonym suitable for this kind of unambitious verse, Ned Ward, Jr. Reynolds was not a John Dryden or an Alexander Pope, and he knew it; instead he was a vigorous and amusing versifier like their contemporary Ned Ward (1667–1731). Something reminded Reynolds of Richard Allen, his boyhood friend and schoolmate at both Shrewsbury School and St.

Paul's, and he addressed his first Ned Ward, Jr. poem to him, "A Parthian Peep at Life." Although the entire contrast between the Parthian or backward look at their boyhood and their current adult sobriety was delightful, the balanced picture of two kinds of dancing was perhaps sharpest:

> Look where we will, joy seems estranged,—
> The dance its very mirth hath changed;
>   Now formal—once how thrilling!
> The limb alive, the spirit supple
> The gallant "casting off two couple"
> All frozen to quadrilling![34]

After Allen's untimely death six months later, Reynolds had to change the tone of his recollection of their childhood sports to poignant elegy in "Stanzas to the Memory of Richard Allen."

Of the other Ned Ward, Jr. pieces—"Spring Song," "Ode to Master Isaac Walton," "Ode to the Printer's Devil," "A Chit Chat Letter," and "Vauxhall Reminiscences"—"A Chit Chat Letter" was the best. Imagining a friend at Oxford to be Anthony Wood, a contemporary of the real Ned Ward, Reynolds urged him to leave his pedantic study at the university and visit him in London to enjoy the indoor pleasures which he detailed sensuously through the course of a full day from breakfast through the final brandy and cigar before retiring. In skipping octosyllabic couplets reminiscent of the original New Ward but without his coarseness, Reynolds showed how enjoyable life could be for the middle-class young Londoner taking a holiday. Shortly before Taylor and Hessey sold the magazine, Reynolds returned to anonymity with "Remonstratory Ode, From the Elephant at Exeter Change to Mr. Mathews" and "Four Sonnets Composed during Ascot Race Week."

One of the unsigned articles was slight, though it probably entertained readers of the *London* with its human interest. "Walking Stewart" sketched the life and character of a recently deceased, eccentric world traveler, who had been a common sight on the streets of London.[35] His biography of John Philip Kemble, who died on 26 February 1823 at Lausanne, was more substantial and showed a real effort to pay tribute to a great actor.[36] He began the article soon after news of Kemble's death reached England, for James Hessey read the first part of it by 17 March and received the last part by about 25 March.[37] In his theatrical reviews for the *Champion* before Kemble retired on 23 June 1817, Reynolds had generally preferred Edmund Kean's fiery, tumultuous style to Kemble's restrained, classical acting, but he never failed to recognize Kemble's supremacy in such parts as Hamlet, Coriolanus, and Brutus. Though he had sometimes censured Kemble rather sharply in 1816 and 1817, in the memoir he praised his achievement with little reservation. He gave only a brief outline of the chief events in Kemble's life and concentrated most of his attention on a few incidents that revealed his character. The description of the quiet happiness of Kemble's domestic life and the emphasis on his habit of reading a chapter from the Bible every morning were reminiscent of Reynolds's favorite Izaak Walton's lives of Herbert and Sanderson. His view of biography argued that if Reynolds had ever written the life of Keats that he planned later, it would have been less than complete: "The private life too, we conceive, of a public man should always be warily told; for who but the veriest fool would crave to have little failings, detracting peculiarities, helpless faults, recorded minutely and with the malice of a biographer, against the children of genius."[38]

The biography of Kemble involved Reynolds in a dispute with William Charles Macready, the leading tragedian at Covent Garden. Remarking that in Kemble's time it had been an honor to perform Hamlet, Reynolds noted that a recent playbill indicated that times had changed. A charitable organization had planned a benefit for the poor with Charles Kemble acting Hamlet; when his brother John Philip Kemble's death prevented him, Macready "condescended to perform the character of Hamlet!!"[39] Macready was so offended that he wrote a letter of protest, which "Lion's Head" printed in May. "Lion's Head"—usually written by Hood, though Reynolds may have been allowed to answer for himself—disposed of all Macready's enraged invective by pointing out the simple truth, that not Macready, but the charitable organization had been blamed for writing that an actor had "condescended to perform the character of Hamlet!!"[40]

In his last unsigned article during the final year of Taylor and Hessey's ownership when Henry Southern was editor, Reynolds responded to Southern's staunch Utilitarianism, which did no violence to his own liberal political view, and wrote a political satire. Using irony to attack the unfairness of the Vagrant Act, Reynolds cited provision after provision and case after case to show that the authorities' power to arrest the unoffending poor was virtually unlimited. Then, after including a letter from a correspondent protesting that the act applied only to the poor and not to the rich, he denied the contention ironically by finding in the records of vagrants common names like James Smith, James Montgomery, and William Hilton and pretending that the affluent authors and painter had also been arrested for vagrancy. He weakened the attack, however, by piling up so many records of arrests and by delaying the climax for so long that many readers may have lost patience and turned elsewhere before arriving at his satirical point.[41]

Part of Reynolds's duty as subeditor was to review new books, and he was useful to Taylor and later to Southern by agreeing to review almost anything; in the dozen book reviews that have been identified, he ranged all the way from the memoirs of a simple Fleet Street spoon-maker to Hazlitt's *Table Talk*. Liveliest of all his reviews was "The Cook's Oracle,"[42] anticipating some aspects of "A Dissertation Upon Roast Pig," which it preceded by a year. Though it began as a review of Dr. Kitchener's cookbook, it developed into a humorous and imaginative personal essay on the naïveté of Dr. Kitchener, the art of cooking, and the pleasures of the table. In general the mingling of irony with gourmandizing suggests Lamb's great essay, and in particular the Swiftian quality of the passage treating the roasting of a goose alive in order to enhance its flavor parallels Lamb's Jesuitical disputation on whether it is justifiable to whip a pig to death if the pain is counterbalanced by the intensification of the pleasure upon man's palate. One of Reynolds's finest comic productions, "The Cook's Oracle" made Dr. Kitchener's book a favorite joke in the Reynolds-Hood circle. Hood wrote an "Ode to Dr. Kitchener" for the "Lion's Head" of the following month and several years later included a longer ode to the same author in *Odes and Addresses to Great People*.

In other reviews Reynolds was censorious more often than not. Noticing George Lambe's translation of Catullus, he protested against Lambe's being allowed "to *traduce* into English some of the sweetest and most natural poems in the Roman language."[43] Reynolds objected to the use of secular melodies in a new hymn book, and he denounced as hypocrisy *Mock Manuscript Sermons* printed in such a fashion that clergymen could pretend to be reading them as their own compositions.[44] Memories of Keats and John Scott inflamed his rage against the immorality of Lockhart's adulterous Presbyterian minister in *Some Passages in the Life of Mr. Adam Blair*.[45] He charged Thomas Moore with impiety in *The Loves of the Angels* and Sarah Siddons with desecrating Milton in her abridgment of *Paradise Lost*.[46]

On the other hand, he recommended warmly Grimm's *German Popular Stories* and gave measured praise to his friend Procter's *The Flood of Thessaly*.[47] As he had always been, he was enthusiastic in his praise of Hazlitt's hard-hitting style and searching intellect in *Table Talk*. Among the quotations, he selected one in which Hazlitt regretted that, unlike wealthy poets, Keats had no protection from attacks.[48]

Because of Reynolds's personal friendship with Hazlitt, Taylor and Hessey relied upon Reynolds for advice and assistance in their sometimes difficult dealings with one of their greatest contributors. In October 1821 they unwisely objected to the forthright, though unsettling, activism of "Guy Faux." When Hazlitt rebuffed their timidity and insisted that it be published, Hessey conferred with Taylor about the problem by letter: "Write about it on Saturday night—let me . . . have your opinion. Reynolds was anxious we should not lose Hazlitt—I wrote to H by his advice, and I have written to him [Reynolds] at Exeter to ask him what he thinks we had better do as he knows Hazlitt and his oddities well."[49] Reynolds's good offices did not succeed in arranging publication in the *London* of "Guy Faux," which Hazlitt printed instead in the *New Monthly,* but Reynolds doubtless helped to limit the friction between the publishers and Hazlitt, who did continue as a contributor, though a less frequent one. A year and a half later Reynolds tried to prevent trouble; when Hazlitt's attack on Scott in his review of *Peveril of the Peak* slipped by Taylor and was printed, Reynolds (and also T. G. Wainewright) called Taylor's attention to it and it was removed, though unfortunately *Blackwood's* managed to get one of the few copies to slip by and caused the kind of difficulty that Reynolds had sought to prevent.[50]

Humble John Clare did not cause Taylor and Hessey the kind of problems that Hazlitt did, but they wanted Clare to be placed at ease during his visits to London as much as possible for one so unassuming, and Reynolds was in the forefront of the magazine's contributors in welcoming him. Clare's account reveals that Reynolds was his favorite of all the Londoners:

Reynolds was always the soul of these dinner parties [given by Taylor and Hessey for contributors] he was the most good-natured fellow I ever met with his face was the three-in-one of fun wit & punning personified he would punch you with his puns very keenly without ever hurting your feelings for if you lookd in his face you could not be offended & you might retort as you pleasd—nothing could put him out of humour either with himself or others . . . he sits as a careless listener at table looking on with quick knapping sort of eye that turns towards you as quick as lightning when he has pun joke or story to give you they are never made up or studied they are flashes of the moment & mostly happy . . . his teeth are always looking through a laugh that sits as easy on his unpuck-erd lips as if he were born laughing he is a man of genius & if his talents were properly applied he would do something I verily believe that he might win the favours of fame with a pun—but be as it will wether she is inclind to smile or frown upon he is quite at home wi content the present is all with him he carries none of the Author about him a hearty laugh which there is no resisting at his jokes & puns seems to be more recom-pense than he expected & he seems startld into wonder at it & muses a moment as if he turnd the joke over agen in his mind to find the merry thought that made the laughter.[51]

Clare was delighted with *The Fancy,* especially with "Stanzas on Re-visiting Shrewsbury," which he thought had a unique rhythm. Puz-zled at first by the pseudonym John Hamilton under which *The Garden of Florence* appeared, his ear for rhythm persuaded him amusingly by degrees that the poem sounded like Reynolds, that it must be Reynolds, that it was Reynolds.

Although Reynolds did not much care for theatrical reviewing, he was the mainstay of the drama department during the first five great years of the *London.* After Hazlitt wrote ten of the eleven reviews during the first year,[52] Scott probably intended for Peter George Patmore to succeed Hazlitt as the regular critic. Patmore wrote the reviews for January and February 1821, but had to flee to France after serving as second in the duel that led to Scott's death. Thomas Noon Talfourd filled in temporarily for March and April. In May Reynolds assumed the post, believing that he would serve only for the summer. After serving as theatrical critic until September 1821, he wrote in November that contrary to his expectation the post had returned to the "summer establishment."[53] He continued to write the large majority of reviews through August 1824. Of the fifty-nine reviews written during the first five years (1820–24), Reynolds wrote thirty-three, while Hazlitt wrote ten and George Darley six.

In quality Reynolds was the *London's* second-best theatrical reviewer; he would have been the first to insist that his imitation of Hazlitt's prose did not equal his master's. But his liveliness and thoughtfulness did make him a better critic than George Darley. When Darley substituted for Reynolds in October 1823, he was not just being modest in praising Reynolds's superiority:

In the temporary *rustication* of our brother Contributor who generally "does the drama," we were invested much against our will, with the ungrateful office. We say, "ungrateful," not with respect to the function of the theatrical critic in general, but in reference to the pecularity of our vicarious situation in the present case. We, who are of the *humdrum* school, one of those plain, honest, stupid kind of people who can see little further than the end of their nose, find the neighbourhood—even on paper—of your witty men, extremely intolerable. Hence, it is not without the utmost repugnance that we have brought ourself to endure a contrast in print with the Gentleman whose brilliancy has heretofore illuminated the dramatic region of this Miscellany. We have neither his keen wit, his playful humour, his tact, nor his discernment in these matters.[54]

Reynolds's "temporary *rustication*" was a fall vacation to escape the hectic pressure of work; he was "living in [a] Cottage near to Plymouth enjoying complete freedom & forgetfulness of all London Matters." He did not even write to members of his family.[55]

As interesting as Reynolds's *London* theatrical reviews were to his contemporaries, they are of less interest to later readers than those in the *Champion* because he did not review nearly as many revivals of dramatic masterpieces from Shakespeare through Sheridan. Though he did criticize performances of *Henry IV, Part I* and *Two Gentlemen of Verona*, for the most part he reviewed new plays, now long forgotten, and focused his attention on the acting. For one example, in January 1822 he criticized the acting of his old favorite, Edmund Kean. Like Hazlitt, Lamb, Keats, Byron, Coleridge, and most of the other Romantics, Reynolds had praised Kean highly during the actor's best years from 1814 through 1819. In the latter year Kean began a two-year tour of America, and, when he returned to resume his old position as chief tragedian at Drury Lane for the season of 1821–22, many London theatrical critics thought that he had lost his earlier power. Reynolds argued that Kean was still the finest living actor, though he admitted that there had been a noticeable decline in the effectiveness of his acting. He believed that the principal reason for Kean's decline lay in his increased use of stage tricks and affected gestures to appeal to mindless spectators. Even the classic restraint of John Philip Kemble would be better than such shallow devices. He was so convinced of the soundness of his basically favorable judgment that "C. Lamb himself has failed to change this studiously weighed opinion of ours; so has Hazlitt (though to differ from him is a good deal presumptuous, and not a little dangerous)."[56]

Reynolds's occasional tongue-in-cheek puffing of his own writing for the stage was amusing, though only the select few who knew of his anonymous work could appreciate it. After censuring Kean's performance in the notice of March 1822, he added, "But who could, with a penny-weight of brains, lay the scene of a tragedy in Wales? The peculiar dialect of the Welch will rise up; and is it tragic?— Alack, no!—We understand that Mathews has a choice specimen of Welch character in his approaching entertainment, in which the dialect is given to the life. The character is described to us as that of a fat Cambrian valetudinarian, who visits every watering place, and talks only of waters, in the hopes of 'getting thinner.' "[57] Reynolds described a character that he doubtless had a hand in creating, for he collaborated with R. B. Peake on *The Youthful Days of Mr. Mathews,* first performed at the English Opera House on 11 March 1822.[58] In April he puffed the same work extravagantly, devoting the entire theatrical section to it. After urging all readers to see the performance, he closed with an amusing *double entendre:* "We need hardly say that this entertainment hits our taste exactly; had we written it ourselves we could not have made it better."[59]

Dilke overstated the case when after Reynolds's death he called the *London Magazine* days "the only true period of his literary life,"[60] because that judgment neglected unfairly Reynolds's substantial achievement from 1816 through the first half of 1820 before his serious work for the *London* began. His *London* years, however, represented a solid accomplishment which he was to recall with satisfaction for the rest of his life. In company with the greatest prose geniuses of the age, Lamb, Hazlitt, and De Quincey, he had been a mainstay for one of the greatest literary periodicals that England has produced.

CHAPTER 14

The Remainder of the Decade—
1822–1829

THE FAVORABLE RECEPTION of *The Youthful Days of Mr. Mathews* encouraged Reynolds to prepare, perhaps with Hood, a more ambitious drama entitled *Gil Blas,* portraying the hero of Le Sage's novel at the ages of seventeen, twenty-five, and fifty-two.[1] No printed version of the play has survived, but it was initially a five-act farcical opera with music by Moss, first performed on 1 August 1822.[2] The theatrical critic who substituted for Reynolds while he was away for his wedding in August of that year summarized it at length in the *London* for August 1822.[3] Problems with a complicated piece of machinery devised to present "the Cavern of the Banditti" delayed the opening of the opera,[4] and critics' objections that it was too long—the first performance ran from seven until midnight—encouraged the authors to cut the opera from five acts to three and to change the title to *The Youthful Days of Gil Blas.*[5] Fanny Kelly, a friend of Reynolds and Hood as well as of Charles Lamb, played Gil Blas both at the age of seventeen and, in the original version, his daughter at a later age. Her expert comic acting was no doubt as much responsible for the long run of thirty-four performances as Reynolds's script.[6]

In the years since his engagement to Eliza Powell Drewe in 1817, Reynolds had earned respectable sums of money from his theatrical and periodical writing and his two profitable books, *Peter Bell* and *The Fancy,* but this kind of income was unpredictable. What he and Eliza were awaiting, and had probably agreed to when he was articled as a law clerk in November 1817, was for him to qualify fully as a solicitor so that he would have reasonable assurance of a steady income to support a wife and family. When he qualified as a solicitor by August 1822,[7] he married Eliza at Holy Trinity Church in Exeter on 31 August 1822.[8] Though the Drewe family was Presbyterian—all the children were christened at the Bow meeting, Presbyterian—the law required that the wedding be performed in the Anglican church.

John Taylor, who had met Eliza Drewe in Bath in the summer of 1820, predicted happiness for the couple in glowing terms to John Clare. "Reynolds is gone off to Exeter to be married, tomorrow is the happy day that is to witness the union of as interesting a couple as I ever met—a fine sensible high-spirited generous warm-hearted young fellow in the prime of youth and health, and a pretty intelligent, modest, interesting young girl, warmly attached to him as he is to her—'tis a pretty picture is it not? Each of us is to send him a letter on his wedding, and you must contribute your offering in Poetry or Prose or both."[9]

Hood's offering was an amusing parody of the program of a state procession, "A Progress from London to Wedlock through Exeter."[10] Not yet having met Eliza and her family, he included "The People of Exeter" only in a general way and particularized the Reynolds family (except that he omitted the married Eliza Reynolds Longmore), the *London Magazine*'s publishers and chief contributors, and personal friends like Rice and Woodhouse. Hood's verbal playfulness abounded in such items as "1st, 2nd, and 3rd Times of Asking and Their Axes" and "Lion's Head with His Two Pages" (the usual length of that department in the *London*).

After a month's honeymoon, the couple returned to London late in September to lodgings at 24 Great Marlborough Street. Charlotte Reynolds and her daughter Charlotte, or Lotte as she was usually called, were away at Upwell, visiting Eliza Reynolds Longmore. On Monday, 30 September, the other Reynoldses—George, Jane, and Marianne—gave a party for the newlyweds in Little Britain inviting as guests Hood, Rice, Mrs. Butler, and John Lincoln and William (probably Mrs. Butler's sons). Hood sketched a picture memorably in a letter to Lotte, imagining that she could see the scene in the family living room with telescopic eyes:

with her eyes like compressed stars, and her eloquent brows—but your father will tell you about those—and her mouth like somebody's you have never seen, and with her easy grace of manner which Jane will tell you of— and her smile which herself will show you—sits the unimaginable reality—the tantalizing mystery—the still-undiscovered Mrs. Reynolds—Mrs. John—John's wife—with a great thick misty veil between her and Upwell— which Jane is trying to fan away with a very circumstantial piece of paper—but it won't do—you must still wish to see her, and then see her to your wish—as I have done.—Only look at John—what a talk he makes! With the horns of his mouth upwards like a fair moon—laughing like a fugleman [soldier acting as model for recruits at drill] to let off our laughters. . . . There—between me and the teapot—her cheek the very colour of content, and her eyes how earnest, sits Jane, the kindly Jane—hugging her own hands for very happiness—she on one side of me—I beside myself—and on the other hand gentle maid Marianne, making go[od] tea as if for Robin Hood and smiling as if her heart drank cream and sugar. How the tea dimples in the cup and the urn sings for joy! Now if you look through the urn you will see your father smiling towards the sofa, and there is Rice smiling towards nine o'clock.[11]

John and Eliza's happiness radiated through the whole family circle in Hood's sustained pretense that the two Charlottes were with them in spirit, though absent in body. "Mrs. John R. is said to have felt the kisses she knew not wherefrom—but I say, Upwell. . . . and didn't John look well!—so merry, and so happy, and so like a fly in a honey-pot, as Rice says—and I'm sure he loves the taste of his wings. And we have been so joyous round him as if he were a common centre of sweets like a sugar cask with all the little loves round it."[12]

On Thursday, 3 October, Rice gave a card party and supper at his place for the new couple which proved to be less enjoyable—at least James Hessey did not enjoy it much. He thought that Rice had not managed to place people effectively at supper. He wrote to Taylor of Eliza, not knowing or forgetting that Taylor had already met her: "I had no opportunity of seeing much of M[rs] R. but she seems a sensible pleasant Woman. She is not pretty, and scarc[e]ly to be called handsome though more of that quality than of the former— She has a very fine eye and eyebrow, & the rest of her face is not unlike her husbands—She is rather tall, & thin, & rather older looking than I expected, but they all said she was not in her best looks that Evening as she had been much fatigued during the Day."[13] Hessey, who visited often at Little Britain, had no doubt heard Reynolds's fiancée spoken of in glowing terms and had expected that Eliza would be several years younger than her husband. Eliza would not have advertised the fact that she was a year and two months older than Reynolds.

Reynolds's happy marriage provided an opportunity to patch up a yearlong breach with the Dilkes, which probably resulted from the Reynoldses' sustained hostility to Fanny Brawne. The Dilkes themselves had initial reservations about Fanny, but they had grown close to her after Keats left England. On 29 October 1822 Fanny Brawne wrote Fanny Keats, "There is, I think, every prospect of a reconciliation between Mrs Dilke and the Reynolds'; for M^r J Reynolds is married, the Dilkes have called on him and have been informed that his sisters are very anxious to make up the quarrel, fine fun it will be to see them together."[14] The reconciliation was effected and the Dilkes and Reynoldses remained lifelong friends.

Perhaps Jane was the more inclined to be sympathetic toward Fanny for the tragic loss of her lover Keats because at this time Jane was thoroughly in love with Hood and had accepted his proposal. In late October (or possibly early November), with Jane at his side at the Butlers', Hood wrote Mrs. Reynolds for the first time as his future mother-in-law a letter that glowed with their complete love and happiness.[15] Although they were not to be married for another three years, their engagement became generally known; by 5 November James Hessey had learned of it.[16]

After the festivities on his return to London, Reynolds settled down to his mundane work as a solicitor in partnership with Rice. In addition to Reynolds's substantial contributions to the *London,* the firm of Rice and Reynolds also represented Taylor and Hessey in some legal matters. In January 1823 Taylor and Hessey started negotiations to move the offices of the *London Magazine* from 93 Fleet Street to 13 Waterloo Place. Reynolds acted for the publishers in a disagreement over rent with a man named Oakley. The details are not clear, but presumably the dispute was settled in some way before Taylor and Hessey moved the *London* offices to 13 Waterloo Place by 15 August 1823.[17] Around this time Reynolds labored hard and long on his double duties of legal work and writing for the *London.* He was at his desk between seven and eight in the morning, worked throughout the day, and then returned to work from eight to ten in the evening on a client's account, his "worst subject."[18]

Despite such hard work, Reynolds caused some problems for Taylor and Hessey. He annoyed Hessey by failing to return the marked copy for a review of Hazlitt's *Table Talk,* and he had to apologize for his "cursed habit of procrastinating the Drama."[19] Though he insisted on paying the extra charges of the printer because of the lateness, he nevertheless caused inconvenience. De Quincey thought it unfair that Taylor and Hessey were not considerate of his difficulties, while they tolerated much greater inconveniences from Reynolds, as they had earlier from Hazlitt: the reasons Reynolds and Hazlitt gave, he said, were frivolous, "that they got drunk—went to the play,—had a cold,—gave a party, or any other reason why!"[20]

By the summer of 1824, Taylor's patience was sorely taxed. When Reynolds requested an advance of £200 on future work, he responded with "a Petition for the Redress of Grievances." He stipulated that, if Reynolds were to continue with the drama, he must have the notices in by the twenty-fifth of each month without fail.[21] He did, however, advance the money, making clear that he valued Reynolds's services by the friendly tone of the carefully revised letter (only the original draft is preserved) and by the invitation to submit as often as possible "articles, to suit your own Taste."

The public reception of the Edward Herbert papers was sufficiently favorable for Reynolds to plan in 1823 and 1824 to publish through Taylor and Hessey a reprint of the collected essays in book form. Charles A. Elton's praise of "Herbert's vein" in "The Idler's Epistle to John Clare" was doubtless characteristic of readers, as well as of fellow contributors.[22] Several steps were taken to further the projected book. Five booksellers subscribed to the proposed edition, though Longmans refused to cooperate.[23] George Cruikshank, with whom Reynolds became close friends some time after his brother Robert illustrated *One, Two, Three, Four, Five, by Advertisement* in 1819, agreed to prepare an etching for each essay and completed the two which survive, one for "Exmouth Wrestling" and the other for "Greenwich Hospital."[24] The book was advertised, but seems never to have been published.[25]

During the last year of his work for the *London*, Reynolds also contributed at least one article to the *Westminister Review*, the new organ of the Benthamites edited by John Bowring, whom Reynolds knew as a contributor to the *London*.[26] In the *Westminster* for July 1824, he attacked John Wilson in a mock review of *The Danciad*, a poem by a dancing master named Thomas Wilson, which admirably suited his purpose because it was so ridiculously bad.[27] In *Blackwood's* for the preceding month, "Christopher North" (most often John Wilson) had confused Reynolds with P. G. Patmore by assigning the authorship of Edward Herbert's letter on the Thurtell trial to Tims, a nickname *Blackwood's* had used earlier for Patmore.[28] Reynolds replied in kind. By pretending to mistake the dancing professor for the Professor of Moral Philosophy at Edinburgh, he satirized Wilson amusingly and effectively:

An inspired work—a good book—as Mawworm calls it,[29] has very recently appeared, entitled "The Danciad, or Dancer's Monitor," and written by Mr. Professor Wilson, to whom we believe we are already indebted for several pleasing poetical as well as dramatic performances, the Isle of Palms, the Children's Dance, the City of the Plague,[30] and other interesting publications. The present production is not exactly in the style of the works we have enumerated; but in moral philosophy, pointed invective, and dramatic spirit, it perhaps far outstrips any of them.[31]

Reynolds struck at Wilson's scandalous attacks in *Blackwood's,* referring to Wilson's personal abuse of the cockneys. "Mr. Wilson appears to be very familiar in this, as in some of his other works, which we have not here specified, with London persons, London vices, and London manners." He thought it unusual, however, for the dancing professor not to reveal the names of his victims, "The only fault we find with Mr. Professor Wilson in the Danciad—and it is a fault which has seldom been laid at his door—is his proneness to conceal the names of persons whom he wishes to hold up to shame, and the particulars of their private lives and connexions. We always admired the pleasant searching truth of the professor, when he chose to indulge in the private history of his offenders." In conclusion Reynolds commented on the quality of Wilson's work with biting, double-edged satire. "That this work is worthy of the pen of the great professor, no one we think will be rash enough to question. . . . Those who have thought his buoyant spirits and pliant abilities a little unbecoming the chair, will now see that not without an object have those amiable gaieties been encouraged. The present work is a key to many of those extravagant sallies, which, until its appearance, were unaccountable even to his friends."[32]

Of course Reynolds had ample reason for attacking Wilson. Lockhart had written the most objectionable articles on Hunt, Hazlitt, and Keats in 1817 and 1818, but as coeditor of *Blackwood's* Wilson shared the responsibility. Furthermore, as Christopher North, he had continued to make scurrilous comments from 1818 to 1824 on the liberal writers who lived in London. For the most part, *Black-*

wood's had spared Reynolds, but it had not spared his friend Keats, and within the last two years it had directed a stream of invective against another friend, Bryan Waller Procter. Indeed it is somewhat surprising that Reynolds used so much restraint; he struck sharply, as any good satirist must, but he did not descend to the kind of personal abuse which his opponents used. Except for the one transparent falsehood on which the article was based, he told nothing but the truth.

That truth hurt. The *Blackwood's* authors did not hesitate to attack others violently, but they could not bear a counterattack against one of their own group. John Scott had been killed in 1821 because he dared to call Lockhart the liar that he was. Now in *Blackwood's* for August 1824, a month after Reynolds's article in the *Westminster,* Wilson's uncle, Robert Syme, wrote a blustering reply:

The *Danciad,* a silly poem, by a London dancing-master of the name of Wilson, is here attributed to Professor Wilson, as the ground-work of a dull joke. The writer is evidently actuated by some low spite against that eminent man, and goes as far to indulge it as he dares. I wonder Mr. Baldwin, who owns this Review, did not recollect that he formerly had another editor in his wages, who began the same slanderous trade. If he remembered it, he would, I think, have paused a little before he made room for another of the same unfortunate gang to yelp to the same tune.[33]

Baldwin, Cradock, and Joy published the *London Magazine* while John Scott was editor. Reynolds's satire must have stung very bitterly indeed to cause Syme to recall an episode so discreditable to *Blackwood's.*

Just as Reynolds's acquaintance with John Bowring, contributor to the *London,* led to his article in the *Westminster,* so his friendship with Henry Southern, who succeeded John Taylor as editor of the *London* and later bought the magazine, led to several articles in the *Retrospective Review,* also edited by Southern.[34] The one of those articles that can be identified was "Sir Thomas Parkyns' Progymnasmata," published in 1825. There Reynolds described at length a favorite bibliographical discovery, a rare and eccentric old book on wrestling which he had treated briefly five years before in "Exmouth Wrestling."

Reynolds's friendship with Hood, now long engaged to Jane, continued to be warm. Only one possible example of temporary coolness in the early years has been discovered. Hessey wrote Taylor on 22 February 1823, "Thomas [the servant] will tell you whether Reynolds can come—if he does not you may as well bring Hood with you, but it would not be comfortable to bring them purposely together."[35] But the disagreement between them, if it was that, passed quickly. In the autumn of 1824 Hood conceived the idea of a set of comic odes addressed to people famous or notorious at the time and persuaded Reynolds to collaborate. Although already beginning to make his way as the outstanding comic versifier of his day, Hood still regarded Reynolds as the master of this minor craft. Sending Reynolds his third specimen for the book, Hood wrote, "I think the thing is likely to be a hit—but if *you* do some, I shall expect it to run like wildfire."[36]

Reynolds did contribute five of the fifteen odes—those to McAdam, Dymoke, Sylvanus Urban, Elliston, and Ireland.[37] *The Ode to Mr. McAdam* is now deadened somewhat by dependence on the many London place names where the streets had been macadamized, but the ingenious joking about the McAdam as son of the biblical Adam is still amusing. Except for a theatrical historian, the *Address to Elliston, the Great Lessee* [of Drury Lane] is too embedded in details of the theater to be of much interest to later readers. *The Address to Mr. Dymoke, Champion of England* shows the laughable incongruity of a nineteenth-century rural squire's attempt to preserve medieval tradition, but Reynolds and Hood had worn out that joke in the five years since the coronation of George IV.

The *Address to Sylvanus Urban* was the best poem in the book, including Hood's, though the appropriate audience may be limited to those familiar with the venerable *Gentleman's Magazine*. Reynolds had taken great delight in publishing his youthful verse and prose in its ponderous pages, and he and his family had always read it as a national institution. He may well have forgotten that the *Gentleman's* reviewed *The Garden of Florence* most harshly of all the journals several years earlier, because his mockery was not vindictive. He laughed at the soporific solemnity of the obituaries and vital statistics:

> Lives of Right Reverends that have never liv'd—
> Deaths of good people that have really died,—
> Parishioners,—hatch'd,—husbanded,—and wiv'd,
> Bankrupts and Abbots breaking side by side!

and at the triviality of much of the antiquarianism:

> X. sends the portrait of a genuine flea,
> Caught upon Martin Luther years agone;—
> And Mr. Parkes, of Shrewsbury, draws a bee,
> Long dead, that gather'd honey for King John.[38]

Reynolds felt most strongly about his subject in *Address to the Very Reverend John Ireland, D.D. . . . The Dean and Chapter of Westminster,* in which he protested against charging admission to view the tombs of the nation's honored dead in Westminster Abbey. Goldsmith had objected to the practice in *The Citizen of the World,* and recently Lamb had castigated the authorities in *Letter to Robert Southey.* Reynolds's satirical tone here was the sharpest in the book, as he set in ironic contrast the grandeur of the dead against the petty greed of the "reverend showmen," whom he advised caustically to contract with living poets like Wordsworth, Coleridge, and Scott for their future remains to ensure a continued thriving business. He suggested that they erect flamboyant pictured signs outside and act as pitchmen to lure the customers into the side show, "All dead! All dead! Walk in! Walk in!"[39] The *Address* is more forceful, if less amusing, than *Sylvanus Urban.*

The hit that Hood predicted when he asked Reynolds to collaborate, *Odes and Addresses* went through two editions by Baldwin, Cradock, and Joy in 1825 and a third by Colburn in 1826. At least nine newspapers and magazines praised it, usually judging it the best comic and satirical collection since the Smith brothers' *Rejected Addresses* in 1812.[40] Coleridge, enthusiastic about the anonymous book, thought that no one but Charles Lamb could have written such a work which was "the *exemplum sine exemplo* of a volume of personalities and contemporaneities, without a single line that could inflict the infinitesimal of an unpleasance on any man in his senses."[41] Lamb replied that they were not his but Hood's and Reynolds's and that he had reviewed the "hearty good-natured things" favorably in a newspaper (the *New Times*).[42]

Reynolds's friendship with Hood, cemented by the success of the book as well as by Hood's marriage to Jane on 5 May 1825, continued through the 1820s.[43] When Hood republished *Lycus the Centaur* in 1827 in *The Plea of the Midsummer Fairies* he replaced his original dedication to Lamb with a new dedication to Reynolds in which he expressed "regret that your pen goes now into far other records than those which used to delight me."[44] Hood's letters show that they spent much time together, sharing new friends, enjoying the parties at Reynolds's house on Golden Square, and conferring about their writing.[45]

Reynolds managed the legal work to which Hood referred in the dedication with more the appearance of success than the reality. Rice and Reynolds represented both George Keats and Fanny Keats Llanos in the disposition of their grandmother's estate.[46] George had some difficulty in communicating with Rice and Reynolds over the great distance from America, but the only serious problem with the account before 1830 was that after Rice informed George that he had a balance of £500, George wrote a draft for £350 that Rice and Reynolds left unpaid, much to George's embarrassment.[47] That problem seems to have been solved satisfactorily, for when Georgiana made the long trip to London in the last half of 1828, nothing interfered with the cordial welcome and extensive hospitality she received from Reynolds, his mother, Marianne, Hood, and Jane. From the seeming affluence she saw, Georgiana concluded that Reynolds enjoyed considerable success in the law. On her return to Kentucky, George wrote Dilke that for Reynolds's mother "it must be gratifying . . . to witness the s{uc}cess of John, whose start in life was by no means so promising."[48] But if the apparent affluence had any foundation at the time, which seems doubtful, it was not to last long, for within a few years Dilke was to write George that "Reynolds' affairs . . . have long been desperate."[49]

The decade closed with the friendship between Reynolds and Hood as warm as ever. Reynolds published a comic poem addressed to Hood in the *Literary Gazette*.[50] The Hoods attended parties at the Reynolds place in Golden Square.[51] Reynolds contributed a sonnet to Hood's *Gem* in late 1828 and in the next year remained close enough to Hood to write to Hartley Coleridge about Hood's departure from the *Gem*.[52]

CHAPTER 15

Journalism, the Theater, and the Law—1830–1839

AFTER 1825 Reynolds's work for periodicals became progressively more journalistic; he wrote for many journals and only a fraction of his work there can be traced. It is significant that when he sent R. M. Milnes a list of his works in 1848, he did not bother to mention any writing after *Odes and Addresses* of 1825.[1] He owned a part of the *Athenaeum* from 1828 until 8 June 1831 and undoubtedly contributed to it from the time he acquired a share, but only a very little of his work can be identified before 5 June 1830 when his old friend Charles Dilke became editor.[2] During many of the years of his editorship, Dilke kept a special file of the magazine in which he recorded the names of the contributors. He marked the file for the years 1830, 1831, 1833, 1834, 1839, and for the years thereafter, though he did not write the authors' names after all the articles during those years.

Reynolds, a frequent contributor in 1830, was much interested in the management of the magazine. Early in 1831 Dilke planned a drastic reduction in the price from eightpence to fourpence in order to increase the circulation. Reynolds and Hood, who also owned a share, were so shocked by the proposal that Reynolds wrote twice in one day to protest that Dilke risked making the magazine "Two-penny Trashish."[3] When Dilke insisted on the radical cut, Reynolds sold the editor his share of the magazine in protest on 8 June 1831, an action which he must have regretted, for the *Athenaeum* became increasingly prosperous after the reduction in price on 6 August and Reynolds needed money badly.

After disposing of his share, Reynolds continued as an important contributor through 1833, furnishing routine work like art criticism. A number of his other articles in 1830 and 1831 were a part of a campaign by the *Athenaeum* against deceitful practices of publishers. Several publishers who owned magazines would arrange to have their books reviewed favorably by writers in their pay and then insert in advertisements laudatory extracts from the reviews. The worst offender was Henry Colburn, who owned the *New Monthly Magazine,* the *Court Journal,* the *United Service Journal,* and a share in the *Literary Gazette.* These periodicals could not be trusted, for their reviews of books published by Colburn were really paid advertisements.[4]

When Dilke became editor of the *Athenaeum* with the 5 June 1830 issue, he set out to remedy this evil. Determined to keep the magazine impartial, he usually insisted that no one review a book who was acquainted with the author. Once, when Reynolds requested permission to criticize a new book, Dilke asked whether he knew either the author or the publisher; Reynolds, who was irritated, returned the book, "that you may consign it to some independent hand, according to your religious custom. I, alas! know author and book-seller."[5] Although this strict policy could be irksome to members of the staff, the *Athenaeum's* reviews gained a reputation as trustworthy.

In addition to preserving its own integrity, the *Athenaeum* conducted a vigorous campaign against the deceitful practices of its rivals. The leader of the attack was Reynolds, who opened fire on 17 July 1830 with a scathing review of *Lives of Remarkable Youths of Both Sexes,* the first volume of a juvenile series published by Colburn and Bentley.

People who keep disorderly houses,—attend boxing matches,—vend wicked pictures or books, are indictable and occasionally indicted; but publishers who infest the newspapers with their own speculative productions, are amenable to no law and escape punishment. No one will have the hardihood to say that the "Juvenile Library" is not become a positive nuisance in the newspapers; for it is scarcely possible to get through a single column of *Chronicle* or *Herald,* without having to suffer a Burlington Street [location of Colburn and Bentley] paragraph. Nothing can be so moral and edifying as the "Juvenile Library"; nothing so pure and pleasant as its style; nothing so disinterested and generous as its object. The paragraphs, which are paid for, say all this; and some persons in London, and many credulous country readers, cannot read the same mystic hymn to the breeches-pocket day after day, without believing that things are as they are said to be.[6]

Reynolds proceeded to expose the book as cheap hackwork derived from standard biographies that were readily available. He pointed out a number of grammatical errors that he considered inexcusable in a book designed for the instruction of young people. Always a clever punster, he seized upon the ambiguity in the title, *Lives of Remarkable Youths of Both Sexes,* and used it as a horrible example of careless writing. He announced the *Athenaeum*'s policy on puffing to the publishers and to the public: "It is the duty of an independent journal to protect as far as possible the credulous, confiding, and unwary, from the wily arts of the insidious advertiser."

His attack roused the author and publisher of *Lives of Remarkable Youths of Both Sexes* to a fighting mood. In a review of the second volume of the Juvenile Library series, Reynolds reported that the author of the first "was for having it out with us at fisty-cuffs" and that the publishers had considered a lawsuit.[7] But the threats of retaliation did not deter him from his duty, for he condemned the second volume as strongly as the first and warned the publishers that they could expect the same treatment until they mended their ways.

In September 1830 Reynolds attacked another publication of Colburn and Bentley, John Galt's *Life of Byron,* arguing that Galt was prejudiced against Byron, that his book was full of errors, and that he contributed no new biographical facts.[8] After this attack Colburn and Bentley received unpaid assistance from a writer in *Fraser's Magazine,* who charged that the *Athenaeum* was biased against the publishing house. Although he was not unfriendly toward the *Athenaeum,* he thought that for several months its writers had attacked the publications of Colburn and Bentley indiscriminately. In a subsequent defense of his earlier articles, Reynolds quoted the criticism of *Fraser's* and accepted it in good spirit, for he was able to refute it easily. He listed the Colburn and Bentley books that the *Athenaeum* had commended after Dilke became editor and those that it had censured; the fact that it had praised twice as many as it had condemned answered his critic effectively. Reynolds reasserted his own independence and continued the attacks on the puffing of other journals, particularly that of the *Literary Gazette,* which he said avoided all unpleasantness by reviewing every book favorably.

Reynolds's criticism so worried Colburn and Bentley that they delayed publication of the third volume of the Juvenile Library. When it finally appeared, a preface explained that every effort had been made to avoid the grammatical errors that had caused hostile criticism of the first two volumes. The text of _The History of Africa_ was satisfactory, and Reynolds reviewed it rather kindly, but unfortunately either the editor of the series had neglected to revise or he was incapable of writing correct English, for his preface contained the same kind of faulty grammar that had marred the first two volumes. Reynolds demolished the preface, and with it the entire Juvenile Library, for shortly thereafter Colburn and Bentley decided to discontinue the series.[9]

Early in 1831 Reynolds directed his last antipuffing articles against another large publishing house.[10] Longmans and Company had advertised widely the first volume of a new Cabinet Library series with laudatory extracts from the _Literary Gazette,_ of which Longman was a principal owner. The first volume of the series, Captain Moyle Sherer's _Military Memoirs of Field Marshal the Duke of Wellington,_ was for the most part a history of the peninsular campaigns. The marked file assigns the first and third installments to Reynolds, but attributes the second to "Swane and Reynolds." Since all three installments bear the distinctive characteristics of Reynolds's style, however, it seems likely that Swane was someone with a knowledge of military history who supplied Reynolds with the facts that he needed for the second notice. In any event, Reynolds and Swane found a host of errors in the book: it mentioned a nonexistent university, reported a man then living to have been killed, confused Spanish geography, and misrepresented Spanish customs. It was an unreliable history, and the reviewers attacked it accordingly.

Reynolds deserves much of the credit for the attacks on the shady publishing practices. The _Athenaeum_ established its reputation through its independence, and its independence became known through its attacks on puffing. Of course the editor Charles Dilke deserves the most praise, for he set the policy requiring strict impartiality and enforced it even when it seemed too rigorous to Reynolds. Yet though Reynolds was only one among a number of critics who attacked puffing, his writing was the liveliest, and his attacks were the sharpest. An advertisement the _Athenaeum_ ran in its own pages in 1830 and 1831 reveals that Reynolds's work attracted the most attention.[11] In a group of testimonials to the _Athenaeum_'s courage and independence extracted from periodicals throughout the country, the only articles praised specifically were Reynolds's attacks on Galt's *Life of Byron.*

Reynolds, of course, had been anything but Simon Pure on the issue of puffing before his connection with the *Athenaeum.* Realizing the importance of friendly notices, he had been no more squeamish than Hazlitt about exerting his influence to have his own work reviewed favorably. He had hoped the critics might "be lured into an admiration" of *The Naiad;*[12] he had asked Keats to use his influence with Hunt to have the spurious *Peter Bell* praised in the *Examiner;* and he had puffed his own dramatic productions in the theatrical section of the *London Magazine.* Nevertheless, it may be said to Reynolds's credit that he never paid for a laudatory review, and he attacked in the *Athenaeum* publishers who had developed puffing into a regular business.

Aside from Reynolds's articles in the campaign against puffing, his most interesting contribution was a review of Hazlitt's *Conversations of James Northcote,* where Dilke relaxed his usual rule against a reviewer's noticing the work of a friend. Hazlitt had died shortly before the publication of this last book, and Reynolds began the review with a survey of the accomplishment of the man who had been his idol in early years. Although Reynolds had been somewhat disillusioned by Hazlitt's divorce and unseemly love affair, his great admiration for Hazlitt still shone through the brief account of his life and works. He observed that many of Hazlitt's fine essays had not been reprinted from magazines and predicted that "Posterity in its slow but sure course of justice" would "collect and value" all his works.[13]

In the same review Reynolds quoted a passage in which Hazlitt had recorded Northcote's harsh judgment of Benjamin Robert Haydon. For over a year Reynolds, Haydon, and Keats had been a triumvirate of close friends, but Reynolds and Haydon's friendship had ended with the bitter quarrel of January 1818. Now, after twelve years, the quarrel had faded, and Reynolds partially defended his former friend against the censure of Northcote:

This is severe work upon a painter whose genius, however, is distinguishable through all his faults. He certainly abandons himself to the excessive in whatever he attempts or achieves;—he paints in the gigantic, and tortures nature; his writings on Art are arrogant and disputatious; his assertions and his complaints are "i' the Hercles vein";—but then his disappointments, his sufferings, aggravate his discontent and egotism; and in contemplating his character, it is impossible not to see and grieve over great misdirected powers, and to feel and acknowledge that circumstances might have made him as pre-eminently superior in Art, as they have unfortunately conspired to fret, baffle, and destroy him![14]

Reynolds saw Haydon's faults clearly, but after the lapse of years was more sympathetic than hostile toward him.

Another passage of some interest appeared in Reynolds's review of Thomas Moore's *Letters and Journals of Lord Byron,* where Reynolds objected to Moore's allowing "all the ill-nature and sarcasm against Keats to be perpetuated,—without regard to the feelings of surviving relations and friends." Reynolds denied Byron's claim that Keats was snuffed out by the *Quarterly Review,* insisting "that consumption, and not criticism, destroyed him."[15]

In his numerous other reviews for the *Athenaeum* from 1830 through 1833, Reynolds criticized novels, annuals, picture books, and one volume of poor verse. His interest in sports was reflected in reviews of publications like *The Horseman's Manual* and the *New Sporting Magazine.* He judged such unusual books as *The Catechism of Whist* and *A History and Description of Modern Wines.* All these reviews were competent journalism, but contain nothing of lasting interest.

In the early 1830s Reynolds was looking backward instead of forward. In a review of Moore's edition of Byron's works, he published the letter in which Byron had acknowledged the dedication of *Safie* in 1814, with a nostalgic comment that he had long ceased trying to win fame as a serious poet.[16] In 1832 he attempted to resume the type of writing with which he had been most successful in the *London Magazine.* "The Letters of Edward Herbert, New Series, No. I" showed careful preparation for a second sequence of letters. Edward Herbert wrote that he had retired to Devonshire after the publication of the first series and that he had only recently returned to London. He promised his correspondent Russell Powell that in future letters he would discuss literature, painting, music, and the drama.[17] But no more letters were forthcoming, and we can only wonder why he discarded the plan.

While he contributed regularly to the *Athenaeum* in the early 1830s, Reynolds also wrote occasionally for the *New Sporting Maga-*

zine. The Honorable Fitzroy Stanhope, a fellow Garrick Club member, introduced him to the editor, Robert S. Surtees, who described his curious manner of writing:

The worst of Reynolds was that there was no getting him to work. He put everything off till the very last moment. . . . When he did sit down he went at a pace and with a power that I never saw surpassed. His accounts of Newmarket, Epsom, and Ascot Races in the opening numbers of the work are perfect models for beginners in that line on which to form their style. I cannot say the same for the shape in which he sent in his MSS. I shall never forget seeing his manuscript arrive at the printers' at the last moment: it would be delivered in the most extraordinary state of confusion—scribbled on letter-backs, old play-bills, anything he could get hold of,—written in a hand that seemed impossible to decipher. After several attempts to read it I was obliged to give it to the printer, with, I confess, no great expectation of its merit. Most agreeably surprised I was to find it read so well. Hamilton Reynolds—there were two Reynolds—was a very clever fellow.[18]

After 1833 Reynolds ceased to contribute regularly to the *Athenaeum,* though he continued to submit occasional pieces for years. The names of the contributors are marked in the file for 1834, and Reynolds's name appears after only one review and two short poems. He probably supplied also an article unmarked in the file, "Unpublished Letters of Coleridge," containing the poet's correspondence with Taylor and Hessey about Reynolds's *Peter Bell* with an introduction giving details likely to have been known only by Reynolds.[19] In the 1835 volume, which is not marked in the file, he wrote one poem and two reviews.[20] For the years 1836 through 1838, also not marked in the file, only three poems and two reviews have been identified.[21] In all his remaining years he contributed only one other poem.[22]

During the years in which he wrote regularly for the *Athenaeum,* Reynolds also assisted Hood with the *Comic Annuals.* To the 1830 volume Reynolds contributed two sonnets and an article entitled "The Pillory," in which he imagined that he had spent a day in the stocks and related how boys and old women had pelted him with vegetables and stones. The pieces are amusing and not inferior to much of the similar work by Hood. Reynolds also designed two of the woodcuts for the 1830 volume and one for 1835.[23] Moreover, according to Charles Dilke, Reynolds deserves further credit for work on these pleasant volumes, for he "lent occasional assistance to the Comic Annual, in suggesting, finishing and polishing, rather than in separate and substantive contributions."[24] He not only lent a hand in preparing the books, but also helped to popularize them by writing favorable reviews in the *Athenaeum*. Where Hood was concerned, Dilke's usual insistence on impartiality apparently did not apply, since he could hardly have found a more biased critic of Hood than Reynolds.

In the thirties Reynolds maintained the theatrical interests from which he had profited earlier. The formation of the Garrick Club in 1831 by Francis Miller and Henry Broadwood under the patronage of the Duke of Sussex allowed Reynolds to combine his love of the theater and his lifelong sociability. The club was founded as "a society in which actors and men of education and refinement might meet on equal and independent terms."[25] When notified of his selection as a charter member, Reynolds accepted on 16 September 1831.[26] For some fifteen years he spent many hours lounging, dining, drinking, smoking, and talking at the club's comfortable quarters with other members: Frank Fladgate, who had known Keats and who was for many years solicitor, barrister, and intimate of James Smith,[27] James Robinson Planché, John Poole, Clarkson Stanfield, Richard Harris Barham, and William Makepeace Thackeray. These were Reynolds's particular friends and companions from the more than three hundred members.[28]

Having shared Fanny Kelly's friendship with Lamb and Hood since the early 1820s, Reynolds wrote in 1833 *Miss Kelly's New Entertainment entitled Dramatic Recollections*. The entertainment, with music by T. P. Cooke, a fellow member of the Garrick Club, was performed at the Strand Theatre from 26 January through 25 March 1833, though there is no record of the number of performances.[29] The script was not published, but Henry Crabb Robinson, who attended on 31 January 1833, provided an account of parts of it:

I had a pleasant few hours in the Strand Theatre. Miss Kelly gave a performance by herself of dramatic recollections and imitations. She looked old and almost plain, and her singing was unpleasant, but some parts of the performance were very agreeable indeed. I am sure that the prologue and a great part of the text were written by Charles Lamb. Other parts, especially a song, I believe to be by Hood. What I particularly enjoyed were the anecdotes of John Kemble, and his kindness to her when a child. Her eulogy of him was affecting. . . . The comic scenes were better, I thought, than the sentimental. I liked particularly an old woman, a Mrs. Parthian, who had lost her memory, and spoke of *Gentleman* Smith, whom she had known in her youth. "His name was Adam Smith. He wrote some pretty songs on political economy, and people used to whisper about his addresses having been rejected,—I forget by whom; but it was some one at Drury Lane." This I thought like one of Lamb's jokes; as well as another, in which the keeper of a caravan of wild beasts asks for orders, as being of the profession. She condescends to notice Miss Kelly as the best in her line, but makes a comparison of her "beastesses" with actors in favor of her own. Is not this Lamb's?[30]

Robinson learned later that Reynolds wrote the script, not Lamb.[31] The jokes probably served their purpose of providing light amusement, though not everyone was as amused as Robinson. Henry Barton Baker reported the piece as "an utter failure."[32] Hood was so pleased by it that he wrote an "Ode to Miss Kelly on her opening at the Strand Theatre," in which he promised to attend the performance three times a week as long as it lasted,[33] but as a close friend of both Reynolds and Fanny Kelly he was anything but impartial.

During these years Reynolds wrote miscellaneous poems for or about actresses and singers—Madame Vestris, Frances Kemble, and Grisi—which did not rise above the usual magazine verse. After Charles Kemble retired on 23 December 1836, his fellow members of the Garrick Club gave him a memorial dinner, for which Reynolds wrote a "Farewell to Charles Kemble," set to music and sung by the composer Michael William Balfe.[34] The *Athenaeum* printed the poem and reported that it was "unanimously encored" when Balfe sang it at the dinner on 10 January 1837.[35] The secretary, James Winston, wrote Reynolds the club's formal thanks, which he acknowledged on 12 January.[36] He was gratified by the hearty success of his "trifle," but he would have been surprised if he could have known that James R. Planché valued it enough to reprint it as late as 1872, twenty years after Reynolds's death.

Reynolds very likely wrote other anonymous and ephemeral theatrical works in the thirties that have, probably mercifully, vanished. His letter of 31 August 1833 to someone in authority at the Haymarket Opera House, almost certainly the manager Pierre F. Laporte, requesting the use of Laporte's private box for the evening, indicates a close connection with that theater.[37] In 1837 Laporte's theater owed Reynolds the large sum of £200, probably for writing the popular theatrical scripts at which he was adept.[38]

His last known theatrical venture was *Confounded Foreigners* in 1838. The farce was skillful, shallow theater, so thoroughly clichéd that it is impossible not to describe the work itself in clichés, though Reynolds showed considerable ingenuity in manipulating them. He mocked Irishness enough to make the English laugh, and represented it favorably enough to warm the hearts of those with Irish inclinations. O'Phelan, the comic hero, is a stage Irishman with a heart of gold. Mr. Western, a London stockbroker whose speech is filled incongruously with the language of his trade, is a thin urban imitation of Fielding's bluff Squire Western. He favors Ireland and an Irish suitor for his daughter Rose, who by a dead aunt's will must marry in a few weeks to get her dowry. After ten days in Calais, Rose's Aunt Martha becomes an affected francophile who is determined to have her niece marry a Frenchman. On her return from Calais, Aunt Martha is deceived by a shady French croupier, named La Folie, from a Boulogne gambling hell. She supports La Folie's suit for her niece and her niece's fortune. But Rose has already fallen in love with the Irishman O'Phelan, who of course is a half-pay lieutenant. In an attempt to win Mr. Western's favor, La Folie pretends to be Irish, and in an effort to placate Aunt Martha, O'Phelan pretends to be French, as Reynolds butchers Irish brogue and French for the simplest comic effects. In the predictable dénouement, La Folie is exposed, Aunt Martha is mollified by O'Phelan's slight knowledge of France, Mr. Western is pleased by Ireland's success, and love triumphs.

Taking no chances, Reynolds fractured the French so obviously that even those in the audience with only a smattering of the language could not miss the point, as in Aunt Martha's "Fermez la porte, I say; open the door, girl." The puns were equally obvious, not to say strained:

La Folie. Sar! you rouse my heart—my *coeur de lion!* You shall be in great danger.
O'Phelan. You'll be in danger. You'll get under arrest.
La Folie. A rest—what is dat?—a rest.
O'Phelan. A rest—oh! you don't know—but a musician wou'd tell you—*it's a long pause in a particular place.*[39]

As a clever and shallow farce for popular enjoyment, it will do, though Reynolds was no Samuel Foote.

After its first performance on 6 January 1838 at the Theatre Royal in the Haymarket, the *Athenaeum* praised the piece as "a smart and sharply written one-act farce, . . . the joint production of Mr. George Dance and Mr. Hamilton Reynolds" and regretted that the closing of the Theatre Royal's season on 15 January would prevent this "completely and deservedly successful" entertainment from having a longer run.[40] Reynolds explained in a letter to the editor the next week that though Dance had suggested the original idea, the two had differed about the development of it, and Reynolds had written the farce alone.[41] The printed version credits J. H. Reynolds, Esq. as author with no mention of Dance.

Reynolds continued to labor at the law; by 7 May 1830 Rice had withdrawn from the firm and Rice and Reynolds became Reynolds and Simmons. Thereafter Rice retired to his father's country place in Putney, where he died in early December 1832. Reynolds angered Valentin and Fanny Keats Llanos by his management of the residue of the Keatses' grandmother's estate. Valentin protested to George Keats that Reynolds had paid him only half of the £780 he thought due him, that he refused to pay the rest, and that he would not answer letters or see him. Valuing his long friendship with Reynolds and grateful for the warm hospitality all the Reynoldses had extended to Georgiana during her visit in London, George did his best to smooth things over. He was sorry that Reynolds had withheld money from them on the basis that his (George's) share must be preserved; he regretted that Reynolds had behaved in such an unaccountable manner; and he even offered to pay the Llanoses half of any loss caused by Reynolds's inattention.[42]

Valentin charged that Reynolds's conduct was "disgraceful,"[43] and the absence of sufficient evidence to extenuate Reynolds must leave the probability of mismanagement. Reynolds argued that the withheld money was for "his account,"[44] that is, his own legal fees, and it is possible that a man like Valentin unacquainted with legal charges could not comprehend the expense. On the other hand, the strongest evidence that Reynolds ought to have paid the Llanoses more was Dilke's statement to George that Reynolds was utterly incapable of paying because his affairs had "long been desperate" and that he declined to intermeddle because he knew that Reynolds could not pay.[45] The implication from the always judicious Dilke was that Reynolds should have paid but could not.

In addition to the distraction of his journalistic and theatrical work, Reynolds's gregariousness and sociability interfered with steady application to his legal work. John Payne Collier recorded the unfortunate effects in his diary on 27 October 1833. "Reynolds has lost his position and his money very much by sitting up late at night. He is very cheerful company, but somewhat prone to satire. . . . He is too much in the habit of thinking that conversation is only good as a vehicle for ridicule; consequently he makes no friends, though few want them more."[46]

Nevertheless, Reynolds did enjoy occasional success with some aspects of his legal practice. Representing his friend and fellow Garrick Club member John Poole, he succeeded in protecting his client from a continuation of misleading advertising by the publisher Richard Bentley. Bentley had advertised *Romances of Many Lands* ambiguously as "by John Poole," whereas Poole had been paid merely to edit the work of others. Reynolds was firm, but polite and tactful, in requiring Bentley to withdraw the advertisement.[47]

As with Keats earlier, though to a lesser degree because of the difference in stature between the two poets, Reynolds's intimacy with Hood continues to be of lasting interest. Tracing the friendship to 1835 is frustrating because almost no letters from either to the other—and there must have been many—have been preserved.[48] The Hood children disregarded Reynolds's letters to Hood after Eliza Reynolds refused to let them have Hood's letters to Reynolds. But scattered references in their letters to others show that they remained intimate during these years. The Reynolds and Hood families vacationed together in February 1831 in Brighton, where the two men consulted about Dilke's proposed price reduction of the *Athenaeum* and Reynolds wrote Dilke their astonished opposition.[49] The Hood family visited Little Britain and the Reynolds home in Golden Square often and kept in close contact with Reynolds and Eliza.[50] Hood dedicated to Reynolds the separate publication of *Eugene Aram* in 1831. Reynolds's writing for *New Sporting* no doubt led to Hood placing his pieces there. Hood advertised Reynolds's *Miss Kelly's New Entertainment* with a poem to Fanny Kelly, while Reynolds returned the favor by puffing the *Comic Annuals* in the *Athenaeum*.

The two attended social gatherings together where others recognized the intimate bond between the two by treating them as a pair. John Payne Collier wrote of a parody Hood composed at a dinner on 26 July 1832, "This was voted very good for the extemporaneous attempt of a bashful versifyer, who spoke so low that he could not do justice to his own performance. Hamilton Reynolds wrote it down, and read it aloud." Meeting them on a visit to London in 1833, James Hogg contrasted the personalities of the two friends: "Hood, from whom I expected a continued volley of wit, is a modest, retiring character. Reynolds more brilliant."[51]

Hood's relations with the Reynoldses until 1835 had been not just amicable, but loving; then in that year came a crisis after the birth of his third child Tom. Married at the rather late age of thirty-three, Jane had a very difficult first pregnancy at thirty-six; after two days of "intense suffering" in labor, the baby girl had to be sacrificed to save the mother. No special difficulty is recorded for the birth of Fanny on 11 September 1830 when Jane was thirty-eight. But Jane was forty-three when she bore her second surviving child Tom on 19 January 1835, and all the Reynolds family and Hood had to be concerned about the delivery in middle age. Mrs. Reynolds no doubt came to attend her daughter as soon as labor began. Instead of a normal recovery after delivery, Jane's condition worsened about 30 January, and her sisters Lotte and Marianne along with Marianne's husband H. G. Green, their two sons, and a nursemaid, came to the Hood house at Wanstead to be with Jane during her extreme illness.[52]

On the verge of financial collapse and exhausted from completing two books, Hood was already approaching the breaking point before Jane's illness. To tax him further, five-year-old Fanny came down with the measles, and he had the seven additional Reynolds and Green mouths to feed for weeks—he called the latter a "trifle," but he was irritated enough by the expense to describe the drain on his larder sarcastically to Dilke.[53]

Jane declined into such a terrible state and suffered so much that the Reynoldses and Greens became convinced that she was going to die. Loving her, but resigned to what they thought certain death, they hoped that her suffering would not be prolonged. They told Hood that they did not believe Jane could survive, and by their countenances and demeanor, even if they did not tell her outright, they let Jane know that they thought she was dying. Hood, on the other hand, struggled successfully to restrain his grief and maintain his composure so that Jane would not lose hope. He maintained reasonable amity with Mrs. Reynolds; "if sometimes wrong headed," she was "always right-hearted."[54] And he sustained civility with Marianne until the final scene. The family's reactions were understandable—who has attended upon apparently terminally ill loved ones without hoping as they did that death would be merciful? Lotte could not muster the self-restraint to keep quiet. When Dr. William Elliot reported that "Jane was in a good sleep—the best thing for her," Lotte said in Hood's hearing, "I hope she will wake sensible, & then pass away quietly." Later John Wright heard her say, "What gave her horror was, that if Jane had been let alone she would have died days ago!"[55] Hood, determined to save his wife, was incensed.

To the surprise of the Reynoldses and Greens, after ten days of delirium and agony, Jane took a turn for the better. Mrs. Reynolds stayed on to help, but the Greens and Lotte, afraid that the Green children might catch Fanny's measles, prepared to leave. Green defended Lotte against Hood, charging Hood with "disgraceful caballing" against her. Hood mocked the charge—he could not cabal because all the rest of the family were in Lotte's camp. But his own account disproves his claim: he had attacked Lotte to John Wright, secured damning evidence from Wright against her, complained to Dr. Elliot, and had Dr. Elliot write a note to justify him against any possible charge from Lotte or the others that he was hardhearted. He tried to placate Marianne, who until this time had been friendly, but she sided with her husband and Lotte. As the Greens and Lotte left the house, Hood remarked sarcastically that since they had given Jane up for dead, they would surely forgive him for restoring her to them again recovered. Making a "contemptuous reply," they left without Hood's even saying goodbye.[56]

It was doubtless Mrs. Reynolds, staying on with Hood's approval, who told Hood the next day that Lotte planned to return. He would not forbid her to see her bedridden sister, but he was determined that Lotte should not remain in the house along with her mother.

Hood's furious letter to Dilke describing the quarrel becomes fine unpremeditated literature as it alternates between white-hot rage and freezing venom, searing with its invective and at the same time scintillating with weird metaphor and analogy.

I am becoming Coleridgean, Kantean, high Metaphysical,—but common-place suits not my present mood. There is much of positive & negative moral electricity to work off & I make you one of my conductors. God bless you,—I feel tonight a Rothschild who might have been a beggar, supposing ones purse of wealth carried somewhere about the left breast pocket. But I have learned to know the true metal from the base,—no Marian flash notes, no Lotte smashing, none of Green's flimsies for me. . . . Another morning—and Jane is better. She may now be thought out of danger. I took a whole sleep last night for the first time,—& did not dream. If I had it would have been of Jane trying to swim in the River of Life with sisterly Millstones round her neck,—or to fly in the vital air, with a deep-sea lead to each leg, like those encumbered pigeons of S. Mark,—I mean those turned out from the Basilica on Palm Sunday at Venice, with weights tied to their legs. I shall love Clark's fly [which took the Greens and Lotte away] for ever—the man who drove & the horses that drew it. Sweetly did it diminish in distance, & lose itself thro that gate at Can Hall Lane. Then did I feel with Shandy—"Go poor fly—there is room in the world for thee & me." There is no magic nowadays—or had I known a formula for transforming that onehorse vehicle into the Andromeda, or the Amphitrite, bound any where,—say New South Wales,— God forgive me, but I fear I should have pronounced it on the spot! What *could* be their sports when children?—Did they dramatize De Foe's History of the Plague & go about with a tiny go cart & a bell & a cry of bring out your dead! I shall never believe in hearts,—they have but two of those stone urns in their bosoms, as funereal & unfeeling. In strict justice & consistency, ought not such death-doing thoughts & feelings to turn homeward,—making them suicidal,—felo de se—ought not one to take laudanum, or deadly nightshade & hellebore, & the other to drown herself in the blackest pool that can be found search England thorough—some pond in a cut-throat lane, with water as still as death & as black as a coffin, from running thro the sable mud of the Slough of Despond. Or is the despairing feeling only a show—an affectation,—born of a damnd pride— disdaining to have been mistaken,—& resenting the idea of being outgone in firmness, common sense, age & good feeling for the sufferer,—by such a thing as a Sister's husband—a brother-in-law?

Hood had reason to feel aggrieved, and every reader's primary sympathy must lie with him in this near tragedy, but one should remember his state of mind and guard against viewing the letter as anything resembling a fair judgment of the Reynolds women, even Lotte. In his rage Hood lashed out at what he charged was female domination in the Reynolds family. "The male sex stand not on a high pedestal in L.[ittle] B[ritain]. Fathers—Brothers—& so forth are but hewers of wood & drawers of water,—domestic spaniels to fetch and carry—& verily that Green is the pet lapdog of the house, with an ignoble collar round his neck to show to whom he belongs."[57]

Hood spared John Hamilton Reynolds from his wrath; indeed he valued Reynolds's friendship so much that he took an unusual step to protect himself from the attacks he feared the Reynolds women would make upon him. While the others, wittingly or unwittingly, had allowed Jane to sense that they thought she was dying, Hood had kept a firm grip on himself ,and preserved the appearance that he thought everything was all right. As a result, he feared that the sentimental Reynolds women would report to Reynolds that he had been unfeeling and hardhearted. To counter that, he sent Reynolds the first copy of Dr. Elliot's note that he had kept up his "courage surprisingly under the severe & tedious trial" to contradict "the sinister reports they persisted in spreading."[58]

Hood felt all the closer to Reynolds because his own suffering made him sympathize with Reynolds's grief at the recent death of his only child, ten-year-old Lucy, "I have still a Wife—a comfort I would have poor J.H.R. hug to his heart as I do—poor fellow, I pitied him in the midst of my own seeming calamity,—for I thought of my next Star of Magnitude, my own Fanny."[59]

By early March 1835, after Jane was out of danger, Hood fled from England to escape his creditors and to reestablish himself financially on the Continent by living more economically as he continued to write. Waiting for Hood to make living arrangements and hardly able to travel, Jane took Fanny and the baby to Golden Square, where they stayed with John and Eliza and waited for further directions from Hood. Reynolds represented Hood legally in his crumbling financial affairs.[60] Jane had been caught in the middle of Hood's quarrel with her sisters; while still extremely ill, she had worried about how she was "to decide between [Hood] . . . & 'her family.' "[61] It was politic that she stay with John rather than at Little Britain so soon after Hood's rage against Lotte and the Greens; Golden Square would allow her to visit and receive visits from her family and smooth over injured feelings without alienating Hood.

After his anger subsided, Hood did not expect Jane to break with her family; he asked her to get help from her father in understanding foreign currencies on 19 March 1835, and later he occasionally referred pleasantly to her mother. He remained close to John, whom he invited to visit him in Germany during the summer, but John and Eliza did not make the trip. He asked Jane to tell John that he would write him a long letter as soon as he heard from London about his affairs. After Jane and the children joined Hood in Koblenz by May, she corresponded with Lotte and presumably with her parents and other sisters.[62]

There were minor irritations between John and the Hoods. He either did something while Jane was living with him or wrote something after she joined Hood for which she found it necessary to "forgive his treatment of me not liking to nourish anger against those I love when we are so far apart." John was vexed that Hood delayed so long in writing; Jane thought he ought to understand that Hood had been too busy to write. But the old affection was not seriously disturbed. In January 1836 Hood learned that Reynolds had written the review of the *Comic Annual,* a review with which he had been so delighted that he wrote Dilke, "I could not have been better pleased had I *reviewed myself.*" He wrote Reynolds and learned, probably from letters of other Reynoldses to Jane, that Reynolds planned to write him. Reynolds, who had enjoyed fishing ever since he was a boy, seemed expert in the sport to Hood, who mentioned Reynolds twice in connection with it after he became fond of fishing in Germany. Reynolds's writing was so much a part of Hood's thinking that he quoted from Reynolds's preface to his mock Peter Bell.[63]

Later Hood, for some unexplained reason, did not want Reynolds to see a set of his drawings; he wrote John Wright on 30 April 1837, "You may show them to Harvey [an engraver] if you like—but mind— not J.H.R." But other references were friendly. He asked Reynolds to send him copies of the *London Magazine* to use in writing his *Literary Reminiscences,* and Reynolds complied with the request.[64]

In the spring of 1836 Reynolds's thoughts turned to a friend he had known years before he met Hood. On his way to Liverpool on business, he stopped off at Shrewsbury on 11 May and scratched out a hasty note to Dovaston. After twenty-one years he still felt warm friendship for Dovaston and had forgotten what the difference was that caused them to break off. Planning to return to Shrewsbury from Liverpool in a day or two, he asked Dovaston to send a note to the post office if he shared his wish to spend an hour talking over old times. It is not clear whether Dovaston responded to his cordial offer and met with him; Dovaston endorsed the note with the nickname that he had used so often in the days of their friendship, Jack Reynolds, but he did not indicate whether he replied, as he did for some letters.[65] Eliza Reynolds's letter to him after Reynolds's death to solicit a contribution perhaps suggests that Dovaston did reply and the two did meet.

After spending some eight years in the house at 27 Golden Square, Reynolds moved to 10 Great Marlborough Street some time between 4 February 1835 and 12 January 1837.[66] From the latter address he thanked Rowland Hill warmly on 16 January 1837 for sending him confidentially a prepublication copy of Hill's pamphlet on postal reform. He approved enthusiastically (as Hood did later) of Hill's plan to reduce the postal rates and offered, as soon as released from silence, to champion the cause "in some public Print."[67] Hill, originally a schoolmaster who had attracted national attention by his rigorous educational methods, shared an interest with George Reynolds and had visited the Reynolds home often in the 1820s and 1830s.[68]

In 1837 Reynolds proposed to collect a number of his own pieces from periodicals and publish them in book form. He wrote John Taylor for permission to publish from the *London Magazine* and explained, "There is a wish amongst a few of my private friends that some of my papers should be housed into volumes—and I who have walked through life with a skeleton of reputation without a particle of name, enter into this wish."[69] Recalling the collection he had planned in 1823 or 1824 but never published, he probably intended to reprint for the most part his essays from the *London.* What he had written since was lively and effective journalism, but little of it was suitable for republication. The book did not materialize, and he continued to publish before 1840 prose pieces and a few poems that no doubt satisfied contemporary readers, but with only a few exceptions fell short of the standard he had set in the *London.* Writing only rarely now for the *Athenaeum,* as in the "Farewell to Charles Kemble" and two pieces on Lady Mary Wortley Montagu in 1837 and a review of Dickens's edition of *Grimaldi* in 1838, he turned to other journals. He contributed to *Bentley's Miscellany,* the *New Monthly Magazine,* a special volume entitled *Sporting,* and the *New Sporting Magazine,* which he edited.

Bentley's Miscellany began publication under the editorship of Dickens a month before Reynolds started to write for it. An advertisement of it in the *Athenaeum* showed that he overstated when he told Taylor that he was "without a particle of name"; the advertisement included Hamilton Reynolds along with Dickens, Theodore Hook, and Douglas Jerrold in the list of authors.[70] His "Gossip with Lady Mary Wortley Montagu" does little more than reveal his mastery of and enthusiasm for early eighteenth-century literature, but it impressed his friend Richard Harris Barham, who singled it out for special mention in *The Garrick Club*.[71] "Monosania. Mr. Klünchünbrüch" achieved limited success as a loose tale. Klünchünbrüch, a German grocer with a large family, seemed to his neighbors to be a sober tradesman whose greatest pride was his position as secretary to a charitable association, but he was a gambler at heart, and his financial ruin in the stock market drove him insane. To the surprise of his friends, who expected that the charitable agency would discharge him, he recovered his sanity on the two days every year when required to serve as secretary and kept his position. Reynolds sought to combine pathos and comedy, but the sadness is so strong that the humor seems doubtfully appropriate.

Reynolds made a sustained effort in "Some Passages in the Literary Life of Olinthus Jenkinson, Barrister-at-Law" in four installments. Though exaggerated, the account of the lawyer Jenkinson's accumulation of lifeless, rejected manuscripts in the first part had some slight autobiographical basis, since *Bentley's* rejected some of his work.[72] The burlesque summaries of the naval novel, the fashionable novel, and the sentimental novel in subsequent parts of the article have lost whatever effect they may have had at the time because the targets satirized have faded from view. Thackeray thought enough of the series to draw four illustrations for it, but *Bentley's* did not grant Reynolds's request to print them from woodcuts. In the last installment Reynolds included rather pedestrian translations from Italian, Latin, Spanish, and Greek verse.

His last original poem of the decade in *Bentley's* was a sonnet on the anniversary of Trafalgar, where his attempt to expand the scope by linking Nelson's death with other tragic English deaths—Ridley's, Latimer's, and Lady Jane Grey's—did not succeed in distinguishing it from the usual magazine verse. The ordinariness of the sonnet showed how far he had declined from the success of the two fine sonnets renouncing poetry in *The Fancy* almost twenty years earlier.

While he was contributing to *Bentley's Miscellany* during the last three years of the decade, he also wrote three pieces for the *New Monthly Magazine.* "A Hazy Night" attempted to develop eccentric characters without much success; one suspects that Dilke's kindness was responsible for the *Athenaeum's* calling it "whimsical and true to life."[73] "Trade-itional Confessions. The Pawnbroker" was perhaps a little better. In this sketch, which did not become a tale because no plot developed, the pawnbroker Drurylane explained to a miller interested in investing in the business how he profited by lending to all kinds of people—the explanations were the confessions mentioned in the title. Some of the accounts were genuinely pathetic: for example, the poverty-stricken laundress who pawned her irons to buy breakfast, then pawned her kitchenware to redeem the irons, and at he end of the day reclaimed her cooking utensils with her wages to prepare the evening meal. But the humor attempted in most of the accounts did not blend successfully with the grimness.

A newspaper advertisement asking for bids for the removal of dust and ashes from the streets in the parish of St. Martin's-in-the-Fields triggered Reynolds's verse "A Legend of a Committee of Paviours." The chance connection between the phrase "dust and ashes" and the conventional association with death led to his plot. He may have remembered that ten years earlier in one stanza of "Death's Ramble" in *Whims and Oddities* Hood had played with the same connection:

> He met a dustman ringing a bell,
>   And he gave him a mortal thrust;
> For himself, by law, since Adam's flaw,
>   Is contractor for all our dust.

Reynolds writes in his poem that when the Committee of Paviours advertised for potential contractors, Death, lest his province be invaded, bid for the contract, won it, and then proceeded to will the deaths of the parish officials so that he could claim his "dust and ashes." Reynolds succeeded with his stark depiction of Death, as he stalked from one grotesque scene to another. The conventionality of the abstraction played off against the sharpness of the images, expected though they were, somewhat in the manner of Beddoes. The somberness and gloom make it a curious poem that might still be of some interest to those who like macabre twists.

To *Sporting,* an anthology edited by Nimrod (pseudonym for Charles James Apperley) in 1838, Reynolds contributed a light poem and a mediocre essay that included two competent sonnets. "Stanzas on two fox-hounds in the pack of J. C. Bulteel, Esq., M.P." presented lively verses with the bustling activity that one would expect from the title. In the essay "Epsom Races," Reynolds succeeded even better than he had six years before in the "Letters of Edward Herbert, New Series. No. I" for the *Athenaeum* in recapturing the manner and tone of his Edward Herbert papers in the *London*. Without using his best-known pseudonym, he made the speaker the same kind of person as Herbert, a pensive man "of studious habits," whose reticent character set in sharp relief the exciting scene that he described. Reynolds's use of the outside observer to distance the description was no accident; the speaker likened himself to Goldsmith's oriental citizen of the world observing the celebrated sights of London. Reynolds described his quaint companions on the coach to Epsom Downs, the bustling road crowded with all kinds of vehicles, the brightly dressed people eating picnic lunches on the grounds, the beauty of the horses, and the excitement of the race.

Probably Reynolds's desperate financial straits drove him to edit the *New Sporting Magazine*. His affairs had "long been desperate" as early as 1833.[74] His failure to meet monetary obligations caused quarrels with his friends. Hood's close friend John Wright, an engraver who long collaborated on the *Comic Annuals,* wrote Hood on 17 March 1837, "Reynolds and I are friends again but that says all. Dilke has been very serious with me on this matter and says if I ever put my neck into nooses again I ought to suffer he said he should set me down as past redemption but concluded by gravely saying 'but you will, now if I asked you to accept a bill, you'd do it directly'!" Wright had unwarily signed notes for Reynolds and had suffered for it. An author Francis Coghlan had trouble with Reynolds which may also have involved money; on 31 May 1837 Wright wrote of him to Hood, "Reynolds and him are friends again."

On 8 September 1837 Wright described a financial disaster. "I have been sorry to hear that John Reynolds is in some scrape about Price's affairs. I do not know how but hear that he had become possessed some time since of 7 or 800 pounds in the business which the creditors now claim to be divided it was money in Chancery and paid over by the court I believe to John and he now has to refund it. Fy! Now! poor John sooner or later you must break up, your friends all foresee it and almost wish it in the hope that it may clear away the mist that has so long obscured you."[75] Stephen Price (1782–1840) was an American, owner of the Park Avenue Theater in New York for many years, who leased and managed Drury Lane for the season of 1826–27. Hood dealt with him about plays and mentioned him several times.[76] In the 1830s Price spent much of his time in England, arranging for English actors to perform on the American stage. At this time he was in straitened financial condition.[77] Reynolds knew him as a fellow member of the Garrick Club. The necessity of repaying £700 or £800 to his creditors brought Reynolds, as Wright predicted, ever closer to bankruptcy.

Maria Dilke wrote on 21 April 1838 that Eliza Reynolds was ill. "I fear it is worry—for she talks of Persons *not* paying *their* Bills to Reynolds—and then how is he to pay *his*."[78] He could not. After a fiat against him on 14 May 1838, his bankruptcy was gazetted on 22 May, and a certificate of bankruptcy was issued on 26 October. Eventually on 13 June 1839, the dividend was set at one shilling, ten pence.[79]

Desperate for an income while the bankruptcy proceedings dragged on, Reynolds secured the place of editor of *New Sporting Magazine* about August 1838 and continued to serve at the post until December 1840. He had written occasionally for the magazine for years—the accounts of the Newmarket, Epsom, and Ascot races in 1831[80] and a commentary on racing called Turfiana in 1834.[81] Now as editor he also wrote a considerable body of the material printed in the magazine, though it is possible to identify with any confidence only his continuation of the Turfiana series[82] and a combined sporting and theatrical essay entitled "Lamb and Pitman's Racquet Match. Van Amburgh the Lion Tamer."[83] A footnote in the latter remains of some small interest because there Reynolds reported an incident involving Keats not elsewhere recorded. The note followed from a discussion of "Eye-fascination" necessary for managing animals:

We intimately know a gentleman, who, with two others—one of them being Keats the deceased poet, and the other a gentleman now distinguished in the wise advancement of cheap and valuable literature—was once put in imminent peril in a field where a dangerous bull was pastured. The cows were feeding leisurely around, but the bull met the party with his nose to the earth and with growls of fearful threatening. The trio only escaped by settled nerve, and *the power of the eye;* for they walked round the beast's lowered and menacing head within two yards of it's terror—composedly, slowly, and with fixed gaze on his eyes. Here the power of the well-nerved and *basilisk* organ perfected safety; for on reaching the farmhouse, or a man from it, it was ascertained that a person had been previously (and but a short time previously) frightfully gored and savaged.—And he suffered this from attempted flight.[84]

The other gentleman was Charles Cowden Clarke, whose advancement of valuable literature was *Tales from Chaucer* (1833) and whose advancement of cheap literature was *Adam the Gardener* (1834) and an edition of Nyren's *Young Cricketer's Tutor* (1833). If not merely a joking disguise for himself, the intimately known gentleman was Charles Dilke, the only one of Keats's personal friends with whom Reynolds was still intimate in 1838. If the gentleman was Dilke, the incident occurred between 1817 when Dilke met Keats and December 1818, after which time Clarke saw Keats rarely, if ever.

Hood must have been worried by Wright's reports to him of Reynolds's financial irresponsibility, but the old friendship remained strong enough for Hood to allow Reynolds to capitalize on his name and pen by reprinting old pieces—"Sonnet on Steam" from *Hood's Own* and extracts from *Up the Rhine*—in the magazine.

CHAPTER 16

Last Years—1840–1852

REYNOLDS remained as sociable as indifferent health permitted in 1840, as Thomas De Quincey revealed when he remarked that the portrait prefixed to Talfourd's *Lamb* "far more resembles Mr. Hamilton Reynolds, the distinguished wit, dressed for an evening party, than Charles Lamb."[1] Reynolds continued to meet his friends Thackeray and Richard Harris Barham at the Garrick Club. A note from Thackeray to Barham indicated the closeness of the friendship, "Reynolds has just raised a wonderful objection to an important article, (of a few lines) w^h I have submitted to him. Would you be good-natured and hear the passage read?—It must be in secret."[2] Thackeray also sought unsuccessfully on 14 January 1840 to help Reynolds place an article in *Fraser's Magazine* by recommending it to James Fraser.[3]

Though *Fraser's* did not welcome him, Reynolds contributed to *Bentley's Miscellany* in February an essay, "Greenwich and Greenwich Men," once again looking to the past, for he had written an Edward Herbert letter on Greenwich Hospital for the *London,* and a decline in his power can be seen from the contrast between a quotation from it and the rest of the article in which it is set. The late essay did not equal the early one in animation and grace of style. Nevertheless "Greenwich and Greenwich Men" made pleasant reading. The old sailors at the hospital reminded him of Nelson, whom he recalled seeing come out of a London shop shortly before Trafalgar in October 1805. He reported a long conversation with a Greenwich pensioner, who described his part in the battle of Trafalgar. The appended "Song of Trafalgar and Nelson," based on the account in Southey's *Life of Nelson,* was burdened with excessive footnotes and too rhetorical to be very effective. Recollection of the past reminding Reynolds of Keats, he compared the extraordinary quietness and repose of the old Greenwich sailors staring fixedly out to sea with Keats's stopping of time in the "little town" in *Ode on a Grecian Urn.*

Reynolds represented Hood legally for a time after Hood fled from England in 1835, but from that time through 1839 he had no hand in Hood's dealings with his publisher, Alfred Head Baily. John Wright, Hood's engraver and close friend, managed the negotiations for the *Comic Annuals* with the advice of Dilke. Hood had long suspected that Baily was taking advantage of him. When Jane came alone to London in October 1839, she feared from what she could learn that Baily's accounts were false, and unfortunately the man upon whom they had long depended for the transactions, John Wright, died while she was there.[4] His distrust of Baily increasing, Hood himself came secretly to London for five weeks in January and February 1840 to investigate Baily's accounts and to probe further his fears about Baily's dealings with him.

While Hood was staying at the Dilkes', he and Reynolds spent time together, continuing the old friendship and allowing Reynolds to see his five-year-old nephew Tom for the first time since the child was a baby. On his return to Ostend, Hood sent Reynolds a present of sardines and wrote him an affectionate letter, to which Jane appended a few lines. When Reynolds replied in his one letter to Hood that has been preserved, he was in a stable frame of mind, though soured in a few respects by all his misfortunes. He had recovered sufficiently from the ordeal of his bankruptcy to joke about it wryly: "I am now,—or rather my new Residence is—undergoing repair & whitewashing:—I wish I could undergo ⟨the⟩ repair myself; *whitewashing* I have gone through."[5] He wished for bodily repair not likely to be achieved at the age of forty-five. Though most of the pain from an attack of influenza had gone, he still had the disease and spoke of some internal discomfort, but diffidently to one like Hood, whose advancing tuberculosis was much worse.

Reynolds was working steadily. Deadlines for the *New Sporting Magazine* harried him, try as he would to turn the pressure into a joke. "I do seriously believe that the months are very unlike cherubs, and consist *only* of *Latter Ends*. I am no sooner out of the frying pan of one magazine—but I am into the fire of the one immediately following."[6] But he performed his editing duties, and he now had an additional resource in Hood, who had promised original articles for the magazine. Hood sent him the requested first installment of "Fishing in Germany" in time for publication in the next month's issue.

Reynolds still practiced law, though not prosperously. He needed to travel to Westmorland for three or four days on business, but lack of money forced postponement of the trip.

Disgruntled at his lack of literary success, he envied those more successful like Dickens and Ainsworth. He had been so inconsiderate of old friends as to speak in company of the dullness of the *Athenaeum,* the Dilkes' "bread" as Maria Dilke put it when she protested to Eliza after hearing of the disparagement. But the Reynoldses remained on good terms with the Dilkes despite the minor annoyance.

Hood was still undecided on his course of action with Baily. Reynolds did not mention Baily in his letter to Hood of 13 March 1840, and he could not have failed to do so if Hood had proposed legal action when they had met or in his letter to Reynolds. Hood returned to England alone in April and grew very ill at Dr. Elliot's in Stratford. By 17 April he had decided to break with Baily, but he did not at first think any legal action would be necessary.[7] By 23 April neither he nor the Dilkes, who visited him at Stratford, had seen Reynolds.[8] In the middle of May, Jane, leaving the children behind in Ostend, came to London to do the best she could with the business that Hood was too ill to manage; perhaps it was she who carried the message to her brother to institute legal proceedings. Despite Baily's insistence that his accounts showed he owed Hood no balance, the decision was made by 19 May to sue Baily for what Hood, and by now Reynolds, believed Baily owed Hood. On that date Reynolds, as Hood's solicitor, wrote Baily's solicitor that he would shortly claim the Hood stock in Baily's possession and sue for the balance allegedly owed.[9] He filed the suit on 22 May, but could not obtain the stock because Hood's creditor John Follett surprised him and Hood by attaching it on the same day. On 12 June Hood's bankruptcy was docketed, on the thirteenth a fiat was issued against him, and the interminable legal wrangle dragged on.[10]

Hood wrote Baily on 31 July 1840 from Reynolds's address, no doubt after advice from his solicitor, acknowledging receipt of accounts Baily had sent and indicating that the court would decide between them.[11] Reynolds and Hood continued as friends, though Reynolds's unreliability in meeting small obligations sometimes irritated Hood, as shown in his remark to Jane that now that he had written an article for *New Sporting,* he could be sure that Reynolds would not send him the customary printed copy.[12] Reynolds printed the final installment of "Fishing in Germany" and a second article, "An Autograph," in the July issue of *New Sporting*. In the August issue he reported that "Mr. Hood promises us, 'health and weather permitting,' to cruise with us again next month," but by that time Hood had committed his efforts elsewhere—after withdrawing from a tentative arrangement with Richard Bentley for *Bentley's Miscellany,* he agreed with Henry Colburn to contribute regularly to the *New Monthly*—and he wrote no more for *New Sporting*. Reynolds, having fallen out with Charles James Apperley, kept up a steady stream of acrimonious attacks upon "Nimrod" until the attacks and Reynolds's editorship ceased together at the close of 1840 when Nimrod, of all people, replaced him as editor of a new series.

Reynolds's illness at the time may have helped to reconcile him to the loss of the editorship—he might think that a man in his poor health could not continue to bear the strain—but probably such rationalizing would not succeed entirely because he was chronically hard pressed for money and the regular salary made a difference. He turned immediately to other writing in an attempt to compensate for the lost income. Three months earlier he had sent Richard Bentley a long tale for the *Miscellany,* which had evidently been rejected. Now, confined to his room by illness for days, he cast about for some new subject. Remembering his greatest success with a prose series, the Edward Herbert papers, he sounded out Bentley in December 1840 on a set of "papers descriptive of London Scenes Places & Persons,—not yet touched upon," hoping that he might collect them eventually from the *Miscellany* for a volume.[13]

Instead of such out-of-the-way places as Greenwich Hospital and the cockpit of the *London* days, he thought of focusing on a place and a class—the dreary, crowded lodging houses of the city and the financially depressed families who had to inhabit them. At first he considered making the sketches epistolary, as the Edward Herbert series had been, but when he wrote the first and only one, he decided on third-person narration. He drew upon his knowledge of the many law clerks he had encountered in his decades of legal practice who had to subsist with their families in the cramped quarters of dingy lodging houses. He had hired clerks himself in the palmier days of his earlier career; in 1832 he had had at least two in his employ, one of whose names, Baber, he may have echoed faintly in the Mabby and Bibby of his sketch.[14]

In "Messrs. Leach, Battye, and Slug's Managing Chancery Clerk" in *Bentley's Miscellany* for March 1841,[15] Reynolds sought for humor in the clash between the self-satisfaction of the three clerks and their mental limitations; for pathos in the depiction of the fourth-floor, one-room apartment, with only a closet to sleep the five children; and for irony in the three clerks' complacent agreement that the one essential of all legal action was that it be slow and protracted. As the chief clerk Mr. Mabby and his two guests, Mr. Bibby and Mr. Jones, engage in postprandial discussion over their pipes and drinks, they of course condemn one employer, Mr. Slug, for violating tradition and being decisive and demanding quick results, while they praise another, Mr. Battye, as "one o' the old school" who "wouldn't care if a suit never got out of the Master's office in his born days." Reynolds succeeded only moderately in the difficult task of making dull people memorable; his whimsical eccentricity was diffuse and his irony uncomplicated. Though contemporary readers were probably mildly amused, it is not surprising that after this first attempt he did not continue with his original plan for a series.

In 1841 Reynolds continued as Hood's solicitor in the legal contest with Baily, writing Baily on 26 March to demand an account of the stock formerly held by Baily until Hood's creditor John Follett attached it the preceding May and "a proper enquiry into the [Baily's] accounts and an adjustment of them."[16] On 31 March Baily sent Reynolds a list of the stock Follett had attached, but refused to allow an inquiry into his accounts. Reynolds ceased acting as Hood's solicitor in the legal action in May 1841; in June St. P. B. Hook replaced Reynolds and continued to serve for the rest of Hood's life, charging Hood nothing for his services.

The whole matter of Reynolds's relationship with Hood after this time is so cloudy that what evidence there is should be considered carefully. Hood never mentioned Reynolds by name in his letters or other writings after May 1841; he showed animosity against his relatives, but always in the plural. Reynolds never mentioned Hood except in the bare report to R. M. Milnes that he and Hood had collaborated on *Odes and Addresses*.[17]

Frances Freeling Broderip's statement showed that there was a break before Hood died: "A congeniality of pursuits and likings drew them together—a connection that was afterwards by my father's marriage with his sister to be still further strengthened. It was a pity it did not survive to the end, for on one side at least it was characteristically generous and sincere."[18] We know, furthermore, that there was a break between Reynolds and Jane because Walter Jerrold reports their reconciliation: "Within a fortnight of her husband's death [3 May 1845] she learned that her mother was in a serious state from which she was little likely to recover. Six months later Mrs. George Reynolds was again seriously ill, and Jane Hood and John Hamilton met and were reconciled at their mother's bedside, after a quarrel of some years' standing, the occasion of which is not known."[19] Finally, the refusal of Eliza Drewe Reynolds, after her husband's death, to supply the Hood children with Hood's letters to Reynolds may or may not have been grounded in resentment from the quarrel.[20]

The only certain conclusion that the evidence allows is that there was a break several years before Hood died. We cannot be sure when it occurred, though there is a good possibility that it happened when Reynolds stopped serving as Hood's solicitor in May 1841. We do not know whether Reynolds withdrew or Hood discharged him. We do not know what grievance either one may have felt against the other. We do not know which one made the break. It is futile to speculate where there is so little evidence.

The poem "To T. Hood, on Hearing of His Sickness" copied into the Reynolds-Hood commonplace book at the Bristol Library and published in *Memorials of Thomas Hood* must remain a tantalizing puzzle. Frances F. Broderip wrote that "He received besides a copy of very beautiful verses, also anonymous," and Tom Hood added in a note, "If I could place my hand in his hand, and look in the face, of their writer, I should feel deeply gratified."[21] Obviously neither of Hood's children suspected afterward that their dead Uncle John might have written the poem, and it is difficult to understand why they did not. The author addressed Hood as "my brother," and Hood had no other living brother or brother-in-law besides Reynolds when he was on his deathbed. He had sisters-in-law who might have called him brother, but they are not known to have written verse, and it is splendid verse. If the poem is Reynolds's, it shows that he still loved Hood as Hood lay dying in 1844 and 1845. On the other hand, there is no other evidence to confirm the word "brother," which could have been used loosely in the sense of brother Christian or brother author.

From May 1841, when he stopped serving as Hood's solicitor, Reynolds dropped almost completely from sight until January 1844; few references to him during those two and one-half years have come to light. He remained so close to the actress Fanny Kelly, for whom he had collaborated on *Gil Blas* in 1822 and had written *Recollections* in 1833, that she followed his advice on parts that she performed. William Charles Macready recorded in his diary on 6 May 1841, "Went to the theatre; received a note from Serle [a playwright], informing me that Miss Kelly's friend, Mr. J. H. Reynolds, would not consent to her acceptance of an engagement for the Old Women—ergo; Miss Kelly does not come to Drury Lane."[22] He called upon his sister Eliza Longmore's family, but so rarely that his visits seemed marvels. In April 1843, Lizzy Longmore wrote her brother William, "Aunt and Uncle John came. This was a wonder." About this time he appeared in the letters of the Longmore children "as rather a shadowy person in poor health seeking a change of air to do him good from time to time. He also provided tickets for a box at theatre or opera occasionally."[23]

He continued to live at the same address during that time, 10 Adam Street, Adelphi; he wrote to Bentley from that residence on 6 December 1840, and he still lived there when he wrote R. S. Mackenzie on 21 September 1844. In January 1844, he resumed publication in *Ainsworth's Magazine* with an elaborate four-part burlesque of a prose fairy tale. *Oriana and Vesperella* is a puzzling piece concerning the vicissitudes of two fairy princesses; at times Reynolds seemed to revel in sensuousness for its own sake, while at others he clearly intended burlesque. "An Ode-let to Master Izaak Walton" that followed in the June *Ainsworth's* was undistinguished verse.[24]

A brief letter to Thomas Noon Talfourd in May 1845, thanking him for a presentation copy of his last book, showed Reynolds, for that moment at least, in a cheerful frame of mind, recalling that he dined with Talfourd when the latter was called to the bar and that they happened to be married on the same day in 1822.[25] He showed not the slightest envy of Talfourd, who unlike himself had succeeded so well at the law that he had become a judge, while at the same time retaining literary interests as an avocation.

Like any other poet, Reynolds, early and late in his career, often did not rise above competence in verse. But "The Mouser-Monarchy," published in the *New Monthly* in September 1845, proved that in his closing years he had not lost his ability to write superior poetry. One of his finest comic poems and quite different from anything else he had ever done, its largely anapestic swinging rhythm (a little like "The Night Before Christmas") played off against the intricacy of the special ten-line stanza appropriate for the mock-Gothic magnificence. Except for hints of exaggeration, the long introduction seemed an entirely serious depiction of the bleakness, desolation, and gloom of the scenery.

After the fair closed in Lancaster, a wayfarer left his inn late at night to travel on horseback through the dark and foreboding countryside toward the home of a friend he planned to visit. Leaving the highway and following a rude path through the moor, he came upon a weird house without a door, stared in at a curious sight, and proceeded to his friend's place. Sitting down before a cheerful hearth, the wayfarer related to his host, as the host's cat snuggled down on the rug, the miraculous scene he had observed. Illuminated by tapers, a stately funeral procession with full heraldry ("mouse couchant" on the standard "emblazoned with talon and fang") marched in with the coffin of the deceased cat monarch. Before the grieving, widowed queen of the cats, a solemn funeral service was conducted and the dead king's coffin lowered into a cavity in the floor. Reynolds succeeded in making the ceremony fanciful, colorful, and sumptuous. The surprise ending climaxed a splendid poem:

> "I left—I have finish'd,—such scene I'd ne'er seen,
> And shall never again perchance—ah! the poor queen,
>   To lose her great Feline King,—"
> —The host scream'd out, in terror, "What's that?"
> For bolt from the rug up mounted his cat,
>   That seem'd such a soft sleeping thing,—
>   His tail enlarged,
>   His eye appear'd charged
> With dilated green glory—he looked doubly furr'd—
> And he grew majestic in whisker,—and purr'd.
>
> Breathless the Wayfarer stared,—so the Host!
> As though they had suddenly seen the ghost
>   Of the mouser-monarch inurn'd;—
> But 'twas no deception,—the terrible Tom
> Bounced up on the window-sill—and therefrom
>   For a moment haughtily turn'd—

> Then dash'd a mass
> Of hole in the glass—
> And squall'd, leaping down to the garden plats,
> "*He's dead!—Well then* I AM—KING OF THE CATS!"[26]

The Burnsian subtitle, "The 'Owre True Tale,' " guided the reader toward Reynolds's great predecessor, and the bizarre scene in the weird house confirmed the echo of Kirk Alloway in *Tam O'Shanter*. One line, "And,—grammercy, what a sight!," was a variation of Burns's "And, vow! Tam saw an unco sight!" (l. 114). And yet Reynolds achieved the comic grotesque with a difference from Burns. "The Mouser-Monarchy" does not approach the greatness of Burns's masterpiece, but it is a fine poem in its own way. T. S. Eliot would have enjoyed it, and so would many other twentieth-century readers.

Reynolds produced this poem illustrative of his great talent as the time approached for him to make his indispensable contribution to the first major biography of Keats who, Reynolds had always known, soared far above anything he could hope for. The biography had been delayed for more than two decades. Shortly after Keats's death, John Taylor planned to write it, and Reynolds stood ready, as Keats's best friend, to provide all the assistance he could. In the face of Charles Brown's stubborn resistance, Taylor let the opportunity slip away. Reynolds made no concerted efforts to prepare a biography, but he did borrow from Taylor about 1825 Severn's letter to Haslam reporting Keats's safe arrival in Italy—Reynolds had not, however, seen Severn's letter describing Keats's death.[27]

In 1825 and again in 1830 George Keats urged Reynolds or Dilke to write the biography, not only because he knew they had the knowledge and ability, but also because he was sensitive to the possibility of Brown's producing a book that claimed George took financial advantage of his brother. When neither Reynolds nor Dilke complied with his request, in 1836 George, who then enjoyed considerable prosperity, asked Dilke to hire another author at George's expense. In 1838 Dilke negotiated with Brown and Taylor for the life of Keats with Reynolds as the suggested biographer-editor, but Brown delayed giving him a final answer. Instead Brown wrote his own manuscript biography, which Dilke attacked sharply about April 1841 as depicting only Brown's relations with Keats, while ignoring others such as Keats's best friend, Reynolds.[28]

By 1845 Brown's "Life" and materials had passed to Richard Monckton Milnes, who negotiated through his publisher Moxon to secure cooperation from Keats's other friends. At first Taylor wanted Reynolds to write the biography instead of Milnes,[29] and Reynolds signified his willingness by discussing his planned "Recollections" with both Taylor and Dr. George Darling. When Taylor annoyed him by suggesting that his motive might be monetary, he insisted that it would be a labor of love. Surprisingly, he saw at this point for the first time Woodhouse's bound volumes of manuscript poems and letters; Reynolds had not known that during Keats's lifetime Woodhouse had carefully preserved copies of the Keats letters that Reynolds thought he had lent him for perusal only.[30]

In the middle of November 1846, thinking to begin work on his "Recollections of Keats," Reynolds called on Taylor and found to his consternation that Taylor had sold to Moxon for £50 all his Keatsiana, including the copies of Keats's letters to him. Having thought that he had Taylor's full cooperation for his own book, he protested angrily to Taylor. On 27 November Reynolds requested that Moxon not allow Milnes to use any of Keats's letters to him without his consent, and on 15 December he forbade Moxon to use the letters, with clear indication that he would turn to the law to protect his property. Taylor was miffed by Reynolds's tone; he saw Moxon and wrote, in what Reynolds considered an offensive letter, that Reynolds's letters would not be used and his name would not be mentioned in Milnes's biography.[31]

Disturbed by Reynolds's opposition, Milnes wrote Moxon apprehensively on 20 December 1846 that Keats's letters to Reynolds "are by far the best letters in the whole collection I have &, if you don't make some arrangement with Mr Reynolds, the thing will be very incomplete."[32] Milnes need not have worried. Reynolds was only venting his anger at what he considered Taylor's rude and insulting treatment. As soon as his temper cooled, he withheld cooperation only until he could assure himself that Milnes was qualified and likely to produce a book worthy of a subject as close to his heart as Keats. In poor health at the time[33] and evidently unable to leave the house himself, three days after he forbade Moxon to use the letters, and in fact two days *before* Milnes urged Moxon to act to solve the serious problem, Reynolds sent Eliza on 18 December to consult with Dilke about whether he should cooperate with Milnes.[34] Reynolds's last reservation removed by Dilke's approval, he responded on 22 December to Milnes's appeal by letter, offering his enthusiastic cooperation.

Unselfishly dedicated to the memory of Keats, Reynolds insisted that if Taylor did pay him any part of the £50, as he had offered, he would turn it over to Milnes "for the use of the family of George Keats," as he had heard of George's financial crash and death five years earlier. Reynolds climaxed his lifelong high valuation of Keats the poet and man with a remarkable tribute written to Milnes: "But a word or two on the great subject of our correspondence. He was hunted in his youth,—before he had strength to escape his ban-dogs! He had the greatest power of poetry in him, of any one since Shakespere!—He was the sincerest Friend,—the most loveable associate,— the deepest Listener to the griefs & disappointments of all around him,—'that ever lived in the tide of times.' " Confident of Milnes's ability, Reynolds felt relieved at having the duty of writing the life removed from his shoulders.[35]

Within eight days Milnes had replied to welcome his assistance and Reynolds had written a second time to start the flow of invaluable information for the *Life*.[36] Thereafter followed a six-month gap in his letters to Milnes because the two began meeting shortly after the letter of 30 December 1846.

The major writing project of his own which Reynolds valued most from the fall of 1846 through the spring of 1848 was frustrated, was never published, and is now lost. He translated four satires of Juvenal and Persius in the manner of Pope and Johnson, adapting them to the contemporary time by substituting English names and events for the Roman. The four satires (one was Juvenal's fourteenth) came to fifteen hundred lines. Proud of his achievement, Reynolds tried hard to have it published.

He had hated *Blackwood's* for its cockney-school attacks on Keats and refused steadfastly in 1819 all William Blackwood's tempting overtures to write for the magazine. Unlike other liberal Londoners such as Lamb and Hood, Reynolds had never written a word for *Blackwood's* and still regarded the attacks on Keats as "drunken brawls."[37] But after all the intervening years, the founder of the magazine had died, the original editors had long since been succeeded by others, and the magazine had gained respectability even in liberal quarters. The *New Monthly* and *Bentley's Miscellany* were open to him and welcomed most of his work, but neither Colburn nor Bentley would be at all likely to accept controversial satire directed against living public figures. Because it was receptive to satire, Reynolds knew that *Blackwood's* was the logical place for his modernized Juvenal and Persius, and furthermore, if the work were as good as he judged it to be, the publisher might reprint it in book form after first publication in the magazine.

On 22 November 1846, Reynolds sounded out *Blackwood's*, writing to what he thought was its London address to outline the project and to inquire whether he might submit a sample. Led to believe that the London address was a mistake, two days later he wrote again, this time directly to Edinburgh, describing the work at greater length and, to arouse interest, citing Byron's and Lockhart's praise of him.[38] But *Blackwood's* rejected the satires and he turned elsewhere, first on 2 July 1847 to R. M. Milnes, hoping that his influence might secure a publisher, but Milnes kept the manuscript for eight months and did not return it until Reynolds had asked him to do so twice.[39] Finally on 11 March 1848 as a last resort, he tried Bentley, whose rejection did not surprise him.[40]

While still in London, Reynolds was more successful with other pieces, publishing a substantial essay and three poems by the end of the winter of 1846–47. In "On the Opening of the Ports of St. Paul's Cathedral and Westminster Abbey," he returned to a subject that had concerned him for over twenty years, arguing for the abolition of the admission fees to the two great national buildings.[41] A London tradesman had sought entrance to St. Paul's, offering to pay the customary twopence, but discovered to his chagrin that the price had been raised to sixpence because it was Lord Mayor's Day. He protested in a letter to the *Times,* and Reynolds predicted that the excitement caused by the letter would lead to the abolition of all fees. Though he rejoiced at the prospect, he thought it ironic that the tradesman should succeed where great men had failed—Goldsmith in *Citizen of the World* and Lamb in *Letter to Robert Southey.* Noting that satire sometimes succeeded where serious attacks failed, Reynolds reprinted from *Odes and Addresses to Great People* his own "An Address to the *Very* Reverend the Dean and Chapter of Westminster," but admitted that the verses had accomplished nothing. The tradesman, he believed, would succeed, since even *Punch* had joined the attack. With Keats very much on his mind now that he was assisting Milnes, Reynolds included in the article a pleasing sonnet entitled "The Cathedral" with strong echoes from *The Eve of St. Agnes.* Though not so fine as his best papers in the *Champion* and *London,* this last essay was a decent farewell contribution to the genre.

The best of the three poems was "The Wall," sensuously rich with its peach, pear, apple, and jasmine and at the same time oddly amusing. Determined to avoid the softly sentimental that Keats had warned him against in the Robin Hood sonnet, Reynolds did not directly glorify fruits and flowers, but struck the pose of an admirer of the brick and mortar wall that sheltered them, and in the process glorified them the more effectively with the indirection. "Have You Heard a Lute" was a competent song, melodious and restrained in its simplicity. "The Two Enthusiasts," paralleling a Jewish mystic in London certain of the arrival of the Messiah and a Christian mystic in Palestine equally certain in his faith in the imminence of the Second Coming, was overelaborate and strained. Favoring neither over the other, Reynolds revealed his skeptical Unitarianism by overtly celebrating the glorious faith of both, but leaving the thoughtful reader with doubts as to the soundness of such zeal turned to fanaticism—without of course risking the loss of pious subscribers to the magazine by saying so.[42]

In the spring of 1847 Reynolds moved away from London for the last five years of his life. He had always been a liberal in politics from his early friendship with Keats, Hazlitt, and Hunt, though in print at least he was moderate and prudent in declaring his views. Political services he performed for the Liberal cause influenced his fellow Garrick Club member, Lord John Russell, to appoint him assistant clerk to the new county court at Newport on the Isle of Wight.[43] The new court for the recovery of debts of less than twenty pounds opened on 22 March 1847, with C. J. Gale as presiding judge and Reynolds and G. Wansey as clerks, and sat for the first time on 19 April.[44]

Leaving Eliza behind in London, Reynolds arrived in Newport some time between 22 March and 19 April. On the latter date he was in Newport, for on that day he addressed an emotional request to George Cruikshank for an autographed sketch to serve as a memento of their long friendship. Having lived in London for most of his life, except for business trips and vacations away from the city, Reynolds realized that the provincial setting would mean a radical change for "the Evening of life."[45] He would no longer have the sociable interchange with his intellectual peers that had always been an important part of his life, but he hoped that such friends as Cruikshank would visit him occasionally in Newport. Eliza was to complete the move by following from London to the Isle of Wight the Monday after 19 April.

Reynolds continued to assist Milnes with the biography of Keats, chiefly by correspondence. On 2 July 1847 he sent what must have been a large packet of materials, including a copy of Chancery proceedings with the dates of Keats's birth and the death of his mother, a bound volume of manuscript of the last three books of *Endymion,* manuscripts of *Nightingale* and *Psyche,* and copies of a few short poems.[46] Not hearing again from Milnes for two months (though Milnes must have acknowledged receipt of the valuable package) and not realizing that Milnes had traveled to Spain, he inquired on 8 September in the briefest of notes, "What of Keats?" By 26 January 1848, he had learned of Milnes's travels but still had not received a letter from him. Concerned that Milnes might not have time to complete the project that Moxon had announced three years before, Reynolds volunteered what he knew were his lesser services as a substitute, but only as a last resort to keep Keats from being *"unbiographed."* Milnes reassured him so that by 6 March when Reynolds was in London he hoped that the book would be out by Easter. Still in London on 9 March, he was delighted with Milnes's report of his progress on the biography and planned to meet him. Milnes had kindly sent Reynolds a card of admission to a nobleman's series of social affairs; Reynolds could not attend the one on 18 March because he had to leave for Newport, but he hoped to return for a later occasion.[47]

Although Reynolds's hope for an Easter date was too optimistic, the book was moving toward publication, and Milnes, preparing to credit his most valuable assistant, asked Reynolds for an account of his works. Reynolds listed his books, omitting *The Eden* and *The Naiad,* and included the *London* as the only periodical to which he had contributed; his realization of how small his lifelong achievement seemed in comparison with Keats's greatness depressed him into chastising himself as "that poor obscure—baffled Thing,—myself!"[48] Visiting in London on 17 April, he offered to help with the proofs.

Back in Newport on 22 June, he wrote, "I send you, at this late hour (but I *fear* they will be *in time!*) the 3 Sonnets."[49] Rollins conjectured that they were the three Nile sonnets by Keats, Hunt, and Shelley or the three sonnets by Keats in Hunt's *Foliage,* but Reynolds's joking modesty about them makes it more likely that they were his own three Robin Hood sonnets. They were published in *The Garden of Florence,* but he had sent Milnes earlier only the title page and preface, not the book.[50] Reynolds also sent a letter he had written twenty-eight years before urging Keats not to publish *Hyperion* with a work by Hunt, but he could not find Keats's original preface to *Endymion,* which he had dissuaded him from publishing, and concluded mistakenly that it was beyond recovery. He had kept the originals of Keats's letters to him; he would have been glad to lend them to Milnes, but Milnes no doubt found it more convenient to work with Woodhouse's copies in the bound volumes. Reynolds considered whether he might review the book in the *Edinburgh* or *Quarterly,* but his diffidence indicated that the idea was tentative and doubtful.

While the book was being printed, Reynolds chanced in his leisurely reading of Coleridge's *Table Talk* to come upon the passage in which Coleridge reported a meeting with Keats. The editor had substituted a blank for the name of the third person present, Mr. Green, Keats's old demonstrator at Guy's Hospital. Probably remembering that Keats told him he had met Coleridge personally, he wrote Milnes, "The meeting took place, I know." He did not know of Keats's detailed account to George and Georgiana of a meeting with Coleridge. After thirty years his memory was imprecise, and he thought that the third person was Hunt and that the meeting had occurred a year or two earlier than 1819. He therefore doubted the accuracy of Coleridge's claim that he sensed death in Keats's hand when he shook it. Since it was too late to change the text, Milnes added a footnote with the mistaken identification of Green as Hunt and with the mistaken time. Sara Coleridge rightly called the footnote "a little cluster of mistakes" in the 1851 edition of *Table Talk.*[51] That Reynolds's sense of the precise date had faded after thirty years was revealed by his directing Milnes to "the Examiner of 1815, or some year close to it" for Hunt's "Young Poets" article joining his name with that of Keats and Shelley.

To avoid any possible jealousy among Keats's friends, Milnes did not send proofs to Reynolds before publication. When he sent the first copy to Severn, he explained, "Even Reynolds, without whom the thing could not have been done at all, has not seen a word in print."[52] When he received his copy, Reynolds paid enthusiastic tribute on 10 August 1848 and in so doing revealed why Milnes was a better biographer than he would have been. "I do not seem (to myself) to have known half the cheerfulness—half the vigour,—half the goodness of heart & mind of Keats, until I met all his letters & Journals ⟨met⟩ *homed* together, and harmonized as they are now, under your care!"[53] Although he might not have written a volume so narrow as Brown's "Life of Keats," Reynolds could hardly have surmounted what had meant the most to him—his own relationship with Keats.

Evidently Reynolds did not follow his intention to write detailed commentary in a special copy interleaved with blank pages and bound, or, if he did, it has been lost like the bulk of his other books and papers. The inscribed presentation copy from Milnes, owned by the Houghton Library at Harvard, is not that interleaved book. Reynolds wrote to Milnes, "I think after I have seen you,—I might help you to a little point of interest here & there, which might be of service."[54] He placed small strips of paper in the presentation copy to mark certain passages, made a few notes, and took the book with him to talk from when he met Milnes. Gittings's dissatisfaction with the sketchiness of the notes, which he called "drunken scrawls," resulted from a misunderstanding.[55] Such cryptic notes may seem puzzling to others, but they can be satisfactory reminders for the one who made them.

The publication of Milnes's *Life, Letters, and Literary Remains, of John Keats* was the brightest spot in the rather unhappy five years of Reynolds's rustication in Newport. The death of his mother on 13 May 1846 saddened him, though the blow could not have been unexpected at her age of seventy-six. He missed the excitement and stimulation of the city; as his friend and fellow Garrick Club member James R. Planché observed, "it was absolute exile for a man of his town tastes and habits, and he lost no opportunity of running up, if only for a few hours, to London."[56] He drank too much and offended many with his political and religious views, as R. E. Prothero, Lord Ernle, reported:

He was . . . a broken-down, discontented man, whose great literary abilities had brought him no success in life. Few, probably, of the islanders were aware that the assistant County-Court Clerk, who professed himself an Unitarian and a bitter Radical, and whose drunken habits placed him beyond the pale of society, had promised to be one of the stars of English literature at the period of its poetic revival.[57]

The statement was damning, and Lord Ernle was in no doubt about his belief in its accuracy, as his reply to Louis A. Holman's query showed. "It is a fact that for the last few years of his life Reynolds drank habitually, and gradually sank in the social scale. I know this because I lived for nearly thirty years of my life within three miles of the town of Newport, and many of the inhabitants of that town knew Reynolds well. There is no doubt about the fact; but whether it is necessary to rake up such an incident in the close of his career I do not know."[58]

Reynolds was discontented, broken down, and habitually drunk. One must accept Lord Ernle's testimony because he had no reason to report other than the truth, and indeed he repeated the charge with some reluctance. There can be no doubt that Reynolds was discontented, for Planché's comment corroborates that report. There can be no doubt of his heavy drinking because a friend William Robson confirmed it nine years after his death. "I did not see Reynolds for many years before his death, but when I asked Mr. C. Kemble, with whom I was very intimate, after him, he always shook his head, and said—'Brandy & Water! Brandy & Water,' and what was still worse, I was warned if I met him, *not to play at cards with him!*"[59] At the same time, as W. B. Pope suggested, the charges can be tempered, even if only a little. Lord Ernle's father, Canon Prothero, rector of Whippingham near Osborne in the Isle of Wight, was an orthodox Anglican clergyman and a political conservative. He, his friends, and other provincial conservatives may have condemned Reynolds's breakdown all the more strongly because of their reaction against his Unitarianism and political radicalism, views for which others would honor him.[60]

Reynolds's drunken breakdown, however, was not complete, for he continued to function and to earn the respect of some of his fellow townsmen. News items and legal notices in the Hampshire *Independent* reveal that he continued to perform his work as assistant clerk of the county court until his final illness. Soon after his arrival in Newport in the spring of 1847, he helped to expedite improvements in the postal service between Newport and London; his long friendship with Rowland Hill, who headed the postal department at the time, may have been useful in that minor success. The Hampshire *Independent* reported on 8 May 1847, "We understand that the town is considerably indebted to J. H. Reynolds, Esq., the clerk of the New County Court, for his valuable assistance in aiding and hastening the measure." In the fall of 1847 he collected money locally for the preservation of Shakespeare's house in Stratford. He lent his satirical pen to the political cause of the Liberals; W. Self Weeks recorded in the *Isle of Wight County Press* in November 1935 the local tradition, "My father used to say that Reynolds was credited with assisting the Liberal party at election times by aiding in the composition of skits on their opponents, which played a prominent part in the election literature of the period."[61]

Reynolds wrote his last poem for the *Athenaeum* of 29 January 1848. In "The Dead Bird" he lamented in simple verses the death of his pet caged bird, turning for relief to thoughts of wild birds and quoting "full-throated" and "fruit-tree" from Keats's *Nightingale*. It was Reynolds's only publication from the Isle of Wight. In earlier years he had depended on periodical writing as a supplement to his income; the salary as court clerk probably reduced the pressure to continue.

For the last three years Reynolds and Eliza lived at 36 Nodehill; Reynolds signed the seven-year lease for the house owned by Joseph Poore on 23 June 1849 at an annual rent of £35. The Hampshire *Independent* reported his death in 1852: "Reynolds.—November 15, at Node Hill, Newport, Isle of Wight, after a very short illness, and highly respected, J. H. Reynolds, Esq., solicitor, and Clerk of the Newport County Court, aged 58."[62] W. B. Pope noted that the "highly respected" appeared in none of the dozen other death notices on the page; perhaps it was more than obituary form and should qualify Lord Ernle's account. Curiously, instead of "a very short illness," the *Athenaeum* reported "a long and painful illness."[63] The *Independent,* closer to the scene, was more likely to know the fact accurately. If the *Athenaeum* phrase was anything other than a flat erroi, Dilke, whom Eliza would have notified immediately by mail, may have had in mind not the immediate attack that killed him, but the chronic ill health that had dogged him during his last years. Eliza wrote a few months after his death, "His position of late years has been a sad one—& his many losses & troubles affected him greatly, & caused the ill health from which he so long suffered."[64]

He was buried in the old burial ground at Church Litten, his gravestone bearing the original inscription, "In Memory of John Hamilton Reynolds who died November 15th 1852 Aged 58 Years." It was not until 1917 when the lettering was restored after it became barely legible that the well-known "The Friend of Keats" was added.[65]

In addition to the death notices in the Hampshire *Independent* and the *Athenaeum,* the *Examiner* on 20 November noted his death. His friend of forty years, Dilke, wrote a detailed obituary for the *Athenaeum* of 27 November, and "W.R.," probably William Robson who later left the report of his drinking, provided another, almost as detailed, for the *Examiner* of the same date. W.R. was a long-time personal friend who had followed Reynolds's writing career so closely that he could identify even Reynolds's unsigned biography of John Philip Kemble in the *London Magazine*. He wrote in part:

I was surprised to observe that in your paper of Saturday, although you announced the death of J. H. Reynolds, Esq., you afforded him no place in your obituary. Five-and-thirty years ago, few who knew him would have anticipated such an omission in so high a literary paper as yours. At that period John Hamilton Reynolds gave promise of a brilliant career. . . . In habits of constant intercourse with [the contributors to the *London*], he carried amongst them one of the finest natures it has been my chance to meet with in this working day world. With splendid dark eyes, a mobile and intelligent countenance lit up by never-failing good humour, and a quiet, bland, but somewhat arch smile, he was goodly to look at as well as to listen too. . . . The last time but one I saw Reynolds, we stood on a knoll upon Wood Green, contemplating a splendid sunset, and, with a sort of rivalry that was common with us, repeating, from memory Collins's beautiful ode to Evening. That is many, many years ago—But as it reminds me "how pleasant was my friend," it is the impression I will cherish of him.

The Hampshire *Independent* reprinted both the *Athenaeum* and *Examiner* obituaries on 4 December 1852.

Thus passed the charming John Hamilton Reynolds, a compound of failures and limited successes. He did not succeed in the law; he supported his family, but usually at the brink of financial collapse—once falling over the brink. His one recorded major legal success was his collaboration with Rice on the Patmore trial after the Scott-Christie duel. He did not like the legal profession. In the early years he could take a momentary interest and "hobby horse" upon it, as Keats put it, but that was transitory. As the years passed, legal work became his *"worst* subject."[66] According to Dilke, who was always deliberate in his judgments and who knew him best near the end of his life, he "threw away this certain fortune" by not following up the opportunity offered by the partnership with Rice and the succession to Rice's business.[67] Thomas Noon Talfourd, who also combined law and literary interests and started at the same place as Reynolds, achieved a position of eminence by steady application. On the other hand, Reynolds, after thirty years in the profession, settled for the obscure post of assistant clerk to the minor court in Newport. Near the close of his life, the law remained "that dreary profession" into which Rice had drawn him.[68]

He was overshadowed greatly in literature by his intimate friends Keats and Hood and his good friends Hazlitt and Lamb. He was neither a major poet nor a major prose writer, but he did create a valuable body of work that entitles him to a position as a significant minor poet and prose writer. In his strongest genre—satire—*Peter Bell* was his finest poetic work, with "Boswell's Visit" following as his best prose. Although he succeeded only occasionally with nonsatirical poetry, the final accumulation of memorable poems was considerable: *The Eden of Imagination,* "Margaret," "Reproach Me Not," *Devon,* the Robin Hood sonnets, the two sonnets renouncing poetry and "What Is Life?" in *The Fancy,* "Go Where the Water Glideth Gently Ever," and "The Mouser-Monarchy." In the main, his early prose was best: the spirited essays in the *Champion* and the *Yellow Dwarf* and the Edward Herbert papers in the *London*. Only occasionally did the late prose in *Bentley's Miscellany* and *New Monthly* approach his earlier standard.

Though his achievement with his pen was not negligible, his

greater achievement was his sparkling and witty personality that led to intimate friendships with Keats and Hood. He was not wrong when he wrote Milnes with quiet confidence, "Keats will take care of me."[69] His name lives because of his friendship with Keats.

Abbreviations

Clubbe John Clubbe, "The Reynolds-Dovaston Correspondence," *Keats-Shelley Journal*, 30 (1981), 152–181.

CR Charlotte Reynolds, the elder.

DNB *Dictionary of National Biography.*

Dov John Freeman Milward Dovaston.

Gittings, *Ariel* Robert Gittings, "The Poetry of John Hamilton Reynolds," *Ariel*, 1 (1970), 7–17.

Gittings, *John Keats* Robert Gittings, *John Keats* (Boston: Little Brown, 1968).

GR George C. Reynolds.

Hudnall Clayton E. Hudnall, "John Hamilton Reynolds, James Rice, and Benjamin Bailey in the Leigh Browne-Lockyer Collection," *Keats-Shelley Journal*, 19 (1970), 11–37.

Kaier Anne Kaier, "John Hamilton Reynolds: Four New Letters," *Keats-Shelley Journal*, 30 (1981), 182–90.

KC Hyder E. Rollins, ed., *The Keats Circle, Letters and Papers and More Letters and Papers of the Keats Circle*, 2d ed., 2 vols. (Cambridge: Harvard University Press, 1965).

KSJ *Keats-Shelley Journal.*

Letters of Hood Peter F. Morgan, ed., *The Letters of Thomas Hood* (Toronto: University of Toronto Press, 1973).

Letters of Keats Hyder E. Rollins, ed., *The Letters of John Keats*, 2 vols. (Cambridge: Harvard University Press, 1958).

Letters of R Leonidas M. Jones, ed., *The Letters of John Hamilton Reynolds* (Lincoln: University of Nebraska Press, 1973).

Marsh George L. Marsh, *John Hamilton Reynolds: Poetry and Prose* (London: Oxford University Press, 1928).

Morgan Peter F. Morgan, "John Hamilton Reynolds and Thomas Hood," *Keats-Shelley Journal*, 11 (1962), 83–95.

R John Hamilton Reynolds.

Reiman reprint *Romantic Context: Poetry Significant Minor Poetry 1789–1830*, selected and arranged by Donald H. Reiman, John Hamilton Reynolds, *The Eden of Imagination, Safie, The Naiad* (New York: Garland, 1978); *Peter Bell, Benjamin the Waggoner* and *The Fancy* (New York: Garland, 1977); and *The Garden of Florence, The Press, Odes and Addresses to Great People* (New York: Garland, 1978).

Richardson   Joanna Richardson, *Letters from Lambeth* (London: Boydell Press, 1981).

Riga and Prance   Frank P. Riga and Charles A. Prance, *Index to the London Magazine* (New York: Garland, 1978).

Selected Prose   Leonidas M. Jones, ed., *Selected Prose of John Hamilton Reynolds* (Cambridge: Harvard University Press, 1966).

Stillinger   Jack Stillinger, ed., *The Poems of John Keats* (Cambridge: Harvard University Press, 1978).

Letters of Reynolds

1 Margaret, 25 February 1815

AL: No. 1662, Box 5 in the Dovaston Collection in the County Records Office, Shire Hall, Shrewsbury. The enclosure in R to Dov, 25 February 1815, omitted by Richardson, p. 134.

Address: J. Dovaston Esqr/West Felton/Salop/Free/Dims Giddy[?]. [In R's hand above the address]—London March the first 1815. *Postmark:* Free/1Ma 1/ 1815.

Endorsed by Dov: Wrote to Reynolds 21 March 1815.

1

The maiden I remember now,
  Though Time hath travell'd since we met;—
She lived beneath a mountains brow,
  The lightsome Margaret!

2

She was the spirit of the place
  With eyes so wild, & cheek so fair
Her form was playful in its grace
  As her own mountain air

3

The rustic dress became her well
  How dear to trace its beauty now
And rich the natural ringlets fell
  O'er her delightful brow

4

With looks & language innocent,
  She won the heart of Memory;—
Who oft in busy scenes hath sent,
  Thoughts to her silently.

5

There was a music in her speech
  That gave the heart a deep delight

Like murmuring waves that kiss the beach
   In a still summer night

6

Her home I saw in day's decline
   It was in sooth a lovely spot—
And fair the starry jessamine
   Wreathed o'er the little Cot

7

I loved the loud brooks sparkling haste
   I loved the fields and mountains green
And her, whose fairy presence graced
   The wildness of the scene

8

And to remind of her,—the brook—
   The fields, the moon—the Heavens conspire
The suns first, fresh, delighting look
   Is like her eyes bright fire

9

Though many feel life's ruder shocks
   May she escape the storms that lour;
And like the violet on the rocks,
   Live an unbroken flower

10

Perchance dark years before me lie
   But ⟨still⟩ I ⟨two illegible words—many⟩ shall
     ne'er—oh! ne'er forget
   Her loveliness of heart & eye
   The ⟨b⟩ lightsome Margaret!

---

2   *Reynolds to Horace Twiss, c. 26 December 1818* (?)[1]

ALS: Bodleian MS. Don. d. 95. fols. 105–6.
Address: H. Twiss Esq.
Endorsed by Twiss: Reynolds

Dᴿ Sir

   I believe your note is for to day—I shall have great pleasure in making one at the proper hour

                Yrs Truly
                J H Reynolds

3   To Moon,[2] Boys, and Graves, 4 August 1832

ALS: British Library, Graves Papers. Add. MS 46140, f. 33.

Address: Mess^r Moon Boys & Graves/Pall Mall

> 27 Golden Square
> 4 Augt 1832

Gent.

Mr Coney,[3] who brings this, will not longer press his proposal against the terms offered by you. He will therefore make over to you his half share in the work & stock on receiving you[r] receipt for £243. 10.6 the amo^t due by him to you for Copies,—your acceptance for £75 payable at 3 months—and your [three words illegible] to present him with 6 N^os of parts 7 & 8 (two of each part being India Proofs) I am gratified that this business is at length brought to a termination

> I am Gent
> Yr ob Ser
> J. H. Reynolds

To M^css^rs Moon Boys & Graves

4   Reynolds to Dilke, c. 3 July 1832

ALS: British Library, Dilke Collection, ADD. 43899, f. 198b.

Dear Dilke

I send you two pieces[4]—the one by Hood—the other by self—2 for a pair. If you want anything *acknowledged*[5] by me—to bear on it my initials—you shall have a serious something

> Yours
> JHR

5   Reynolds to Dovaston, 11 May 1836

ALS: No. 1662, Box 9 in the Dovaston Collection in the County Records Office, Shire Hall, Shrewsbury.

Endorsed by Dov: Jack Reynolds

> Shrewsbury
> 11 May 1836

Dear Dovaston

I am again in my native Town & cannot but remember old friends. Business leads me to Liverpool—but I return here in a day or two & shall have to pass a day at Oswestry. We had some difference many years ago—which has gone out of my mind & I still feel the friendship alive there in a green old age. I should like to pass an hour with you in my way if you have the same wish—Drop me a line Post Office here—which I shall get on my return. We shall see changes in each. You have been leading a quiet retired life—I have been in the world in all its struggles—

Believe me & C
Dear Dovaston
Yours faithf.
J. H. Reynolds

6 Reynolds to Rowland Hill, *16 January 1837*

ALS: British Library 31, 978, f. 7.
Endorsed by Hill: Reynolds J H January 16. 1837.

10 Great Marlbro St.
16 Jan.y. 1837

My Dear Sir

Many thanks for your Confidence—& many thanks for your pamphlet ⟨of⟩ on Post Office Reform—which *hits the mark*. Oh! that our Legislators could but be convinced that in a matter in which the Public is the great Actor—cheapness (which is the antidote to Poaching—Smuggling and other *illegal* innovations) is the desideratum for the Revenue & the People. You are Palmer the second but I should hope the first in the fair recognition & after reward of the truth. I have shewn your Pamphlet to no-one—Said (as Vulgars say) "nothing to nobody"—but when you absolve me from Silence, I shall be glad to take up the subject, as well as I am able in some public Print or other.

Sincerely yours
J H Reynolds

7 Reynolds to Blackwood's, *22 November 1846*

ALS: Blackwood's Collection, National Library of Scotland.
Private

88 Guildford Street
Russell Square
22d Novr 1846

Gentn

I am inclined to submit to the Editor of your Magazine,—some paraphrases of two or three of the Satires of Juvenal and Persius, adapted to the present times. I think they [illegible word] may start a few of your columns well in the New Year; but your Editor must "have a taste of my quality." Perhaps you will oblige me by letting me know what the amount of remuneration would be to me—in case my verses are thought well of—And in case of my approval of it—You will tell me whether I shall send the M.S. through *you* to the Editor. Does he reside in Edinburgh?

I am Gentⁿ
Your obed serv
J. Hamilton Reynolds

Mess^r Blackwood

8   *Reynolds to* Blackwood's, *24 November 1846*

ALS: Blackwood's Collection, National Library of Scotland.

88 Guildford St
Russell Square
24 Nov 1846

Gentⁿ

I yesterday addressed a note to you, as "Messrs Blackwood, Publishers, *Pall Mall,"* and I am only just now ⟨illegible word⟩ made aware of the error in the direction. As this note may never reach you[6]—I think it the best course, to write you again direct to Edinburgh. I am desirous of offering to your Magazine,—some Paraphrases of certain Satires of Juvenal & Persius, with a few notes—adapted to the present time. ⟨and⟩ I would at once send you my version of Juvenal, fine 14^h Sat.—for the perusal of your Editor—if I should be satisfied with the terms of remuneration you would offer me—Subject of course to the *Editor's* approval of my M.S. It would be necessary to abandon the columns in the setting up of the Poems—And if the text were by leading, made a little more open—it would be better. But this I should of course leave to your Editor.

There will be 4 Satires in all of about 1500 lines with notes. And they might be collected into a small Volume—if they commanded attention Enough to justify it.

I *think* my verses will suit the spirit of your Magazine—And start the New Year in a new Department well.

I know not whether my name is known to you. I apprehend not. It was favorably mentioned in Byron's Letters & in Peter's Letters by Mr Lockhart many years ago—as *one of Promise.* My avocations have prevented me from hitherto making any serious attempts at performance.

Yr obed Serv
J. Hamilton Reynolds

Mess^r Blackwood & sons

Letters to Reynolds

1 Rylance to Dovaston and Reynolds, 23 August 1813

ALS: No. 1662, Box 4 in the Dovaston Collection in the County Records Office, Shire Hall, Shrewsbury.

Address: John F. M. Dovaston Esq/The Nursery/West Felton/near Shrewsbury. *Postmarks:* W—AUG-A/23/1813; Add!/1.

Endorsed: by Dov: Rylance-/wrote to him/9 Sepr. 1813

Edinburgh Monday morning
23^d August 1813

Your letters have transported me beyond the ignorant present, and I feel now the future in the instant. If you had seen me after I had read your folio joint epistle which I received precisely a week ago you would have laughed an hour sans intermission "Call back that bundle of thick coming fancies, that balloon of sighs, that cartridge filled with blasting powder compounded by a file of blue devils, call it back" said I, but the letter was already over the border, and would not be remanded—Here comes another more ardent than the first. I had been from day to day conning a sonnet as a response to yours, but the printer has been pouring in proof-sheets of the Index as thick as shot and the thread of my discourse was repeatedly snapt. Your letter of the 18th came yesterday, Sunday, but I had it not, unfortunately till this morning, or I should have bestowed the whole day in answering it. Thanks, most hearty thanks a hundred times told, to you both for your kind friendship, the assurance of it has cheered & reanimated me. How shall I describe the change you have effected—[7] Imagine a ship at sea, becalmed & lost in a thick fog, sails flagging & flapping to & fro by the mere heaving of the sluggish waters, rudder lash'd & left to itself, hands idling here & there, & piping now & then a faint despairing whistle, but not a cap-full will come—all gloom, sadness & impatience; when behold the ⟨illegible word⟩ sea in the offing begins to curl, the sails swell, the mist & scud clear away—the mariners are roused from their lethargy—haul the mainsail to the wind set the topsail & up with the *fly-by-night*—the breeze that blew fitfully awhile now freshens & bears steadily along—the gallant vessel rustles through the waves, and leans toward her course as if she voyaged rejoic-

304

ing." So it was with me—I felt strength and only wanted wings to make the wind my post horse and be down among you with the afternoon sun at the foot of the dial[8] just as the fume of your pipes were curling through the leaves of the ilex & Mrs. Turner[9] had drawn your high flavoured October "from his dark retreat, mature & perfect" to sparkle in the sun and gladden the wearing hours. Since I can't fly I must write—and this I do with alacrity, that my greeting may reach you ere Reynolds returns and that thus I may make some amends for the uneasiness which my late gloomy, pitchy letter occasioned you both, and for coming into your presence as I then did, with so rueful & so downcast a countenance. Thank him for his address to Sappho, which is finely and pathetically imagined and which I the more admire since it breathes the true music of the noble Spenserian stanza. I cannot but think his projected Eastern tale[10] rather an arduous attempt; but even as an attempt it will do him good, because it must demand a course of reading which will enlarge his store of poetic imagery. Of course I mean if he has not already so prepared himself, and is ⟨not⟩ as great a stranger to the oriental metaphor and allusion as I am. With his ardent mind, he will soon overcome that obstacle. I can easily imagine that, as you say, he finds his fancy impregnated at West Felton. In your delightful retreat, and with your unbounded and unabating flow and range of poetic converse it must be so. I declare I never think of the hours I past with you without getting into a train of ideas that seems to me a new order of existence, equally superior to the heedless hurry or the stupid stagnation of every-day life. And when I feared those hours were never to return, no wonder I was so dejected; but there was no reason for making my dejection contagious—and I reproach myself for it. No more of that—If one glimpse of Autumn remains when I take my departure hence I do design to come & eat a pippin with you, when I hope we shall consecrate our friendship anew and I shall carry with me a cordial shake of the hand for Reynolds that the triad may be united.

Judging by the fine weather we have had here you must have had a glorious season of it. I have often in thought gone over all our old rounds with you and Reynolds, and ⟨illegible words⟩ remembered many things we talked about at each halting-place. The hornets, I suppose, have taken up their old quarters in the gate-post and now & then a straggler comes to share your beverage under the tree. Crony[11] I hear has been in the straw and one of her progeny is destined to go with Mr Wimble[12] to London. The pup if he takes of his dam, will be a great favourite at Lambeth after he has got over the ear-cropping, the distemper and the plagues of whelp-hood. I am sorry for Doll Tearsheet's[13] lameness, which

I hope is only temporary, and not a symptom of declining age. Perhaps it is an accident owing to some of her gamesome tricks in the stable, if so, rest and repentance may bring her about & set her on her legs again.

There is no literary news that I can gather in this literary metropolis wherewith I can occupy this remaining space of my letter. Mr Dugald Stewart, I hear is writing a philosophical work on the active Powers of Man. Jeffrey, I think I told you, is gone to America to fetch a wife. She is a niece or some such relation to the celebrated John Wilkes so that from such a stock the future race of authors may augur a tremendous breed of critics. Walter Scott, they say, has another poem almost ready for the press. Mr Constable who published his Marmion, shewed me the other day, the whole MS. of that poem, which he had taken the trouble to preserve. The first canto appears to have been sent under franks from London; part of the second, from Stewart Rose's at Christ church Hants, the rest from different places in Scotland. Mr. C. intends to have it bound up, along with the Poet's receipt for a thousand pounds, which was paid before the poem was finished so that upon the whole it will form one of the most curious volumes of MS. that ever antiquary preserved.

Again I thank you for your heart inspiring letter which I have thus, (too hastily & carelessly I fear) answered; but no language could have expressed the happiness I feel in the assurance of your friendship after this period of anxious suspense. Yours in heart & soul—

R. Rylance

I have written under the impression that Reynolds is still with you and as your hearts are one so has been the language of mine to you both. Through you I knew him and shall ever be proud of his friendship for its own sake and for yours which is united with it. I look with ardour to a time when we three shall meet again

Remember me to Yates & Wood—I will fulfill my promise to Yates ere I leave Scotland[14]

2 Constable and Company to Reynolds, 15 January 1820

Source: Constable and Company's letter-books in the National Library of Scotland. This and the following items are the office copies of the letters that were mailed.

Address: J H Reynolds Esq/London

15 January 1820

on the day I left London I sent you a check for the Sum you wanted which, in your favour rec^d yesterday you did not acknowledge; but I hope notwithstanding you rec^d it[15]

I should [have] written to you ere this as to your poetry,[16] but as you said you were to be out of town for sometime, I thought it unnecessary to do so till I heard of your return

We have every wish to do your will as to this said favorite—but to be honest, as I told you before we have a hor[r]or at poetry, and decline it at all hands, except where the author pays the paper and print—and this resolution arises from experience—no one poem that we have published having done any [business?] saving Walter Scott—the publick are gorged with Poetry—and the trade will not look at it we therefore return your M.S. with this—but when we do this we are happy you have another channel for it—as the disappointment will not be so great

Mr. Morehead[17] is grumbling at you mightily—You really must try an article for him. Your Books shall be sent, but Good Sir pray send us a good article soon— and follow it with another. The Novels and Poetry come to £10.16/.

Do commence soon with Mr Moyse[18]

3   *Woodhouse to Reynolds, 4 May 1820*

ALS: Adelman Collection in the Bryn Mawr Library.

Address: Jnᵒ Taylor Esq/Fleet St[19]

Dʳ John,

I have just laid hands (not fists) upon the "punishing" letter from Peter Corcoran's fair correspondent.—Take what parts you think best: and if you can, by any little alterations, improve its effect—do so—The copyright is not very sacred—& the Author's reputation will not suffer in your hands.—What think you of making the Correspondence have taken place between P.C. and his *real* Sweet heart, who afterwards turned cruel, & broke his heart & then married to break her husband's. I think it woᵈ. be in Character & give reality to her & him—& poze the *criketts*. Might not her unkindness be supposed to have originated in this reply to her remonstrance?[20]

Yrs truly

Rᵈ W.

May 4. 1820.

Note—The young lady a short time before her Marriage (which it is believed hastened poor Corcoran's death) returned all his letters to her[21]—& this is printed from the original.—

4   Constable and Company to Reynolds, 15 May 1820

Source: Constable and Company's letter-books in the National Library of Scotland.

Address: J H Reynolds Esq/Little Britain

15ʰ May 1820

I was almost on the point of writing to you when your letter of the 10th inst made its appearance—we have [been] certainly much surprised at your silence, we have been at a loss indeed to imagine how you had managed to lose sight of your agreement—I tell you so candidly—this however is clear, you are greatly too late for this season, but we must *have you in October* without fail—of course we must content ourselves without you for the present—but as our arrangements for the next book season are in a train—we beg of you to understand, that we can give you till October but *no longer* we always find it better to be explicit in business operations—and if the work is not ready by the time we mentioned, we shall be constrained to throw it up altogether—but from your known acquirements, we have no idea that such an issue will be called for—

We think it better to allude to the title which it would be well if you could improve—we are not over fond of that already announced Your ingenuity can easily make it better

We would council you to commence at Press soon, this will excite you to exertion and not press hard upon you *near your time*

We beg to hear when you begin with Mr Moyse & are & c

5   Constable and Company to Reynolds, 21 June 1820

Source: Constable and Company's letter-books in The National Library of Scotland.

Address: J. H Reynolds/London

21 June 1820

We wrote you on the 15th May and have been expecting to have had the pleasure of hearing from you ere this—the season gets on—and we have to crave your attention to this We are & c A C & Co[22]

6   Constable and Company to Reynolds, 8 July 1820

Source: Constable and Company's letter-books in The National Library of Scotland.

Address: J. H. Reynolds Esq/London

We have your favor of the 20th June—we count on the book as mentioned in our former letter—and hope you will not lose a day in putting it in the Printers hand, we do not like the 'Tales of the Ferryman' nor the Sempstresses—try another neither are what may be called leading titles— of course ⟨depends⟩ a good deal depends on the book itself—we were lately asked by an author to fix on a title for his book—which we did at rando[m] without knowing what it contained—we must therefore lean on you on this matt[er] We are & c

A.C. & Co   PR.C.

7   Constable and Company to Reynolds, 15 August 1820

Source: Constable and Company's letter-books in the National Library of Scotland.

Address: J. H. Reynolds Esq / London

15 Augt 1820

Still no tidings of your commencement—and the season gets on—we are now obliged to assail you in true earnest, longer delay being fatal to the project

Be so good as say when you ⟨intend⟩ are to put Mr Moyes in motion— we hear to day from town that he has not yet heard from you—

We are still of opinion that the titles you have proposed are not the most fitted for the many headed Monster the public but the Author of P.C.[23] can devise some good sounding name—we crave your *immediate* attention to all this—and beg to hear from you on the subject We are & c

A C & Co

8   Constable and Company to Reynolds, 21 August 1820

Source: Constable and Company's letter-books in the National Library of Scotland.

Address: J. H Reynolds Esq / London

21 August 1820

We have your favor of the 18th Inst, and altho we had resolved upon the period of bringing out your book, we after due consideration, agree to your proposal that it should make its appearance at Christmas—and this we hope as to both Author & Publisher will be *final.*

We are yet astray about the title, but you may go on we can consider of it in the mean time

Mr Morehead is glad at the delay for it gives him an article[24]—we do not rejoice on the score we look for a very good book—We remain & c

A C & Co

P.S. We had almost forgot to say that we had heard from Mr Moyes.

9   Constable and Company to Reynolds, 15 September 1820

Source: Constable and Company's letter-books in the National Library of Scotland.

Address: J. H. Reynolds Esq/London

15 Sepr 1820

Our plan of operations for the winter Campaign are now in progress—and we are of course anxious to array all our forces—pray what shall we finally make your title—? We are not fond of the Sempstresses—the Fairies we do not like either—do favor us, and if possible *in course* with *a rational title*—we have, we think said before that there is some what of *tact* in making titles—but we confess this one bothers us not a little—the public too are so much pamperd that they will not look at any thing of a common Cast do turn all this over in your mind—and instruct us—our Catalogue is almost waiting for it We are & c

A C & Co

10   Constable and Company to Reynolds, 27 January 1821

Source: Constable and Company's letter-books in the National Library of Scotland.

Address: J. H. Reynolds Esq / London

27 January 1821

We are in receipt of your favor of the 22^d Ins^t, it is not our wish to separate from you—but have our book *out*—and soon—as to the title we care not—altho we would certainly wish one as attractive as possible—yet, we have not by our correspondence assumed any right to dictate a title to your work—by all means proceed with a title of your own—not knowing what your book may contain it is impossible that we can make any suggestions—we have no doubt that any thing you write will be good but do pray proceed and with a title such as you think most fitting—

We count of [on] your attending to our wishes—and that without any delay

11   Constable and Company to Reynolds, 13 February 1821

Source: Constable and Company's letter-books in the National Library of Scotland.

Address: J. H. Reynolds Esq / London

13 February 1821

We cannot find out any proper reason—for the line of conduct you are pursuing towards us—we contracted with you for a work in Novem^r 1819 which was to have been published in the following Spring—we are now arrived at spring 1821—and no more doing in your undertaking than when first it was contracted for.—

Our Mr Cadell was not a little amazed at not seeing you when in London in order that the whole might be either off or on—and it is the purpose of this note to express our feelings on this point—we consider ourselves much agrieved the paper has been with the printer for one whole year—and with all this nothing done—if the book is not published by the month of April we must be constrained to throw it up altogether We beg an early answer and Are & c

A C & Co

12   Constable and Company to Reynolds, 23 June 1821

Source: Constable and Company's letter-books in the National Library of Scotland.

Address: J. H. Reynolds Esq / London

Mr Moyes writes us that there is yet no progress made with your work[25]—we must say that this annoys us very much, we would much rather it were to cease altogether, than that you should do any thing evidently against your inclination—Altho the paper is paid for & on it we must sustain loss—we would rather receive back the £80 advanced to you on the projected undertaking & let it drop altogether—we cannot but think this to be your wish from the course you have pursued lately—& on your transmitting ⟨transmitting⟩ us the sum mentioned—we shall hand you the agreement cancelled

We cannot close this letter without expressing our regret at being constrained [to] adopt this course & Remain & —

A C & Co

13   Constable and Company to Reynolds, 2 August 1821

Source: Constable and Company's letter-books in the National Library of Scotland.

Address: J H Reynolds Esq / 18 Poland Street London

2ᵈ Aug 1821

Mr Constable (who has for some months past been much indisposed, and not attending to the detail of business) has handed to me your letter to him of the 26th Inst

I beg most explicitly to state that we we want your book, not the money back, we have again & again ⟨stated⟩ stated this to you—and if you were on the point of going to Mr Moyes on the receipt of my Letter of 23 June

you ought not to have stopped but proceeded with him—the tone[26] [le]t-
ter was written in despair of seeing the book that feeling is in some
degree abated by your letter to Mr Constable just received, therefore pray
proceed & we shall count on it by Xmas—but if not *then* ready, I can assure you we shall then have cause to complain and *shall complain.*—We
are not ignorant that you have written other BOOKS since you Contracted
with us in 1819! The last ("The Garden of Florence") we only knew of
by accident some three or four days ago[27]—and regret to find that you
have been assailed in our Magazine for July, had we known that you
were the Author, we would have suppressed the Review but it was *burely*
[*barely?*] *possible* to suppose that it was from one who was in arrear to
us for a Book so long contracted for We are & c

14 Constable and Company to Reynolds, 17 August 1821

Source: Constable and Company's letter-books in the National Library of
Scotland.

Address: J. H. Reynolds Esq / London

17 August 1821

We have this morning your letter addressed to our Mr Cadell—

On looking over the letters we have written to you from time to time,
we see no cause to regret any part of them—but we regret them only, we
may say, in one view, & that is, that they may cause you to perform a
task—the purport of the present note is to relieve you from that as it
must be anything but agreeable to you, & if on receipt you transmit us
the sum we paid to you in Novem[r] 1819 say £80—(we shall say little
about the interest) & pay to Mr Moyes the expense he has been at, & here
we shall also relieve you from our loss in laying in & paying for paper,
you may, we say, after making good these sums consider yourself relieved
from your task, & your agreement shall be returned cancelled—

However, if the foregoing proposal does not meet your views—you need
not reply to this letter, but proceed with your work—on the condition
stated in your favor just recd that it is to be out by Xmas

A. C. & Co.

P.S. As to your remarks on the Garden of Florence & c—all we have to say
is, that we *did not* know that you were the Author—& perhaps would
never have known but for the transmission of a Critique on it for the
Edinburgh Review

A C & Co

Letters of the Reynolds Family

1 Mrs. Charlotte Reynolds to William Longmore,[28]
26 September 1841

ALS: Photocopy in the Keats House of the original owned by Mrs. G. Dora Hessell of Papakura, New Zealand.

My Dear Willy

I take shame to myself . . . letting your Letter lay so long unnoticed & which gave me so great pleasure in receiving. Illness has stood boldly in my way & it has been that alone which has prevented me from telling you— ⟨with⟩ with many thanks—how pleas'd I was when it came to hand—I like your stile of Letter writing, it is natural, & easy, which to me is more to be admir'd than any of the high sentimental stuff of the present day.—Brother George[29] set off yesterday to the Castle at Hertford to Uncle Philips[30] for a fishing bout, I wish he may be a successful Angler he seems so to enjoy the sport.—It gives me high & mighty delights to learn that you are so comfortable & enter with such energy into yr employments,[31] all your pursuits are good, & sensible, & will I trust end to your advantage—I am too Old to see the day arrive, when you shall have to build new Houses of Parliment, or a Royal Exchange but *you* are Young enough to ⟨live?⟩ have to do similar things ⟨things⟩ which will do honour to yourself & delight to your friends.—Aunt Charlotte returnd from Your Fathers last Night & left all well there.—Aunt Hood spent the day here yesterday & enquir'd after you kindly & *begs you will write to her.* The Hamstead dears I believe are tolerably well but they might as well be at Hanover or else where, as where they are for any thing I shall ever see of them[32]—I suppose you have by this time seen most of the Beauties of Oxford, indeed by the letters sent Home, I perceive you have not been Idle in this way & it gave me great pleasure to find you had employ'd your leisure in making observations on that fair & fine City, for it is worthy notice—Grandpapa & *I* go on in the same John Trot stile as when you were here. we peep thro' our grand Evergreens, & as usual witness a Boy fight, a dog ditto, or a Preacher ranting like Mad. I believe the two first of these exploits I prefer, as having most sense in them.— ⟨pray⟩ pray make my Compliments to Mr & Mrs[33] Case & tell them they have my best wishes for a continuance of their health & happiness, & my thanks

for any kindness they may have conferd on You since you have liv'd under thier Roof—

I am quite aware my dear Boy that I am sending you as stupid a Note
as any Grandmother in the Universe could send. As an excuse for which,
I must inform you that I am assaild by not a few evils that are foes to
good sense. such as want of Memory, the stupidity of Age, the torments of
ill health & c & c, *then* what can You or any other Person expect from
such an helpless ⟨Indivial⟩ Individual as your most obedient correspon-
dant. C—. R—, —— we all unite in kind love to You with every kind
hope for your good, *now* & for ever. I look forward to meeting you "before I go hence & be nomore seen" God bless you Dear Willy & believe me
in truth

Your Affectionate Grandmother
Sincere Friend
and well wisher
C. Reynolds

Septr 26th
1841
Your Sister Liz³⁴ & Lotty spend the Ev^g at the Champs tomorrow M^r
C[h]amps has given Aunt Lotty a Beautiful envelope Case, elegant as it
it well can be

2 *Eliza Drewe Reynolds to Dovaston,*³⁵ *10 March 1853*

ALS: No. 1662, Box 10 in the Dovaston Collection in the County Records Office, Shire Hall, Shrewsbury.

Endorsed by Dov: Mrs Reynolds March 10th 1853

Thursday
March 10th

Sir

I come to you as a stranger—though your name has been so long familiar to me, I have heard of you as the early friend of my dear & lost Husband—& in your retirement you will have heard no doubt of this by bitter
loss. His position of late years has been a sad one—& his many losses &
troubles affected him greatly, & caused the ill health from which he so
long suffered.

I feel strangely in writing to you, & it is very painful to me—but if you
were his friend, I cannot be wrong,—& I have brought my mind to say to
you, that he was unable, from his troubles, to provide for my future—&
that a few friends are trying to raise enough to purchase a small Annuity
for me. I do not dwell upon my own distress of mind in having thus to
write—I have never seen you,—& cannot judge of your feelings in any

way—but if you can & will aid in this from a regard for his Memory,—I seem to feel that you will—& therefore I thus write.

Yours obd[ly]
E P. Reynolds

Will you direct to me—
at A. Symonds Esqu
6. Victoria Terrace
Lee
Blackheath
Kent

Letters of the Keats Circle

1 Woodhouse to Taylor, 1 May 1821

ALS: Adelman Collection in the Bryn Mawr Library.

I and mine go the "English" to see J H R's Jarvey "stand still at the rate of 9 miles an hour." The fabricator of that vehicle (of amusement) having sarved me with *orders* to attend—what we shod. call subpoenas.[36]

Yrs very truly

Rᵈ W

5/1/21

2 John Martin to James Rice, 1 November 1830

ALS: British Library, Eg. 2838, f. 148–49. This note was enclosed in the following letter.

Address: James Rice Esq Junr

Mount Street[37]

Nov. 1. 1830

Dear Rice,

Mr F Madden[38] is on the council of the Royal Society of Literature, whose first meeting is on Thursday next—will you take the trouble of seeing or writing to that gentleman requesting him to favor Dilke with the name of someone who will report the proceedings of the meeting for the Season—

Yours truly

J Martin

3 James Rice to Frederic Madden, 2 November 1830

ALS: British Library, Eg. 2838, f. 146.

Address: F. Madden Esqʳᵉ/British Museum. *Postmarks:* even/2 NO/1830—rest illegible; another illegible mark.

Poland Street

2 Novʳ 1830

Dear Sir,

If the request contained in the inclosed letter is not an improper one,

316

and will not occasion much trouble to yourself, you will much oblige me by so far complying with it as to put my Friend in the way of effecting his object.—M^r. Dilke the gentleman named in the within letter is a particular Friend of mine & the Editor of a Literary Journal devoted to the Arts, Sciences & general literature, called the "Atheneum' in which I also am a little interested & doubtless it would be very useful to that Work (& I take it not undesireable to the Society of Literature) that its proceedings should be *properly* reported

However I have a full reliance on your willingness to oblige me in this matter if you can fairly do it and I leave the mode of doing so to your better Judgment

> I am Dear Sir
> Your's very truly
> J Rice Jun

My Friend Dilke is a Hampshire Man & a precursor of yourself by a year or two at the Same School.[39]

Notes

Chapter 1

1. Guildhall Library, MS 5266, vol. 4; MS 5265, vol. 5; MS 5257, vol. 10. Cited in Robert Gittings, "The Poetry of John Hamilton Reynolds," *Ariel*, 1 (1970), 8, to which I am also indebted for subsequent references to Guildhall Library records and genealogical MSS.

2. R to Dov, 31 December 1808. Joanna Richardson, *Letters from Lambeth* (London: Boydell Press, 1981), p. 30. His middle initial is recorded in the MS Shrewsbury School Register.

3. All the reports of the baptismal date and place by various scholars of the Keats circle derive ultimately from the MS Christ's Hospital record, where he is said to be the "only son." St. Olave's church no longer exists, nor apparently does the baptismal record. He may have had at least one sister, who became the aunt mentioned in CR to Dov?, and 26 November 1808. Clubbe, p. 159. Without the baptismal record, there seems no way to confirm it.

4. Guildhall Library, MS 5257, vol. 11.

5. George L. Marsh, *John Hamilton Reynolds: Poetry and Prose* (London: Oxford University Press, 1928), p. 10.

6. Guildhall Library, MS 5265.

7. MS Account, Hackney Public Library.

8. Phyllis Mann, "The Reynolds Family," *Keats-Shelley Journal*, 5 (1956), 6.

9. CR to Dov, 9 March 1808 and 24 August 1808. Richardson, pp. 12, 22.

10. Gittings, pp. 9–10.

11. Notice in the *Gentleman's Magazine*, cited by Richardson, p. 2.

12. Mann, pp. 6–7.

13. Marsh, p. 9.

14. He was paid a full year's salary of £11 on 29 September 1798. I am grateful to James B. Lawson, librarian of Shrewsbury School, for searching the school's MS records for this and subsequent information.

15. R to Dov, 10 February 1809. Richardson, p. 31.

16. R to Dov, 4 December 1813, 19 July 1814. Richardson, pp. 114, 118.

17. MS Shrewsbury School records.

18. MS Shrewsbury School records for the date and number. Willard B. Pope, "Critical and Biographical Estimates of Benjamin Robert Haydon and John Hamilton Reynolds," Harvard doctoral dissertation (1932), p. 610.

19. *London*, 7 (May 1823), 525–26, and 9 (January 1824), 35–36.

20. *London*, 4 (July 1821), 8–9.

21. John Masefield, ed., *The Fancy* (London: Elkin Mathews, 1905).

22. Peter's tutor was called the Rev. Mr. S—— in *The Fancy*, Leonidas M.

Jones, ed., *Selected Prose of John Hamilton Reynolds* (Cambridge: Harvard University Press, 1966), p. 262n. Sheil's closeness to the Reynoldses is shown in Sheil to Dov, 12 June 1810. He was appointed as third master on 29 September 1799 and continued to serve until 25 March 1808—MS Shrewsbury School records.

23. MS Shrewsbury School records; "Greenwich and Greenwich Men," *Bentley's Miscellany*, 7 (February 1840), 282.

24. Leonidas M. Jones, ed., *The Letters of John Hamilton Reynolds* (Lincoln: University of Nebraska Press, 1973), p. 17.

25. CR to Dov, 9 March 1808, and GR and CR to Dov, 9 June 1808. Richardson, pp. 12, 18–19. Thomas Allen, *The History and Antiquities of Lambeth* (London: J. Allen, 1826), pp. 337–38. Allen shows that the salary was not reduced.

26. R to Dov, 10 Feb. 1809. Richardson, p. 31. It later declined somewhat; in 1826 the number was reported as "from 358 to 380." Allen, p. 338.

27. Allen, *Lambeth*, p. 336. For Blake, David Erdman, *Prophet against Empire* (Princeton: Princeton University Press, 1954), p. 266.

28. Lewis S. Benjamin, *William Makepeace Thackeray* (Garden City, N.Y.: Doubleday, Doran, 1928), pp. 21–22.

29. GR and CR to Dov, 9 June 1808. Richardson, p. 19.

30. Marsh, pp. 10–11.

31. DNB under "Andrew Bell."

32. CR to Dov, 18 August 1809. Richardson, p. 40. Here and hereafter I locate the pages in Richardson, but quote from my own transcription of the MS letters to correct a few small slips. See also Marsh, p. 11.

33. Marsh, p. 10.

34. Thomas Allen, *The History and Antiquities of London,* 5 vols. (London: Cowie and Strange, 1828), III, 593.

35. B.A. 1782, M.A. 1785. Robert B. Gardiner, *The Admission Registers of St. Paul's School* (London: G. Bell, 1906), p. 148.

36. R to Dov, 31 December 1808. Richardson, p. 29.

37. CR to Dov, 24 August 1808. Richardson, p. 20.

38. Richard Harris Barham, *The Garrick Club* (New York: privately printed, 1896), p. 42.

39. Gardiner, p. 232.

40. R to Dov, 11 September 1809, and CR to Dov, 11 September 1809. Richardson, pp. 42, 38. The date of Reynolds's letter can be fixed more precisely than Miss Richardson's "Late August or early September 1809." It was sent along with Miss Richardson's no. 12 (CR to Dov), which she understandably misdates as 11 August 1809 because Charlotte wrote the wrong month (as she did once later—but she caught her own error). The postmark, omitted by Miss Richardson, corrects the date to SE/11[1]809.

41. R to Dov, 11 September 1809. Richardson, pp. 42–43.

42. CR to Dov, 21 April 1808; R to Dov, 31 December 1808 and 10 February 1809. Richardson, pp. 14, 29, 31.

43. R to Dov, 23 September 1808. Richardson, p. 26.

44. R to Dov, 11 September 1809. Richardson, p. 42.

45. CR to Dov, 9 March 1808 and 21 April 1808; GR and CR to Dov, 9 June 1808; R to Dov, 23 September 1808. Richardson, pp. 12, 14, 18, 26.

46. Henry C. Shelley, "A Friend of Keats," *Lamp,* 28 (July 1904), 451.

47. Frances F. Broderip and Tom Hood, *Memorials of Thomas Hood,* 2 vols. (Boston: Ticknor and Fields, 1860), I, 39.

48. GR and CR to Dov, 9 June 1808. Richardson, p. 19.

49. CR to Dov, 18 August 1809. Richardson, p. 40.

50. CR to Dov, 14 February 1810; GR to Dov, 10 October 1809; CR to Dov, 14 February 1810. Richardson, pp. 48, 43–44, 47.

51. R to Dov, 10 February 1809. Richardson, p. 31.

52. R to Dov, 25 February 1815. Richardson, p. 131. R wrote only the first paragraph of this letter on Saturday, 25 February; the eight dots of suspension indicate an interruption. The rest of the letter he wrote on or after Sunday, 26 February, because in the second paragraph he mentioned seeing Hunt's thanks to him in the *Examiner* of that date: "The Editor has received R.'s Letter, and fully appreciates the spirit in which it was written." The postmark was 1 Ma 1/1815.

53. Ralph Rylance to Dov, 23 December 1813, p. 1.

54. CR to Dov, about 8 April 1814. Richardson, p. 116. Dov's endorsement, "wrote a hasty, and free Answer, 10 April 1814," suggests that he replied immediately, so that she wrote only a few days before 10 April.

55. CR to Dov, 9 March 1808, 21 April 1808, and 24 August 1808. Richardson, pp. 12, 15, 22.

56. CR to Dov, 7 and 8 October 1810. Richardson, p. 58.

57. R to Dov, 11 September 1809. Richardson, p. 42.

58. Cr to Dov, 11 September 1809. Richardson, p. 38.

59. CR to Dov, 11 September 1808. Richardson, pp. 24–25.

60. GR and CR to Dov, 9 June 1808. Richardson, p. 18.

61. CR to Dov, 14 February 1810, 12 June 1810, 7 and 8 October 1810, 13 May 1811, 16 August 1812. Richardson, pp. 48, 53, 58, 65, 78–79.

62. CR to Dov, 7 and 8 October 1810, 9 March 1808, 11 September 1808, 12 June 1810, 24 August 1808. Richardson, pp. 58, 12, 25, 53, 22.

63. CR to Dov, 10 February 1809. Richardson, p. 33.

64. R to Dov, 23 September 1808; CR to Dov, 18 August 1809. Richardson, pp. 26, 40–41.

65. The *Post Office London Directory* lists "G. Squibb, Auctioneer, Boyle Street, Saville Row" in 1810, 1811, 1812, 1813, 1814, and 1815. By 1817 his son Frank had evidently succeeded to the family business.

66. He reached 21 in 1812 when R was 18, R to Dov, 15 September 1812. Richardson, p. 89.

67. GR to Dov, 10 October 1809. Richardson, p. 44.

68. R to Dov, 2 November 1809. Richardson, p. 45. R dated the letter 3 November, but he erred for the postmark was NO 2, and Dov received the letter on 3 November.

69. R to Dov, 1 August 1810. Richardson, pp. 54–55.

70. R to Dov, 11–14 March 1810 and 1 August 1810. Richardson, pp. 49, 54. Ellis C. Knight, *Dinarbas* (London: Dilly, 1790) was a continuation of *Rasselas.*

71. R to Dov. 11–14, March 1810. Richardson, p. 49.

72. R to Dov, 10 May 1810, and CR to Dov, 12 June 1810. Richardson, pp. 51, 52–53.

73. CR to Dov, 12 June 1810. Richardson, p. 52. Marsh, p. xiii.

74. R to Dov, about 27 September 1810. Richardson, p. 56.

75. J. J. W. Deuchas, ed., *Peeps into the Past, a Souvenir of the Bi-Centenary*

of the Old Amicable Society (Norwich, 1908), as cited in George L. Marsh, "New Data on Keats's Friend Reynolds," *Modern Philology,* 25 (February 1928), 324.

76. Marsh, "New Data," pp. 324–25.

77. R to Dov, 14 June 1811. Richardson, p. 66.

78. The first piece in time of composition, "Observations on Old Age," in the *Repository,* 2 (August 1809), 74–76 is signed J. H. R. and dated from Sudbury, Suffolk, 12 May 1808. The last piece is dated 4 June 1809 in the *Repository,* 2 (July 1809), 11. Between these outside dates are Sudbury (without date) in 1 (April 1809), 257; Sudbury, 6 March 1809, in 1 (May 1809), 278; Sudbury, 9 May 1809, in 1 (June 1809), 369–70; and Sudbury, 14 May 1809, in 2 (August 1809), 135. Two poems in the *Poetical Magazine* are signed J. H. R. and dated from Sudbury in 1809: 1 (May 1809), 19, and 1 (September 1809), 271.

79. *Repository,* 2 (July 1809), 9–11.

80. Sheil to Dov, 12 June 1810.

81. R to Dov, 14 June 1811. Richardson, p. 66.

82. R to Dov, 1 August 1810, 27 September 1810, 22 November 1810, 24 December 1810, 2 September 1811, and 4 November 1811. Richardson, pp. 55, 56, 61, 62, 67, 70.

83. R to Dov, 4 November 1811, 23 June 1812, and 11 July 1812. Richardson, pp. 70, 73–74, 76.

84. CR to Dov, 2 February 1812; R to Dov, 2 September 1811, 14 June 1811. Richardson, pp. 72, 67, 66.

85. CR to Dov, 13 May 1811. The address was later printed, R to Dov, 14 June 1811. Richardson, pp. 64, 66.

86. First visit—CR to Dov, 11 September 1808 and R to Dov, 23 September 1808. Second visit—CR to Dov, 10 February 1809. Third visit—CR to Dov, 18 November 1809. Richardson, pp. 24, 26, 33, 46.

87. GR to Dov, 10 October 1809. Richardson, p. 43.

88. Quoted by Charlotte in CR to Dov, 7 and 8 October 1810. Richardson, p. 57.

89. CR to Dov, 7 and 8 October 1810. Richardson, p. 57.

90. CR to Dov, 2 September 1811. Richardson, p. 69. Miss Richardson was misled in her note (p. 177) as to how Jane used the room by a later reference to French lessons involving Jane and Ralph Rylance—Richardson thought Jane taught Rylance. As Rylance's letters to Dov reveal, Rylance gave Jane lessons in French.

91. R to Dov, 2 September 1811; CR to Dov, 2 February 1812. Richardson, pp. 68, 71.

Chapter 2

1. R to Dov, 23 June 1812. Richardson, p. 73. Dov's phrase comes from his endorsement of the letter.

2. R to Dov, 2 July 1812 and 11 July 1812. Richardson, pp. 74–75, 75–76.

3. CR to Dov, 16 August 1812. Richardson, pp. 78–79.

4. R to Dov and Rylance, about 2 September 1812 (it is postmarked 3 September 1812). Richardson, p. 81.

5. In the copy of *The Eden* which he sent Dov, now at Yale, R wrote beneath the title of "A Recollection," "This was suggested on Blodwell Rocks."

6. Dov's account is reprinted in Richardson, pp. 139–40. Dov printed the MS

version R sent him in February 1815, not knowing that R had published a revised and expanded version in *The Naiad* (1816).

7. Rylance to Dov, 14 March 1813.

8. Rylance to Thomas Yates, 23 December 1813 and Dov's obituary of Rylance in Dov to Thomas Archer, 31 December 1834.

9. R to Dov and Rylance, about 4 September 1812. Richardson, p. 85. Miss Richardson, who disregarded postmarks, dated this letter August–September 1812. It was sent at the same time as CR's letter of 2 September, which was postmarked 4 September. Dov received the two letters together.

10. R to Dov and Rylance, about 2 September 1812 (it is postmarked 3 September 1812). R to Dov and Rylance, about 4 September 1812. Richardson, pp. 79–85.

11. R to Dov and Rylance, about 2 September 1812; CR to Dov, 2, 3 September 1812. Richardson, pp. 79–80, 86.

12. Rylance to Dov, 6 September 1812.

13. R to Dov, 15 September 1812. Richardson, p. 88.

14. Rylance to Dov, 29 September 1812, 11 March 1813.

15. R to Dov, 15 September 1812, 3 and 5 October 1812, and 21 November 1812. Richardson, p. 89. John Clubbe, "The Reynolds-Dovaston Correspondence," *KSJ,* 30 (1981), 162, 166.

16. R to Dov, 15 September 1812, 3 and 5 October 1812, Rylance to Dov, 15 March 1813, and R to Dov, 3 March 1813. Richardson, p. 88. Clubbe, pp. 162, 176.

17. R to Dov, 29 June 1813. Richardson, p. 101. Miss Richardson dates the letter July 1813; it was postmarked 29 June.

18. R to Dov, 15 September 1812. Richardson, p. 88.

19. R to Dov, 28 December 1812, 3 March 1813, and 9 March 1813. Clubbe, pp. 170, 176, 179.

20. R to Dov, 23 October 1813. Richardson, p. 108.

21. R to Dov, 9 March 1813. Clubbe, p. 179. *Repository,* 10 (November 1813), 311.

22. R to Dov, 9 April 1813 and 15 June 1813. Richardson, pp. 90, 97.

23. R to Dov, 15 June 1813. Richardson, p. 97.

24. R to Dov, 4 September 1813. Richardson, pp. 106–7.

25. R to Dov, 9 March 1813. Clubbe, pp. 180–81.

26. R to Dov, 9 April 1813. Richardson, pp. 89–90.

27. R to Dov and Rylance, about 2 September 1812, R to Dov, 3 March 1813, R to Dov, 24 May 1813. Richardson, p. 81. Clubbe, p. 175. Richardson, pp. 92–93.

28. R to Dov, 15 June 1813. Richardson, p. 97. Rylance to Dov, 23 September 1812.

29. R to Dov and Rylance, 4 September 1812; R to Dov, 2 August 1813, 28 December 1812, and 8 June 1813. Richardson, pp. 82, 102. Clubbe, p. 172. Richardson, p. 95.

30. R to Dov and Rylance, about 2 September 1812; R to Dov, 8 June 1813 and 23 October 1813. Richardson, pp. 81, 95, 109.

31. R to Dov, 14 June 1811. Richardson, p. 66.

32. R to Dov, 24 May 1813. Richardson, p. 94. Published in the *Repository,* 10 (July 1813), 58.

33. *Repository,* 10 (November 1813), 306.

34. R to Dov, 10 October 1814. Richardson, p. 129.

35. *Champion,* 22 December 1816, p. 406.

36. Hyder E. Rollins, ed., *The Keats Circle, Letters and Papers and More Letters and Papers of the Keats Circle,* 2nd ed., 2 vols. (Cambridge: Harvard University Press, 1965), II, 281–82. The girl Bailey meant was not the penitent girl as Rollins thought, but Jairus's daughter because her arms have to be crossed and her eye has to be on Christ: both true of Jairus's daughter and neither of the penitent girl.

37. "Reproach Me Not," *Champion,* 27 April 1817 and "Sonnet on the Picture of a Lady," *The Garden of Florence,* p. 130.

38. R to Dov, 3 March 1813. Clubbe, p. 176. The number was 14 in 1813; it had declined to 12 by 1815 when the society was discontinued.

39. R to Dov, 15 September 1812. Richardson, p. 89. The word looks like Zetosophian to me in all cases. Richardson reads Zetesophian and Clubbe Letasophian. Reynolds's carelessness misled Clubbe about the first letter in 3 March 1813. But the fourth letter perhaps remains doubtful.

40. From a prefatory sheet in John Martin's annotated copy of the *Inquirer* in the Bodleian Library.

41. British Museum Catalogue.

42. Willard B. Pope, ed., *The Diary of Benjamin Robert Haydon,* 5 vols. (Cambridge: Harvard University Press, 1960–63), II, 182n.

43. Richardson, p. 169.

44. R to Dov, 3 March 1813. Clubbe, p. 176.

45. R to Dov, 9 April 1813. Richardson, p. 89.

46. The address is preserved in the Leigh Browne–Lockyer Collection in the Keats House, London.

47. R to Dov, 30 September 1813. Richardson, p. 108.

48. John Martin's prefatory sheet in his annotated copy of the *Inquirer* in the Bodleian.

49. R to Dov, 30 April 1813, 24 May 1813. Richardson, pp. 92, 93.

50. R to Dov, 9 March 1813. Clubbe, p. 181.

51. R to Dov, 15 September 1812. Richardson, p. 89.

52. From the MS book of the constitution, laws, and minutes of the society in the Houghton Library at Harvard.

53. R to Dov, 28 December 1812. Clubbe, p. 172.

54. R to Dov, 9 March 1813. Clubbe, p. 180.

55. R to Dov, 9 April 1813, 30 April 1813, and 8 June 1813. Richardson, pp. 89–90, 91, 96–97. In Notes to Correspondents, the editor of the *Ladies Museum* announced, "In R. we recognize a youth who is an ornament to literature." R began a series of articles in April 1813 and concluded it in October 1813. It included: Letter of intention to write "The Critic," *Ladies Museum,* 14 (April 1813), 214–15; "On Recreation," 14 (April 1813), 219–22; "The Critic, No. I" (on Warton's "Ode on the Approach of Summer"), 14 (May 1813), 276–80; "The Critic, No. II" (on Ossian), 14 (June 1813), 364–67; "The Critic, No. III" (on figurative language), 15 (July 1813), 46–48; "The Critic, No. III" [By mistake there are two No. IIIs and no No. IV] (conclusion on figurative language), 15 (August 1813), 96–97; "The Critic, No. V" (ridicules Dr. Francis's note on the first ode of Horace), 15 (October 1813), 218–21. The essays on figurative language were close to textbook treatment; the essay on Dr. Francis's footnote was pedantic. After the last three essays, the editor realized that ladies were not going to read that kind of material, for he commented in Notes to Correspondents, "Though we decline the insertion of R's last paper from its want of originality; we should be sorry to lose the aid of his promising talents." But he did lose

them; R contributed no more. He had written no essay for September, because he was vacationing with Dov in August.

56. R to Dov, 15 June 1813. Richardson, p. 98. Miss Richardson, disregarding the postmark, dated it only "Late June 1813."

57. *Letters of R.,* pp. xv–xvi.

58. R to Dov, 29 June 1813. Richardson, p. 102. Without reference to the postmark, she dated it "July 1813."

59. R to Dov, 2 August 1813. Richardson, p. 102. He had been back in London for more than a week when he wrote Dov on 4 September 1813.

60. R to Dov, 4 September 1813. Richardson, p. 107.

61. *Repository,* 10 (August 1813), 120.

62. The "Ninth Statue" was less likely a pun on the nine muses, as Miss Richardson surmised, than it was a verse imitation of the ancient Persian prose tale, "Story of the Ninth Statuette" in *Vikrama's Adventures,* ed. and trans. Franklin Edgerton in *Harvard Classical Studies,* vol. 26 (Cambridge: Harvard University Press, 1926), 97–100. "Statue" is used interchangeably with "statuette" in the frame of the story. The story of the fair damsel haunted by a demon who drank the blood of her lovers would have appealed to the future author of *The Naiad.* The puzzle, however, is how Reynolds could have encountered a version of it; Edgerton wrote that not much of the work had been printed in English before the middle of the nineteenth century. When he wrote *Safie,* R shifted from the Ninth Statue, a legendary Persian tale, to a Persian tale of his own devising.

63. R to Dov, 4 September 1813. Richardson, pp. 105–7.

64. R to Dov, 21 November 1812. Clubbe, pp. 167–68.

65. Rylance to Dov, 28 March 1813.

66. R to Dov, 4 September 1813. Richardson, p. 106.

67. R to Dov, 3 and 5 October 1812. Clubbe, p. 164.

68. R to Dov, 29 June 1813, 15 June 1813. Richardson, pp. 100–101, 97.

69. R to Dov, 29 June 1813. Richardson, p. 100.

70. R to Dov, 15 September 1812, 3 and 5 October 1812. Richardson, p. 88. Clubbe, p. 164.

71. R to Dov, 21 November 1812. Clubbe, p. 166.

72. R to Dov, 8 June 1813, 4 December 1813. Richardson, pp. 95, 115.

73. Vol. 82, pt. 2 (October 1812), 366.

74. 9 (March 1813), 82.

75. R to Dov, 3 March 1813. Clubbe, p. 176.

76. R to Dov, 21 November 1812, 29 June 1813. Clubbe, p. 167. Richardson, p. 101.

77. *Repository,* 9 (March 1813), 181, and 10 (August 1813), 120.

78. *Inquirer,* September 1814, pp. 134–36.

79. R to Dov, 4 September 1813. Richardson, p. 106.

Chapter 3

1. R to Dov, 4 September 1813 and 30 September 1813. Richardson, pp. 105, 107.

2. R to Dov, 30 September 1813. Richardson, pp. 107–8.

3. R to Dov, 4 December 1813. Richardson, p. 114.

4. CR to Dov, 20 November 1813. Richardson, pp. 110–11.

5. CR to Dov, 29 November 1813. Richardson, pp. 112, 113. Miss Richardson's overlooking the apostrophe in "wrong'd one" caused her to shift the sense a little to "wrong done."

6. R to Dov, 4 December 1813. Richardson, pp. 114–15.

7. Rylance to Dov, 23 December 1813.

8. CR to Dov, March/April 1814. Richardson, p. 117. Dov's endorsement, "wrote a hasty and free Answer, 10 April 1814," indicates that the date was not many days before 10 April.

9. William Roscoe to Dov, 5 March 1814.

10. David Parkes to Dov, 2 March 1814.

11. Robert Roscoe to Dov, 24 February 1814.

12. William Roscoe to Dov, 5 March 1814.

13. A. Monks to Dov, 5 March 1814.

14. William Roscoe to Dov, 3 May 1814. Rylance's intermittent insanity continued through 1819. On 5 October 1815, the antiquary John Britton wrote Dov, "Poor Rylance, I am sorry to say, is subject to occasional derangement.—From this cause I cannot preserve an intimate acquaintance with him." Between 8 March 1814 and 7 February 1820 there are only two letters from Rylance to Dov in the collection, 4 June 1816 and 26 June 1816. In the former he wrote that he had been under the care of a physician and a surgeon for six months for a disorder of the penis, though he believed it had turned out to be only a simple sore. He managed to visit Dov once later in the summer of 1816. From 1820 through 1828, there is no evidence of any mental disorder in the multitude of letters from Rylance to Dov.

15. CR to Dov, March/April 1814. Richardson, pp. 116–17.

16. The endorsement by Dov, dated 10 April 1814, on CR's letter to Dov of about 8 April 1814.

17. R to Dov, 19 July 1814. Richardson, pp. 117–19.

18. See chap. 2, n. 62.

19. R to Dov, 4 September 1813. Richardson, p. 107. Rylance to Dov, 5 October 1813.

20. R to Dov, 4 December 1813. Richardson, p. 115. Rylance to Dov, 23 December 1813.

21. Rylance to Dov, 23 December 1813.

22. *Letters of R*, p. 65.

23. *Safie* (1814), *The Eden of Imagination* (1814) and *The Naiad* (1816) are reprinted in Donald H. Reiman, *Romantic Context: Poetry, Significant Minor Poetry 1789–1830* (New York: Garland, 1978).

24. CR to Dov, March/April 1814. Richardson, pp. 116–17.

25. Leslie A. Marchand, ed., *Byron's Letters and Journals* (Cambridge: Harvard University Press, 1974), III, 245–46.

26. Marchand, *Byron's Letters and Journals* (1975), IV, 68–69. Deleting his name to remain anonymous, R published this letter in the *Athenaeum*, 31 December 1831, p. 841.

27. *Letters of R*, p. xvi. *Selected Prose*, p. 252.

28. Marchand, *Byron's Letters and Journals*, IV, 74.

29. *British Critic*, 1, new series (February 1814), 210–12; *Anti-Jacobin Review* 46 (February 1814), 180; *Critical Review*, 5, 4th series (March 1814), 318. *Safie* was also reviewed briefly in the *Universal Magazine*, 21, new series (February 1814), 136; the *Theatrical Inquisitor*, 4 (April 1814), 229; and the *New Annual Register* for 1814.

30. *Monthly Review,* 75 (September 1814), 60–65.

31. P. 60.

32. Martin's account in the Bodleian copy of the *Inquirer,* CR to Dov, about 8 April 1814, R to Dov, 19 July 1814. Richardson, pp. 117, 118. Martin wrote in the tables of contents the names of the authors of nearly all the pieces.

33. *Inquirer,* May 1814, pp. 94–104, 17–18, 104–5.

34. R to Dov, 23 August 1814. Richardson, p. 122.

35. Bailey, pp. 7–17; William Squibb, pp. 24–27, 72–82; Frank Squibb, pp. 115–27; Dilke, pp. 82–93.

36. R to Dov, 23 August 1814. Richardson, p. 122.

37. *Inquirer,* September 1814, pp. 136–41. Dov's authorship is revealed by R's request of Dov in R to Dov, 30 July 1814, p. 121 (Miss Richardson overlooked the postmark and dated it July–August) and by Martin's note in the Bodleian copy that it was written by a friend of Reynolds.

38. R to Dov, 19 July 1814. Richardson, p. 118.

39. R to Dov, 30 July 1814. Richardson, p. 121.

40. Pp. 134–35.

41. P. 256 of the Bodleian copy.

42. January 1815, p. 332.

43. Prefatory note in Martin's copy in the Bodleian.

44. R to Dov, 19 July 1814, 30 July 1814, 23 August 1814. Richardson, pp. 119, 120, 122–23.

45. *Selected Prose,* p. 26.

46. R to Dov, 30 July 1814. Richardson, p. 120.

47. Reiman reprint, *The Eden of Imagination,* pp. 30–31.

48. R to Dov, 30 September 1814. Richardson, p. 127.

49. R to Dov, 25 September 1814. Richardson, p. 125. Reiman reprint of *The Eden,* pp. 17, 19–20.

50. R to Dov, 25 September 1814. Richardson, p. 125.

51. R to Dov, 30 September 1814. Richardson, p. 127.

52. Dov's endorsement of R to Dov, 30 September 1814, omitted by Miss Richardson: "Wrote to Reynolds, & told him he had misnomered me in the dedication— ⟨12⟩ 7 Octr. 1814."

53. Inferences from R's reply, R to Dov, 10 October 1814. Richardson, pp. 127–29.

54. R to Dov, 10 October 1814. Richardson, pp. 127–28.

55. Written in Bailey's hand in a copy of the book in the Keats House.

56. *Critical Review,* 4th series, 6 (November 1814), 479. *British Critic,* new series, 4 (July 1815), 95.

57. In his hand in a copy in the Keats House.

58. R to Dov, 30 July 1814. Richardson, p. 120.

59. R to Dov, 25 February 1815. Richardson, p. 132.

60. R to Dov, 23 August 1814. Richardson pp. 136–38. Miss Richardson has mistakenly transferred the enclosure including "The Song of a Spanish Lover" and "Extracts from A Tale" from the 23 August 1814 letter where they are filed in the Dovaston Collection to the 25 February 1815 letter. Possibly the reason for the mistake is that the 23 August 1814 letter does not mention an enclosure, while the 25 February 1815 letter does. But the enclosure R reopened his 25 February 1815 letter to include was "Margaret." R mentions in that letter that the stanzas he sends "take a poetical view of a little incident you may remember" (Richardson, p. 132), that is, his seeing Peg o' the Pant in Wales. "Margaret" is

now filed at the end of the next-to-the-last package in No. 1662, Box 5, "Letters between Michaelmas 1814 & Lady Day 1815," without any evidence as to why it is there. It is in R's hand. What apparently happened was that when Dov decided to publish "Margaret" in the Oswestry *Herald,* he took it out, used it, and then returned it to the box without restoring it to its proper letter. There can not be the slightest doubt that the MS "The Song of a Spanish Lover" was written before 1815 because R revised that MS thoroughly before publishing the poem in the *Inquirer,* January 1815, p. 332—the last half of stanza 4 and all stanza 5 were radically rewritten, and words and phrases were polished throughout. There would be no need for R to copy out a MS of a poem that Dov could read in print. Finally, "The Song of a Spanish Lover" is written on the inside of the wrapper used for R to Dov, 23 August 1814. Dov endorsed it on the outside, "Wrote to Reynolds, 26 Augt. 1814."

61. William Drewe of St. Martin's and Ann Powell of St. George's were married by license on 14 February 1792 at St. George's, Exeter. Witnesses were George Powell, Elizabeth Powell, and Anna Maria Gardiner. The date of Ann Drewe's death comes from her will on file in the county record office, Exeter.

62. I am very much indebted to the ingenuity and tenacity of Mr. J. W. Bastin for the search that finally uncovered these records.

63. R to Dov, 25 September 1814. Richardson, p. 125.

Chapter 4

1. Anne Kaier, "John Hamilton Reynolds: Four New Letters," *KSJ,* 30 (1981), 186. A Mrs. Reynolds had died on 14 January 1813 in her house on Lamb's Conduit Street (*Times,* 16 January 1813); if she was George's mother, Susannah Beardsell Reynolds, he may have inherited the house and postponed moving in for two years. If he inherited it, however, he did so somehow without a will, for there is no will on record.

2. R to Dov, 25 February 1815. Richardson, p. 131.

3. The *Anti-Jacobin Review,* 48 (April 1815), 372, was kind; the *British Critic,* 4, new series (July 1815), 97, was understandably severe.

4. Clayton E. Hudnall, "John Hamilton Reynolds, James Rice, and Benjamin Bailey in the Leigh Browne-Lockyer Collection," *KSJ,* 19 (1970), 13–14. Mary's dates are 1793–1876, Sarah's 1794–1845, and Thomasine's 1796–1883.

5. George L. Marsh, typescript "The Poetical Works of John Hamilton Reynolds," note to *An Ode,* p. 5, in the University of Chicago Library.

6. We know from Keats's letter that the Butlers lived at 2 Spencer Place, Kennington Common—Hyder E. Rollins, ed., *The Letters of John Keats,* 2 vols. (Cambridge: Harvard University Press, 1958), I, 275. For all I have learned of the Butlers, see Chap. 7, note 52.

7. Hudnall, p. 13.

8. R to Dov, 25 September 1814. Richardson, p. 125.

9. Hudnall, p. 14.

10. Hudnall, p. 17.

11. J. H. Reynolds to his friend J. R." in the Leigh Browne-Lockyer Collection, Keats House.

12. "Poems by Two Friends," p. 69 in the Leigh Browne-Lockyer Collection.

13. "Poems by Two Friends," p. 53 in the Leigh Browne-Lockyer Collection.

14. R to Dov, 19 July 1814. Richardson, p. 118.

15. *Examiner*, 26 February 1815, p. 137.

16. R to Hunt, 24 February 1815. Kaier, pp. 183–86. R to Dov, 25 February 1815. Richardson, pp. 131–32. For dating of parts of the second letter see chap. 1, n. 52.

17. Sir Charles Wentworth Dilke, *The Paper of a Critic*, 2 vols. (London: John Murray, 1875), I, 1.

18. Letter of Frederick Madden to James Rice, Sr., 19 October 1823, British Library Eg. 3837, f. 1, and the letter of James Rice, Jr. to Frederick Madden, 2 November 1830, Eg. 2838, f. 146.

19. Leslie A. Marchand, *The Athenaeum* (Chapel Hill: University of North Carolina Press, 1941), p. 27.

20. Stephen Gwynn and Gertrude M. Tuckwell, *The Life of the Rt. Hon. Sir Charles W. Dilke*, 2 vols. (London: John Murray, 1917), I, 6.

21. *An Abstract from the Account of the Asylum or, House of Refuge* (London: Philanthropic Society, 1809), p. 23.

22. *Selected Prose*, pp. 335–50.

23. Hudnall, pp. 31–32.

24. Hudnall, p. 34.

25. KC, II, 281–82. Bailey dates his poem on the resemblance between Reynolds's dead first sweetheart and the girl in *Christ's Entry* 1815–16. Rollins reports erroneously in a note that the copy of the poem in "Poems by Two Friends" is dated 1817; no date at all is included for the poem in the MS volume.

26. *DNB*; Horace Smith, "A Graybeard's Gossip about His Literary Acquaintance," *New Monthly Magazine*, 81 (1847), part 3, 415–16; and Ernest de Selincourt, ed., *The Letters of William and Dorothy Wordsworth, the Middle Years* (London: Oxford University Press, 1937), II, 712.

27. Statement by George Soane, *Champion*, 15 October 1815.

28. He had written *The Fairies* for Hunt's *Examiner* in February 1815, but Hunt could not print it because of the demand for space created by Waterloo. "Stanzas Composed under an Oak," dated August 1815 in "Poems by Two Friends," was not published until 18 February 1816. "Lines (Through these still woods)," "Sonnet. Composed on Seeing an Unexpected Snowy Morning," and "Reproach Me Not" were all written before 25 December 1816 because they are included in "Poems by Two Friends," which Bailey presented to Thomasine Leigh on that date, but they were not published until 1817.

29. A remark by Keats on 22 November 1817 shows that Reynolds was in charge of the poetry section: Keats asked him to lend him some of the laughable poems he had received on the death of Princess Charlotte. *Letters of Keats*, I, 190.

30. It is dated from "Enfield, 27th Feb. 1816" and signed C.C.C.

31. "The Reader, No. XIII," *Champion*, 18 August 1816, pp. 262–63, signed C. B. Brown later reprinted the article in a thoroughly revised form as part of *Shakespeare's Autobiographical Poems* (London: James Bohn, 1838), pp. 230–40. In the later version he omitted the introductory and closing passages and substituted new material to make the article fit the thesis of his book.

32. Walter Jackson Bate, *John Keats* (Cambridge: Harvard University Press, 1963), p. 97.

33. *Letters of R*, p. 5. It may be that he did *not* send it, and R had to send it after he returned from vacation. It was delivered along with a shipment of

books by the publisher Longmans, an economical method of delivery that R had often used to send books and magazines to Dov. Wordsworth does not mention Haydon in his reply to R.

34. Thomas Hutchinson, ed., revised by Ernest de Selincourt, *The Poetical Works of Wordsworth*, Oxford Standard Authors (London: Oxford University Press, 1936), p. 748.

35. Canto XIV, stanza 61, last six lines.

36. (London: Cadell and Davies, 1810).

37. *Champion*, 21 July 1816, p. 230.

38. Reiman reprint, pp. 39–42.

39. 4 August 1816, p. 245.

40. *Letters of R*, p. 5.

41. *European Magazine*, 70 (September 1818), 250; *Augustan Review*, 3 (October 1816), 345; *Critical Review*, 5th series, 4 (October 1816), 344; *Eclectic Review*, new series, 6 (November 1816), 489; *Gentleman's Magazine*, 86, no. 2 (November 1816), 436; *Literary Panorama*, new series, 5 (February 1817), 758; *Monthly Review*, 82 (March 1817), 323; and *British Critic*, new series, 8 (October 1817), 415.

42. *Critical Review*, p. 350.

43. *Eclectic Review*, p. 497.

44. Ernest de Selincourt, ed., 2nd edition, revised by Mary Moorman and Alan G. Hill, *The Letters of William and Dorothy Wordsworth, the Middle Years* (London: Oxford University Press, 1970), pp. 345–46.

45. R to Dov, 9 March 1813. Clubbe, p. 177.

46. *Letters of R*, p. 3.

47. *Selected Prose*, pp. 150–53.

48. Hudnall, p. 20.

49. *Letters of R*, pp. 9–10.

50. *Selected Prose*, p. 153. *Letters of R*, p. 9.

51. *Champion*, 15 September 1816, p. 294.

52. *Letters of R*, p. 11. Only the last page of the letter has been preserved, but the promise can be inferred from one passage: "I know that my character must suffer in your Estimation . . . by this word, which must remain an unredeemed pledge in your hand:—But I cannot avoid it—and I must trust to Time to lend me an opportunity of refreshing my name in your recollections. Will you write to me while I stay here?"

53. Paul Kaufman, "The Reynolds-Hood Commonplace Book," KSJ, 10 (1961), 49–50. *Champion*, 24 November 1816, pp. 373–74.

54. Reiman reprint, *The Garden of Florence*, p. 32. The quotation is a reversal of the phrase from *Ode: Intimations*.

55. Reiman reprint, *The Garden of Florence*, pp. 78–80.

Chapter 5

1. The Reader, No. IV, *Champion*, 26 May 1816, p. 160. *Selected Prose*, p. 53.

2. Review of Hazlitt's *Characters of Shakespeare's Plays*, *Champion*, 20 July 1817, p. 230. *Selected Prose*, p. 114.

3. "The Broken Sword," *Champion*, 13 October 1816, p. 326. *Selected Prose*, pp. 157–58.

4. "Richard Duke of York," *Champion*, 28 December 1817, p. 413. *Selected Prose*, p. 207.

5. "Hamlet," *Champion*, 14 December 1817, p. 397. *Selected Prose*, p. 204. He borrowed the phrase from Hazlitt's *Characters*, P. P. Howe, ed., *The Complete Works of William Hazlitt*, 21 vols. (London: J. M. Dent, 1930–34), IV, 232.

6. "Manuel," *Champion*, 16 March 1817, p. 85. *Selected Prose*, p. 178.

7. Review of Hazlitt's *Characters*, *Champion*, 20 July 1817, p. 230. *Selected Prose*, p. 114.

8. Review of Hazlitt's *Characters*, p. 230. *Selected Prose*, p. 113.

9. *A Course of Lectures on Dramatic Art and Literature*, by Augustus Wilhelm Schlegel, Translated from the Original German by John Black, 2 vols. (London: no publisher, 1815).

10. The Reader, No. V, *Champion*, 2 June 1816, p. 174. *Selected Prose*, p. 62.

11. *Letters of R*, p. 9.

12. The manner in which he echoed Hazlitt, perhaps unconsciously, can be seen from a comparison of two passages. Hazlitt wrote in *The Round Table*: "A journeyman sign-painter, whose lungs have imbibed too great a quantity of white-lead, will be seized with a fantastic passion for the stage" (*Complete Works of Hazlitt*, IV, 59). In describing a similar situation, Reynolds used many of the same words and phrases: "We remember seeing a Mr. Edwards, a journeyman sign-painter we believe . . . his voice fainted from his lips, overcome with turpentine and white lead" ("King Richard. Mr. Fisher," *Champion*, 7 December 1817, p. 389).

13. *Champion*, 16 February, 14 December 1817, pp. 53, 397. For the latter, *Selected Prose*, pp. 204, 205.

14. Review of Hazlitt's *Characters*, *Champion*, 20, 27 July 1817, pp. 230–31, 237. *Selected Prose*, pp. 113–19.

15. R to Dov, 30 September 1813. Richardson, p. 107.

16. "The First Part of Henry the Fourth. Mr. Stephen Kemble in Falstaff," *Champion*, 13 October 1816, p. 325. *Selected Prose*, p. 153.

17. *Champion*, 14 December 1817, p. 397. *Selected Prose*, p. 203.

18. "Essay on the Early Dramatic Poets," *Champion*, 7 January 1816, p. 6. *Selected Prose*, p. 34.

19. "Mr. Hazlitt's Lectures," *Scots Magazine*, December 1818, p. 548. *Selected Prose*, p. 243.

20. John Aikin, *Vocal Poetry* (London: J. Johnson, 1810), p. 166n., quoted in R's "Ben Jonson," *Champion*, 4 May 1817, p. 14. *Selected Prose*, p. 108.

21. William Cartwright, "In the Memory of the Most Worthy Benjamin Jonson," l. 104, included in *Jonsonus Virbius* (1638).

22. *Champion*, 17 December 1815, p. 405.

23. *Champion*, 3 March 1816, p. 70. *Selected Prose*, pp. 42–44.

24. Reynolds's "To Spenser," *Champion*, 10 March 1816, p. 78. Bailey's "To Milton," *Champion*, 30 June 1816, p. 206.

25. "Sonnet to a Friend," first published in the *Athenaeum*, 7 July 1832, p. 432, but dated 1817.

26. "Mr. Kemble," *Champion*, 29 June 1817, p. 206.

27. *Champion*, 7 April 1816, p. 110. *Selected Prose*, pp. 45–50. He had evidently written a first version of the article several years earlier, for a letter of Thomas Winstanley of Liverpool to Dovaston on 20 April 1816 contains on a separate sheet in a different hand an extract from another version of the article containing lavish praise of Dovaston not in the *Champion* version (Dovaston Collection, Shropshire County Record Office). Winstanley was a close friend of William Roscoe, Ralph Rylance's mentor and close friend since boyhood. Rylance

regularly sent Roscoe a large volume of his own poetry and prose. Apparently when Rylance and Reynolds were warm friends, Rylance sent Roscoe a manuscript copy of the Reynolds essay sometime before the spring of 1814 when the Reynoldses broke all communication with Rylance. When Winstanley became acquainted with Dovaston in 1816, he sought to please him by sending the lavish praise from the manuscript essay in the Roscoe family papers. After his friendship with Dovaston faded, Reynolds deleted the passage in praise of Dovaston.

28. R's quotation from the General Prologue, l. 748 in *Champion*, 26 May 1816, p. 166. *Selected Prose*, p. 58.

29. *Champion*, 12 May 1816, p. 151. *Selected Prose*, pp. 51–52.

30. *Champion*, 1, 15 December 1816, pp. 381–82, 397–98. *Selected Prose*, pp. 84–96.

31. The Reader, No. V, *Champion*, 2 June 1816, pp. 173–74. *Selected Prose*, p. 62.

32. R to Dov, 30 July 1814. Richardson, p. 120.

33. Hudnall, p. 21.

34. *Champion*, 9 December 1815, p. 398. *Selected Prose*, pp. 25–27.

35. Ernest de Selincourt, ed., 2nd ed. revised by Mary Moorman and Alan G. Hill, *The Letters of William and Dorothy Wordsworth, the Middle Years* (London: Oxford University Press, 1970), p. 283.

36. *Champion*, 21 April 1816, p. 125.

37. *Champion*, 13 October 1816, pp. 326–27. *Selected Prose*, pp. 70–76. John Scott wrote Wordsworth on 29 May 1816 that he planned to review the *Thanksgiving Ode* himself (MS in Dove Cottage), but the review five months after his statement could not be his because its author wrote that "our publisher will see it [a long quotation] with grief of soul" (p. 79), and Scott was the publisher, who was in Paris and would not see it until after publication. Mr. Patrick O'Leary, who is preparing a biography of John Scott, notes that in a number of cases Scott's stated intentions to write pieces went unfulfilled. I am grateful to Mrs. Winifred F. Courtney and Professor Robert Woof of the University of Newcastle upon Tyne for helpful correspondence in this matter.

38. *The Faerie Queene*, I, v, 1–2. R supplied the italics. Keats quoted the same lines, *Letters of Keats*, I, 134.

39. *Champion*, 20 October 1816, pp. 334–35. *Selected Prose*, pp. 76–84. The cartoons were paintings by Raphael.

Chapter 6

1. *Letters of R*, p. 60. A little uncertain of the time, "at the close of 1816 or early in 1817," he remembered the place clearly thirty years later.

2. R to Dov, 19 July 1814. Richardson, p. 118. R to Hunt, 24 February 1815. Kaier, p. 183.

3. KC, I, 4–5, 281.

4. "Bless thee, my Bell!—Again with sincere joy," *Champion*, 21 April 1816, p. 126. Signed C.C.C. and dated from Enfield, 27 February 1816.

5. Robert Gittings, *John Keats* (Boston: Little, Brown, 1968), pp. 83–84.

6. KC, I, 4–6; *Letters of R*, xxi; Gittings, *John Keats*, pp. 92–93.

7. Bailey's poem, "Written in Jane Reynolds's Album, previously to my going to Oxford on her Birth day," in "Poems by Two Friends," p. 163.

8. *Letters of Keats*, I, 119–20.

9. *Examiner*, 1 December 1816, p. 761.

10. *Champion*, 8 December 1816, p. 390.

11. Hunt's holograph of the sonnet is in the British Library.

12. *Alfred*, 13 October 1818.

13. *Letters of Keats*, I, 121; KC, II, 267. More than thirty years later Bailey wrote, "It was, I think, about the end of 1816, or the beginning of 1817, that my friend, Mr Reynolds, wrote to me at Oxford respecting Keats, with whom he & his family had just become acquainted" (KC, II, 267). The probability is that the Reynolds family met Keats in December 1816 rather than January 1817. Bailey implies that the family made Keats's acquaintance not very long after R did. If the family had not met Keats by the end of December, they would not have met him until the last half of January, because R was in Devonshire during the early part of January 1817. Finally, it is very unlikely after Keats had invited R into his home that R would have missed the chance to invite Keats. CR did not behave that way with her son's good friends: when R first met Rylance, she invited Rylance to dinner in London while he was still in Shropshire.

14. Hudnall, p. 21.

15. Oliver Elton, *A Survey of English Literature, 1780–1830*, 2 vols. (London: Edward Arnold, 1912), II, 293.

16. Reiman reprint, *The Garden of Florence*, p. 34.

17. R to Dov, 24 May 1813. Richardson, p. 93.

18. Reiman reprint, *The Garden of Florence*, p. 33.

19. For a more detailed argument, see my "Reynolds' *The Romance of Youth*, Hazlitt, and Keats's *The Fall of Hyperion*," *English Language Notes*, 16 (June 1979), 294–300.

20. Willard B. Pope, "Studies in the Keats Circle: Critical and Biographical Estimates of Benjamin Robert Haydon and John Hamilton Reynolds" (Harvard doctoral dissertation, 1932), p. 745 and Gittings, *Ariel*, p. 14.

21. Reiman reprint, *The Garden of Florence*, stanzas LVII–LIX, pp. 67–68.

22. Stanzas XCIV–XCVI, pp. 87–88.

23. *The Fall of Hyperion*, I, 216–18, 228–33, 251–58. Jack Stillinger, ed., *The Poems of John Keats* (Cambridge: Harvard University Press, 1978), pp. 483–84. All subsequent passages from Keats are from this text.

24. Another influence by R on the diction of *Ode to a Nightingale* is possible. In his essay on Chaucer five months before he met Keats, R wrote of the nightingale's "*pouring forth . . .* her *soul*" (*Champion*, 26 May 1816, p. 160. *Selected Prose*, p. 54. Italics supplied). Cf. "thou art pouring forth thy soul" (*Nightingale*, l. 57).

25. F. L. Jones, *Mary Shelley's Journal* (Norman: University of Oklahoma Press, 1947), p. 76.

26. Harry Buxton Forman, ed., *The Complete Works of John Keats*, 5 vols. (Glasgow: Gowans and Gray, 1900–1901), II, 176n.

27. KC, II, 141; *Letters of Keats*, I, 125. Haydon's letter is dated only March 1817, but in it he says that he has just read *Sleep and Poetry*, published in *Poems* on 3 March.

28. KC, II, 267; *Champion*, 9 March 1817, p. 78. *Selected Prose*, pp. 99–108.

29. *Champion*, 1 December 1816, pp. 382–83.

30. Woodhouse wrote that Keats's first brief note to Reynolds was "sent by hand." The rest is inference from the note itself. Keats scribbled "a few mono-sentences" hurriedly, agreed to the time of meeting, and commented briefly on the anonymous new tragedy that had excited them the night before.

31. *Letters of Keats,* I, 123.

32. *European Magazine,* May 1817, p. 434; Dorothy Hewlett, *A Life of John Keats,* 2nd ed. (New York: Barnes and Noble, 1950), pp. 82–83; *Anti-Gallican Monitor,* 18 June 1817, as reported by Lewis Schwartz, "Keats's Critical Reception in Newspapers of His Day," *KSJ,* 21 and 22 (1972 and 1973), 173.

33. *Letters of Keats,* I, 124. Keats sends his "brother's"—doubtless a slip for "brothers' "—remembrances to Reynolds's kind sisters.

34. Maria Pearse's Commonplace Book, No. 2, p. 72. Leigh Browne-Lockyer Collection.

35. Probably Jane for two reasons. "Miss" without Christian name normally, though not invariably, meant the eldest daughter. The sonnet was first published by Thomas Hood, Jane's husband, in the *Gem.*

36. *Letters of Keats,* I, 125–26.

37. *Letters of Keats,* I, 127.

38. *KC,* II, 475.

39. *Letters of Keats,* I, 134, 200.

40. *Letters of Keats,* I, 125.

41. Reiman reprint, *The Garden of Florence,* pp. 143, 135.

42. *Letters of Keats,* I, 129.

43. *Letters of Keats,* I, 134. *The Faerie Queene,* I, v, 1.

44. *Letters of Keats,* I, 133, 133n.

45. *Champion,* 20 April 1817, p. 125.

46. *Letters of R,* p. 9.

47. *KC,* II, 267.

48. *Letters of R,* pp. 8–10.

49. *Champion,* 27 April 1817. The copy in "Poems by Two Friends" shows that the bracketed dropped *s*'s in the last stanza were printer's errors.

50. *The Poetical Works of Lord Byron,* Oxford Standard Authors (London: Oxford University Press, 1904), pp. 55, 65.

51. *Letters of Keats,* I, 147.

52. His "Small Talk from Paris" appeared in the *Champion* of 11 August 1816 with that date.

53. Horace Smith, "A Graybeard's Gossip about His Literary Acquaintance," *New Monthly Magazine,* 81 (1847), part 3, 415–16.

54. A remark that Keats made to R later confirms the inference that R visited Paris in May or June 1817. When R planned a later trip to the Continent, Keats wrote him on 28 February 1820, "You will not meet with so much to hate at Brussels as at Paris" (*Letters of Keats,* II, 268).

55. Hazlitt had contributed dramatic reviews and a series of articles on the fine arts in 1814 and 1815.

56. *Letters of Keats,* I, 147. The postmark shows where he mailed it.

57. *Letters of Keats,* I, 276. Gittings, *John Keats,* p. 144.

58. *Champion,* 20 July 1817, p. 230. *Selected Prose,* p. 114.

59. P. 238. Revised and reprinted in *The Garden of Florence,* Reiman reprint, pp. 95–103.

60. Reiman reprint, *The Garden of Florence,* pp. 98–99, 102–3.

61. *KC,* I, 63.

62. *Champion,* 3 August 1817, p. 245. Loyal supporters of Reynolds, the Leigh girls copied Pierre's poems into their commonplace books.

63. *Champion,* 17 August 1817, p. 261.

64. *Letters of Keats,* I, 149.

65. *Letters of Keats*, I, 148–49.
66. *Selected Prose*, pp. 430–31.
67. *Letters of Keats*, I, 149.
68. *Letters of Keats*, I, 160.
69. Rollins neglected to include the address from the Woodhouse transcript in *Letters of Keats*, I, 162. He had included it for Bailey's letter written on the doublings in KC, I, 6. I am grateful to Miss Rae Ann Nager, then of the Houghton Library, for verifying this detail for me.
70. *Letters of Keats*, I, 190.
71. *Letters of Keats*, I, 160.
72. *Letters of Keats*, II, 11n.
73. *Letters of Keats*, I, 169. Files of the two newspapers reveal the date and place of the meeting. For 14 September R and Hunt reviewed the same performance, and both mention attending on the same night, 10 September.
74. *Letters of Keats*, I, 162.
75. *Letters of Keats*, I, 162.
76. See stanza 8, "You never saw a wiser man, / He knows his Numeration Table; / He counts the sheep of Harry Gill," and stanza 15, "Four brown bugs are feeding there" with its footnote, "I have a similar idea in my Poem on finding a Bird's Nest:—'Look! five blue eggs are gleaming there.'" (Reiman reprint, pp. 12, 15.)
77. Jeremy Taylor, *A Discourse of the Nature, Offices, and Measures of Friendship* . . . In a Letter to Mrs. K[atherine] P[hilips] (London: R. Royston, 1671).
78. *Letters of Keats*, I, 165. The line is not italicized in any of the seventeenth-century editions in the Houghton Library.
79. *Letters of Keats*, I, 166.
80. KC, I, 6–7.
81. Hudnall, p. 16.
82. *Letters of Keats*, I, 168, 172.
83. *Letters of Keats*, I, 169, 171.
84. In the *Champion* of 7 December 1817, p. 389, he echoed the opening line, "There are who lord it o'er their fellowmen" in the sentence, "The part of Richard is exactly suited to him [Edmund Kean] . . . placing him in a seat of solitary grandeur, and forcing him to lord it over his fellow men."
85. *Letters of Keats*, I, 172.
86. *Letters of Keats*, I, 190.
87. *Letters of Keats*, I, 197.
88. *Letters of Keats*, I, 172.
89. *Letters of Keats*, I, 166, 181. The story was not *The Fancy*, as Rollins thought, because the three extracts from letters included there were a direct reply to Nan Woodhouse's letter, not written until 6 April 1820. The two letters Keats mentions may be two of the Edward Herbert letters later published in the *London Magazine*, but it seems doubtful that Keats would call the Edward Herbert series "a little Story" any more than one would call Lamb's Elia essays a story.
90. *Letters of Keats*, I, 174, 171.
91. *Letters of Keats*, I, 181.
92. *Letters of Keats*, I, 187. Gittings, *John Keats*, p. 160.
93. *Letters of Keats*, II, 11.
94. *Letters of Keats*, I, 187n. Andrew Lang, *The Life and Letters of John Gibson Lockhart* (London: J. C. Nimmo, 1897), I, 199.

95. *Letters of R*, p. 61. That MS has not survived—see Stillinger, p. 574.
96. *Letters of Keats*, I, 38, 196, 201.

Chapter 7

1. *Letters of Keats*, I, 188.
2. *Letters of Keats*, I, 193; 196 and note.
3. KC, II, 279. Italics supplied.
4. Gittings, *John Keats*, p. 183.
5. The only times Bailey and George were in London together were April 1817 and late summer 1817 before George and Tom went to France.
6. Gittings, *John Keats*, p. 150.
7. Peter F. Morgan, ed., *The Letters of Thomas Hood* (Toronto: University of Toronto Press, 1973), pp. 34, 39.
8. *Letters of Keats*, I, 38.
9. *Letters of Keats*, I, 195–96, 202.
10. *Letters of Keats*, I, 188. The "Heart" should not mislead. Keats is not talking about any disruption in Reynolds's love affair because he says he is exposed to the same kind of vexation. Both have met with irritation from Haydon, for whom they both have affection.
11. *Letters of Keats*, I, 205, 206.
12. *Letters of Keats*, I, 202–3.
13. *Letters of Keats*, I, 210.
14. *Letters of Keats*, I, 200–201.
15. *Letters of Keats*, I, 219–22.
16. *Letters of Keats*, I, 216–17.
17. Reiman reprint, *The Fancy*, p. 51. He probably wrote the poem as a separate piece long before he devised the Peter Corcoran hoax and added the two parenthetical stanzas addressed to Peter's sweetheart Kate on p. 77 just before he published it in 1820. It seems unlikely that he kept the Peter Corcoran joke to himself for two and a half years.
18. *The Fancy*, stanza XXX, p. 68.
19. *The Fancy*, stanza II, p. 54.
20. For the surname, R gave a cockney spelling to a famous member of the Fancy who lived in Tothill Fields, William Habberfield or "Slender Billy." In this poem and later in "The Jewels of the Book," he described the bear baitings and dogfights held in Habberfield's house, The Four Chimbleys.
21. William H. Marshall has shown that Hazlitt, not Reynolds, wrote the fourth unsigned concluding essay of the series, in "An Addition to the Hazlitt Canon," *Papers of the Bibliographical Society of America*, 55 (Fourth Quarter 1961), 347–70.
22. *Letters of Keats*, I, 221.
23. KC, I, cxxiii.
24. Reiman reprint, *The Garden of Florence*, stanzas LXXXVIII–XC, pp. 84–85.
25. *Selected Prose*, p. 212.
26. *Selected Prose*, pp. 211–12.
27. *Selected Prose*, p. 215.
28. *Selected Prose*, p. 213.

29. *Selected Prose,* p. 223n.

30. He does not use the word in the "Pulpit Oratory" series, but it recurs frequently in the theatrical reviews in the *Champion.*

31. *Selected Prose,* pp. 219–20.

32. *Letters of Keats,* I, 206.

33. *Letters of Keats,* I, 225n.

34. For a full account, see my "The Date of 'Lines on the Mermaid Tavern,'" *English Language Notes,* 15 (March 1978), 186–88.

35. *Selected Prose,* pp. 50, 51.

36. *Selected Prose,* p. 101.

37. See the last illustration of *filbert* in the *Oxford English Dictionary.*

38. *Letters of Keats,* I, 223–25.

39. *Letters of Keats,* I, 223.

40. Reiman reprint, *The Garden of Florence,* pp. 124–25.

41. P. 64. Copies of the three sonnets in Lamb's hand were found among his papers after his death.

42. John Masefield, ed., *The Fancy* (London: Elkin Mathews, 1905), p. 23.

43. *Letters of Keats,* II, 207–8.

44. R to Dov, 4 September 1813. Richardson, p. 105.

45. P. P. Howe, ed., *The Complete Works of William Hazlitt,* 21 vols. (London: J. M. Dent, 1930–34), V, 82.

46. Jack Stillinger, *The Texts of Keats's Poems* (Cambridge: Harvard University Press, 1974), p. 85.

47. *Selected Prose,* pp. 59–63.

48. Gittings, *John Keats,* p. 192.

49. *Letters of Keats,* I, 236, 288.

50. KC, I, 13; *Letters of Keats,* I, 247.

51. *Letters of R,* pp. 11–12.

52. *Letters of Keats,* I, 268, 236, 267, 275. Not much can be ascertained with certainty about the Butlers, in care of whom Keats addressed his letter to 2 Spencer Place, Kennington Common. Mr. Vaughan Heis, assistant borough archivist of the Minet Library in London to whom I am grateful, reported that the rate books stop at 1816 and that the name Spencer Place was not used in the records, but that "in the approximate area of the terrace (north part of Brighton Road) in 1815 and 1816 there is a Charles Butler. No house numbers are used and no occupations given so I cannot be more definite than that." Approximate though the location of the house is in the records, it is clear that Butler's first name was Charles. But he was not the Charles Butler identified by Maurice Buxton Forman as Keats's classmate at Guy's Hospital (*Letters of Keats,* I, 236n.), though the medical student may possibly have been the son of an older Butler. The Reynolds family friend was old enough to have the three-year-old daughter (or possibly granddaughter) Fanny to whom R addressed his verse epistle while convalescing there and another daughter at least fourteen, probably the Sarah to whom Keats asked to be remembered (*Letters of Keats,* I, 275). Thomas Hood, who stayed in the Butler house along with Jane and wrote letters from there in 1824 while the rest of the family was away in the country with the married daughter Eliza, compared the older Butler daughter with Miss Fenton in Elizabeth Inchbald's *A Simple Story* (*Letters of Hood,* p. 59). Miss Fenton in the novel is an adult young woman evidently in her twenties; therefore the older Butler daughter was fourteen or older in 1818 and was not the daughter of a

young medical student. Walter Jerrold, who conferred with descendants of the Reynolds family, mistakenly thought Mrs. Butler was Eliza Drewe's mother (*Thomas Hood* [London: Alston Rivers, 1907], p. 126n.). Edmund Blunden suggested that she was Eliza Drewe's aunt (*Letters of Keats*, I, 236n.), but no one has discovered evidence to establish a relationship between the Butlers and Eliza. A reasoned guess would be that Mrs. Butler was R's aunt, George Reynolds's sister. Charlotte mentioned an aunt who lived close enough so that the Reynolds children could visit with her (Clubbe, p. 159), and R reported that he had both an uncle and cousins, at whose house he performed in private theatricals (Richardson, pp. 88, 31). The difficulty in identifying this Charles Butler is that the name was almost as common as Charles Brown, who found it desirable to adopt a middle name to individualize himself. Several other Charles Butlers proving not to fit for one reason or another, the remaining candidate emerges as the Charles Butler who published two textbooks, one in 1812 (*Gentleman's Magazine*, 82, part 1 [February 1812], 136) and the other in 1828 (British Museum Catalogue). It is likely that a fellow teacher would be a long-time friend of George Reynolds, but where he taught remains a mystery—it was *not* at Lambeth Boys Parochial School, the Lambeth Female Asylum, Christ's Hospital, or Westminster School.

53. *Letters of Keats*, I, 234. Early in 1820 Smith wrote that they were intimate— Josephine Bauer, *The London Magazine, 1820–1829* in Anglistica, I (Copenhagen: Rosenkilde and Bagger, 1953), 63n.

54. *Letters of R*, pp. 11–12.

55. *Letters of Keats*, I, 233, 246, 256.

56. *Letters of R*, p. 11.

57. *Letters of Keats*, I, 259–63, ll. 97, 94–95.

58. *Letters of R*, p. 61.

59. *Letters of Keats*, I, 266–67, 268.

60. *Letters of Keats*, I, 269. William H. Bond corrected the date by printing the holograph which had been unavailable to Rollins. See KSJ, 20 (1971), 17–19.

61. *Bentley's Miscellany*, 7 (1840), 280.

62. *Letters of Keats*, I, 277, 278.

63. *Letters of Keats*, I, 280, 282.

64. *Letters of Keats*, I, 282n.

65. Howe, ed., *Complete Works of Hazlitt*, VI, 166 and note; *Selected Prose*, p. 464, n. 45.

66. Reiman reprint, *The Garden of Florence*, pp. 144–49. The poem clashes with the reticence of the title by giving the child's first name, Fanny.

67. P. 377.

68. *Letters of Keats*, I, 41, 276, 288, 294.

69. *Letters of Keats*, I, 294.

70. KC, II, 15. Gittings, *John Keats*, p. 215.

71. *Letters of Keats*, I, 293.

72. *Letters of Keats*, I, 296, 326.

73. KC, I, 31.

74. *Letters of Keats*, I, 322.

75. *Letters of Keats*, I, 325.

76. *Letters of Keats*, I, 341.

77. *Letters of Keats*, I, 288.

78. *Letters of Keats*, I, 341.

79. KC, II, 418; *Letters of Keats*, I, 366.

Chapter 8

1. KC, II, 417–18.
2. Reiman reprint, *The Garden of Florence*, pp. 132–33.
3. *Letters of Keats*, I, 368, 369.
4. *Letters of Keats*, I, 395.
5. *Letters of Keats*, I, 371.
6. *Letters of Keats*, I, 366.
7. *Letters of Keats*, I, 371, 394.
8. *Selected Prose*, pp. 225–30.
9. *Champion*, 2 February 1817, p. 30. *Selected Prose*, p. 173.
10. "On Egotism in Literature," *Champion*, 2 June 1816, pp. 173–74. *Selected Prose*, pp. 59–63.
11. *Blackwood's*, 3 (August 1818), 519–24 (the August issue had appeared well before Reynolds's defense of 6 October, for John Taylor mentioned it on 8 September—KC, I, 37); *Letters of R*, p. 12.
12. KC, I, 63; II, 418. Hunt's holograph of the sonnet is in the British Library. This was the only publication in the nineteenth century.
13. Joanna Richardson, *The Everlasting Spell* (London: Jonathan Cape, 1963), p. 223.
14. *Letters of Keats*, I, 274. Keats made a fair copy in late August (*Letters of Keats* I, 371, and Stillinger, pp. 604–5), which he would have been glad to lend R to take with him on vacation, but R left sooner than Keats thought he would. However, R must have read the draft in the six weeks that Keats was in London before the Scottish tour, as eager as Keats was to show it to R and as interested as R was in it.
15. *Letters of Keats*, I, 274.
16. *Letters of R*, pp. 12–13. The letter survived because it was one of those Keats sent in a packet to George and Georgiana (*Letters of Keats*, I, 401). George Keats's daughter, Mrs. Philip Speed, showed it to E. L. Madden, who quoted two sentences from it in *Harper's New Monthly Magazine*, 55 (1877), 361.
17. *Letters of Keats*, I, 402; Reiman reprint, *The Garden of Florence*, pp. 130–31.
18. Richardson, *The Everlasting Spell*, p. 223. It was not published in the *Scots Magazine*, the *Edinburgh Review*, or the *Literary Gazette*.
19. *Letters of Keats*, I, 402. Gittings, *John Keats*, p. 257.
20. *Letters of Keats*, I, 407.
21. Now in the Bristol Central Library. For my argument for redating the Induction to *The Fall of Hyperion*, see "The Dating of the Two *Hyperions*," *Studies in Bibliography*, 30 (1977), 120–35.
22. KC, I, 63–65.
23. Reiman reprint, *The Garden of Florence*, p. vii.
24. *Letters of Keats*, II, 7.
25. (London: Rodwell and Martin, and Colburn, 1818). In the *Edinburgh Review*, 16 (December 1818), 80–93. For Reynolds's authorship, see my "Reynolds, Hazlitt, and the *Edinburgh Review*," *Studies in Bibliography*, 29 (1976), 342–46.
26. *Edinburgh Review*, XVI, 83.
27. *The Works of Horatio Walpole, Earl of Orford*, 5 vols. (London: G. G. and J. Robinson and J. Edwards, 1798)—13 letters from vol. II, 25 from vol. IV, and 338 from vol. V. The rest of the volumes consisted of printed works.

28. *Letters of Keats,* II, 27.

29. *Letters of Keats,* II, 271.

30. London, 1820. The June publication date is revealed by "Works Lately Published," *London Magazine,* 1 (June 1820), 715. The *British Museum Catalogue* does not specify the publishers, but the first volume of the set in the British Library, which was all that could be located, supplies them. The introduction reads in part, "the Prefatory Index, in which the most striking subject of each letter is briefly noticed, will facilitate the reader's references "(I, ix). The index covers 49 pages, a task to keep Dilke busy.

31. *Letters of Keats,* II, 213; *Edinburgh Review,* XVI, 88.

32. *Letters of Keats,* II, 15.

33. Bodleian MS Don. d. 95 fols. 105–6. I am grateful to Mr. J. C. Grigeley for sending me the note.

34. *Letters of Keats,* II, 15. KC, I, 74.

35. *Alfred,* Tuesday, 17 November 1818, p. 3.

36. *Alfred,* Tuesday, 29 December 1818, p. 3.

37. Heavitree record, Exeter.

Chapter 9

1. P. P. Howe, *The Life of William Hazlitt* (New York: R. R. Smith, 1930), p. 266.

2. Gittings, *John Keats,* p. 273n.

3. *Letters of Keats,* II, 78; John G. Lockhart, *Peter's Letters to His Kin-Folk,* 2nd ed., 2 vols. (Edinburgh: W. Blackwood, 1819), II, 227–28; Alan Lang Strout, "Knights of the Burning Epistle," *Studia Neophilologica,* 26 (1953–54). 85.

4. Andrew Lang, *The Life and Letters of John Gibson Lockhart,* 2 vols. (London: J. C. Nimmo, 1897), I, 226; *Letters of Keats,* II, 178–79.

5. *Letters of Keats,* II, 60.

6. *Letters of Keats,* II, 20.

7. He did not wish to see the Reynolds girls there, but he quite possibly had been polite to Charles Butler when he was in Bedhampton on 24 January 1819, when Brown wrote that he and Keats would call on Mr. Butler and Mr. Burton that morning (*Letters of Keats,* II, 35). Heretofore everyone has assumed that they were residents of Bedhampton. Just as possibly, Charles Butler and William Burton made the trip from London to attend the opening of Stanstead Chapel, along with the host of other spectators from all over England, and Keats and Brown called upon them at their temporary quarters. William Burton (1774–1825), London printer, bookseller, and author of *Researches into the Phraseology, Manners, History and Religion of the Ancient Eastern Nations,* 2 vols. (London: W. Burton, 1805), had a special interest in Judaism which would have attracted him to the affair.

8. *Letters of Keats,* II, 59.

9. *Letters of Keats,* II, 66–67.

10. *Letters of Keats,* I, 369.

11. *Letters of Keats,* II, 66n. Gittings, *John Keats,* p. 291.

12. Gittings, *John Keats,* p. 291.

13. I now believe that I misinterpreted the evidence in my introduction to the *Letters of R,* pp. xxvi–xxvii, where I inferred that Marianne and her family

were angry because they expected Bailey to persevere in his suit until he overcame Marianne's maidenly reservations.

14. KC, I, 232.

15. *Letters of Keats,* II, 46.

16. *Letters of Keats,* II, 65.

17. *Letters of Keats,* II, 78.

18. *Letters of Keats,* II, 90.

19. *Letters of Keats,* II, 82.

20. KC, I, 74, 75.

21. Giovanni Boccaccio, *The Decameron,* trans. John Payne (New York: Triangle Books, 1931), p. 226.

22. Reiman reprint, *The Garden of Florence,* stanza XV, p. 14.

23. Oliver Elton, *A Survey of English Literature, 1780–1830* (London: Edward Arnold, 1912), II, 293.

24. Ian Jack, *English Literature, 1815–1832* in *The Oxford History of English Literature* (London: Oxford University Press, 1963), X, 150.

25. *Letters of Keats,* II, 83–84. The motto is from Susannah Centilevre, *Bold Stroke for a Wife* (1718), V, i. Colonel Fainwell impersonates Simon Pure, a Quaker preacher, only to have Simon Pure appear on the scene to expose him.

26. *Notes and Queries,* 3rd Series, 9 (10 February 1866), 127.

27. Reiman reprint, *Peter Bell,* p. v.

28. P. 17n.

29. Stanzas 39–40, p. 24. Gerald J. Pyle, Jr. showed that R took the "W.W.–trouble you, trouble you" from a letter from "Sexton" on epitaphs in the *Literary Gazette,* 6 December 1817—*Notes and Queries,* 24 (July–August 1977), 323–324.

30. Pp. vii–viii. Willard B. Pope, "Studies in the Keats Circle: Critical and Biographical Estimates of Benjamin Robert Haydon and John Hamilton Reynolds" (Harvard doctoral dissertation, 1932), p. 707.

31. *Letters of Keats,* II, 84n.

32. Henry Shelley, "A Friend of Keats," *Lamp,* 28 (July 1904), 457.

33. Earl L. Griggs, ed., *Collected Letters of Samuel Taylor Coleridge* (London: Oxford University Press, 1959), IV, 938.

34. Edmund Gosse, *Gossip in a Library* (New York: J. W. Lovell, 1891), p. 210; *Letters of Keats,* II, 84n.

35. Marsh, p. 27; *Theatrical Inquisitor,* 14 (June 1819), 449.

36. *Times,* 24 April 1819; *Literary Journal,* 24 April 1819, p. 243; *Morning Chronicle,* 24 April 1819; *Examiner,* 25 April 1819, p. 270 (by Keats); *Champion,* 25 April 1819; *New Times,* 26 April 1819; *Literary Gazette,* 1 May 1819, p. 275; Exeter *Alfred,* 11 May 1819 (probably by R himself); *Eclectic Review,* new series 11 (May 1819), 473; *Gentleman's Magazine,* 89, part 1 (May 1819), 441; *Scots Magazine,* 4 (May 1819), 425; *Theatrical Inquisitor,* 14 (June 1819), 449; and *Monthly Review,* 89 (August 1819), 422.

37. *Examiner,* 25 April 1819, p. 270. The *Examiner* ruined Keats's metaphor by changing "Samplers" to "samples."

38. Marsh, "The Writings of Keats's Friend Reynolds," p. 496.

39. *Alfred,* 11 May 1819.

40. Leslie A. Marchand, ed., *Byron's Letters and Journals* (Cambridge: Harvard University Press, 1977), VII, 171.

41. E. H. Coleridge, ed., *The Works of Lord Byron* (London: John Murray, 1898–1904), VII, 63–64. And *Don Juan,* III, stanzas 98–100.

42. See Jack B. Gohn, "Who Wrote *Benjamin the Waggoner?* An Inquiry," *The Wordsworth Circle,* 8 (Winter 1977), 69–74.

43. George L. Marsh, *Modern Philology,* 40 (February 1943), 267–74.

44. *Letters of Keats,* II, 94.

45. *Letters of Keats,* II, 93.

46. Stillinger, p. 651.

47. *Letters of Keats,* II, 208.

48. *Letters of R,* p. 26.

49. *Letters of Keats,* II, 128.

50. *Letters of Keats,* II, 210–11.

51. *The Georgian Era: Memoirs of the most eminent persons who have flourished in Great Britain, from the accession of George the First to the demise of George the Fourth* (London: Vizetelly, Branston, 1832–34), IV, 464.

52. (London: John Cumberland, 1819) included in *Cumberland's British Theatre* (London: John Cumberland, 1833), xxxi.

53. John Genest, *Some Account of the English Stage from the Restoration in 1660 to 1832* (Bath: T. Rodd, 1832), IX, 325.

54. *Letters of Keats,* I, 199–200. Rollins did not notice that the "Loveless" on p. 200 was the title of the farce mentioned in the preceding page.

55. *Letters of Keats,* II, 136.

56. *Letters of R,* p. 65; *Notes and Queries,* 2nd series (4 October 1856), p. 275.

57. *Letters of Keats,* II, 146.

58. *Letters of Keats,* II, 165.

59. *Letters of Keats,* II, 152.

60. *Letters of Keats,* II, 162.

61. *Letters of Keats,* II, 168.

62. *Letters of Keats,* II, 165.

63. *Letters of Keats,* II, 166–68.

64. *Letters of Keats,* II, 173–74.

65. *Letters of Keats,* II, 174.

66. *Letters of Keats,* II, 176, 179. Brown suppressed R's name when he printed his letter.

67. *Letters of Keats,* II, 176–77.

68. *Scots Magazine,* October 1819, pp. 304–310.

69. P. 308 (italics supplied).

70. P. 310.

71. Constable's Letter Books, Letter to R of 17 August 1821 in the National Library of Scotland. See appendix B for the full text.

72. *Letters of Keats,* II, 230, 267.

73. *Letters of Keats,* II, 235. Keats does not say that R gave him the "regular reports," but the mention of R immediately afterward suggests it.

74. *Letters of Keats,* II, 230.

75. Constable and Co. to R, 15 January 1820 (see appendix B). "Winter. Bath," *London Magazine,* I (January 1820), 63. Attributed to R in Frank P. Riga and Charles A. Prance, *Index to the London Magazine* (New York: Garland, 1978), p. 4.

76. Charles W. Dilke, ed., *The Papers of a Critic,* 2 vols. (London: John Murray, 1875), I, 14 and Gittings, *John Keats,* pp. 374, 377.

Chapter 10

1. Constable's Letter Books, 15 January 1820, National Library of Scotland. See the appendix B for full text. Constable did not mention the title of the collection of poems, but it must have consisted of those eventually published as *The Garden of Florence and Other Poems* in 1821. It could not have been *The Fancy* because most of it was written after this date.

2. Josephine Bauer, *The London Magazine, 1820–1829,* in *Anglistica,* I (Copenhagen: Rosenkilde and Bagger, 1953), 62n.

3. *Letters of Keats,* II, 244.

4. *Letters of Keats,* II, 245. Very little is known of Thomas Richards.

5. *Letters of Keats,* II, 250.

6. *Letters of Keats,* II, 252.

7. *Letters of Keats,* II, 260–61.

8. Stillinger, pp. 677, 679.

9. Gittings, *John Keats,* p. 372.

10. *Letters of Keats,* II, 268.

11. *Letters of Keats,* II, 61.

12. *Letters of Keats,* II, 268.

13. *Letters of Keats,* II, 279.

14. *London Magazine,* I (March 1820), 254–63. Attributed correctly to R by Riga and Prance, p. 8. In *Letters of R,* p. 16, I erred in identifying the article as "On Fighting," *London,* I (May 1820), 519–22, and I (June 1820), 640–45. A letter from Bryan Waller Procter to Scott in the National Library of Scotland identifies Procter as the author of that article.

15. *Letters of Keats,* II, 245.

16. *Boxiana,* 19 August 1812, p. 82; Reiman reprint, *The Fancy,* pp. xx–xxiii; KC, I, 107.

17. *The Fancy,* p. 6.

18. Date of George's departure—*Letters of Keats,* II, 248. R failed to acknowledge receipt of the book or was very slow in doing so, for George wrote Keats on 8 November 1820, "I sent Reynolds Waverley, has he received it?" (*Letters of Keats,* II, 357).

19. Reiman reprint, *The Fancy,* p. xiv.

20. *The Fancy,* p. xxix.

21. *The Fancy,* p. 1.

22. *The Fancy,* pp. 4–5.

23. *The Fancy,* pp. 41–43.

24. George L. Marsh, "The Writings of Keats's Friend Reynolds," *Studies in Philology,* 25 (October 1928), 498, lists seven reviews: *Blackwood's,* 7 (June 1820), 294–306; *London,* 2 (July 1820), 71–75; *European Magazine,* 78 (July 1820), 61; *Scots Magazine,* 7 (July 1820), 64; *Literary Chronicle and Weekly Review,* 8 July 1820, pp. 437–40; *New Monthly Magazine,* 14 (1 August 1820), 174–77; and *Lonsdale's Magazine or Provincial Repository,* 1 (August 1820), 358.

25. In the *Letters of R,* p. 19, I printed from the London *Times,* which omitted the word "Fancy" as illegible. Sudie Nostrand discovered the letter in the Berg Collection of the New York Public Library, found the word to be legible, and included it in "The Keats Circle: Further Letters," New York University doctoral dissertation, 1973, authorized facsimile by University Microfilms International, Ann Arbor, Michigan, p. 158.

26. KC, I, 137.

27. *Blackwood's,* VII, 305.
28. KC, I, 116.
29. *The Fancy,* p. 92n. KC, I, 117–18. Rollins's conjectural date for this letter of 30 June (?) 1820 is a week too early. The *London* usually came out on the first of each month, and Woodhouse discusses the review in the July issue.
30. KC, I, 120.
31. KC, I, 106–7. Woodhouse's letter to Reynolds of 4 May 1820 shows how closely Woodhouse was involved in the preparation of Reynolds's book: "I have just laid hands (not fists) upon the 'punishing' letter from Peter Corcoran's fair correspondent.—Take what parts you think best: and if you can, by any little alterations, improve its effect—do so" A.L.S., Adelman Collection, Bryn Mawr Library. See appendix B for the full text of the letter.
32. KC, I, 116–17.
33. *New Monthly,* 14 (August 1820), 177.
34. KC, I, 117; Adelman Collection, Bryn Mawr Library.
35. (New York: J. W. Lovell, 1881).
36. (London: Elkin Mathews, 1905).
37. W. C. Macready, *Reminiscences and Selections,* ed. F. Pollock (London: Macmillan, 1875), I, 209.

Chapter 11

1. Gittings, *John Keats,* p. 402.
2. *Letters of R,* p. 66. R wrote R. M. Milnes on 22 June 1848 that he found the letter "28 years old! amongst the originals of Keats's Letters." It is unclear how he retrieved the letter he had sent to Keats. It could have been a first draft from which he transcribed the copy actually sent to Keats, but it would be a little unlike him to be so careful. Or like Haydon he could have recovered some of his letters to Keats after Keats's death.
3. *Letters of R,* pp. 21–22, 66.
4. *Letters of R,* p. 18; R to William Jerdan, 25 August 1820. Kaier, p. 186.
5. *Letters of R,* p. 19.
6. Keats House MS, No. 63.
7. *Edinburgh,* XXXIV, 203–13.
8. *Scots Magazine,* October 1820, p. 316. Italics supplied. *The Scottish National Dictionary,* William Grant and David D. Murison, eds. (Edinburgh: Scottish National Dictionary Association, 1960), V, 265–66: "in I. prep. Sc. usage where mod. Eng. uses a different preposition . . . A. 3. Of place, position: on, upon, along . . . 'He had been murdered in that hill.' . . . 'A bit ring he had hinging in a black ribbon.' . . . 'A house in fire.' "
9. *Letters of Keats,* II, 132.
10. *Letters of Keats,* II, 8, 13.
11. KC, II, *More Letters,* p. 20.
12. KC, II, *More Letters,* p. 20.
13. Gittings, *John Keats,* pp. 361–62.
14. *Letters of Keats,* II, 345.
15. Charles W. Dilke, ed., *The Papers of a Critic,* 2 vols. (London: John Murray, 1875), I, 11. The date was probably shortly after 5 July 1820 when the doctor gave the order. Reynolds knew it before 13 July when he reported it to

Francis Jeffrey, and he surely told his family immediately. Jane was evidently discussing news that she had heard recently.

16. *Letters of R,* p. 21.

17. *Letters of Keats,* II, 292–93.

18. *Letters of Keats,* II, 298.

19. *Letters of Keats,* II, 181, 346.

20. *Letters of Keats,* II, 176.

21. *Letters of Keats,* II, 360. Harry Buxton Forman filled in Reynolds's name for the five *X's* in *The Complete Works of John Keats,* 5 vols. (Glasgow: Gowans and Gray, 1900–1901), V, 203. The passage can be interpreted to mean that Keats regretted only not writing, but the tone implies more sorrow than the failure to write would warrant.

22. *Letters of Hood,* pp. 210, 219, 223, 253, 282, 621.

23. "Exmouth Wrestling," *Selected Prose,* p. 275.

24. *Letters of R,* p. 21.

25. *Letters of R,* p. 22.

26. *Letters of R,* p. 22.

27. *Letters of R,* pp. 17–18.

28. Thomas Allen, *The History and Antiquities of the Parish of Lambeth* (London: J. Allen, 1826), p. 337.

29. *Letters of R,* pp. 19–20.

30. *London,* 2 (August and September 1820), 155–61, 268–76.

31. *Memoirs of Richard Lovell Edgeworth, Esq.—Begun by himself, and concluded by his Daughter Maria Edgeworth,* 2 vols. (London: R. Hunter, 1820).

32. Riga and Prance, p. 16.

33. "Lion's Head," *London,* 2 (August 1820), 123.

34. *London,* II, 269.

35. *London,* II, 270, 273. In the first, R was also thinking of B. W. Procter's *A Sicilian Story,* published earlier in 1820.

36. *London,* II, 242.

37. *London,* II, 325–26.

38. Rylance's letter to Dov of 5 December 1820 noted that Constable's prepublication catalogue advertised it as being in two volumes.

39. Constable and Co. to R, 8 July 1820. See appendix B.

40. Constable and Co. to R, 21 August 1820.

41. Reverend Robert Morehead, junior minister of St. Paul's Episcopalian Church in Edinburgh, later became rector in Edsington, Yorkshire.

42. "Pilgrimage," *Champion,* 17 April 1816, p. 110. *Selected Prose,* pp. 45–50. "Living Authors," *Scots Magazine,* August 1820, pp. 133–40. *Selected Prose* (in part), pp. 251–58.

43. *Champion,* 16 February 1816, p. 53, and "Notes Written in a Commonplace Book after Reading the Play of Othello," 21 January 1816, pp. 21–22.

44. *Scots Magazine,* August 1820, pp. 135–36. *Selected Prose,* p. 256. R mentioned in a footnote that Leigh Hunt had also remarked on Hazlitt's weak handshake in the *Indicator.* He explained that he was not plagiarizing from Hunt, but copying from his commonplace book into which he had made the entry before Hunt's article.

45. Percival P. Howe, *The Life of William Hazlitt,* 3rd ed. (New York: R. Smith, 1930), p. 291.

46. *Letters of R,* pp. 21–22.

47. *Scots Magazine,* October 1820, p. 290.
48. Kaier, p. 186.
49. *London,* 2 (December 1820), 608–18. *Selected Prose,* pp. 274–92.
50. *Selected Prose,* p. 277.
51. *Selected Prose,* p. 278.
52. KC, I, 171, 174.
53. *Letters of Keats,* II, 365.
54. KC, I, 232.
55. Leonidas M. Jones, "Reynolds and Rice in Defence of Patmore," *Keats-Shelley Memorial Bulletin,* 21 (1970), 12–13.
56. *Selected Prose,* p. 291n.
57. *London,* 2 (November 1820), 474.
58. Sir Thomas Parkyns, *Progymnasmata: or, Treatise on Wrestling,* 2nd ed. (Nottingham: W. Ayscough, 1714).
59. All the letters drawn upon for this paragraph are in the Dovaston Collection, No. 1662, Box 5.
60. The letters stopped there in the boxes made available to me when I studied the Dovaston Collection in the summer of 1980. Since that time other materials (probably including additional Rylance letters after 1828) have turned up, as I know because the archivist very kindly sent me two additional Reynolds letters.

Chapter 12

1. Gordon N. Ray, ed., *The Letters and Private Papers of William Makepeace Thackeray,* 4 vols. (Cambridge: Harvard University Press, 1945–46), III, 127.
2. KC, II, *More Letters,* p. 111.
3. William Sharp, *The Life and Letters of Joseph Severn* (New York: Charles Scribner's Sons, 1892), p. 100. The brackets are Sharp's.
4. KC, I, cxxi.
5. Keats House MS, No. 63.
6. Sharp, p. 109.
7. KC, I, 261, 264.
8. Sharp, p. 109.
9. *Letters of Keats,* II, 293. Certainly written before 22 June 1820, this undated letter is conjecturally dated by Rollins as June, but it may have been written in either May or June.
10. *Letters of Keats,* II, 289–90.
11. *Letters of Keats,* II, 292n.
12. Jack Stillinger, ed., *The Letters of Charles Armitage Brown* (Cambridge: Harvard University Press, 1966), pp. 125–26.
13. *Letters of Keats,* II, 365.
14. For detailed accounts of the duel and its aftermath, see my "The Scott-Christie Duel," *Texas Studies in Literature and Language,* 12 (Winter 1971), 605–29 and "Reynolds and Rice in Defence of Patmore," *Keats-Shelley Memorial Bulletin,* 21 (1970), 12–20.
15. *Times,* 3 March 1821.
16. *Morning Chronicle,* 2 March 1821. The names of R and Rice were not given, but they fit the descriptions exactly. The third man was probably Thomas Noon Talfourd because he was a friend of Scott and a barrister; he had been

admitted to the bar on 10 February 1821, and R attended a dinner to celebrate the occasion.

17. *Times,* 3 March 1821.

18. *Times,* 3 March 1821.

19. The facts in this paragraph and the following four paragraphs come from *Letters of R,* pp. 23–33.

20. Basil Champneys, *The Memoirs and Correspondence of Coventry Patmore,* 2 vols. (London: G. Bell, 1900), II, 415.

21. So the prosecutor Walford said at the trial, *Times,* 14 April 1821.

22. *Letters of R,* p. 31.

23. *Times,* 14 April 1821.

24. Derek Patmore, "A Literary Duel," *Princeton University Library Chronicle,* 16 (Autumn 1954), 16. Like Silas Tomkyn Comberback, Patmore could change his name, but not his initials: first P. G. Pitt and then P. G. Preston.

25. *Times,* 14 April 1821. Subsequent quotations from the first trial derive from the same source.

26. Champneys, II, 418. She wrote of Reynolds's being responsible "on the first occasion" and Rice's being responsible "in the last."

27. *Morning Chronicle,* 9 June 1821.

Chapter 13

1. Josephine Bauer, *The London Magazine, 1820–1829,* in *Anglistica,* I (Copenhagen: Rosenkilde and Bagger, 1953), 119.

2. Rylance to Dov, 22 March 1821.

3. Reiman reprint, *The Garden of Florence,* pp. xi–xii.

4. *The Garden of Florence,* p. 35.

5. *London,* 2 (July 1821), 57–61.

6. *The Garden of Florence,* pp. 104–5.

7. *Examiner,* 17 June 1821, p. 381; *New Edinburgh Review,* 1 (July 1821), 273–77; *New Monthly Magazine,* n.s. 3 (October 1821), 523; *Literary Gazette,* 13 October 1821, pp. 643–44; and *Literary Chronicle and Weekly Review,* 24 November 1821, pp. 736–37.

8. *Gentleman's Magazine,* 91 (October 1821), 341.

9. *Scots Magazine,* 9 (July 1821), 52–55.

10. Constable and Co. to R, 2 August 1821.

11. Constable and Co. to R, 17 August 1821.

12. Constable and Co. to R, 2 August 1821.

13. Edmund Blunden, *Keats's Publisher: A Memoir of John Taylor* (London: Jonathan Cape, 1936), pp. 123–25.

14. *London,* 3 (June 1821), 628–32. See Riga and Prance, p. 36. No doubt need linger as to R's authorship, for he added a word within the quotation marks to the passage he had quoted from Keats's epistle "To J. H. Reynolds, Esq." in "Exmouth Wrestling," "weaves their untumultuous fringe of silver foam" (p. 630).

15. *London,* 3 (June 1821), 632–33. Riga and Prance, p. 36. Mrs. William Davies, quoted by Riga and Prance, did not know R as well as she thought she did when she offered to secure R's services for *Blackwood's.* At this very time, R was defending Patmore as a result of the duel caused by *Blackwood's.*

16. Rylance to Dov, undated but noted by Dov as received on 30 May 1821.

17. Rylance to Dov, 30 June 1821, 18 August 1821.
18. Blunden, *Keats's Publisher,* p. 246.
19. Hood's dedication to Reynolds of *Lycus, the Centaur,* published in *The Plea of the Midsummer Faeries* (1827).
20. British Library Egerton MS 2245 f. 374, quoted by Peter F. Morgan, "John Hamilton Reynolds and Thomas Hood," KSJ, 11 (1962), 83.
21. Richard Woodhouse's "Notes of Conversations with Thomas De Quincey" in *Confessions of an English Opium Eater,* ed. Richard Garnett (London: Kegan Paul, Trench, 1885), p. 213.
22. *London,* 5 (January 1822), 52.
23. Thomas Hood, Jr., ed., *The Works of Thomas Hood, Comic and Serious, in Prose and Verse,* 7 vols. (London: E. Moxon, 1862–63), II, 380–81. The quotation comes from R's "Sonnet on the Nonpareil" in *The Fancy,* p. 91.
24. James T. Fields, *Charles Dickens, Barry Cornwall, and Some of His Friends* (Boston: Houghton Mifflin, 1876), p. 59.
25. Riga and Prance, p. 38.
26. Sudie Nostrand, "The Keats Circle: Further Letters," New York University doctoral dissertation, 1973, authorized facsimile by University Microfilms International, Ann Arbor, Michigan, p. 201.
27. *London,* 4 (September 1821), 235.
28. *London,* 4 (October 1821), 351.
29. *London,* 8 (September 1823), 235.
30. *London,* 4 (July 1821), 12.
31. *London,* 9 (February 1824), 165.
32. Edith J. Morley, *Henry Crabb Robinson on Books and Their Writers,* 3 vols. (London: J. M. Dent, 1938), I, 302.
33. Riga and Prance, pp. 53, 56, and 58, are no doubt correct in attributing "A Bachelor's Soliloquy" and "Don Giovanni the XVIII" to R. They are certainly correct in assigning him *The Princess of Moonland,* where the scene opens in Shrewsbury and the speaker recalls fishing in the Severn as R did when a boy. The last is the least slight of the three, but is no more successful than Keats's *The Cap and Bells,* which it resembles a little in its extravagance and its form—the Spenserian stanza. Thomas Hood, Jr. reprints it as one of Hood's poems, another of his errors.
34. *London,* 7 (May 1823), 525.
35. *London,* 6 (November 1822), 410–13.
36. *London,* 7 (April 1823), 449–60.
37. KC, II, 435, 440.
38. *London,* 7 (April 1823), 450.
39. *London,* 7 (April 1823), 451.
40. *London,* 7 (May 1823), 490.
41. "The Vagrant Act," *London,* New Series 1 (January 1825), 7–15. Riga and Prance are correct in assigning the article to R. The presentation of the pretended offenders on p. 15 is too similar to that in "The Literary Police Office" to be coincidental.
42. *London,* 4 (October 1821), 432–39. *Selected Prose,* pp. 292–306.
43. *London,* 4 (July 1821), 86.
44. *London,* 4 (September 1821), 323–25, and 4 (November 1821), 516–17.
45. *London,* 5 (May 1822), 485–90.
46. *London,* 7 (February 1823), 212–15, 215.
47. *London,* 7 (January 1823), 91–92, and 7 (June 1823), 669–72.

48. *London,* 7 (June 1823), 689–93.

49. Blunden, *Keats's Publisher,* pp. 137–38.

50. Bauer, p. 239.

51. J. W. and Anne Tibble, eds., *The Prose of John Clare* (London: Routledge and Paul, 1951), pp. 86–87.

52. There was no review for November 1820, and the October review cannot be assigned—it was not by R as Riga and Prance conjecture because he was in Devonshire while the reviewed plays were performed.

53. *London,* 4 (November 1821), 549.

54. *London,* 8 (October 1823), 432–33.

55. Hessey to Taylor, 9 October 1823, Brooke-Taylor MS, quoted by Morgan, p. 85.

56. *London,* 5 (January 1822), 91. "Dangerous" because Hazlitt had recently chastised Janus Weathercock (T. G. Wainewright) for differing from him.

57. *London,* 5 (March 1822), 292.

58. "The Manager's Note-Book," *New Monthly Magazine,* 52 (1838), 73.

59. *London,* 5 (April 1822), 397.

60. *Notes and Queries,* 4 (October 1856), p. 275.

Chapter 14

1. Walter Jerrold, *Thomas Hood, His Life and Times* (London: Alston Rivers, 1907), p. 115. Alvin Whitley has questioned Hood's share, in "Thomas Hood as a Dramatist," *University of Texas Studies in English,* 30 (1951), 187–88.

2. Reginald Clarence [pseudonym for H. J. Eldredge], *The Stage Cyclopaedia* (London: no publisher, 1909), p. 173.

3. Reprinted in Jerrold, *Thomas Hood,* pp. 116–18.

4. Playbill of the Theatre Royal, English Opera House, Strand, 5 August 1822, as cited in Willard B. Pope, "Studies in the Keats Circle" (Harvard doctoral dissertation, 1932), p. 754.

5. *The Drama, or Theatrical Pocket Magazine,* 3 (August 1822), 138, and Playbill of the English Opera House, 6 September 1822, as cited in Pope.

6. Playbill of the English Opera House, 25 September 1822, as cited in Pope.

7. Gittings, *Ariel,* p. 13. He did not report how he knew the date of R's qualification; probably the time span for an articled law clerk was about five years.

8. For the license, R gave his address as St. James, Westminster. The witnesses were Eliza's sisters, Anne and Lucy Drewe, and J. (?) Crocker.

9. Edmund Blunden, "New Sidelights on Keats, Lamb, and Others from Letters to J. Clare," *London Mercury,* 4 (June 1921), 141.

10. Henry C. Shelley, *Literary By-Paths in Old England* (Boston: Little, Brown, 1906), pp. 325–26.

11. *Letters of Hood,* pp. 34–35.

12. *Letters of Hood,* p. 33. Morgan followed Jerrold in reversing the order of the two undated letters to Mrs. Reynolds and Lotte. The letter to Lotte was written first, on Thursday, 3 October 1822. Hessey reported to Taylor that he attended the party at Rice's on that date (KC, II, 423). Hood writes Lotte that he plans to attend the party at Rice's that night. Hood wrote the letter to Mrs. Reynolds later in October or possibly in November. In his letter to Lotte, he said he intended to write her mother later about John and Eliza; in the letter

to Mrs. Reynolds he apologized for not writing about John and Eliza as he had promised. Furthermore, he wrote the letter to Mrs. Reynolds on Eliza Reynolds Longmore's birthday (p. 32). She was baptized on 20 November 1799; her birthday was not recorded, but all the other children were baptized within a month of birth. Morgan did not notice that the letter was written from the Butlers' house at Kennington, as Hood's remarks on p. 32 show.

13. KC, II, 423.

14. Fred Edgcumbe, ed., *Letters of Fanny Brawne to Fanny Keats, 1820–1824* (New York: Oxford University Press, 1937), pp. 81–82.

15. *Letters of Hood,* pp. 31–32.

16. KC, II, 319.

17. KC, II, 430, 432. Joanna Richardson, *The Everlasting Spell* (London: Jonathan Cape, 1963), pp. 224–25.

18. KC, II, 462–63.

19. KC, II, 436, 463. Rollins erred in identifying the *Table Talk* as Coleridge's; R's review of Hazlitt's *Table Talk* was finally printed in the *London* of June 1823.

20. Horace A. Eaton, *Thomas De Quincey: A Biography* (New York: Oxford University Press, 1936), p. 301.

21. KC, II, 457–60.

22. *London,* 10 (July 1824), 143.

23. KC, II, 468.

24. Albert M. Cohn, *A Few Notes upon Some Rare Cruikshankiana* (London: Karslake, 1915), p. 23. Cohn reproduced the two Herbert etchings in *George Cruikshank, A Catalogue Raisonné of the work executed during the years 1806–1877* (London: Office of "The Bookman's Journal," 1924), p. 271.

25. Marsh, p. 28.

26. KC, II, 433, 435. Riga and Prance, p. 179.

27. Thomas Wilson, *The Danciad* (London: the author, 1824).

28. The name Tims came from R's *King Tims: An American Tragedy,* but *Blackwood's* applied it to Patmore in the summer of 1820.

29. Character in Isaac Bickerstaffe's *The Hypocrite.*

30. The first and third were by John Wilson, the second an earlier book by Thomas Wilson.

31. *Westminster Review,* 2 (July 1824), 214. *Selected Prose,* p. 400.

32. *Selected Prose,* pp. 400, 402, 411.

33. "Letters of Timothy Tickler, Esq., No. XVII, On the Last Westminster Review," *Blackwood's,* 16 (August 1824), 226. In the same issue, an earlier essay by R was censured in a footnote: "In a stupid attempt at wit in the same number [of the *London*], a poor devil, who signs himself Edward Herbert, calls Sir Walter Scott 'alias the Great Unknown, alias Bill Beacon, alias Cunning Walter.' London Magazine for February 1823, p. 160. Poor Driveller!" (p. 183). R had not been severe on Sir Walter Scott in "The Literary Police Office."

34. Charles Dilke, *Notes and Queries,* 2nd series, No. 40 (4 October 1856), p. 275.

35. Brooke-Taylor MS, quoted by Morgan, p. 84. Morgan suggested that staid Taylor and Hessey would not have been comfortable with the high spirits of both at once, but it seems more likely that a meeting between the two would have been awkward because of some rift.

36. *Letters of Hood,* p. 62.

37. They shared equally the "Ode to Maria Darlington," and each also added

touches to the poems of the other. Seven different divisions of the poems with a multitude of conflicting claims have been reported in the following works: Walter Jerrold, *Thomas Hood: His Life and Times* (London: Alston Rivers, 1907), pp. 163–65; M. Buxton Forman, ed., *The Letters of John Keats,* 4th ed. (London: Oxford University Press, 1952), p. xxxix; Marsh, p. 31; Alvin Whitley, "Keats and Hood," KSJ, 5 (1956), 36; and Morgan, pp. 86–87. The vexing problem will probably never be solved beyond dispute, but the *written* records of Hood and Reynolds are most reliable and they agree in assigning McAdam, Dymoke, Elliston, Sylvanus Urban, and Ireland to Reynolds. They agree that Maria Darlington was a joint production, but, since it is impossible to identify R's part of it, I do not discuss it. The marked copy in the Houghton Library, the account of John Payne Collier, and the account of Hannah Lawrance are demonstrably untrustworthy. Collier assigned Sylvanus Urban to Hood; a note from Hood to R of 1825, kindly sent me by Peter F. Morgan, proves R's primary responsibility for that poem: "You may set up for a Prophet as soon as you like. There never was a prediction in Moore more to the point than a line in your Verses to Sylvanus Urban indicating the mischance of an Official Assignee—viz: 'Bankrupts and Abbots breaking side by side.' Now, walk about like Sir Oracle and say you predicted it" (from a sale catalogue of Ximenes: Rare Books Inc., New York; the letter is inserted in a first edition of *Odes and Addresses* at p. 71 where the line appears). The marked Houghton Library copy, Collier, and Lawrance all assign Ireland to Hood; R reprinted all the poem in the *New Monthly* in 1847, signing it J. H. R. The point is that the evidence argues strongly for the falsity of particulars in all the attributions which disagree with the written records of Hood and R, and they are therefore untrustworthy. R may, as he claimed to Milnes, have made some contributions to Hood's poems, but it is impossible to be certain about them.

38. Reiman reprint, *Odes and Addresses,* p. 71 for both passages.

39. *Odes and Addresses,* p. 134.

40. *Literary Chronicle and Weekly Review,* 26 February 1825, p. 129; *Literary Gazette,* 5 March 1825, p. 147; *Times,* 9 March 1825, p. 2; *London Magazine,* n. s. 1 (March 1825), 47; *British Critic,* n. s. 23 (March 1825), 295; *John Bull,* 10 April 1825, p. 116; *New Times,* 12 April 1825—by Charles Lamb; *Literary Magnet,* 3 (April 1825), 103; and *Monthly Magazine,* n. s. 1 (January 1826), 72.

41. Earl L. Griggs, ed., *Collected Letters of Samuel Taylor Coleridge,* 6 vols. (London: Oxford University Press, 1971), V, 473.

42. E. V. Lucas, ed., *The Letters of Charles and Mary Lamb,* 3 vols. (New Haven: Yale University Press, 1935), III, 8.

43. R joined his father, his sister Charlotte, and Rice as witnesses for the marriage register—*London,* n. s. 2 (1825), 317, and *Notes and Queries,* 8th series 5 (1894), 397. [The Dr. Edward Rice who performed the ceremony was George Reynolds's colleague, head grammar master at Christ's Hospital—Robert B. Gardiner, *Admission Registers of St. Paul's* (London: G. Bell, 1906), p. 296, where he is included because his son attended St. Paul's.]

44. Walter Jerrold, ed., *The Complete Poetical Works of Thomas Hood* (London: Oxford University Press, 1920; rpt. Westport, Conn.: Greenwood Press, 1980), p. 161.

45. *Letters of Hood,* pp. 96, 108, 113.

46. George Keats to Dilke, 4 March 1826, KC, II, *More Letters,* p. 32.

47. George Keats to Dilke, 23 May 1827; George Keats to Fanny, 25 March 1828. KC, II, *More Letters,* pp. 38–39, 40.

48. George Keats to Maria Dilke, 19 March 1829, KC, I, 320.

49. KC, II, 9.

50. The Reynolds-Hood commonplace book at the Bristol Central Library has a clipping of the poem with J. H. R. written in MS beneath the pseudonym. William Jerdan, editor of the *Literary Gazette*, listed R as a contributor to the magazine in *The Autobiography of William Jerden*, 4 vols. (London: Hall, Virtue, 1852–53), III, 282. In *Thomas Hood, His Life and Times* (London: Alston Rivers, 1907), p. 187, Walter Jerrold quoted from the poem, though he did not know the author and he erred in giving the date as 1827 instead of 1828 and in reporting the signature as Sam Wildfire instead of Sam Wildfun.

51. *Letters of Hood*, p. 96.

52. G. E. and E. L. Griggs, eds., *The Letters of Hartley Coleridge* (London: Oxford University Press, 1936), p. 100.

Chapter 15

1. *Letters of R*, p. 65.

2. A sonnet in the issue of 12 January 1829, p. 23, is signed Edward Herbert. In *The Athenaeum, a Mirror of Victorian Culture* (Chapel Hill: University of North Carolina Press, 1941), p. 122n., Leslie A. Marchand wrote that after May 1829, "It is easy to see the hand of John Hamilton Reynolds in the satirical attacks on the game of puffery." Perhaps he had in mind two articles in which the style resembles Reynolds's: "Memoir of a Popular Author Lately Deceased," 24 June 1829, pp. 393–94, and "An Hour at a Publisher's," 1 July 1829, pp. 401–2.

3. Charles Wentworth Dilke, ed., *The Papers of a Critic*, 2 vols. (London: J. Murray, 1875), I, 25–26.

4. For an extensive account of puffing practices and the *Athenaeum's* war against them, see Marchand, *The Athenaeum*, pp. 97–156.

5. Dilke, *Papers of a Critic*, I, 45.

6. *Athenaeum*, 17 July 1830, p. 440.

7. *Athenaeum*, 14 August 1830, p. 497.

8. *Athenaeum*, 4 and 11 September 1830, pp. 552–55 and 568–69.

9. *Athenaeum*, 23 October 1830, pp. 657–58. A week after R's review, the *Athenaeum* reported Colburn and Bentley's decision to discontinue, 30 October 1830, p. 680.

10. *Athenaeum*, 8, 15, and 22 January 1831, pp. 17, 33–36, and 57.

11. First printed 25 September 1830, p. 608.

12. *Letters of R*, p. 5.

13. *Athenaeum*, 2 October 1830, p. 612.

14. *Athenaeum*, 23 October 1830, p. 661. *Selected Prose*, pp. 414–15.

15. *Athenaeum*, 1 January 1831, p. 6. *Selected Prose*, p. 417.

16. *Athenaeum*, 31 December 1831, p. 841.

17. *Athenaeum*, 7 January 1832, pp. 5–6. *Selected Prose*, pp. 418–22.

18. *Robert Smith Surtees, by Himself and E. D. Cuming* (Edinburgh: William Blackwood, 1924), pp. 65–66. The other Reynolds was Frederick Reynolds, the dramatist.

19. *Athenaeum*, 18 October 1834, p. 771. Attributed to R in George L. Marsh, "Newly Identified Writings of John Hamilton Reynolds," KSJ, 1 (1952), 52–53.

20. B. W. Procter's *Life of Edmund Kean* and Hood's *Comic Annual*, *Athe-*

naeum, 30 May and 6 June 1835, pp. 401–3 and 428–30; 12 and 19 December 1835, pp. 928–29 and 942–44.

21. "Attic Philosophy," *Athenaeum,* 31 December 1836, pp. 918–19; "Farewell to Charles Kemble," 14 January 1837, p. 33; "The Letters and Works of Lady Mary Wortley Montagu," 21 and 28 January 1837, pp. 48–50 and 61–63; "Lines to Lady Mary Wortley Montagu," 28 January 1837, p. 64; and a review of Dickens' *Grimaldi,* 17 February and 3 March 1838. R's authorship of the last is revealed in Madeline House and Graham Storey, eds., *The Letters of Charles Dickens* (London: Oxford University Press, 1965), I, 376–77.

22. "The Dead Bird," *Athenaeum,* 29 January 1848, p. 211.

23. Attributed to R in the tables of illustrations are "Neglecting to Join in a Catch" and "O, Nothing in Life Can Sadden Us," 1830, pp. 137 and 147, and "Navy Stock," 1835, p. xx.

24. *Notes and Queries,* 2nd series, No. 40 (October 1856), p. 275.

25. Richard Harris Barham, *The Garrick Club* (New York: privately printed, 1896), p. vi.

26. *Letters of R,* p. 38.

27. Arthur H. Beavan, *James and Horace Smith* (London: Hurst and Blackett, 1899), pp. 238–39.

28. A printed "List of Members" for 1833 with several penned additions in the Houghton Library at Harvard lists 367 members. Francis Fladgate is listed as Barrister.

29. From playbills in the Shaw Theater Collection in the Houghton Library at Harvard.

30. Henry Crabb Robinson, *Diary, Reminiscences and Correspondence,* ed. Thomas Sadler (Boston: Fields, Osgood, 1869), II, 179.

31. Edith J. Morley, ed., *Henry Crabb Robinson on Books and Their Writers,* 3 vols. (London: J. M. Dent, 1938), I, 424.

32. Henry Barton Baker, *History of the London Stage* (London: G. Routledge, 1904), p. 439.

33. Walter Jerrold, ed., *The Complete Poetical Works of Thomas Hood* (London: Oxford University Press, 1920; rpt. Westport, Conn.: Greenwood Press, 1980), pp. 462–63.

34. James R. Planché, *The Recollections and Reflections of J. R. Planché,* 2 vols. (London: Tinsley Brothers, 1872), II, 30.

35. *Athenaeum,* 14 January 1837, p. 33.

36. *Letters of R,* pp. 41–42.

37. Kaier, pp. 187–88. Laporte joined the Garrick Club some time after 1833; he is not in the 1833 list of members, but is included in R. H. Barham, *The Garrick Club* (New York: privately printed, 1896), p. 36.

38. *Letters of R,* pp. 42–43.

39. Benjamin Webster, ed., *Confounded Foreigners,* in *The Acting National Drama,* vol. III (London: Chapman and Hall, 1838), pp. 15, 19. There is a MS of the farce in R's hand, partly illegible, in the Larpent Collection in the British Library.

40. *Athenaeum,* 13 January 1838, p. 36.

41. *Athenaeum,* 20 January 1838, p. 52.

42. KC, I, 330; *Letters of Keats,* I, 89; KC, II, *More Letters,* pp. 60, 63–65, and 70; KC, II, 5.

43. KC, II, *More Letters,* p. 71.

44. KC, II, *More Letters,* p. 71.

45. KC, II, 9.

46. John Payne Collier, *An Old Man's Diary* (London: printed by T. Richards, 1872), IV, 62, as quoted in Morgan, p. 90.

47. *Letters of R,* pp. 40–41.

48. *Letters of Hood* includes one letter on pp. 62–63, and Peter Morgan discovered a brief note after publication of his book. He kindly sent me a copy of the latter, which is printed in Chap. 13, n. 37.

49. *Letters of R,* pp. 37–38.

50. *Letters of Hood,* pp. 96, 104, 108, 113, 133, 137, 143, and 156.

51. Collier, *Diary,* II, 19; James Hogg, *A Series of Lay Sermons* (London: J. Fraser, 1834), p. 83, quoted by Morgan, p. 90.

52. *Letters of Hood,* p. 77 and note; pp. 160–68.

53. John Clubbe reports that George Reynolds was also present, but cites no evidence, *Victorian Forerunner: The Later Career of Thomas Hood* (Durham, N.C.: Duke University Press, 1968), p. 21. Hood does not mention him. J. C. Reid says that Marianne and Lotte blamed Hood for the poverty of the household and Jane's state, but cites no evidence, *Thomas Hood* (London: Routledge and Kegan Paul, 1963), p. 127. Apparently following Reid, Clubbe makes the same statement, p. 21. The speculation is of course possible, but it seems unlikely.

54. *Letters of Hood,* p. 160.

55. *Letters of Hood,* p. 167.

56. *Letters of Hood,* pp. 160–161.

57. *Letters of Hood,* pp. 163–64, 165–66.

58. *Letters of Hood,* p. 167.

59. *Letters of Hood,* p. 163.

60. Charles MacFarlane, *Reminiscences of a Literary Life* (New York: Scribner's, 1917), p. 107. MacFarlane was erroneous on so many points that one must be careful. Hood's letter to Jane of 19 March 1835 corroborates him here, "I hope Reynolds may be able to beat the receivers about the house" (*Letters of Hood,* p. 179).

61. *Letters of Hood,* p. 163.

62. *Letters of Hood,* pp. 179, 175, and 182; Jane to Lotte, 25 August 1835, Morgan, p. 91.

63. Jane to Lotte, 25 August 1835, Morgan, p. 91; *Letters of Hood,* pp. 237, 239, 217, 297, and 246.

64. *Letters of Hood,* pp. 307, 370, and 399n.

65. The letter is included in appendix A.

66. *Letters of R,* pp. 40–41.

67. British Library 31, 978 f. 7. Printed in appendix A.

68. Frances F. Broderip and Thomas Hood, Jr., eds., *The Complete Works of Thomas Hood,* 11 vols. (London: Ward and Lock, 1882–84), X, 25n.

69. *Letters of R,* p. 43.

70. *Athenaeum,* 7 January 1837, p. 24.

71. R. H. Barham, *The Garrick Club* (New York: privately printed, 1896), p. 42.

72. *Letters of R,* pp. 47, 64, 67.

73. "Our Weekly Gossip on Literature and Art," *Athenaeum,* 4 February 1837, p. 88.

74. KC, II, 9.

75. All the quotations from Wright are from MSS in the Bristol Reference Library, quoted by Morgan, p. 91.

76. *Letters of Hood*, pp. 81, 385, 395.

77. *Dictionary of American Biography*.

78. Bristol MS, quoted by Morgan, p. 91.

79. *Perry's Bankrupt and Insolvent Weekly Gazette*, XI, 332, 335, 365, 402, 445, 453, 492, 653, 679, 706; XII, 327, 354, 445. The account of the bankruptcy with the documentation is derived from Morgan, pp. 91–92.

80. *New Sporting*, 1 (May, June, July 1831), 17, 113, 198.

81. *New Sporting*, 6 (January 1834), 153–60.

82. *Turfiana*, No. II, *New Sporting*, 16 (February 1839), 132–40; No. III, 16 (April 1839), 253–65; No. IV, 17 (September 1839), 196–200; and No. V, 18 (February 1840), 127–30.

83. *New Sporting*, 15 (October 1838), 245–56.

84. *New Sporting*, 15 (October 1838), 245. *Selected Prose*, p. 424.

Chapter 16

1. From *Tait's Magazine* (December 1840), reprinted in *Collected Works of Thomas De Quincey* (Edinburgh: A. and C. Black, 1890), III, 85.

2. Gordon N. Ray, ed., *The Letters and Private Papers of William Makepeace Thackeray*, 4 vols. (Cambridge: Harvard University Press, 1945–46), IV, 307.

3. *Letters of Thackeray*, I, 407.

4. J. C. Reid, *Thomas Hood* (London: Routledge and Kegan Paul, 1963), p. 170.

5. *Letters of R*, p. 49.

6. *Letters of R*, p. 49.

7. *Letters of Hood*, pp. 425–426.

8. *Letters of Hood*, p. 431.

9. *Letters of R*, pp. 51–52.

10. *Letters of Hood*, pp. 431–32n. Charles MacFarlane's statement that R had a large hand in Hood's return to London should be rejected: "I do not remember how long he [Hood] remained in Germany, but I think it was not quite a year. He could get nothing there, and at that distance, do much with the London publishers. Some arrangements were made with his creditors, by means of his brother-in-law, Reynolds, himself a poet and debtor, and by some other friends, and Tommy returned to London with his wife and children" (*Reminiscences of a Literary Life* [New York: Scribner's, 1917], p. 107). The demonstrable errors in the passage discredit MacFarlane's testimony. Hood lived abroad for five years, not less than one, and he returned to England to stay weeks before R knew he was there. MacFarlane, who wrote his account seventeen years after Hood's return while living as a mental case in the Charterhouse, had heard some tales about Hood and R, but his knowledge was hazy and faulty and should not be trusted without corroboration from some other source.

11. *Letters of Hood*, pp. 425–26.

12. *Letters of Hood*, p. 426.

13. *Letters of R*, pp. 52–54.

14. In an assignment of rent charges on 3 March 1832, witnesses were "George Baber and Benjamin Keenan both of 27 Golden Street in the county of Middle-

sex, clerks to John Hamilton Reynolds of the same place Solicitor"—Greater London Record Office MDR 1832/2/330.

15. *Bentley's Miscellany*, 9 (March 1841), 293–301. Signed H. R. for Hamilton Reynolds.

16. *Letters of R*, p. 55.

17. *Letters of Hood*, pp. 631, 666, 678; *Letters of R*, p. 65.

18. Frances Freeling Broderip and Thomas Hood, Jr., eds., *The Complete Works of Thomas Hood*, 11 vols. (London: Ward, Lock, 1882–84), X, 261.

19. Walter Jerrold, *Thomas Hood, his Life and Times* (London: Alston Rivers, 1907), p. 396.

20. Frances Freeling Broderip, *Memorials of Thomas Hood*, with preface and notes by his son, 2 vols. (Boston: Ticknor and Fields, 1860), I, 10n.

21. *Memorials of Thomas Hood*, II, 237. Paul Kaufman printed the poem from the commonplace book in "The Reynolds-Hood Commonplace Book: A Fresh Appraisal," KSJ, 10 (1961), 50–51.

22. William Toynbee, ed., *The Diaries of William Charles Macready*, 2 vols. (London, 1912; rpt. New York: Benjamin Blom, 1969), II, 134.

23. I am grateful to Mrs. G. Dora Hessell of Papakura, New Zealand, a descendant of the Longmores, for sending me this information from her collection of as yet unpublished letters of the Longmore family. The generosity with which she responded to my time-consuming requests was remarkable.

24. It was, however, reprinted in *Passages from Modern English Poets illustrated by the Junior Etching Club* (London: no publisher, 1862), with an illustration by Whistler.

25. *Letters of R*, p. 66.

26. *New Monthly Magazine*, 75 (September 1845), 23.

27. *Letters of R*, pp. 36–37.

28. KC, I, 288, 329; II, 23, 33, 105.

29. KC, II, 116.

30. *Letters of R*, pp. 58–59.

31. *Letters of R*, pp. 58–59.

32. KC, II, 167n.

33. Obituary of Jane Hood, *Literary Gazette*, 12 December 1846, p. 1059.

34. KC, II, 176. Dilke said she called ten days before the date of his letter to Milnes, 28 December.

35. *Letters of R*, p. 59.

36. *Letters of R*, pp. 60–61.

37. *Letters of R*, p. 68.

38. Both letters are included in appendix A.

39. *Letters of R*, pp. 63–64; Donald Lange, "The Keats Circle: Four Reynolds-Milnes Letters," *Notes and Queries*, 24 (January-February 1977), 13–14.

40. *Letters of R*, pp. 64, 67.

41. *New Monthly*, 69 (February 1847), 162–72.

42. "The Wall," *New Monthly*, 78 (December 1846), 469–70; "Have You Heard a Lute?" *New Monthly*, 79 (February 1847), 248; and "The Two Enthusiasts," *Bentley's Miscellany*, 21 (February 1847), 209–12.

43. R. E. Prothero, ed., *Letters and Journals of Lord Byron* (London: J. Murray, 1899–1901), III, 46n.

44. Willard B. Pope, "John Hamilton Reynolds, the Friend of Keats," *Wessex* (1935), 11, drawing the information from the Hampshire *Independent*.

45. R to Cruikshank, 19 April 1847, Kaier, p. 190.

46. *Letters of R,* pp. 62–63.
47. Lange, "The Keats Circle," pp. 13–14.
48. *Letters of R,* p. 65.
49. *Letters of R,* p. 66.
50. *Letters of R,* p. 63.
51. Cf. Donald Lange's scrupulous examination of all the evidence in "A New Reynolds-Milnes Letter: Keats and Coleridge," *Modern Language Review,* 72 (October 1977), 769–72. Although it is possible that Reynolds remembered another, earlier meeting, it seems unlikely. Lange calls it "a nuance of uncertainty."
52. William Sharp, *The Life and Letters of Joseph Severn* (New York: Scribner's, 1892), p. 196.
53. *Letters of R,* p. 68.
54. *Letters of R,* p. 68.
55. Gittings, Ariel, p. 17.
56. James R. Planché, *The Recollections and Reflections of J. R. Planché* (London: Tinsley, 1872), I, 101.
57. R. E. Prothero, ed., *Letters and Journals of Lord Byron* (London: J. Murray, 1899–1901), III, 46n.
58. Pope, *Wessex,* p. 9. Prothero had earlier shown no reluctance to paint the picture darkly in the *Athenaeum,* 20 April 1901, p. 501: "As to the later days of Reynolds in Newport . . . his drunken habits were, in my childhood, the talk of the neighbourhood, and the legends of his doings innumerable. My father, who was a clergyman within three miles of Newport, knew him well, and the fact is incontestable."
59. KC, I, cxxiii.
60. Pope, *Wessex,* p. 9.
61. Pope, *Wessex,* pp. 11–12.
62. Pope, *Wessex,* p. 12 for the lease; p. 9 for the death notice.
63. *Athenaeum,* 20 November 1852, p. 1272.
64. Eliza to Dov, 10 March 1853. See the Appendix.
65. J. L. W. Ventnor, *Notes and Queries,* 12th series, 3 (September 1917), 360.
66. *Letters of R,* p. 36.
67. Dilke's annotated copy of R. M. Milnes, *Life, Letters, and Literary Remains, of John Keats* (London: Moxon, 1848), I, 169, in the Morgan Library in New York.
68. *Letters of R,* p. 60.
69. Lange, "A New Reynolds-Milnes Letter, " p. 770.

Appendixes

1. The note is undated, but Keats wrote on 29(?) December 1818 that R "dined a few days since at Horace Twisse's" (*Letters of Keats,* II, 15).
2. Francis Graham Moon (1796–1871), publisher and printseller.
3. I have not traced this client for whom R arranged the compromise settlement.
4. The first is Hood's "Miss Fanny's Farewell Flowers" (ADD. 43899, f. 194–96) and the second R's "Lines to Miss F Kemble on the Flower-scuffle at Covent Garden Theatre" (ADD. 43899, f. 197–99). Both were published in the *Athenaeum,* 7 July 1832, p. 436.

5. R signed his poem Curl-Pated Hugh.

6. It did, however, for *Blackwood's* filed it so that it was preserved.

7. Rylance probably intended to use beginning quotation marks here for the ship metaphor that he closed with quotation marks some dozen lines below.

8. Dov's sundial, a favorite place for their outdoor lounging.

9. Either a neighbor or possibly the surname of Dov's servant Molly.

10. First planned as the tale of the ninth statue from the legendary *Vikrama's Adventures,* but written as the original story, *Safie.*

11. Dov's dog.

12. The part R took when the three enacted the *Spectator* the previous summer.

13. Dov's mare.

14. Thomas Yates, the friend for whom Dov swore undying friendship at this time, but against whom he turned bitterly later. John Clavering Wood, Dov's neighbor.

15. An advance of £80 on a book of prose tales never completed.

16. Substantially, the collection of poems that later comprised *The Garden of Florence and Other Poems.*

17. Reverend Robert Morehead, editor of Constable's *Scots Magazine.*

18. For Moyes, Constable's London printer.

19. Woodhouse sent the letter to Taylor's office for R. What he says in it makes clear that the John addressed inside is John R, not John Taylor. It has to be addressed to the author of *The Fancy.*

20. Neither Nan Woodhouse's letter nor a fictitious reply to it that accompanied Woodhouse's letter to R by way of Taylor has been preserved. It would seem that R based Peter Corcoran's reply to Kate (*The Fancy,* pp. xxii–xxiii) on a reply that Woodhouse wrote and sent along with Nan's letter.

21. R did not adopt Woodhouse's suggestion entirely. He had Kate refuse to supply the editor with Peter's first letter (*The Fancy,* pp. xxi–xxiin).

22. Archibald Constable and Company.

23. Peter Corcoran.

24. "Living Authors, a Dream."

25. In a letter of the same date to their London printer, Moyes, Constable and Co. noted that "the Post for Mr Reynolds book is the only unused paper."

26. Nothing shows in a blank space of half a line. Possibly Constable's agent wrote something like "the tone [you complain of was because the le]tter was written in despair of seeing the book."

27. The agent in charge during Archibald Constable's illness could not know that R had offered Constable the poems that went into *The Garden of Florence and Other Poems.* Indeed Constable himself had returned the poems so automatically that it is doubtful whether he read them.

28. William Alexander Longmore (1825–1907). I am very grateful to Mrs. G. Dora Hessell for a detailed family tree that supplied names and dates.

29. George Moody Longmore (1824–55).

30. Philip Longmore (1799–1876).

31. Studying architecture at Oxford.

32. The Hamstead (for Hampstead) dears were the Hood children, Fanny and Tom, who were living with their parents at Camberwell. Charlotte had missed them while they were in Germany and felt cheated that she still did not see them now that the family had returned to England.

33. I believe she meant to write "Mr & Mrs," though both the courtesy titles look alike and seem to be "Mrs."

34. Eliza Skinner Longmore (1822–97).

35. The letter has a black, mourning border.

36. R wrote the script for a theatrical piece at the English Opera House and sent Woodhouse "orders," or tickets, to attend a performance. Woodhouse's metaphor of the Jarvey, or hackney coach, was suitable for hackwork.

37. This address confirms that the John Martin was Keats's old friend, sometimes called the bibliographer, rather than John Martin, the painter. On 14 May 1833, John Martin the bibliographer wrote the Reverend Francis Wrangham from the same address—British Library Add. 45918, f. 181.

38. Frederic (later Sir Frederic) Madden (1801–73), official at the British Museum and family friend of James Rice, Sr. See the letter of Frederic Madden to James Rice, Sr., 19 October 1823, British Library Eg. 3837, f. 1.

39. Portsmouth Grammer School.

Index of Works by Reynolds and Keats

Reynolds

Index